Call DBPR for Renewal!

Post-Licensing Education for Florida Real Estate Sales Associates

Ninth Edition Update | Edward J. O'Donnell

Dearborn
Real Estate Education

John.Platt@myfloridalicense.com
561-315-4694

This publication is designed to provide accurate and authoritative information in regard to the subject matter covered. It is sold with the understanding that the publisher is not engaged in rendering legal, accounting, or other professional advice. If legal advice or other expert assistance is required, the services of a competent professional should be sought.

President: Dr. Andrew Temte
Chief Learning Officer: Dr. Tim Smaby
Executive Director, Real Estate Education: Melissa Kleeman-Moy
Development Editor: Evonna Burr

POST-LICENSING EDUCATION FOR FLORIDA REAL ESTATE SALES ASSOCIATES NINTH EDITION UPDATE
©2016 Kaplan, Inc.
Published by DF Institute, Inc., d/b/a Dearborn Real Estate Education
332 Front St. S., Suite 501
La Crosse, WI 54601

Printed in the United States of America

ISBN: 978-1-4754-3778-2
PPN: 1610-3010

CONTENTS

INTRODUCTION

Before their first license renewal, Florida real estate sales associates must complete a Florida Real Estate Commission–approved 45-hour post-licensing education course. The Commission has approved the use of this book in the course. Licensees who take the course have an opportunity to build on the principles and practices learned in the prelicensing course and to obtain new, hands-on training in many important areas.

Because nearly 75% of licensees sell residential real estate, the topics covered in this course book focus primarily on that part of the real estate business. Many of the principles and practices described in this book also apply to the commercial and investment sectors.

We've included learning objectives at the beginning of each chapter to help you focus on important points. We have prepared discussion questions for each chapter to help you acquire a more complete understanding of the material. We have also included a quiz at the end of each chapter for additional review of the material.

The book is divided into five sections arranged in the typical sequence of real estate activities:

- Section I updates the licensee on the important laws that regulate the licensee's daily activities. A chapter on business planning helps the new licensee get organized.

- Section II focuses on building a strong listing portfolio, including prospecting, pricing the property, making the listing presentation, and getting the listing agreement signed.

- Section III describes how to work with buyers, from the initial contact with a buyer to analyses of the buyer's needs and ability to purchase to showing the property. A section on sales and option contracts is included, as well as information on writing and presenting the offer.

- Section IV concentrates on obtaining financing and closing the sale. The coverage starts with an evaluation of current lending practices and programs, and it continues with a step-by-step discussion of how a loan is processed after a contract is written. Another chapter gives the new practitioner a step-by-step guide to getting the contract to closing. The responsibilities of each cooperating sales associate are covered in detail. The section ends with coverage of how to close a transaction.

- Section V describes economic principles and the processes used to analyze real estate investments. The section also describes the important field of property management.

We have attempted to make this text as thorough and practical as possible and included many features that we hope you find helpful.

Forms To Go

A Forms To Go section is in Appendix B. Symbols such as the one on the left show you when a form is available there. The section includes Florida Real Estate Commission (FREC) forms, brokerage relationship disclosures, and other forms you might find useful in your daily practice.

WEBLINK

We have included weblinks throughout the book with an icon like the one shown on the left, so you can use the internet to find more resource material.

While it is difficult to design one book to meet the needs of every real estate sales associate, it is our intention to provide a bridge from basic classroom education to deeper understanding and practical hands-on training in real estate.

Edward J. O'Donnell

ACKNOWLEDGMENTS

The author is indebted to the many real estate professionals who have provided advice and the assistance necessary for the completion of this edition, particularly to Valleri Crabtree for her review of this new edition.

The author would like to acknowledge those who reviewed previous editions of this book:

- John Anderson
- Mary Basler
- Jack R. Bennett
- Ronald O. Boatright
- Audrey M. Conti
- Linda Crawford
- Deborah Diesing
- Terrance M. Fitzpatrick
- Richard T. Fryer
- Andy Gray
- John L. Greer
- Lawrence D. Greer
- Anthony L. Griffon
- Ron Guiberson
- Robert L. Hogue
- John F. Phillips, Ph.D.
- Michael Rieder
- Donald L. Ross
- Roger L. Satterfield
- James Sweetin
- Mary E. Sweetin
- Donald E. Tennant
- Audrey Van Vliet
- Curtis H. Wild

LAYING THE FOUNDATION FOR A SUCCESSFUL CAREER

Chapter 1 will familiarize licensees with the important license law changes relating to the broker's relation-ships with customers. It describes the disclosure forms that licensees must give to their clients and customers and lists those situations when the disclosure requirements do not apply.

State and federal laws that affect real estate are also described to help the licensee stay current on important laws such as property condition disclosure, federal income taxes, and lead-based paint disclosures.

Chapter 2 describes the important provisions of the Fair Housing Act and the Americans with Disabilities Act.

In chapter 3, the student will learn the basics of developing a business plan, setting goals, and time management. ■

CHAPTER 1

LEGAL ISSUES AND RISK MANAGEMENT

LEARNING OBJECTIVES

When you finish reading this chapter, you will be able to:

- list and describe the duties of the four authorized brokerage relationships in Florida,
- describe the responsibilities of a licensee as they relate to do-not-call laws, and
- describe the duties of a licensee when showing a house where a death occurred.

KEY TERMS

agency	designated sales associate	No Brokerage Relationship
agent	dual agency	Notice
buyer brokerage agreement	false or misleading	principal
community association	statement	property condition
Consent to Transition	fiduciary relationship	disclosure
to Transaction Broker	innocent purchaser status	radon gas
Notice	material fact	single agent
customer	misrepresentation	transaction broker

OVERVIEW

Chapter 1 will update new licensees on laws and trends in the real estate industry. The first section of this chapter describes how to renew a real estate license. The second section is designed to help licensees avoid charges of misrepresentation. A discussion of brokerage relationships describes the duties and disclosures required of licensees in their dealings with customers. The final section of the chapter is a review and update of important state and federal laws.

Students should be familiar with Florida real estate license law and stay current on important changes to the law. This section covers license renewal and brokerage relationships.

RENEWING YOUR FLORIDA REAL ESTATE LICENSE

The Department of Business and Professional Regulation (DBPR) is required to send a renewal notice to the last known address of the licensee at least 60 days before the expiration date.

Licensees should send the renewal notice and a check to the DPBR before the renewal date or renew online with a credit card. Be sure your renewal request is postmarked on or before the renewal date to avoid a $45 late renewal fee. The late fee does not apply to the first renewal because the initial license will become void if not renewed by the renewal date.

In Practice

Licensees who do not receive a renewal notice should ensure that the DBPR has their current address on file. If not, they should send a change of address to the DBPR using Form DBPR 0080-1. Licensees may also visit www.myfloridalicense .com to change their address and to renew their license.

Required Education for Renewing the Initial License

The initial real estate license expires on the first of two dates after 18 months have elapsed following issue: March 31 or September 30.

A sales associate must successfully complete a 45-hour sales associate post-licensing course before the first renewal. A new broker must complete 60 hours of broker post-license education before the first renewal. If the licensee does not successfully complete the post-license requirement, the license becomes void. A sales associate wanting to continue in real estate would have to take the prelicense course again and pass the state exam. The license of a broker who does not complete the required post-license course will become void. The broker may, however, take a 14-hour continuing education course and apply for sales associate status. The licensee who wishes to become a broker again must successfully complete the broker prelicense course and pass the state exam.

Students failing the post-licensing education end-of-course examination prescribed by the Florida Real Estate Commission (FREC) must wait at least 30 days from the date of the original examination and pass a different end-of-course examination. A student may retake the prescribed end-of-course examination only one time, and that exam must be taken within one year of the original end-of-course examination. Otherwise, students failing the Commission-prescribed end-of-course examination must repeat the course before retaking a different form of the examination.

In Practice

Take your first exam more than 30 days before your renewal date. That way, if you fail, you can take the second exam before the expiration date. If you fail the exam and don't have 30 days before expiration, enroll in another course immediately. There's no limit to the number of times you can take the course. Save your license.

A licensee who has received a four-year degree in real estate from an accredited institution of higher education is exempt from the post-license education requirements.

Required Education for Subsequent Renewals

After the first renewal, the license will expire on the same date every two years. If a licensee fails to renew the license, the license will become involuntary inactive, and the licensee may not perform real estate services. After the first renewal, a licensee must complete an FREC-approved 14-hour continuing education course.

The DBPR will not renew a license until the required education course has been posted to the database at www.myfloridalicense.com. Course providers must submit an electronic roster of course attendees to the department within 30 calendar days of the course completion date or prior to the renewal date, whichever occurs sooner.

AUTHORIZED BROKERAGE RELATIONSHIPS

A real estate licensee may work with potential buyers and sellers:

- as a transaction broker (this relationship is presumed under state law unless the licensee enters into a different relationship with the customer),
- as a single agent,
- with no brokerage relationship, or
- as a designated sales associate (but only in a nonresidential transaction).

Florida law prohibits **dual agency** because a licensee cannot fairly represent both parties in a transaction.

If a single-agency relationship is established with a residential seller, all licensees in that brokerage firm have single-agent duties to that seller. It is not legal for another sales associate in the firm to represent a buyer when selling that property, nor can that sales associate be a transaction broker. It would, however, be legal for the sales associate to work with the buyer in a no-brokerage-relationship role.

If a broker has a single-agent relationship with a principal, the broker may change (transition) to a transaction broker relationship. The licensee must make the appropriate disclosure of duties to the buyer or the seller. The principal must give written consent before the change. A **customer** is not required to enter a brokerage relationship with any real estate licensee (475.278(1)).

DISCLOSURE REQUIREMENTS FOR RESIDENTIAL PROPERTY TRANSACTIONS

A licensee in a residential sales transaction must give a brokerage relationship notice to potential buyers or sellers before or at the time of entering into a listing agreement or before the showing of property, whichever occurs first. *Residential sale* is defined as:

- property with four units or fewer,
- unimproved residential property intended for use of four units or fewer, or
- agricultural property of 10 acres or fewer.

The three types of required residential brokerage notices include the following:

- No Brokerage Relationship Notice
- Single Agent Notice
- Consent to Transition to Transaction Broker Notice

Brokers must keep copies for at least five years of the disclosure notices for all residential transactions that result in a written sales contract.

Property Transactions That Do Not Require Disclosure Notices

A licensee need not give a brokerage relationship notice when:

- the licensee is acting as a transaction broker;
- the licensee knows that a single agent or a transaction broker already represents the potential seller or buyer;
- an owner is selling new residential units built by the owner and the circumstances or the setting should reasonably inform the potential buyer that the owner's employee or single agent is acting on behalf of the owner, whether because of the location of the sales office or because of office signage or placards or identification badges worn by the owner's employee or single agent;
- selling nonresidential property;
- renting or leasing real property, unless the buyer has an option to purchase all or a portion of the property improved with four or fewer residential units;
- holding a bona fide open house or model home showing that does not involve eliciting confidential information, executing a contractual offer or an agreement for representation, or negotiating price, terms, or conditions of a potential sale;
- engaging in unanticipated casual conversations with a seller or a buyer that do not involve eliciting confidential information, the execution of a contractual offer or agreement for representation, or negotiations concerning price, terms, or conditions of a potential sale;
- responding to general factual questions from a potential buyer or seller concerning properties that have been advertised for sale;
- the licensee's communications with a potential buyer or seller are limited to providing general factual information, oral or written, about the qualifications, background, and services of the licensee or the licensee's brokerage firm; or
- auctioning, appraising, or disposing of any interest in business enterprises or business opportunities, except for property with four or fewer residential units.

TRANSACTION BROKER RELATIONSHIP

Licensees are presumed to be working as transaction brokers unless they have entered into another brokerage relationship with a customer. Because of this legal presumption, the licensee need not provide a brokerage relationship notice to the customer. A **transaction broker** provides limited representation to a buyer, a seller, or both in a real estate transaction, but does not represent either in a fiduciary capacity. The customer is not responsible for the acts of the transaction broker. A recent survey by the Florida REALTORS® showed that nearly 70% of the REALTORS® worked exclusively as transaction brokers.

Transaction Broker Duties

A transaction broker owes the following seven duties to the customer:

1. Dealing honestly and fairly.
2. Accounting for all funds.
3. Using skill, care, and diligence in the transaction.
4. Disclosing all known facts that materially affect the value of residential real property and are not readily observable to the buyer.
5. Presenting all offers and counteroffers in a timely manner, unless a party has previously directed the licensee otherwise in writing.
6. Limited confidentiality, unless waived in writing by a party. The transaction broker may not reveal to either party:

   ■ that the seller might accept a price less than the asking or list price,

   ■ that the buyer might pay a price greater than the price submitted in a written offer,

   ■ the motivation of any party for selling or buying property,

   ■ that a seller or buyer will agree to financing terms other than those offered, and

   ■ any other information requested by a party to remain confidential.

7. Any additional duties that are entered into by this or a separate agreement.

SINGLE AGENT RELATIONSHIP

Agency is a relationship created when one person, the **principal**, delegates to another, the **agent**, the right to act on his or her behalf in business transactions. A **single agent** represents either the buyer or the seller, but not both, in a transaction. The principal relies on the single agent to give skilled and knowledgeable advice and to help negotiate the best terms in dealings with the customer. Because only single agency creates a **fiduciary relationship**, only single agents may call their customers "principals." The principal is responsible for the acts of his single agent.

Single Agent Duties

A single agent owes the following nine specific duties to a buyer or a seller:

1. Dealing honestly and fairly
2. Loyalty
3. Confidentiality

4. Obedience

5. Full disclosure

6. Accounting for all funds

7. Skill, care, and diligence in the transaction

8. Presenting all offers and counteroffers in a timely manner, unless a party has previously directed the licensee otherwise in writing

9. Disclosing all known facts that materially affect the value of residential real property and are not readily observable

Single Agent Notice

Forms To Go

The Single Agent Notice (see Appendix B) must be given before, or at the time of, entering into a listing agreement or an agreement for representation or before the showing of property, whichever occurs first. It may be a separate and distinct disclosure document or part of another document, but it is most often made part of a listing agreement or a **buyer brokerage agreement**.

The notice should be signed. If a principal who wants the single agent form of representation refuses to sign a Single Agent Notice, the licensee may still work as a single agent for that person but should note on the licensee's copy that the principal declined to sign.

Role of Sales Associates

Sales associates are agents of their registered brokers. If a seller's broker has a listing, that broker and all the sales associates in that firm represent the seller.

Transitioning from Single Agent

When a single agent for one party begins working with the party on the other side of the transaction, the single agent must either have no brokerage relationship with the other party or transition to transaction broker for both parties. The agent may not disclose to the other party any confidential information learned while a single agent.

> **EXAMPLE:** As their single agent, broker James listed the Smiths' house. Sally, a licensee in James's office, is working as the single agent for a buyer, Mr. Farley. Farley becomes interested in the Smiths' house. Because he cannot represent both parties (dual agency), the broker must get permission from the principal to become a transaction broker.

In Practice

When you're taking a listing, how do you answer a seller who wants you to remain a single agent throughout the transaction? Maybe you could explain that if you're not a transaction broker, it's unlikely that a buyer will buy the property through you and may decide to use another licensee for help. The other licensee may want to show their listings first, and the buyer would be lost.

**Forms
To Go**

Consent to Transition to Transaction Broker Notice

The **Consent to Transition to Transaction Broker Notice** (see Appendix B) allows a single agent to change his or her brokerage relationship to that of a transaction broker. The principal must sign this notice before the single agent becomes a transaction broker.

NO BROKERAGE RELATIONSHIP

A buyer or a seller can choose to not be represented by a real estate broker. In this case, the buyer or the seller would be a "customer" of the broker. Licensees working with no brokerage relationship to the customer owe the following three duties:

1. Dealing honestly and fairly
2. Disclosing all known facts that materially affect the value of the residential real property that are not readily observable to the buyer
3. Accounting for all funds entrusted to the licensee

A single agent for one party in a transaction may decide to work with the other party as a nonrepresentative. If a broker does not have a brokerage relationship with a customer and is a single agent for the other party, the customer is at a disadvantage. It is the duty of the single agent to work diligently for his principal and to get the best price and terms for the principal.

**Forms
To Go**

The duties of a licensee who has no brokerage relationship with a buyer or a seller must be fully described and disclosed in writing to the buyer or the seller. The **No Brokerage Relationship Notice** (*see* Appendix B) must be given to prospective buyers and sellers of residential property before showing a property. The notice need not be signed.

DISCUSSION EXERCISE 1.1

Nonrepresentation. Broker Helen lists the Smiths' home as a single agent. Later, Helen shows it to Mr. Jones, a prospective buyer, and gives him a No Brokerage Relationship Notice.

While Helen is writing his offer for the property, Jones says, "I'll pay the asking price of $200,000 if I have to, but I would like to start the negotiations at $185,000."

When Helen presents the offer, she must tell the Smiths that Jones has said he will pay up to the listed price. Failure to make this disclosure would expose her to disciplinary action and civil liability for violation of her fiduciary duty of full disclosure.

THE DESIGNATED SALES ASSOCIATE

A broker may legally appoint one sales associate in the firm to act as the agent for the buyer (or lessee) and another sales associate in the firm to act as the agent for the seller (or lessor). This status may be used only in a nonresidential transaction. In this status, each **designated sales associate** is an advocate for the party she represents in the transaction and can actively help in the negotiations. The broker, however, must remain neutral. To meet the requirements of the law, buyers and sellers must have personal assets of at least

**Forms
To Go**

$1 million, must sign disclosures that their assets meet the requirement, and must request this representation status. The licensees must give the parties a Designated Sales Associate Notice (see Appendix B).

DISCUSSION EXERCISE 1.2

Designated Sales Associate. FatBurgers Inc. is searching for five store locations in Pompano. It engages Mary Stevens of Pompano Commerce Realty as single agent because of her knowledge and expertise in the Pompano fast-food field. Jack Wilson, of the same firm, represents the seller of one of the potential sites.

Because FatBurgers Inc. wants Mary to be its single agent, the broker appoints Mary as a single agent for FatBurgers Inc. and Jack as single agent for the seller. Mary and Jack are now designated sales associates.

SELECTED LAWS REGULATING REAL ESTATE PRACTICE

Notifying DBPR of Convictions or Pleas

Florida licensees who are found guilty of, or plead nolo contendere to, any crime (misdemeanors included) must report this fact to the FREC within 30 days after the plea or after being found guilty. Formerly, real estate licensees had a duty to report only felonies. If the plea or conviction took place before the effective date of this law (July 1, 2009), the licensee must have reported it within 30 days after the effective date of the law (455.227(1)(t), F. S).

In addition to Chapter 475, Florida Statutes, state and federal laws regulate the professional practice of real estate licensees, as well as the rights and duties of consumers. This section is intended to focus on those requirements. More information can be found using the weblinks provided.

Homeowners Association Disclosure (Chapter 689, F.S.)

Some homebuyers in Florida have been surprised shortly after the purchase when they discovered that they must pay dues to a **community association**. If owners must be members in a community association, the developers or owners of the parcel must disclose before a buyer signs a purchase contract:

- that the property owner must be a member of the community association;
- that recorded covenants govern the use and occupancy of the property;
- that the property owner is obligated to pay an assessment to the association and that the failure to pay the assessment could result in a lien being placed on the property; and
- that there is no obligation to pay rent or land use fees for recreational or other commonly used facilities (not applicable to any condominium, cooperative, or time-share association).

Any contract or agreement for sale must refer to and incorporate the disclosure summary and must include, in prominent language, a statement that the potential buyer should not sign the contract or agreement before receiving and reading the disclosure summary required by this section.

Each contract entered into for the sale of property governed by covenants subject to disclosure required by this section must contain in conspicuous type a clause that states the following:

> ### HOMEOWNERS ASSOCIATION DISCLOSURE
>
> *If the disclosure summary required by section 689.26, Florida Statutes, has not been provided to the prospective purchaser before executing this contract for sale, this contract is voidable by buyer by delivering to seller or seller's agent written notice of the buyer's intention to cancel within 3 days after receipt of the disclosure summary or prior to closing, whichever occurs first. Any purported waiver of this voidability right has no effect. Buyer's right to void this contract shall terminate at closing.*

This section does not apply to any association regulated as condominiums (Chapter 718), cooperatives (Chapter 719), vacation and time-sharing (Chapter 721), or mobile home park lots (Chapter 723). It also does not apply if disclosure regarding the association is otherwise made in connection with the requirements of those Chapters.

Ad Valorem Tax Disclosure (Chapter 689, F.S.)

The Save Our Homes Amendment to the Florida Constitution limits the annual increases in the assessed value of a homestead property. The assessment can increase annually by 3% or the percentage of increase in the Consumer Price Index, whichever is less. When the property is sold, it is reassessed at full market value. Many buyers are shocked when their first tax bill is much higher than what the former owner paid.

Before the buyer signs a contract to purchase, Florida real estate licensees must give a property tax disclosure that includes the following wording:

> ### PROPERTY TAX DISCLOSURE SUMMARY
>
> *Buyer should not rely on the seller's current property taxes as the amount of property taxes that the buyer may be obligated to pay in the year subsequent to purchase. A change of ownership or property improvements triggers reassessments of the property that could result in higher property taxes. If you have any questions concerning valuation, contact the county property appraiser's office for information.*

Radon Gas Protection Act (Chapter 404.056, F.S.)

Radon gas may be the second most common source of lung cancer in the United States. Radon results from decaying uranium in the soil. Radon gas is everywhere, but because of very low concentrations in the atmosphere, it is rarely a problem. When uranium decays under a home, the gas can seep into the home through foundation cracks and plumbing lines. Improved building techniques and insulation intended to provide energy-efficient homes have the unintended side effect of trapping the gas inside the home.

1 Testing is the only way to learn whether radon levels are a health hazard. The EPA
2 recommends intervention if testing shows radon levels at four picocuries per liter of air.
3 This would be a concentration approximately 10 times that of outdoor air. Exposure to
4 radon inside the home can be reduced to an acceptable level by sealing foundation cracks
5 and other openings.

6 The radon levels in a building can also be reduced by mitigation systems. Such systems
7 use polyvinyl chloride (PVC) pipes installed through the slab with a fan that draws air from
8 beneath the building and vents it above the roofline. Such systems may cost from $1,000 to
9 $3,500. The electric cost for running the fan is only about five dollars per month.

10 The following wording must be on every sale contract and on every lease contract for
11 more than 45 days:

> **RADON GAS**
>
> *Radon is a naturally occurring radioactive gas that, when it has accumulated in a building in sufficient quantities, may present health risks to persons who are exposed to it over time. Levels of radon that exceed federal and state guidelines have been found in buildings in Florida. Additional information regarding radon and radon testing may be obtained from your county health department.*

WEBLINK

The EPA pamphlet *A Citizen's Guide to Radon* is available at www.epa.gov/radon/pubs/citguide.html.

12 ## Federal Residential Lead-Based Paint Hazard Reduction Act

13 Because of the danger of neurological damage, the Residential Lead-Based Paint Hazard
14 Reduction Act requires that disclosure be made to purchasers of residential buildings that
15 were built before 1978. The seller, landlord, or licensee must provide the following before
16 the contract is signed:

17 ■ A lead hazard information pamphlet
18 ■ Information about the presence of any known lead-based paint or lead-based
19   paint hazard
20 ■ A 10-day period to conduct an inspection (does not apply to rentals)

21 The Lead-based Paint Warning Statement (see Appendix B) must be attached to the
22 contract.

**Forms
To Go**

23 Because renovations and demolitions of properties built before 1978 can create lead
24 dust and chips that would be harmful to children and adults, the Environmental Protec-
25 tion Agency (EPA) requires contractors who disturb paint in these properties to be certi-
26 fied and follow specific work practices. To become certified, a renovator must successfully
27 complete an eight-hour training course offered by an accredited training provider.

WEBLINK

The EPA's lead website is at www2.epa.gov/lead.

HUD's Office of Healthy Homes and Lead Hazard Control (OHHLHC) is at http://portal.hud.gov/hudportal/HUD?src=/program_offices/healthy_homes.

Comprehensive Environmental Response, Compensation, and Liability Act of 1980

The Comprehensive Environmental Response, Compensation, and Liability Act (CER-CLA) of 1980 imposes substantial liability on owners of real property that has been contaminated with toxic or hazardous substances. The liability also extends to other parties in a transaction, such as attorneys, developers, lenders, and real estate brokers. The liability in the act is joint and several, which means that all present or former property owners may be forced to pay (joint) or only one owner may be required to pay (several).

A purchaser who wishes to avoid liability under the statute must do intensive research, usually in the form of a Phase I environmental audit. The audit is expensive and time-consuming. The statute allows the purchaser to defend against any later action by claiming **innocent purchaser status**, provided that the purchaser exercised due diligence to investigate the property. Licensees should be particularly careful when listing or selling sites such as former gas stations or dry cleaning establishments. Residential properties built on former farmland have been contaminated by pesticide use (e.g., Dioxin, DDT, etc.) or old farm gas tanks that have leaked. Other problem areas for residential licensees are old, leaking heating oil tanks buried in the ground.

WEBLINK

The EPA's Superfund site is at www.epa.gov/superfund/.

The National Do Not Call Registry

The National Do Not Call Registry is a list of phone numbers belonging to persons who do not want to be contacted by commercial telemarketers. It is managed by the Federal Trade Commission (FTC) and enforced by the FTC, the Federal Communications Commission (FCC), and individual states.

The registry now includes more than 221 million phone numbers. Numbers placed on the registry remain on the list for five years.

Telemarketers must pay an annual subscription fee to access the FTC list to ensure that no calls are made to protected numbers. The companies also must update their own calling lists every 31 days to ensure that no numbers from the registry are on them. The current annual subscription fee for the list is $58 for each area code, with a maximum cost of $15,963 for access to all U.S. numbers on the list.

The rules of the do-not-call registry cover the sale of goods or services by telephone.

Political organizations, charities, telephone surveyors, or companies with which a consumer has an existing business relationship are exempt from the rules of the do-not-call registry. A company that has an existing business relationship with the consumer may place a call, even if that consumer is on the registry, for up to:

- 18 months after that consumer's last purchase, delivery, or payment, even if the consumer's number is on the registry; or
- three months after that consumer makes an inquiry or submits an application to the company.

If the consumer asks the company not to call again, the company must honor the request.

Accessing the Do-Not-Call Registry. Only sellers, telemarketers, and other service providers may have access to the registry. The registry may not be used for any purpose other than preventing telemarketing calls to the telephone numbers on the registry. The only consumer information available from the registry is telephone numbers. The numbers are sorted and available by area code. Companies may access as many area codes as needed (and paid for), by selecting, for example, all area codes within a certain state.

Sellers or telemarketers may not call into any area code before paying for the protected numbers, even if those consumers whose telephone numbers are not on the registry. The only exceptions are for telemarketers who call only consumers with whom they have an existing business relationship or written agreement to call and that do not access the do-not-call registry for any other purpose.

A seller or telemarketer could be liable for placing any telemarketing calls (even to numbers not on the do-not-call registry) unless the telemarketer has paid the required fee for access to the registry. Violators may be subject to fines of up to $11,000 for each call placed. In 2013, a large mortgage refinancing company was fined $7.5 million for many violations of the law.

To successfully avoid penalties for violations of the law (safe harbor), the seller or telemarketer must demonstrate that it:

- has written procedures to comply with the do-not-call registry requirements,
- trains its personnel in those procedures,
- monitors and enforces compliance with these procedures,
- maintains a company-specific list of telephone numbers that it may not call,
- accesses the National Do Not Call Registry no more than three months before calling any consumer and maintains records documenting this process, and
- erred unintentionally if it did make any call in violation of the do-not-call registry rules.

The best source of information about complying with do-not-call registry rules is the FTC's website. It includes business information about the registry.

WEBLINK

Visit the National Do Not Call Registry at https://donotcall.gov.

The Florida Do Not Call Program

The National Do Not Call Registry did not eliminate Florida's do-not-call law. Florida continues enforcing this law and accepts new consumer telephone numbers. The national registry supersedes portions of the Florida law that are less strict. Sellers and telemarketers must consult both lists to ensure that a consumer is not on either list before placing a sales call. Florida's law allows licensees to contact for sale by owners (FSBOs) to solicit a listing, but this is still permissible only if the owner is not in the National Do Not Call Registry.

In Practice

Review the list and check it twice.

Before placing a call, you should be sure that the consumer is not on any of the following three lists:

- National Do Not Call Registry
- Florida Do Not Call list
- Your own in-office do-not-call list

You can call a FSBO in the national registry if you have a buyer who wants to purchase the property, but you may not use the call to discuss listing the property. If the FSBO is on the Florida list but not on the national registry, you may solicit the listing if the property was advertised or has a sign in front.

WEBLINK

Visit the Florida Do Not Call Program at www.fldnc.com.

Junk Fax Protection Act

The law requires the person who sends a fax to:

- have an established business relationship (EBR) with the recipient or written consent from the recipient,
- have voluntarily received the recipient's fax number,
- provide the recipient the right to opt out of getting more faxes, and
- remove the numbers of persons who opt out within 30 days.

Federal law prohibits most unsolicited fax advertisements to any machine, either business or personal. An unsolicited advertisement is defined under the act as "any material advertising the commercial availability or quality of any property, goods, or services which is transmitted to any person without that person's prior express invitation or permission, in writing or otherwise."

An exception to the rules allows faxes to be sent to recipients with whom the sender has an EBR. If the sender had an EBR with the recipient and possessed the recipient's fax number before July 9, 2005 (the date the Junk Fax Prevention Act became law), the sender may send the fax advertisements without demonstrating how the number was obtained.

Fax Opt-Out Notice Requirements. Senders of fax advertisements must provide specified notice and contact information on the fax that allows recipients to opt out of any future faxes from the sender and specify the circumstances under which a request to opt out complies with the act.

The rules provide that it is unlawful to send unsolicited advertisements to any fax machine, including those at businesses and residences, without the recipient's prior express invitation or permission. Fax advertisements, however, may be sent to recipients with whom the sender has an EBR, as long as the fax number was provided voluntarily by the recipient. Specifically, a fax advertisement may be sent to an EBR customer if the sender also:

- obtains the fax number directly from the recipient through, for example, an application, contact information form, or membership renewal form; or
- obtains the fax number from the recipient's own directory, advertisement, or site on the internet, unless the recipient has noted on such materials that it does not accept unsolicited advertisements at the fax number in question; or
- has taken reasonable steps to verify that the recipient consented to have the number listed, if obtained from a directory or other source of information compiled by a third party.

To stop unwanted fax advertisements, your opt-out request must:

- identify the fax number or numbers to which it relates; and
- be sent to the telephone number, fax number, website address (URL), or email address identified on the fax advertisement.

If you change your mind about receiving fax advertisements, you can subsequently grant express permission to receive faxes from a particular sender, orally or in writing.

Fax Broadcasters. Fax advertisements are often sent in bulk on behalf of a business or entity by separate companies called fax broadcasters. Generally, the person or business on whose behalf a fax is sent or whose property, goods, or services are advertised is liable for a violation of the junk fax rules, even if the person or business did not physically send the fax. A fax broadcaster also may be liable if it has a "high degree of involvement" in the sender's fax message, such as supplying the fax numbers to which the message is sent, providing a source of fax numbers, making representations about the legality of faxing to those numbers, or advising about how to comply with the junk fax rules. Also, if a fax broadcaster is "highly involved" in the sender's fax messages, the fax broadcaster must provide its name on the fax.

WEBLINK

Visit the FCC's Fax Advertising: What You Need to Know webpage at www.fcc.gov/guides/fax-advertising.

The Controlling the Assault of Non-Solicited Pornography and Marketing Act

The Controlling the Assault of Non-Solicited Pornography and Marketing Act (CAN-SPAM Act) of 2003 establishes requirements for those who send commercial email, spells out penalties for spammers and companies whose products are advertised in spam if they violate the law, and gives consumers the right to ask emailers to stop spamming them.

The law makes a distinction between commercial email and transactional or relationship email. The act covers only commercial electronic mail messages and regulates emailers whose primary purpose is to advertise a commercial product or service.

Transactional or relationship messages include, for example, emails informing sellers about the progress on marketing a listed property or emails thanking past customers and updating the relationships. As long as these emails don't contain false or misleading routing information, they are exempt from most provisions of the act. Informational messages, such as newsletters that don't contain advertisements are also exempt.

The law bans false or misleading header information, meaning that the "From," "To," and routing information must be correct and identify the person who sent the email. It requires that the email give recipients an opt-out method. It also requires that commercial email be identified as an advertisement and include the sender's valid physical postal address.

The new rules define the primary purpose of the rule as commercial if the email is exclusively an advertisement for a commercial product or service, if a reasonable interpretation of the subject line would lead to the conclusion that a message is commercial, or a transactional or relationship message does not appear in whole or in part at the beginning of the message's body text.

The act is enforced by the FTC and the Department of Justice (DOJ). Each violation is subject to fines up to $11,000.

WEBLINK

Visit the FTC website on spam at www.onguardonline.gov/articles/0038-spam/.

INCOME TAX REGULATIONS AFFECTING RESIDENTIAL REAL PROPERTY

Real estate licensees are not expected to be income tax experts, but they should be knowledgeable about basic provisions of the Internal Revenue Code as they relate to real estate transactions. Licensees always should advise consumers to seek professional tax advice. An important benefit to homeowners is that interest and property taxes are deductible if the taxpayer itemizes. Additionally, all or part of the gain on sale of the property is exempt from taxes.

> **In Practice**
>
> **Be careful what you tell buyers about tax deductions.**
>
> Don't tell buyers that they can deduct property taxes and interest to get them to purchase a home. You must be certain that they have enough other deductions (e.g., combined deductions exceeding $11,400 for a married couple filing jointly in 2014) so they can take full advantage of the realty-related deductions.

Exclusion of Gain From the Sale of a Personal Residence

A taxpayer currently may exclude up to $250,000 ($500,000 for a married couple filing jointly) of gain on the sale of a personal residence if the taxpayer owned and occupied the residence for at least two of the previous five years. If the taxpayer held the home less than two years, a prorated portion of the exclusion may apply. The number of times a homeowner may use this exclusion is unlimited, except that the exclusion can be used only once every two years. The law is advantageous to most families because it allows them to earn large profits on their residences tax free.

EXAMPLE: The Wilsons bought their home in 1992 for $50,000. In 1992, they added a deck and pool for $25,000. They lived in the home until they sold it for $300,000 in March of this year. Selling costs were $20,000. They would calculate their taxes as follows:

Selling price		$300,000
Less selling expenses		– $ 20,000
Equals amount realized		$280,000
Basis		
Original cost	$50,000	
Plus improvements	+ $25,000	
Equals adjusted basis		$75,000
Gain on sale ($280,000 – $75,000)		$205,000
Less exclusion on sale of residence		– $500,000
Taxable capital gain		**$0**

The exclusion is available only once every two years, but there are several exceptions. Under the old rules, if the home has been held fewer than two years and if the move is job-related or health-related or there were other unforeseen circumstances, the taxpayer was allowed a prorated portion of the exclusion. The IRS ruled that unforeseen circumstances could include:

- divorce, legal separation, or death of a spouse;

- becoming eligible for unemployment compensation;

- a change in employment that makes it impossible to pay the mortgage or basic living expenses;

- multiple births resulting from the same pregnancy;

- damage to the home from a natural disaster, act of war, or terrorism; and

- condemnation, seizure, or involuntary conversion of the property, such as foreclosure.

Taxation of Gain From Sale of Real Estate

Short-term capital gains (for property held for one year or less) are taxed at the investor's ordinary income tax rate. Long-term capital gains (property held for more than 12 months) are taxed at different rates, depending on the taxpayer's income:

- 0% for taxpayers who are in the 10% to 15% tax brackets

- 15% for taxpayers in the 25%, 28%, 33%, or 35% tax brackets

- 20% for taxpayers in the 39.6% tax bracket. This includes single filers earning more than $400,000 and married couples filing jointly making more than $450,000

Capital gains income is subject to an additional 3.8% Medicare tax for single filers making more than $200,000 or married couples filing jointly who make more than $250,000.

Taxation of Independent Contractors

Most real estate brokerage firms contract with their sales associates to be independent contractors. If the broker meets all requirements, this results in substantial savings, primarily from the employer's share of Social Security taxes, workers' compensation insurance, unemployment taxes, and other fringe benefits. There are three major requirements to qualify for independent contractor status:

- ■ The sales associate must hold a real estate license.

- ■ The sales associate's gross income must be based on production rather than on the number of hours worked.

- ■ The sales associate's work must be done based on a written contract that states, among other things, that the sales associate will not be considered an employee for federal tax purposes.

However, if the broker reimburses the sales associate for business costs such as automobile expenses and pays for business cards, insurance plans, or licensing or board dues, the IRS may determine that the sales associate is an employee. The broker would then be liable for Social Security and Medicare taxes and income taxes.

ANTITRUST LAWS

Brokers risk their assets and careers by attempting to get other brokers to charge a standard commission. Antitrust laws prohibit any action by a party to fix prices or inhibit competition by using unfair practices. Some of the prohibited actions under antitrust laws include:

- ■ conspiracy to set prices,

- ■ splitting up competitive market areas,

- ■ conspiring to boycott cut-rate brokers or otherwise interfering with their business, and

- ■ requiring a minimum commission before allowing listings to be circulated in any service, such as through a multiple listing service (MLS).

Certain of these acts are considered so harmful to competition that they are almost always illegal. These acts are called "per se" violations of the Sherman Antitrust Act, so that no defense is allowed.

Violating the Sherman Antitrust Act carries severe penalties, both civil and criminal. Criminal penalties may carry fines of up to $100 million for corporations and $1 million for individuals.

DISCUSSION EXERCISE 1.3

Boycotting. Gloria, president of Big Tree Realty, Inc., had a luncheon meeting with Samuel, president of Statewide Residential Brokers, Inc. The subject of the meeting was Southern Discount Realty and the increased market share it had achieved since it announced its new discount fee structure. Big Tree and Statewide previously had a 47% market share between them, but their combined share was now 39%.

They agreed to tell their sales associates not to show Southern Discount Realty listings to their buyers. Also, they agreed to call several other brokers in the area to do the same.

"A broker simply cannot give good service by charging that little. It's unprofessional," Gloria said.

If you were a sales associate for Statewide Realty and your sales manager suggested that you boycott Southern Discount listings, what would your response be?

AVOIDING MISREPRESENTATION

While the legal definition is much broader, the common definition of **misrepresentation** is the act of a licensee who, either intentionally or unintentionally, fails to disclose a **material fact** or makes a **false or misleading statement** that is justifiably relied on by another, resulting in damage. Intentional misrepresentation is actionable as fraud. Unintentional misrepresentation is negligence.

When a property experiences problems after the closing that were not disclosed by the brokers, buyers sometimes file a claim for misrepresentation. All licensees, regardless of their brokerage relationship, have the duty to disclose known facts that materially affect the value of residential property that are not readily observable. Buyers frequently ask brokers to describe a property and to make representations about the condition of the property or other facts associated with the sale.

To win a fraudulent misrepresentation case against a broker, the plaintiff must prove that:

- the broker made an error in giving information, oral or written, to the buyer or failed to disclose a material fact to the buyer;
- the broker knew the statement was not accurate or the information should have been disclosed;
- the plaintiff reasonably relied on such statement; and
- the plaintiff was damaged as a result.

The buyer is entitled to relief if the representation was a material inducement to the contract. The broker's duty stems from the seller's duty not to misrepresent.

In establishing liability or in applying remedies, it does not make a difference whether the misrepresentation was fraudulent (intentional) or negligent (unintentional). The most common remedies available to the offended party include monetary damages, rescission of the contract, forfeiture of the broker's commission, and disciplinary action by the FREC.

In Practice

Don't make any of the following statements to a buyer:

- "No need to get a title search. I sold this house last year and title was fine." Chapter 475 requires that you tell buyers to get an attorney's opinion or purchase title insurance.
- "Don't worry, the seller told me by phone that I could sign the contract for her." A contract for sale of real property is not enforceable unless the person has a power of attorney. A sales associate or broker should avoid using a power of attorney because of representation issues.
- "I won't be able to present your offer until the seller decides what to do about the offer I submitted yesterday." Chapter 475 requires you to present all offers.
- "That roof is in great condition—I can tell just by looking at it." If it's not OK, you may get to repair it at your expense.

Practical Steps for Sales Associates

A real estate licensee can take several practical steps to decrease the risk of misrepresentation claims:

1. Have the seller complete a **property condition disclosure** form and discuss any potential problem areas.

2. Inform the seller of the legal duty to disclose material facts that affect the value of residential property and are not readily observable.

3. Find out about the following common problem areas with respect to condominiums:

   - House rules regarding children, pets, and waterbeds
   - Location of lockers and parking stalls
   - Existence of special assessments (for what and how much)
   - Maintenance fee(s) (what is included, proposed increases)
   - Planned future capital improvements
   - Existing reserves and purpose of reserves
   - Historical information as to when capital improvements were completed

4. Ask about factors external to the property that might influence its value and affect a person's decision to buy, such as the following examples:

   - Abutting and nearby uses (present and proposed), such as a rock band venue next door
   - Highway expansion or rerouting of a bus line

5. Do not make statements concerning matters about which you do not have first-hand knowledge or that are not based on expert opinion or advice. Have a list of government agencies from which you can get information. Suggest that the buyer check things out, too, by providing the telephone numbers and website addresses of the appropriate government agencies. It is best that important technical information come directly to the buyer from the government agency.

6. Do not participate with the seller in nondisclosure of required information. If the seller refuses to disclose material defects, decline the listing. Taking a listing of this nature is not worth damage claims, loss of reputation, and loss of license.

7. Avoid exaggeration. If you wish to venture a quick opinion about things you are not certain about, make sure the buyer understands that it is only a guess, and be certain the buyer does not rely on it in making a decision.

8. Disclose pertinent information in writing, such as in a property condition disclosure form from the sellers. The buyers should sign the disclosure indicating that they have received it. A confirmation letter would confirm earlier discussions in which you pointed out a leaky roof or the need to consult with a soil engineer, and it would affirm that neither you nor the seller makes any warranty as to the condition of the roof or the foundation. Keep copies of these documents in the transaction file.

9. When using email for discussing important items, request that the customer reply to the email. Keep the email and reply for documentation.

Home Inspection

One of the most effective risk-management tools available to licensees is to suggest that the buyer order a home inspection. The inspection is intended to disclose defects in a building. It is better to identify problems before the closing so the parties can negotiate a settlement. If a material defect is discovered after closing, the buyer may sue the licensee rather than the seller, who may now live in a distant city.

Home inspectors must be licensed by the DBPR. They must have a high school diploma, be of good character, complete a minimum of 120 hours of prescribed education, and pass a state examination.

In Practice

Have buyers select their own inspector so there's no question about collusion. Give your buyers a list with names and phone numbers of qualified home inspectors in your area.

WEBLINK

Visit the American Society of Home Inspectors website at www.ashi.org.

Death in a Property

A seller or a licensee has no duty to disclose a death in the property (see 689.25(1)(b), F.S.):

(1) (a)   The fact that an occupant of real property is infected or has been infected with human immunodeficiency virus or diagnosed with acquired immune deficiency syndrome is not a material fact that must be disclosed in a real estate transaction.

(b)   The fact that a property was, or was at any time suspected to have been, the site of a homicide, suicide, or death is not a material fact that must be disclosed in a real estate transaction.

(2)   A cause of action shall not arise against an owner of real property, his or her agent, an agent of a transferee of real property, or a person licensed under Chapter 475 for the failure to disclose to the transferee that the property was or was suspected to have been the site of a homicide, suicide, or death or that an occupant of that property was infected with human immunodeficiency virus or diagnosed with acquired immune deficiency syndrome.

QUICK REFERENCE CHART FOR REQUIRED DISCLOSURES

Figure 1.1 shows numerous required disclosures. It is intended to be a quick reference guide to help licensees understand some of the many requirements, but it should not be considered all-inclusive.

FIGURE 1.1 ■ Florida Real Estate Disclosure Chart

Subject	Disclosure Trigger	To	Disclosure Requirement
Ad Valorem Tax Disclosure	Contract to purchase	Buyer	Disclosure that property taxes may increase after the purchase from reassessments
Brokerage relationship disclosures	Entering into a representation agreement or showing a property	Buyer or seller	Review this chapter for detailed disclosure requirements
Condominium Act— purchase cancellation	Contract to purchase	Buyer	15-day cancellation privilege when buying from a developer; 3-day cancellation privilege when buying a resale unit
Condominium Act— recreation lease	Contract to purchase	Buyer	Whether a recreational lease exists; when membership in a recreation facilities club is required; description of the facilities and the charges
Federal Reserve's Regulation Z	When advertising financial terms on real property, a trigger item is included in ad	Readers of ads	Full disclosure of all material factors in financing, including price, down payment, monthly payment, finance costs, and annual percentage rate of interest
Florida Building Energy-Efficiency Act	Contract to purchase	Buyer	Energy-efficiency rating system description and how to get the building rated
Homeowners Association Disclosure	Contract to purchase	Buyer	Notification that the owner is required to be a member of an association; there are covenants and restrictions; there is a required assessment; there may be a land use fee
Landlord and Tenant Act	Within 30 days of signing lease	Tenant	Where deposit is being held; whether it is in an interest-bearing account and the interest rate, if any
Land use disclaimer— some jurisdictions, but not statewide	Contract to purchase	Buyer	Restrictive covenants for the neighborhood; buyer's responsibility to investigate whether the anticipated land use conforms to comprehensive plan, zoning, building codes, etc.; public or private street and drainage maintenance
Lead-based paint	Contracts for purchase or lease	Buyer or tenant	Lead hazard information pamphlet; disclosure of any known hazards; 10-day inspection and cancellation privilege
Property condition disclosure	When listing property; at time of showing property	Seller Buyer	Any material defects that affect the property's value
Radon gas	Contracts for purchase or lease	Buyer or tenant	Statement as to the nature of the gas and how to get more information
Roof inspection ordinance— some jurisdictions	Closing of a real estate transaction	Buyer	Disclosure of condition of roof covering, decking, and framing, usually made within 30 days before closing

F I G U R E 1.1 ■ Florida Real Estate Disclosure Chart (continued)

Subject	Disclosure Trigger	To	Disclosure Requirement
Time-Share Act—purchase cancellation	Contract to purchase	Buyer	All material aspects of the property; rights and obligations of buyer and seller; 10-day cancellation privilege; notification that purchase is a leisure time activity, not an appreciating investment
Time-Share Act—unit assessments	Contract to purchase	Buyer	Annual assessment for common expenses
Wood-destroying organisms report	Closing of a real estate transaction that includes commercial or residential buildings	Buyer	Wood-destroying organisms report signed by a licensed pest inspector, made within 30 days before closing date

SUMMARY

- Before renewing a license for the first time, licensees must complete a post-license course, or the license will be void.

- After the first renewal, a licensee must complete 14 hours of continuing education before renewing.

- Three brokerage relationships are available to licensees who sell residential property:

  - Single agent brokers represent either the buyer or the seller, but not both, in a transaction. Only single agent brokers may call their customers "principals." Principals are responsible for the acts of their single agent. The broker must give a Single Agent Notice before showing property or before entering a representation agreement. The notice should be signed, but if the principal declines to sign the notice, the licensee may note the fact on the form and work with the principal.

  - Transaction brokers provide limited representation but do not have a fiduciary relationship with the customer. The customer is not responsible for the acts of the transaction broker. Transaction brokers need not give a brokerage relationship notice to customers. A single agent may enter into a transaction broker relationship by having the principal sign a Consent to Transition to Transaction Broker Notice.

  - Brokers who will not represent the customer as a single agent or a transaction broker must give the customer a No Brokerage Relationship Notice before showing property. The notice need not be signed.

- Brokers in nonresidential transactions may work with a customer in one of the ways shown but need not give a brokerage relationship notice.

- Nonresidential brokers may appoint one sales associate in the firm to represent the seller and one sales associate to represent the buyer.

  - As designated sales associates, they act as single agents for their principal. The broker must remain neutral.

  - The buyer and the seller must each have at least $1 million in assets and agree to the relationship.

  - A Designated Sales Associate Notice and a Single Agent Notice must be given to each party.

- The law specifically forbids dual agency.

- Florida licensees who are found guilty or plead nolo contendere to any crime, including misdemeanors, must report this fact to the FREC within 30 days.

- If a home is in a subdivision that requires membership in a community association, a written disclosure must be attached to the contract for sale, or the contract may be voidable by the buyer.

- Before a buyer signs a contract to purchase a homestead property, owners must give an ad valorem tax disclosure form to the buyer that states that the property taxes may increase in the year following the sale.

- A radon gas disclosure must be part of every sale and lease contract. The disclosure describes the gas but does not require an inspection.

- If a residential property was built before 1978, the seller or the landlord must provide a lead warning statement, a lead hazard information pamphlet, information about the presence of any known lead-based paint, and a 10-day period to conduct an inspection. Contractors who disturb paint in these properties must be certified and follow specific work procedures.

- The Comprehensive Environmental Response, Compensation, and Liability Act of 1990 (CERCLA) imposes substantial toxic waste cleanup liability on buyers, sellers, attorneys, and brokers. A buyer who wants to avoid liability must exercise due diligence. Licensees should be careful when listing or selling sites such as former gas stations or dry cleaning establishments.

- Brokers may not call consumers on federal or state do-not-call lists unless the consumer purchased or listed property no more than 18 months or made an inquiry no more than 3 months ago.

- Persons who send a fax must have an established business relationship with the recipient and offer a way for the recipient to opt out of future faxes.

- Taxpayers may exclude up to $250,000 ($500,000 for married couples filing jointly) of the gain on the sale of a principal residence.

- In real estate transactions, licensees must be careful to disclose fully any facts that materially affect the property's value. A licensee must avoid making statements that could result in a claim of misrepresentation. The licensee should use a property condition disclosure statement and having the home inspected by a licensed home inspector to reduce liability.

REVIEW QUESTIONS

1. A broker need NOT give a brokerage relationship disclosure when the property being shown is a
    a. triplex.
    b. single-family home valued at more than $1 million.
    c. seven-acre tract zoned for agricultural use.
    d. nonresidential property.

2. A principal is legally represented by a
    a. single agent.
    b. dual agent.
    c. transaction broker.
    d. nonrepresentative.

3. Which statement to a prospective buyer is NOT likely to increase a licensee's liability?
    a. "The title to the property is clear; I checked the courthouse yesterday."
    b. "I used to be in construction, so I can tell you that the roof is in perfect condition."
    c. "You should be able to get information from the school board about which school your child would attend if you purchase this home."
    d. "You don't need a home inspection because the house is only five years old."

4. A licensee is legally required to disclose to a prospective homebuyer that
    a. there was a recent murder in the house.
    b. the roof occasionally leaks.
    c. the occupant of the property is infected with human immunodeficiency virus.
    d. the former owner was killed when he fell from the roof.

5. A broker may not legally work with a buyer or a seller as a
    a. transaction broker.
    b. single agent.
    c. dual agent.
    d. nonrepresentative.

6. A principal is responsible for the acts of her
    a. transaction broker.
    b. dual agent.
    c. single agent.
    d. nonrepresentative.

7. A student failed her sales associate post-licensing course for the second time. What are her options if she wishes to maintain her license?
    a. She must wait 30 days and pass a different end-of-course exam.
    b. She must take the 63-hour prelicense course for sales associates and pass the course exam and the state exam.
    c. She must retake at least 45 hours of the sales associate prelicense course and pass a course exam.
    d. She must retake the course and pass the end-of-course exam.

8. Which term is found in the Junk Fax Protection Act?
    a. Innocent purchaser
    b. Established business relationship
    c. Estimate of settlement costs
    d. National register

9. Licensed sales associates working at the seller's single-agent brokerage firm
    a. may represent either the seller or the buyer in a transaction.
    b. are legally bound to represent the seller.
    c. may have another principal in the transaction.
    d. may be transaction brokers for the buyer to ensure limited confidentiality.

10. If a broker sells commercial property exclusively, she
    a. must give the customer a No Brokerage Relationship Notice before showing property.
    b. may be a single agent, a transaction broker, a designated sales associate, or have no brokerage relationship with the customer.
    c. must give the customer a Single Agent Notice before showing property.
    d. may not be a single agent.

11. In which status does a licensee NOT need to provide a written brokerage relationship disclosure notice?
    a. Single agent broker
    b. Transaction broker
    c. Designated sales associate
    d. When acting with no brokerage relationship

12. A broker must disclose known facts that materially affect the value of residential property when that broker is
    a. a licensee with no official brokerage relationship.
    b. a single agent.
    c. the transaction broker.
    d. all of these.

13. A single agent for the seller has a no brokerage relationship with a buyer. The buyer agrees to pay up to the listed price, if necessary, but first wants to submit an offer 10% below that price. The broker should
    a. tell the seller, "The buyer said he will pay up to the listed price."
    b. refuse to disclose the statement because of the broker's duty of limited confidentiality.
    c. suggest that the seller counteroffer, if desired.
    d. tell the seller, "The buyer is qualified."

14. For how many years must a broker retain required brokerage relationship disclosures?
    a. One
    b. Three
    c. Four
    d. Five

15.   Two sales associates work for a commercial broker. The broker allows one sales associate to act as a single agent for the buyer and the other sales associate to act as a single agent for the seller. Both the buyer and the seller have assets of more than $1 million and each agrees to this form of representation. The situation describes a
   a.   transaction broker relationship.
   b.   designated sales associate.
   c.   single agency.
   d.   dual agency.

16.   A real estate association's conspiracy to set prices violates
   a.   fair housing acts.
   b.   the Americans with Disabilities Act.
   c.   the do-not-call laws.
   d.   antitrust laws

17.   A man has a capital gain of $197,000 on the sale of his home, which he owned for three years. The sales price was $425,000. Sales costs were $7,000, qualified fix-up costs were $1,000, and moving costs were $2,000. How much must Henry pay in capital gains taxes on this sale if his normal tax rate is 25%?
   a. $0
   b. $39,400
   c. $98,500
   d. $197,000

18.   New concern about the presence of radon gas is the result of the increase in
   a.   radon levels at large factories.
   b.   the number of energy-efficient buildings.
   c.   the depletion of the ozone layer.
   d.   Freon® in air-conditioning systems.

19.   If a broker shows property built before 1978, that fact will require disclosures about
   a.   coastal management zones.
   b.   lead-based paint.
   c.   asbestos poisoning.
   d.   radon gas.

20.   To claim innocent purchaser status under the hazardous substance statutes, a purchaser should
   a.   refuse to purchase former gas stations.
   b.   pay for and obtain an environmental audit.
   c.   show that the seller did not reveal any problems.
   d.   ask the real estate agent for a property warranty.

2 FAIR HOUSING AND THE AMERICANS WITH DISABILITIES ACT

LEARNING OBJECTIVES

When you finish reading this chapter, you will be able to:

- list the categories of persons protected under the Fair Housing Act,
- list at least five discriminatory practices prohibited by the Fair Housing Act, and
- describe at least four requirements of the Florida Americans with Disabilities Act.

KEY TERMS

accessible
accommodation
Americans with Disabilities
 Act (ADA)
blockbusting
Civil Rights Act of 1866
codes

disability
Fair Housing Act
Fair Housing Amendments
 Act of 1988
Florida Americans with
 Disabilities Act
Florida Fair Housing Act

handicap
Housing for Older Persons
 Act
modification
redlining
steering

OVERVIEW

Title VIII of the Civil Rights Act of 1968, commonly known as the Fair Housing Act, prohibits discrimination in the sale, rental, and financing of dwellings based on race, color, religion, sex, and national origin. In 1988, Congress passed the **Fair Housing Amendments Act of 1988** (FHAA). The amendments expand coverage of Title VIII to prohibit discriminatory housing practices based on disability and familial status. The Florida Fair Housing Act is modeled after the federal act and affords victims of discrimination another, perhaps easier, remedy than suing in federal court.

Another law directly affecting real estate practitioners is the Americans with Disabilities Act. This act sets the standards for building accessibility, goods, services, and employment. Florida has a law that mirrors this act.

Florida statutes prohibit housing discrimination against persons with human immunodeficiency virus (HIV) or acquired immune deficiency syndrome (AIDS).

PUBLIC PERCEPTIONS ABOUT FAIR HOUSING LAWS

Before going further, it may be interesting to take the short quiz in Figure 2.1 that the Department of Housing and Urban Development (HUD) has used to evaluate the general public's familiarity with the fair housing laws. When you have completed the quiz, you can check your answers and compare your scores.

FIGURE 2.1   ■   A Short Quiz on Fair Housing

True or False?

1. Under federal law, it is legal for an apartment building owner to assign families with younger children to one particular building.   ☐ True   ☐ False

2. An apartment building owner has the right to reject an applicant because of poor housekeeping habits.   ☐ True   ☐ False

3. Not allowing the construction of a wheelchair ramp on the apartment building owner's property is permissible, even if the tenant agrees to remove it at her own expense upon leaving.
    ☐ True   ☐ False

4. Under federal law, indicating a preference based on religion in advertising an available apartment is perfectly legal.   ☐ True   ☐ False

5. An apartment building owner may legally reject an applicant with a history of mental illness, though he is not a danger to others.   ☐ True   ☐ False

6. A rental application may be rejected by the landlord because of the applicant's religion.
    ☐ True   ☐ False

7. When using a real estate agent, a family may sell their house only to a white buyer.   ☐ True   ☐ False

8. A real estate agent is allowed to limit a home search to certain neighborhoods based on the client's race/ethnicity.   ☐ True   ☐ False

9. A loan officer may turn down a black applicant because of the applicant's lack of steady job and income.   ☐ True   ☐ False

10. It is legal for a loan officer to require higher down payments from Hispanic families in order to get a mortgage.   ☐ True   ☐ False

Answer Key: 1. False   2. True   3. False   4. False   5. False   6. False   7. False   8. False   9. True
    10. False

Source: U.S. Department of Housing and Urban Development

Only 63% of those surveyed answered more than seven questions correctly. This survey demonstrates that many buyers and sellers of real estate don't understand fair housing laws. Customers sometimes make requests for licensees to act illegally on their behalf. It is the licensee's duty to describe the law and to scrupulously follow its requirements.

CIVIL RIGHTS ACT OF 1866

The **Civil Rights Act of 1866** was passed just after the Civil War to prohibit discrimination based on race. For many years, the law was not widely enforced, but in 1968 the U.S. Supreme Court upheld the law in the case of *Jones v. Mayer*. Subsequent court actions requiring compliance with the law have been numerous and successful.

THE FAIR HOUSING ACT

The Civil Rights Act of 1968 included Title VIII, the **Fair Housing Act**. The act, as amended, protects against discrimination in housing based on race, color, religion, sex, national origin, handicap and familial status. A discussion of each protected class follows.

Race and Color

Real estate advertisements should not indicate the racial makeup of a neighborhood. An ad that says, "Excellent area with many Asian families" would be a clear violation. Sales associates may never steer buying prospects into a neighborhood based on the buyer's description of racial or ethnic characteristics.

> **EXAMPLE:** An owner agrees to sell a house, but after discovering that the buyers are black, pulls the house off the market, then promptly lists it for sale again. If the buyers file a discrimination complaint, HUD may authorize the U.S. Department of Justice to seek an injunction in federal district court to prevent the owner from selling the house to anyone else until HUD investigates the complaint.

> **In Practice**
>
> Don't advertise using the words *Negro, Black, Caucasian, Oriental, American Indian, Asian, African American, Colored,* et cetera.

Religion

Licensees should not advertise that a home is "near St. Thomas Catholic Church" or that the neighborhood is "within walking distance of Temple Israel Day School."

> **EXAMPLE:** A Jewish person responds to a landlord's advertisement to rent an apartment. The owner says, "As a matter of principle, we rent to Christians only and do not rent to Jews, Muslims, or Hindus. There's a nice apartment down the street whose landlord will rent to you, and it has several vacancies."

> **In Practice**
>
> Don't advertise using the words *Protestant, Christian, Catholic, Jew, Muslim,* et cetera.

Sex

Advertisements for single-family dwellings or apartments may not describe a preference or limitation based on sex. "Single female roommate wanted" is allowed as an exception for shared living advertising.

National Origin

Steering a Cuban family into an area because they want to live in a Spanish-speaking area is a violation. Advertising for "English-speaking tenant only" is a limitation and is illegal.

> **In Practice**
>
> Don't advertise using the words *Mexican-American*, *Puerto Rican*, *Filipino*, *Polish*, *Hungarian*, *Irish*, *Italian*, *Chicano*, *African*, *Hispanic*, *Chinese*, *Indian*, *Latino*, et cetera.

Handicap

A **handicap** is defined in the act as:

- a physical or mental impairment that substantially limits one or more of a person's major life activities, such as walking, seeing, hearing, learning, breathing, caring for oneself, or working;
- a record of having such an impairment; or
- being regarded as having such an impairment.

Not only can housing providers not discriminate against a person with a disability, but they must make reasonable accommodations to rules, policies, and practices to provide that person with the same enjoyment of a dwelling; to allow the person to make reasonable physical modifications of premises; and to require multifamily housing built since March 1991 to have basic wheelchair accessibility.

An **accommodation** is a change that the housing provider must provide. An example would be a tenant's request for a handicapped-accessible parking space close to the tenant's unit. A **modification** is a change that the housing provider must allow the tenant to provide at the tenant's expense. An example would be lowering cabinets and countertops for accessibility.

The Fair Housing Act's protection covers not only home seekers with disabilities but also buyers and renters without disabilities who live or are associated with individuals with disabilities.

A number of cases have involved housing providers' responsibility to allow service or companion animals for people with disabilities even when they have a "no pets" rule in place. Licensees who advertise "not wheelchair accessible" violate the law. However, it is acceptable to advertise that a residence is "handicapped accessible," or "wheelchair ramp for accessibility."

> **In Practice**
>
> Don't advertise using the words *crippled*, *blind*, *deaf*, *mentally ill*, *retarded*, *impaired*, *handicapped*, *physically fit*, et cetera.

Familial Status

Familial status is the presence or anticipated presence of children under age 18 in a household. Before the 1988 amendments were passed, a HUD study showed that 25% of apartment complexes had a "no children" policy. The policy decreased housing options for families with children.

The act defines *familial status* as:

- a parent or another person having legal custody of such individual or individuals; or

- the designee of such parent or other person having such custody, with the written permission of such parent or other person. The protections afforded against discrimination based on familial status apply to any person who is pregnant or is in the process of securing legal custody of any individual who is not at least 18 years old.

Housing providers may not refuse to deal with families with children, segregate children into certain housing units, restrict children's activities with special rules, charge higher security deposits, restrict families with children only to some areas or floors of a property, restrict the number of children in a unit, or refuse to rent to children of a certain age. Owners may set reasonable rules for maximum occupancy in an apartment building, but owners should obtain legal advice before establishing such rules.

Under the **Housing for Older Persons Act**, certain 55-and-older communities are exempt if at least 80% of the units have at least one occupant who is at least 55 years of age. While such communities can legally ban children, they still may not discriminate based on race, color, national origin, religion, sex, or disability.

In Practice

Don't advertise the words *children*, *adults*, *singles*, *mature persons*, et cetera.

Persons Covered by the Fair Housing Act

The law applies to persons who own four or more homes, multifamily properties (except properties with fewer than four units, one of which is occupied by the owner), brokers and sales associates who sell two or more homes in a year, and transactions in which a broker is involved. While it appears that a private owner may be able to discriminate under the 1968 act, the 1866 act clearly prohibits discrimination based on race.

Who Is Not Covered by the Act?

The Fair Housing Act does not apply to all persons or organizations, as seen in the following three categories:

- Religious organizations may limit the sale, rental, or occupancy of dwellings that they own or operate for other than a commercial purpose to persons of the same religion, and they may give preference to such persons, unless membership in such religion is restricted because of race, color, or national origin.

- Private clubs that provide lodgings that they own or operate for other than a commercial purpose may limit the rental of such lodgings to its members.
- Owners of any single-family house may restrict the sale or rental of the house, provided the following conditions are met:
    - The owner does not own or have any interest in more than three single-family houses at any one time.
    - The house is sold or rented without the use of a real estate broker, agent, or salesperson. If the owner selling the house does not reside in it at the time of the sale or was not the most recent resident of the house prior to such sale, the exemption applies to only one such sale in any 24-month period.
    - The rooms or units in dwellings contain living quarters occupied or intended to be occupied by no more than four families living independently of each other, if the owner actually maintains and occupies one of such living quarters as her residence.

Students and smokers are not protected. Income status, sexual orientation, marital status, and age are also not protected groups. These classes may, however, be protected under a local ordinance. Therefore, before drafting a fair housing policy, a housing provider should determine whether local ordinances protect individuals that are not protected by state or federal law.

Sexual Orientation

The Fair Housing Act does not specifically include sexual orientation and gender identity as prohibited bases. However, a lesbian, gay, bisexual, or transgender (LGBT) person's experience with sexual orientation or gender identity housing discrimination may still be covered by the Fair Housing Act. In addition, housing providers that receive HUD funding, have loans insured by the Federal Housing Administration (FHA), as well as lenders insured by FHA, may be subject to HUD program regulations intended to ensure equal access of LGBT persons.

Violations

The following acts violate fair housing laws:

- Refuse to sell or rent a dwelling after a bona fide offer has been made, or to refuse to negotiate for the sale or rental of a dwelling because of race, color, religion, sex, familial status, or national origin, or to discriminate in the sale or rental of a dwelling because of handicap.
- Discriminate in the terms, conditions, or privileges of the sale or rental of a dwelling, or in the provision of services or facilities in connection with sales or rentals, because of race, color, religion, sex, handicap, familial status, or national origin.
- Engage in any conduct relating to housing that denies dwellings to persons because of race, color, religion, sex, handicap, familial status, or national origin.
- Make, print, or publish any notice, statement, or advertisement with respect to the sale or rental of a dwelling that indicates any preference, limitation, or discrimination because of race, color, religion, sex, handicap, familial status, or national origin.

- Represent to any person because of race, color, religion, sex, handicap, familial status, or national origin that a dwelling is not available for sale or rental when such dwelling is in fact available.

- Induce for profit or attempt to induce a person to sell or rent a dwelling by representations regarding the entry into the neighborhood of persons of a particular race, color, religion, sex, familial status, or national origin or with a handicap. In establishing a discriminatory housing practice under this section, it is not necessary that there was, in fact, a profit as long as profit was a factor for engaging in the **blockbusting** activity.

- Deny access to or membership in any multiple listing service, real estate brokers' association, or other service organization or facility relating to the business of selling or renting a dwelling because of race, color, religion, sex, handicap, familial status, or national origin.

- Engage in **steering**, an illegal practice against a person or persons in a protected class. It is possible to be guilty of steering, even when trying to be helpful. For example, a Hispanic woman asked a sales associate to find a Spanish-speaking area so her children could retain part of their culture. Steering is performed by:

  - discouraging that person from inspecting, purchasing, or renting a dwelling;

  - discouraging the purchase or rental of a dwelling by exaggerating drawbacks or failing to inform the person of desirable features of a dwelling or of a community, neighborhood, or development;

  - communicating to any prospective purchasers that they would not be comfortable or compatible with existing residents of a community, neighborhood, or development; or

  - assigning any person to a particular section of a community, neighborhood, or development, or to a particular floor of a building.

- Engage in prohibited activities relating to dwellings, including but not limited to:

  - discharging or taking other adverse action against an employee, broker, or agent because he or she refused to participate in a discriminatory housing practice;

  - employing **codes** (such as an asterisk in the upper right corner of a rental application) or other devices to segregate or reject applicants, purchasers, or renters;

  - refusing to take or to show listings of dwellings in certain areas because of race, color, religion, sex, handicap, familial status, or national origin;

  - refusing to deal with certain brokers or agents because they or one or more of their clients are of a particular race, color, religion, sex, handicap, familial status, or national origin;

  - denying or delaying the processing of an application made by a purchaser or renter or refusing to approve such a person for occupancy in a cooperative or condominium dwelling because of race, color, religion, sex, handicap, familial status, or national origin.

- Discriminate against any person in making loans for a dwelling, or which is or is to be secured by a dwelling, because of race, color, religion, sex, handicap, familial status, or national origin. Prohibited practices include, but are not limited to, failing or refusing to provide to any person the availability of loans, application requirements, procedures, or standards for the review and approval of loans or financial assistance, or providing information that is inaccurate or different from that provided others, because of race, color, religion, sex, handicap, familial status, or national origin. This violation is called **redlining**.

The Equal Credit Opportunity Act (ECOA) gives additional protection to consumers who apply for mortgages to purchase, finance, or make home improvements and is covered in more detail in chapter 12.

In Practice

Refuse to engage in discriminatory behavior with a buyer. If a buyer asks you about the ethnic characteristics of a neighborhood, don't get involved in the conversation. This response may keep you out of trouble:

> I appreciate having the opportunity to work with you in finding a home. The law and our company's policy do not allow me to show you homes based on the racial, religious, or ethnic characteristics of a neighborhood. So I won't be able to place any such restrictions on showings or information about the availability of homes for sale or for rent.

ADVERTISING

Selective Use of Advertising Media or Content

The selective use of advertising content can violate the Fair Housing Act. For example, the use of the English language alone or the exclusive use of advertising catering to the majority population in an area, when there are also non-English-speaking persons or other minority persons, may be discriminatory. The following are examples of the selective use of advertisements that may be discriminatory:

- *Selective geographic advertisements.* Such selective use may involve the strategic placement of billboards, brochure advertisements distributed within a limited geographic area by hand or in the mail, or advertising in particular geographic-coverage editions of major metropolitan newspapers.

- *Selective use of equal opportunity slogan or logo.* When placing advertisements, such selective use may involve placing the equal housing opportunity slogan or logo in advertising reaching some geographic areas but not others.

- *Selective use of human models when conducting an advertising campaign.* Selective advertising may involve an advertising campaign using human models primarily in media that cater to one racial or national origin segment of the population without a similar advertising campaign directed at other groups.

Evidence of Compliance with Fair Housing Laws

In the investigation of complaints, HUD will consider, as evidence of compliance, among other things:

- the use of the equal housing opportunity logo, statement, or slogan stating that the property is available to all persons regardless of race, color, religion, sex, handicap, familial status, or national origin; and

- that when photographic ads are used, human models should be representative of the majority and minority populations in the area, including both sexes and children, where appropriate.

The choice of logo, statement, or slogan will depend on the type of media used (visual or auditory) and, in space advertising, on the size of the advertisement (see Figure 2.2).

F I G U R E 2.2 ■   Advertising Guide for Fair Housing Logos

As a guide to advertising the equal housing opportunity logo, licensees can use this simple formula:

Size of advertisement	Size of logo in inches
½ page or larger	2 × 2
⅓ page up to ½ page	1 × 1
4 column inches to ⅓ page	½ × ½
Less than 4 column inches	Do not use

In any other advertisements, if other logotypes are used in the advertisement, then the equal housing opportunity logo should be of a size at least equal to the largest of the other logotypes.

In space advertising that is less than 4 column inches (one column 4 inches long or two columns 2 inches long) of a page in size, the equal housing opportunity slogan should not be used.

Such advertisements may be grouped with other advertisements under a caption stating that the housing is available to all without regard to race, color, religion, sex, handicap, familial status, or national origin.

Forms To Go

Brokers should post the fair housing poster (see Appendix B) in all offices. Failure to do so shifts the burden of proof in discrimination actions to the broker. It is the broker's responsibility to provide training and supervision to ensure compliance with the law.

In Practice

HUD says it's all right to use these words in your advertising: *master bedroom, desirable neighborhood, Santa Claus, Easter Bunny, St. Valentine's Day, Merry Christmas, Happy Easter, mother-in-law suite, bachelor apartment, great view, fourth-floor walk-up, walk-in closets, jogging trails, walk to bus stop, nonsmoking, sober, wheelchair ramp, two bedroom, cozy, family room, no bicycles allowed,* and *quiet streets.*

DISCUSSION EXERCISE 2.1

Examples of Fair Housing Violations. Match the letter of the prohibited action to the appropriate example.

Prohibited Action	Letter	Example of Violation
A. Advertising any discriminatory preference or limitation in housing or making any inquiry or reference that is discriminatory in nature	_____	A man owns an apartment building with 160 residential units. When a Hispanic family asks to look at some of the apartments, he tells them to go away.
B. Denying membership or participation in a multiple-listing service, a real estate organization, or another facility related to the sale or rental of housing as a means of discrimination	_____	A woman is quite religious, and when a Muslim family asks to look at a $900 apartment, she tells them that the $900 price is a discount for Christians. Their rent would be $1,000.
	_____	A real estate developer runs a full-page ad in the *Tampa Tribune* that says, "Be a happy homeowner in Bellair Gardens." The only photo shows several African American families.
C. Falsely representing that a property is not for sale	_____	A woman is a person with disabilities. When she looks at a single-family home for rent, the owner says the home is not available. The next day, the house is advertised and a For Rent sign is posted.
D. Altering the terms or conditions of a home loan, or denying a loan, as a means of discrimination		
E. Profiting by inducing property owners to sell or rent based on the prospective entry into the neighborhood of persons of a protected class	_____	A sales associate sends a newsletter to homeowners in a predominantly white neighborhood. The cover of the newsletter has a photo showing several black persons. The title of the newsletter is *The Changing Face of Sunland Station.*
F. Refusing to sell, rent, or negotiate the sale or rental of housing	_____	A landlord requires that a divorced mother of three children pay for a credit report and have her father cosign her lease. A male friend had lower income than she did and poor credit but was not required to do either of those things.
G. Changing the terms or conditions or services for different individuals as a method of screening	_____	The Indian River Realty Council meets weekly to market available properties. The council has restricted membership to Caucasian males, rejecting applications from women and African Americans.

FAIR HOUSING ENFORCEMENT

HUD's Fair Housing Complaint Process

People have one year to file a complaint with HUD. The complaint should include:

- the complainant's name and address,
- the name and address of the person or company who is the subject of the complaint,
- the address or other identification of the housing involved,
- a short description of the facts that caused the complainant to believe his or her rights were violated, and
- the dates of the alleged violation.

A more detailed discussion of the complaint process is described below.

Intake. After HUD has received the initial information, an intake specialist will contact the complainant by phone to collect facts about the alleged discrimination. The specialist will then review the allegations to determine whether the matter is within HUD's jurisdiction.

Filing. If HUD accepts the complaint for investigation, the investigator will draft a formal complaint on HUD's standard form and mail it to the complainant. The complainant must sign the form and return it to HUD.

Within 10 days after receiving the signed complaint, HUD will send the respondent notice that a fair housing complaint has been filed against him along with a copy of the complaint. Within 10 days of receiving the notice, the respondent must submit to HUD an answer to the complaint.

Investigation. As part of the investigation, HUD will interview the complainant, the respondent, and pertinent witnesses. HUD has the authority to take depositions, issue subpoenas and interrogatories, and compel testimony or documents.

Conciliation. The Fair Housing Act requires HUD to bring the parties together to attempt to resolve every fair housing complaint. If the parties sign a conciliation agreement, HUD will end its investigation and close the case.

No Cause Determination. If, after a thorough investigation, HUD finds no reasonable cause to believe that housing discrimination has occurred or is about to occur, HUD will issue a determination of "no reasonable cause" and close the case. A complainant who disagrees can request reconsideration of the case.

Cause Determination and Charge. If the investigation produces reasonable cause to believe that discrimination has occurred or is about to occur, HUD will issue a determination of reasonable cause and charge the respondent with violating the law.

After HUD issues a charge, a HUD administrative law judge (ALJ) will hear the case unless either party elects to have the case heard in federal civil court. Parties must elect within 20 days of receipt of the charge.

Hearing in a U.S. District Court. If the court finds that a discriminatory housing practice has occurred or is about to occur, it can award actual and punitive damages as well as attorneys fees.

Hearing Before a HUD ALJ. When the ALJ decides the case, the ALJ will issue an initial decision.

If the ALJ finds that housing discrimination has occurred or is about to occur, the ALJ can award a maximum civil penalty of $11,000, per violation, for a first offense, in addition to actual damages for the complainant, injunctive or other equitable relief, and attorneys' fees.

WEBLINK

To report fair housing violations online, go to http://portal.hud.gov/hudportal/HUD?src=/program_offices/ fair_housing_equal_opp/online-complaint.

Testing

As part of its investigative process, HUD, as well as other organizations, visit rental and sales offices to monitor compliance with the law. The testers are usually organized in teams that have different ethnic, religious, or disability characteristics. Sometimes a black couple visits a real estate office in response to an ad for a specific house. A white couple wanting to see the same house would follow them sometime later. Of course, the test is to see whether the sales associate asks the same questions, establishes different financing requirements, shows the same houses, and offers equal service to both couples.

The fair housing test forms ask the following questions:

- What was the date and time of visit?
- What is the name of the sales associate, as well as the associate's ethnicity, gender, and age?
- How long did you wait to meet with the person?
- What were you told about the availability of the home in the ad?
- Were any other homes recommended to you? (Can you provide a list of those homes?)
- Did the agent talk about fair housing laws?
- Were you referred to another associate?
- Did the agent tell you that you must go to a lender to be prequalified for financing?
- Can you list the qualifying questions you were asked, such as family size, income, savings, debts, reason for moving, et cetera?
- Can you list comments made by the agent about neighborhoods and areas, such as noise, safety, schools, rising or declining values, racial characteristics, et cetera?
- Did the agent make any remarks about race, religion, persons with disabilities, or families with children?
- What arrangements were made regarding future contact?

HUD also tests for violations against disabled persons. Of course, HUD is expecting that both couples would enjoy the same considerations.

WEBLINK

Visit the National Fair Housing Advocate Online at www.fairhousing.com.

HUD's fair housing bookshelf is available at http://portal.hud.gov/hudportal/HUD?src=/library/bookshelf08.

HUD's fair housing and equal opportunity website is at http://portal.hud.gov/hudportal/HUD?src=/program_offices/fair_housing_equal_opp.

FLORIDA FAIR HOUSING ACT (CHAPTER 760, F.S.)

The **Florida Fair Housing Act** is modeled after the federal Fair Housing Act and prohibits discrimination based on race, color, religion, sex, national origin, familial status, or handicap. The principal reason that states have their own fair housing laws is that suing in a state court gives victims of discrimination another, perhaps easier, remedy than trying to bring a federal case. Also, the states are able to add additional protected classes.

AMERICANS WITH DISABILITIES ACT

The **Americans with Disabilities Act (ADA)** prohibits discrimination based on disability in employment, programs, and services provided by state and local governments; goods and services provided by private companies; and commercial facilities. **Disability** is defined by the ADA as a physical or mental impairment that substantially limits a major life activity, such as walking, seeing, hearing, learning, breathing, caring for oneself, or working. The Department of Justice administers the law.

The ADA does not cover temporary impairments such as broken bones, nor sexual or behavioral disorders. Sexual orientation is not covered under the law. The act does protect persons who are recovering from substance abuse, but it does not protect persons who are currently engaging in the current illegal use of controlled substances. Juvenile offenders and sex offenders, by virtue of that status, are not persons with disabilities protected by the act. Additionally, the act does not protect an individual with a disability whose tenancy would constitute a direct threat to the health or safety of other individuals or result in substantial physical damage to the property of others unless the threat can be eliminated or significantly reduced by reasonable accommodation.

Full compliance with ADA is required for new construction and alteration. Existing structures must be made **accessible** when that goal is readily achievable, meaning that the goal can be carried out without much difficulty or expense. The factors for determining whether changes are readily achievable are described in more detail in the ADA regulations issued by the Department of Justice, and the ADA regulations should be consulted for more detail. A tax deduction of up to $15,000 is available for removing barriers at existing places of business. Some of the ADA compliance requirements for various building areas are described on the following page.

Parking Areas

Parking areas should have one accessible space for every 25 total spaces. The accessible parking space should be 8 feet wide for a car, with a 5-foot access aisle. At least one space must be van accessible (8 feet wide with an 8-foot access aisle, and at least 98 inches of vertical clearance). The accessible spaces should be the closest available to the accessible entrance.

Access to Buildings

People with disabilities should be able to approach a building and enter as freely as everyone else. Curbs at the entrance should have curb cuts. The route of travel should be at least 36 inches wide, stable, and slip-resistant. An object must be within 27 inches of the ground in order to be detected by a person using a cane. Overhead objects must be higher than 80 inches for head room.

Ramps

For every inch of height, ramps should have at least 1 foot of length (1:12) and have a railing at least 34 inches high. There must be a 5-foot-long level landing at every 30-foot horizontal length of ramp, and at the top and bottom of the ramp and at switchbacks.

Entrances

Inaccessible entrances should have signs showing the closest accessible entrance. A service entrance should not be used as the accessible entrance unless there are no other options. Entrance doors should have at least 32 inches of clear opening, with at least 18 inches of clear wall space on the pull side of the door. Door handles should be no higher than 48 inches and operable with a closed fist. Doors in public areas should have at least a 32-inch opening.

Aisles and Pathways

Aisles and pathways to services should be at least 36 inches wide. Spaces in auditoriums should be distributed throughout the hall. Tops of tables or counters should be between 28 and 34 inches high.

Restrooms

Restrooms should be accessible to people with disabilities. If a restroom is inaccessible, there should be a sign giving directions to an accessible restroom. A wheelchair-accessible stall that is at least 5 feet square is necessary to make turns. Grab bars should be behind and on the side wall nearest the toilet. At least one lavatory should have a 30-inch-wide by 48-inch-deep clear space in front. The bottom of the lavatory should be no lower than 29 inches; the rim should be no higher than 34 inches. The faucets should be operable with one closed fist.

The ADA also requires that state and local governments provide access to programs offered to the public. The ADA also covers effective communication with people with disabilities and eligibility criteria that may restrict or prevent access, and the ADA requires reasonable modifications of policies and practices that may be discriminatory.

WEBLINK

Visit the U.S. Department of Justice's website at www.justice.gov.

The Americans with Disabilities (ADA) webpage is at www.ada.gov.

FLORIDA AMERICANS WITH DISABILITIES ACT (CHAPTER 760, F.S.)

The **Florida Americans with Disabilities Act** implements and mirrors portions of the Americans with Disabilities Act and includes other important provisions. Florida has its own act because suing in a state court gives victims of discrimination another remedy for violations.

AIDS VICTIMS AND HOUSING (CHAPTERS 689.25 AND 760.50, F.S.)

The fact that an occupant of real property is infected with HIV or diagnosed with AIDS is not a material fact that must be revealed in a real estate transaction. An owner of real property or his agent may not be sued for the failure to disclose to the buyer or tenant that an occupant of the property was infected with HIV or AIDS (689.25, F.S.).

Such disclosure also would violate the law that prohibits discrimination against persons who have acquired immune deficiency syndrome (AIDS) and a human immunodeficiency virus (HIV). Any person with or perceived as having AIDS or HIV is entitled to every protection available to handicapped persons, including fair housing protections (760.50, F.S.).

SUMMARY

- The Civil Right Act of 1866 prohibits discrimination based on race.
- Title VIII of the Civil Rights Act of 1968, as amended (the Fair Housing Act) prohibits discrimination based on race, color, religion, sex, and national origin, disability, and familial status.
- The Florida Fair Housing Act is modeled after the federal act and affords victims of discrimination another, perhaps easier remedy than suing in federal court.
- The Fair Housing Act applies to persons who own four or more houses, any multifamily property, except properties with four or fewer units when one is occupied by the owner. Brokers and sales associates who sell more than two homes a year are also required to abide by the law.
- Religious organizations may restrict sales or rentals of their property to members of the organization. Private clubs that offer lodgings may restrict the use of the property to only their members. Other characteristics that are not covered by the law include smokers, students, low income persons, sexual orientation, marital status, and age.
- Steering, blockbusting, and redlining are discriminatory practices that violate the laws.
- When advertising, it is best to describe the attributes of the property. Avoid advertising the characteristics of the likely buyer or tenant. Selective advertisements, such as to certain geographic areas, or photos with models showing only one racial, sex, or ethnic characteristic are violations.
- The Americans with Disabilities Act prohibits discrimination based on disability in employment, programs, and services provided by the government; goods and services provided by private companies; and commercial facilities.
- New construction must fully comply with ADA guidelines. Existing structures must be made accessible when that goal is readily achievable.

- Owners may be required to make accommodations to existing structures, policies, and practices to provide equal accessibility, and to allow tenants to make reasonable modifications to the premises.

- The fact that an occupant of real property is infected with HIV or diagnosed with AIDS is not a material fact that must be revealed in a real estate transaction and could violate fair housing laws is disclosure is made.

R E V I E W   Q U E S T I O N S

1. Which two classes were added to Title VIII of the Civil Rights Act of 1968 by the Fair Housing Amendments Act of 1988?
    a. Religion and sex
    b. Familial status and sex
    c. Familial status and age
    d. Handicap and familial status

2. Which is NOT a fair housing advertising violation?
    a. Home is close to the First Baptist Church and downtown.
    b. No university students!
    c. House is not modified for handicap access.
    d. Hispanic buyers welcome.

3. A lender has stopped making any loans in a minority area of Tampa. This is an illegal practice called
    a. redlining.
    b. blockbusting.
    c. steering.
    d. hammering.

4. It is NOT a potential violation of fair housing laws to advertise using
    a. the equal opportunity logo in some areas, but not in others.
    b. all black photographic models advertising for a housing development in a predominantly black area.
    c. human models that are representative of majority and minority populations in the area.
    d. a message such as "We specialize in sales to Asians."

5. A licensee is the single agent for a minority couple. He says, "Are you more comfortable buying a home in a neighborhood with people of your race?" Does this question violate any laws?
    a. Yes. This is an illegal act called blockbusting.
    b. Yes. This is an illegal question that is considered steering.
    c. No. If he is a single agent, he needs to know their housing needs.
    d. No. It is legal as long as the agent does not decide which neighborhoods to show.

6. A broker manages a single-family home. A disabled person wants to rent the property and wants to make alterations, including installing a ramp at the entrance, lowering the kitchen counters, and widening some of the doorways. He agrees to pay for the remodeling and for restoring the premises at the end of the lease term. Which is TRUE?
    a. Owners of single-family homes are not required to comply with the Americans with Disabilities Act.
    b. The broker should suggest that Harry find another home that has already been renovated for the disabled.
    c. The owners could refuse to allow the alterations, but they must do so by stating that the renovations are "not readily achievable."
    d. The broker would violate the law if he tells the prospective tenant that the owner will not allow the alterations.

7. The vertical height for a wheelchair-accessible ramp is 30 inches. How many feet must the ramp be to meet the ADA guidelines?
    a. 18
    b. 24
    c. 30
    d. 36

8. If a broker complies with an owner's instructions to restrict prospective tenants to Christians, will the broker violate the Fair Housing Act?
    a. Yes, because it shows a preference or limitation based on religion.
    b. No, because single homeowners are not exempt from the act.
    c. No, because single homeowners are exempt from the act when using a broker.
    d. No, because religious preference is not a legal violation.

9. Which advertising term would be a violation of fair housing laws?
    a. Cool bachelor apartment
    b. Third-floor walkup
    c. Apartment for sober person
    d. English-speaking tenant wanted

10. A prospective tenant asks a landlord to provide a reserved handicapped-accessible parking space at the entrance to the apartment building. This is a request for
    a. an accommodation.
    b. a modification.
    c. a waiver.
    d. a conditional permit.

11. Which is NOT discrimination based on familial status?
    a. Requiring a couple to be married before occupancy
    b. Refusing to rent to a pregnant woman
    c. Refusing to show an apartment to a grandmother who has custody of two children
    d. Setting aside a section in the apartment complex near the playground for families with children

12. Which person or entity is covered by the Fair Housing Act?
    a. A religious organization renting its own property
    b. An owner of five single-family houses
    c. A private club providing lodging at its own property for a noncommercial purpose
    d. A duplex when the owner occupies one of the units

13. An example of steering is
    a. persuading a person to sell a dwelling by saying that persons of a particular race, color, religion, sex, familial status, or national origin, or with a handicap are moving into the area.
    b. discouraging the purchase or rental of a dwelling by exaggerating drawbacks or failing to inform the person of desirable features of a dwelling.
    c. representing to any person because of race, color, religion, sex, handicap, familial status, or national origin that a dwelling is not available for sale or rental when such dwelling is in fact available.
    d. refusing to sell or rent a dwelling after a bona fide offer has been made.

14. When the parties involved in a HUD complaint are brought together to attempt to resolve the issues, it is called
    a. mediation.
    b. arbitration.
    c. adjudication
    d. conciliation.

15. Unless either party elects to have a discrimination case heard in court, the case will be heard by
    a. a HUD attorney.
    b. an assistant attorney general.
    c. an administrative law judge.
    d. civil court judge.

16. Which is NOT correct about accessible parking requirements of the Americans with Disabilities Act?
    a. Parking areas should have one accessible space for every 40 total spaces.
    b. The accessible parking space should be 8 feet wide for a car, with a 5-foot access aisle.
    c. The accessible spaces should be the closest available to the accessible entrance.
    d. At least one space must be van accessible (8 feet wide with an 8-foot access aisle, and at least 98 inches of vertical clearance).

17. Which is NOT correct about access to buildings under the Americans with Disabilities Act?
    a. Curbs at the entrance should have curb cuts.
    b. The route of travel should be at least 24 inches wide.
    c. Overhead objects must be higher than 80 inches for head room.
    d. An object must be within 27 inches of the ground in order to be detected by a person using a cane.

18. Accessibility standards for restrooms do NOT require that
    a. the bottom of the lavatory be no lower than 21 inches and the rim no higher than 42 inches.
    b. a wheelchair-accessible stall that is at least 5 feet square is necessary to make turns.
    c. grab bars should be behind and on the side wall nearest the toilet.
    d. at least one lavatory should have a 30-inch-wide by 48-inch-deep clear space in front.

19. Which parties are protected under the Americans with Disabilities Act?
    a. Juveniles who violate the law
    b. Persons who are abusing alcohol
    c. Persons with broken legs
    d. Persons recovering from drug abuse

20. A broker is showing her listing to a man. The seller has been diagnosed with AIDS. What should the broker do with respect to disclosure?
    a. The broker should not volunteer the information but, if asked, is permitted to disclose the information.
    b. The broker has the duty to make disclosure because the information may materially affect the value of the property.
    c. Disclosure of the fact would be a violation of the law.
    d. The broker must ask the seller when taking the listing if it is all right to disclose the information to prospective buyers.

BUSINESS PLANNING AND TIME MANAGEMENT

LEARNING OBJECTIVES

When you finish reading this chapter, you will be able to:

- describe three types of communication skills that the professional real estate sales associate must master,

- list the three types of knowledge a real estate sales associate needs and distinguish the differences between each type, and

- list at least 10 services that an unlicensed personal assistant can perform.

KEY TERMS

jargon	prioritize	time management
marketing knowledge	product knowledge	to-do list
nonverbal communication	professional ethics	written communication
oral communication skills	technical knowledge	skills

OVERVIEW

Probably the most important characteristics of a successful real estate licensee are professionalism and the ability to plan and manage time. The level of professionalism comes from following strong ethical guidelines and enhancing communication skills.

Because professionals are normally paid for their time and expertise, it is important to understand the benefits of goal-setting, business planning, and time management. A business plan sets goals and tells how those goals are to be achieved. Goals should be written, measurable, and attainable, and should contain deadlines.

Once the business plan has been completed, it's up to the licensee to make the most efficient use of time to maximize results and achieve all the goals.

ACHIEVING PROFESSIONALISM

Customers of real estate licensees expect them to be knowledgeable, organized, and effective in their duties. The Florida Real Estate Commission (FREC) has established the requirement for post-licensing education to help new sales associates become proficient in the day-to-day practice of real estate.

Professionalism is not easily achieved. Professional knowledge and behavior result from additional study and hard work and go beyond minimum legal requirements.

The sales associate who provides honesty, service, diligence, and knowledge tends to be more successful than the stereotypical "hard sell" sales associate who "closes" with manipulative techniques. This chapter deals with the basic qualities that better serve clients and customers:

- Professional ethics
- Communication skills
- Professional education
- Goal setting
- Time management

PROFESSIONAL ETHICS

A distinct difference exists between what is ethical and what is legal. License laws set a minimum standard of professional behavior, while codes of ethics set the higher standard of what is honest and fair to all parties involved in a real estate transaction.

Even the appearance of impropriety may cause customers to avoid doing business with a sales associate and her brokerage firm. The expression "perception is reality" is true; such shortcomings are very damaging to a real estate career.

The National Association of REALTORS® (NAR) has standardized a code of **professional ethics**, so that all members are aware of and follow their professional responsibilities. NAR's Code of Ethics is extremely influential, not only for REALTORS® but also for other licensees because ethical codes often later become license laws. The code may be the best available guideline for ethical behavior, whether or not a licensee is a member of NAR.

COMMUNICATION SKILLS

Communication is the core of the real estate brokerage business. A licensee may be knowledgeable, competent, and ethical, yet because of a lack of communication skills, be unable to help customers successfully. The four types of communication skills necessary are the following:

- Listening skills
- Oral communication skills
- Written communication skills
- Nonverbal communication skills

Listening Skills

One of the most important communication skills is listening. Good listening takes practice and has three basic steps:

1. *You must hear.* For example, if your customers say, "The price of the house is too high," you would be able to repeat the thought.

2. *You must understand.* Think about what the customers are saying. What do they mean when they say that? Should you ask some questions? Do they believe it's overpriced or that it's more than they can afford?

3. *You must evaluate.* Do the customers' comments make sense? Based on the information, should you change the type houses you show?

In Practice

Focus. Don't let your mind wander. Give your full attention. If you feel your mind wandering, lean forward into the conversation. Don't think about what you're going to say while the customers are still speaking.

Hear them out. Don't talk until they have finished. Let them say everything they want to say without being interrupted.

Listen for the main points. This is what they really want to say. The main points may be repeated. Pay special attention when they say, "The point of this is …"

Ask questions to be certain you have it right. For example, you could say, "When you said that it's too high, did you mean that it's overpriced or that it's more than you'd be comfortable buying?"

Oral Communication Skills

Talking to buyers, sellers, appraisers, surveyors, and other licensees enables the professional to share information, ask questions, and better understand the needs of others. The professional must be able to express information completely, honestly, and clearly. The individual who fails to master **oral communication skills** may be misunderstood, appearing incompetent or even dishonest.

Community colleges and universities offer communication and public speaking classes to the public. One inexpensive way to learn to speak effectively is by joining Toastmasters International, a nonprofit service organization devoted to enhancing oral communication skills. Many real estate licensees point to their years in Toastmasters as a key factor in their success.

WEBLINK

The Toastmasters International website is at www.toastmasters.org.

When licensees prepare for oral presentations, they should know exactly what they are going to say and organize the presentations logically.

Word choice is important. For instance, the statement "We can finish the deal by the end of the month" would sound better as "We should be able to close the transaction by the end of the month."

Jargon is a word or an expression related to a specialized vocation that a layperson might not understand. Licensees should avoid using jargon. By avoiding jargon, real estate professionals help clients and customers better understand the information they are trying to relate.

Written Communication Skills

Letters, emails, flyers, and other forms of written communication are often the first impression licensees make on members of the public. Bad grammar and misspellings may reflect poorly on the licensee and the brokerage firm. Written communications skills are even more important for writing a contract provision. An ambiguous clause may result in a lost sale, a lawsuit, and disciplinary action by the FREC.

DISCUSSION EXERCISE 3.1

Les shows a townhome to a married couple interested in purchasing it despite the fact that the property has been poorly maintained. The seller has told Les that he would be willing to make reasonable repairs if the buyers include them in the sales contract. So Les writes the following special clause in the contract:

"Seller agrees to remodel the townhome and put everything into first-class condition."

Based on this clause, what will the buyer expect?

What will the seller want to do?

Is there a possibility for miscommunication here?

How should this clause have been written?

Written communication skills may be enhanced by taking courses at community colleges, by reading books to improve writing skills, or by purchasing a book of ready-made real estate letters. A dictionary, a spell-checker, and a grammar checker on a software program are minimum requirements for achieving better written communication.

Nonverbal Communication Skills

Nonverbal communication, often called body language, can be very important in sales. The real estate sales associate who understands body language will be better able to read the attitudes of customers and develop body language that can make a customer comfortable and establish rapport. Often, nonverbal communication can be far more revealing than what a person says. Some obvious body language styles include those described in Figure 3.1.

F I G U R E 3.1 ■ Body Language Indicators

Body Language	Probably Means . . .	Comments
Pyramiding fingertips—the classic "banker" look	I'm superior to you, and I'm making some judgments about you	Don't do this when talking to a customer
Pyramiding, leaning back in the chair with hands joined behind the head—the "boss"	I'm superior to you; you have less status here	Don't do this when talking to a customer
Arms folded across the chest	Closed, defensive	Bad sign; you'll get nowhere in this presentation until you get the listener loosened up
Legs crossed at the knee away from the listener with body facing to the side	Closed, defensive	Bad sign; you'll get nowhere in this presentation until you get the listener loosened up
Customer looking away (no eye contact) during a sales presentation	Closed, often unfriendly	Bad sign; unlikely to buy until you can establish rapport
Palms toward the person just before speaking	Stop talking; I have more important things to say	Don't do this when talking to a customer
Stroking the chin (mostly males); fingertips to the neck (mostly females)	Sign of seriously considering the proposal	Get ready to write the offer
Scratching the head	Thinking; may be about to make a decision	Ask to help with any questions the customer may have
Staring at the ceiling	Thinking; trying to remember a fact	Ask to help with any questions the customer may have
Leaning forward into sales presentation	Interested, attentive	Good sign; you're doing something right

Reflecting. When reflecting what the other person has said, you show not only that you have understood, you indicate interest in the other person and help establish rapport.

Testing Understanding. The best way to use reflection is to test your understanding of what the customer has said. This could also help to build rapport. If you repeat the words exactly, it's called parroting. Rephrasing in your own words is called paraphrasing.

Creating Rapport. Reflecting what a person says can create a bond of agreement. You can reflect their words by echoing what they say. You can reflect their style by using their modes of speech. However, poor use of this technique can have the opposite effect.

Nonverbal Reflecting. You can also reflect nonverbal body language by repeating what they do, rather than what they say.

Mirroring is displaying the same body language as the other person. If they lean forward, you lean forward. However, it's easy to recognize and may backfire. A better way to relate is by matching. Matching reflects nonverbal signals, but it is less obvious and not copying. If they cross their arms, you can cross your legs. If they nod in agreement, you can smile and occasionally nod.

1   Matching will build rapport only when the customer registers it intuitively and not
2   consciously. There is a limit to how much matching will help in the sales presentation.

In Practice

To be more effective with your customers:

- Your handshake should be firm, but not too hard.
- Usually, direct eye contact when you are talking or listening is good. Staring without blinking or looking away occasionally may be disconcerting to the listener. Persons from certain cultures may perceive constant direct eye contact as disrespectful.
- Don't cross anything. Arms and legs should be open and relaxed.
- Lean forward into the conversation to display your interest. If you lean backward, especially if hands are joined behind the head, it may be perceived as a sign of superiority or aloofness.

WEBLINK

The Center for Nonverbal Studies website is rich in observations of nonverbal communication.
Visit http://center-for-nonverbal-studies.org.

DISCUSSION EXERCISE 3.2

In this exercise, fill in the box denoting the message you are receiving from a customer, and then discuss your answers.

Customer Action	Aggressive	Bored	Closed	Ready to Buy	Deceptive
Arm around your shoulders	☐	☐	☐	☐	☐
Leaning forward	☐	☐	☐	☐	☐
Ignores distractions	☐	☐	☐	☐	☐
Doodling as you talk	☐	☐	☐	☐	☐
Sweating	☐	☐	☐	☐	☐
Stifled yawn	☐	☐	☐	☐	☐
Hands on hips	☐	☐	☐	☐	☐
Biting inside of mouth	☐	☐	☐	☐	☐
Looking down	☐	☐	☐	☐	☐
Drumming fingers	☐	☐	☐	☐	☐

PROFESSIONAL EDUCATION

Licensees enhance their professionalism through continuing education. The law requires continuing education before renewal of a license, but many professionals take more courses than are required by the law. National organizations award professional designations to graduates of their educational programs. The designations make consumers aware of those persons who have exceeded the legally required continuing education.

Other types of education, when combined with formal instruction, also enhance a licensee's competence. Sales associates need three types of knowledge:

- Technical knowledge
- Marketing knowledge
- Product knowledge

Technical Knowledge

Technical knowledge provides the tools of the business, such as completing contracts properly, knowing sellers' and buyers' costs, and understanding the comparative market analysis process.

This course includes technical knowledge in the following areas:

- State and federal laws
- Preparing a comparative market analysis (CMA)
- Preparing a listing contract
- Qualifying a buyer
- Understanding financing plans
- Preparing a sales contract
- Reviewing closing statements
- Analyzing real estate investments

Sales associates should not work in the field without the appropriate technical knowledge. For example, sales associates will feel quite incompetent if they cannot fill out the cost disclosure statement or a contract form. One of the purposes of this course is to provide the new licensee with the technical knowledge to become competent and confident with consumers. Technical knowledge also includes knowledge about state and federal laws, such as fair-housing and antitrust laws.

DISCUSSION EXERCISE 3.3

Traci has been in the real estate business for about a month and is working with her first buyer customers, referred to her by a close friend. She shows them a home listed by another sales associate in her office. The buyers immediately start to talk about where to place their furniture. "We think this is the one," they tell Traci.

It is Saturday afternoon, and Traci is unable to contact the broker to answer some questions about how to complete the required forms. Nervously, she tells the buyers, "You know, I hate to see you rush into anything. You might like some other houses out there better. I can show them to you tomorrow, if you like. That'll give you time to think about it all, too!"

What is Traci's main objective at this moment?

How could Traci have been better prepared for this situation?

Marketing Knowledge

Learning how to sell real estate comes from **marketing knowledge**. It encompasses the knowledge of psychology and the ability to assess a consumer's specific housing needs. This course includes marketing knowledge in some of the following areas:

- Business planning (section on self-marketing)
- Prospecting for listings
- Making an effective listing presentation
- Prospecting for buyers
- Showing and selling the property

Many sales training books and tapes are available commercially. Institutes and societies of the National Association of REALTORS® as well as local boards of REALTORS® offer sales training classes. Many brokerage firms and franchise companies hold regular sales training courses for sales personnel. Marketing knowledge is an important tool and a major part of the service consumers expect when buying and selling real estate.

Product Knowledge

Customers expect their real estate sales associates to know the market. They want the benefits of that product knowledge in marketing a property or finding the right property for purchase. A new practitioner should work hard to get that knowledge as quickly as possible to best serve the consumer. This course cannot help you acquire **product knowledge**.

In Practice

If you really want to know the market, see lots of property.

If you don't know the inventory, take as much time as you can to see as many listings as possible, then schedule at least a half-day each week to update your knowledge with new listings. Make a list of the best properties in each price range.

SETTING GOALS, BUSINESS PLANNING, AND TIME MANAGEMENT

Setting realistic goals is extremely important in real estate sales. Because real estate sales associates are usually independent contractors, they receive little supervision. Without a clear set of goals and a strong plan, the licensee may lose focus and direction. Goals should be written, measurable, attainable, and flexible, and they should contain deadlines. Once goals have been set, a business plan should show how to achieve the goals. Time management is an important part of that plan.

A distinction can be made between goals, plans, and time management. For example, an automobile trip from Orlando to St. Louis requires all three:

1. The goal is St. Louis.
2. The plan is the road map on which is drawn the route and mileage.
3. **Time management** consists of the daily objectives: When do we leave, when do we stop for food, and how far should we go today?

Goal setting should begin with a long-term view: What accomplishments does a person want to achieve in his lifetime? Once this long-term view is established, the next step is to work back to the present, using smaller increments of time. By working from the long term to the short term, it becomes clear what a licensee must do this year, this week, and today to achieve the long-term goal.

When setting these goals, the professional should always include personal and family objectives. An example of professional goal setting follows (see Figure 3.2).

F I G U R E 3.2 ■   Sample Long-Range Plan

Year 5	CRS designation	Own brokerage firm	$150,000 net worth
Year 3	Finished 2 courses	Open office	$90,000 net worth
Year 1	Finished first course	Pass course and state exam	Must save at least $30,000 this year
Month 1	Check class schedule	Check class schedule	Must save at least $2,500 this month

A licensee's five-year goals are:

- earning the professional education designations CRS and CRB,
- obtaining a broker's license,
- owning a brokerage firm with 15 associates, and
- acquiring $150,000 in additional net worth.

Once the licensee establishes her one-year goal, she converts it into monthly and weekly goals—short-term tasks.

In Practice

Remember, because you're not salaried, you'll have to pay your own taxes, health insurance, advertising expenses, board of REALTORS® dues, and license fees. Estimate those costs at about 35% of gross income. So if you need to make $50,000 annually, you'll have to set your goal at about $77,000!

**Forms
To Go**

Use the worksheet shown in Figure 3.3 to see what you must do today to achieve a $48,000 income. If the assumptions shown are appropriate for your market area, it is simple to project how you can accomplish the goal. This example focuses on income goals, but the same exercise could be completed for other goals. A blank worksheet for your personal goals is included in Appendix B.

F I G U R E 3.3 ■ Goals Worksheet

1.	During the next 12 months, I want to earn	$48,000
2.	That works out to be monthly earnings of (line 1 ÷ 12)	$4,000
3.	Probably 60% of my earnings should come from listings sold (line 2 × .60)	$2,400
4.	Probably 40% of my earnings should come from sales made (line 2 × .40)	$1,600

Achieving my listing income:

5.	In my market area, the average listing commission amount is (Figure used here should be changed to fit your market.)	$1,800
6.	So I must have the following number of listings sold (line 3 ÷ line 5)	1.5
7.	If only 75% of my listings sell, I have to get this many listings (line 6 ÷ .75)	2
8.	It may take this many listing appointments to get a listing (Get this number from your broker.)	5
9.	So I need to go on this many listing appointments (line 7 × line 8)	10
10.	It may take this many calls to get an appointment (Get this number from your broker.)	15
11.	So I have to make this many calls per month (line 9 × line 10)	150
12.	Which means I must make this many calls per week (line 11 ÷ 4.3 weeks per month)	35

Achieving my sales income:

13.	In my market area, the average sales commission is (Figure used here should be changed to fit your market.)	$1,800
14.	So I've got to make this many sales per month (line 4 ÷ line 13)	0.9
15.	It takes about this many showings to make a sale (Get this number from your broker.)	20
16.	So I must show this many properties per month (line 14 × line 15)	18

Source: O'Donnell, Edward J. *30-Day Track to Success*. Tallahassee: O'Donnell Publishing, 2013.

When the licensee is aware of what she must do today to achieve her long-term goals, she writes out the goals in contract form. It can be a private contract or a public document, with copies delivered to the broker and a mentor. Giving a copy to another person usually strengthens a commitment to succeed in the goals. A sample goals contract might look like the one in Figure 3.4.

F I G U R E 3.4 ■ **Goals Contract**

I, _____, have determined my career and financial goals
voluntarily, independently, and without coercion. I now formally commit to the following:

During the next 12 months, I will earn (from line 1)	$48,000
I will obtain at least this number of listings per month (from line 7)	2
I will go on this number of listing appointments weekly (line 9 ÷ 4.3)	2.3
I will make this many listing calls weekly (from line 12)	35
I will make this many sales each month (from line 14)	0.9
I will show this many properties each week (line 16 ÷ 4.3)	4

If I begin to fall behind, I request that my broker remind me of this commitment and prod me to stay on schedule
so that I can achieve my goals.

Date _____   My signature _____

Date _____   My broker's signature _____

Date _____   My mentor's signature _____

Source: O'Donnell, Edward J. *30-Day Track to Success.* Tallahassee: O'Donnell Publishing, 2013.

The licensee then posts the goals where they are visible. "Out of sight, out of mind"
can be a problem. The licensee should review and update the goals regularly.

Daily Goals and Time Management

Time management goes hand in hand with goal setting. Goals don't work without a schedule. Besides being measurable and attainable, a deadline must be set for achieving the
goals. For example, the goal of "making as many calls as possible to prospective sellers" is
attainable, but it is also immeasurable because no time deadline has been established. The
statement "I will make five calls to prospective sellers by 6 pm today" is clear, measurable,
and more likely to accomplish the goal.

The licensee should make a **to-do list** before each workday starts. The licensee should
keep the list nearby and check off each item as it is completed. This provides a sense of
accomplishment and motivation to continue. Some helpful points to remember about the
list are as follows:

- Transfer unfinished tasks from the previous day.
- Include those daily tasks from the goals worksheet that are necessary to achieve
  long-term goals.
- **Prioritize** items on the list.
- Put the least pleasant items at the beginning of the list ("Eat the frog first").
  Completing the tough tasks results in the ability to get on with achieving impor-
  tant goals.
- Establish times for completing each task. Even if they need to be adjusted later,
  you have established a basic guideline to follow.
- Make notes for items to include on tomorrow's list.

Time Management Hints

A licensee can do many things to help manage time more effectively:

Forms To Go

- Schedule time off for family, recreation, exercise, and relaxation. Failing to plan for these items can result in guilt feelings, discontent, poor health, or burnout.

- Make a time log of all activities in 15-minute segments for about two weeks. This will show where time is wasted and may give clues for being a more effective time manager. Time can be rated as *A*, *B*, or *C*, with respect to productivity. A time is most productive because it represents time actually spent with customers. B time is necessary work that can sometimes be handled by a personal assistant. C time is wasted time. Doubling your income may require only moving more of your workday to A time, not working twice as many total hours. See Figure 3.5 for a sample daily activity log. A blank worksheet is in Appendix B.

- Qualify sellers and buyers based on their financial ability to complete a transaction, as well as on their motivation. Working with unqualified buyers and sellers is both a disservice to the consumers and a nonproductive use of time.

- Be on time for appointments. Being late is a quick way to lose the confidence of customers. Plan for contingencies such as rush-hour traffic, last-minute phone calls, and weather-related inconveniences.

- Understand how much each hour of your day is worth. For example, if you earn $48,000 per year and work 290 days per year, nine hours per day, you work 2,610 hours, and the hourly rate is approximately $18.39.

- Make cost-effective decisions. If you make $18.39 per hour, hiring a personal assistant for $10 per hour is more cost-effective than doing your own mail-outs and clerical work. Going home to wash the car Monday afternoon may cost you $18.39 versus $9.95 at a car wash.

- Use technology to increase productivity.

- Keep one calendar that includes work, social, family, and personal appointments.

Time Management and the Use of a Personal Assistant

Personal assistants are becoming more and more valuable and popular in the real estate business. According to the Florida REALTORS®, 17% of REALTORS® use the services of a personal assistant. Of those assistants, 43% have a license.

Licensed Personal Assistants. Licensed personal assistants are very valuable and can provide all real estate services for the customers of the employing licensee, including showing and listing properties, calling prospects, and providing access to a listed property. A licensed personal assistant must be registered under the employing broker and may be paid for brokerage activities only by the broker. A sales associate may pay the licensed personal assistant for nonselling activities but may not compensate a personal assistant for performance of brokerage activities that require a license.

Unlicensed Personal Assistants. Many licensees now employ unlicensed assistants to help complete routine office activities, such as mass mailings, writing ads, and preparing comparative market analyses. Sales associates who employ such assistants and their brokers must ensure that the assistant does not perform any activities that violate the law. A list of FREC-approved activities that may be performed by unlicensed personal assistants is shown in Figure 3.6.

FIGURE 3.5 ■ Sample Daily Activity Log

A Direct $	Hours [Goal]	Hours [Actual]	Comments
Prospecting for sellers	1	1	Pretty good. Got a lead for a listing.
Prospecting for buyers	1	0	Just couldn't get to this.
Make appointments with buyers or sellers			
Showing homes			
Presenting offers			
Making listing presentation			
Other activities that will directly produce $:			
Calling friends for referrals	1	1	Jane said she has a good friend who needs to sell a house. Maybe I'll call her tomorrow.
TOTAL	3	2	I need to do better at this.
B Office and Administrative			
Prepare CMAs			
Write ads	.5		
Attend office meetings	1	0	
Look at properties	2	1	Just didn't have time to see more.
Attend education meeting		1	
Other administrative activities:			
Prepare announcement and mail out	1	0	I'll try to do this tomorrow.
TOTAL	4.5	2	
C Wasted Time			
Stopped to shop at Dillard's	0	1	Had a sale; shouldn't have, but . . .
Friend stopped by office	0	1	She had a day off and wanted to talk. Should have arranged to see her at lunch.
TOTAL		2	Makes me mad at myself.
? Personal			
Scheduled time off			
Other (describe):			
Renew driver's license	.5	1.5	Went to tax collector's office, traffic snarled. Should have
TOTAL	.5	1.5	just mailed it.
GRAND TOTAL HOURS	**8.5**	**7.5**	

FIGURE 3.6 ■ Unlicensed Personal Assistant Activities

1. Answer the phone and make telephone calls.
2. Fill out and submit listings and changes to any multiple listing service.
3. Follow up on loan commitments after a contract has been negotiated and generally secure the status reports on the loan progress.
4. Assemble documents for closing.
5. Secure documents (public information) from courthouse, utility district, etc.
6. Have keys made for company listings and order surveys, termite inspections, home inspections, and home warranties with the licensed employer's approval.
7. Write ads for approval of licensee and supervising broker (newspaper ads, website updates, etc.), and prepare flyers and promotional information for approval by licensee and supervising broker.
8. Receive, record, and deposit earnest money, security deposits, and advance rents.
9. Only type the contract forms for approval by licensees and supervising brokers.
10. Monitor licenses and personnel files.
11. Compute commission checks.
12. Place signs on property.
13. Order items of repair as directed by the licensee.
14. Prepare flyers and promotional information for approval by licensee and supervising broker.
15. Act as a courier service to deliver documents, pick up keys.
16. Place routine telephone calls on late rent payments.
17. Schedule appointments for licensees to show listed property.
18. Be at an open house
    a. for security purposes, and
    b. to hand out materials (brochures).
19. Answer questions concerning a listing for which the answer must be obtained from the licensed employer–approved printed information and is objective in nature (not subjective comments).
20. Gather information for a comparative market analysis (CMA).
21. Gather information for an appraisal.
22. Hand out objective, written information on a listing or rental.

An unlicensed individual may not negotiate or agree to any commission split or referral fee on behalf of a licensee.

Unlicensed personal assistants, because they are paid by salary and may not be paid commissions, are under the control of their licensee employers. Except in special circumstances like a large mail-out project, they are not usually classified as independent contractors. The employers must withhold and pay FICA and income taxes and file withholding tax reports on a timely basis. Penalties for noncompliance can be substantial. Licensed personal assistants may be paid a commission, but only the broker may pay commissions. If the licensed assistant is paid a salary or assigned specific working hours or told how to do the work, she would be an employee rather than an independent contractor.

A licensee also should be aware of the liability of having employees. An accident on the job could make the licensee's employer liable, as could an employee who injures another person while running errands for the licensee.

Do a role-playing session, assigning parts to Sharon, John, and the broker.

Sharon:
[*Excited*] I did it! I got that FSBO over on Killearney Way! Now I have another showing appointment. I *love* this business. Gotta go! See you later!

John:
[*Dejected, shaking head*] How does she keep doing it? She seems to get one appointment after another. I'm still slogging along trying to finish up my daily plan. I've got eight more things to do!

Broker:
[*Sympathetically*] Tell me what you have done today, John.

John:
Well, I had to make copies of the plat book pages for my farm area, make up a list of all the people on Scenic Drive, take my clothes to the cleaners, shop for a financial calculator, go to the title insurance company to get a rate card, and get my car washed. I did all that.

Broker:
What is still on the to-do list?

John:
I still need to find some listings for the guy who called on my floor duty yesterday and tell him about some property. I've got to get back in touch with the buyer I showed property to last week to set up another appointment.

Oh! And I need to get a market report back to my wife's friends who said they're interested in selling their house. I also got a response to the notice of sale cards I mailed last week. I need to call those people back. They said they might consider selling. And the tenants on Jackson Bluff Road think they may be ready to buy. I need to call them and set up a time.

There's just not enough time in the day!

Can you help John evaluate his time management skills so he can be as productive as Sharon?

SUMMARY

- A real estate sales associate must develop a strong set of ethical standards. The National Association of Realtors has established the REALTORS® Code of Ethics for its members.

- The four types of communication skills a sales associate should master are as follows:

  - Listening: hear, understand, evaluate
  - Oral: public speaking class, join Toastmasters
  - Written: take courses at community college, study books of business letters
  - Nonverbal: Body language

- Professional education has three major parts: technical knowledge, marketing knowledge, and product knowledge.

- Technical knowledge provides the tools of the business, such as completing contracts and preparing comparative market analyses.

- Marketing knowledge helps a sales associate prospect for listings, show the property, and write effective advertising.

- Product knowledge is acquired only by seeing properties on the market.

- A business plan helps a sales associate to set goals.

- Goals should be written, measurable, attainable, and flexible, and that establish deadlines.

- Licensed personal assistants must be registered under the employing broker and paid by the broker for brokerage activities. The sales associate may pay salary to the assistant.

- Unlicensed personal assistants are not independent contractors. They may not perform any of the eight services of real estate.

R E V I E W   Q U E S T I O N S

1. A sales associate hires an unlicensed personal assistant for $7 per hour. The unlicensed assistant may NOT
    a. write ads for approval by the licensee and her supervising broker and place classified advertising.
    b. place signs on properties.
    c. show a buyer several listed properties, provide complete information, and help the buyer write the offer.
    d. gather data for preparation of a CMA.

2. When a sales associate pyramids his fingers during a meeting, the customer is likely to perceive that the sales associate is
    a. listening carefully.
    b. closed and defensive.
    c. not speaking honestly.
    d. acting in a superior way.

3. A sales associate wants to have $50,000 in cash by the end of five years. Currently, she has just enough cash available for her living expenses. How much cash should she have by the end of year three to be on target to reach her goal?
    a. $24,000
    b. $30,000
    c. $32,000
    d. $35,000

4. To make the best impression, a sales associate would NOT
    a. keep his arms open and relaxed.
    b. fold his arms across the chest.
    c. have a firm handshake.
    d. lean forward into the conversation.

5. A sales associate can improve written communication skills by
    a. attending a community college course on writing.
    b. joining Toastmasters.
    c. reading books on the subject.
    d. attending a community college course on writing and reading books on the subject.

6. A prospective buyer calls a real estate company to speak with a listing agent. The agent's secretary tells him, "She is on the caravan." Puzzled, the buyer hangs up with thoughts of the desert. This expression is an example of
    a. the buyer's lack of communication skills.
    b. jargon.
    c. nonverbal communication.
    d. a common expression that buyers and sellers of real estate should understand.

7.   A new sales associate gets a call from a property owner who wants to list her home. The associate is uncertain about how to do a CMA and how to complete the necessary forms. Based on this information, the associate lacks
    a.   technical knowledge.
    b.   product knowledge.
    c.   marketing knowledge.
    d.   communication skills.

8.   What is FALSE about an unlicensed personal assistant who works for a sales associate?
    a.   The associate may be financially liable for accidents involving the personal assistant.
    b.   The associate may be responsible for violations of the license law or FREC rules.
    c.   The associate's employing broker may be financially responsible for acts of the personal assistant, as well as for violations of the license law or FREC rules.
    d.   Assistants rarely help increase the income of the sales associate enough to cover the assistant's compensation.

9.   Setting and meeting goals does NOT involve
    a.   starting with short-range increments.
    b.   starting with long-term goals, then breaking them down into short-term objectives.
    c.   writing the goals down.
    d.   giving a copy of the goals to a mentor to help strengthen commitment.

10.   A sales associate's goal is to make $58,000 in gross collected commissions next year. He feels that his listings should contribute about 50% of the required income. The average commission per transaction in his office is $1,200, and about two-thirds of his listings are expected to sell. He gets about three listings in five listing presentations. Approximately how many presentations must he make monthly to stay on target?
    a.   2
    b.   3
    c.   5
    d.   10

11.   A sales associate's goal is "to make as much money as I can next year." What is TRUE about her goal?
    a.   As long as she works toward the goal, it is effective.
    b.   It is not measurable.
    c.   It is not attainable.
    d.   It should be combined with a time management plan that says "I'll work until I get tired most days."

12.   An effective method of finding out where time is wasted in a daily schedule is to
    a.   keep good goal sheets.
    b.   make a time log of activities.
    c.   ask your spouse.
    d.   measure the distance from appointment to appointment.

13. Sales associates should make a log of daily activities and
    a. try to move most activities into section B (Office and Administrative).
    b. attempt to move hours spent on section A (Direct $) to Personal Time.
    c. spend more time on section A (Direct $).
    d. reduce personal time to 0 hours.

14. A sales associate needs to earn $40,000. If expenses such as Social Security, Medicare, and operating expenses average 35% of gross income, what should the sales associate's goal be for gross income?
    a. $14,000
    b. $29,630
    c. $56,615
    d. $61,538

15. Guilty feelings, discontent, and burnout are likely to result from
    a. wasting time in the office.
    b. working too hard.
    c. failing to schedule time off for family, recreation, and exercise.
    d. not staying focused on business.

16. Which is LEAST likely to be one of a sales associate's five-year goals?
    a. Obtaining names of customers who are likely to list their homes
    b. Earning a GRI designation
    c. Increasing net worth by $100,000
    d. Opening a brokerage firm

17. A sales associate works nine hours every day but Sunday. Last year he made $68,000. What is his gross hourly rate, assuming he worked 50 weeks?
    a. $17.92
    b. $22.35
    c. $25.19
    d. $34.00

18. When making a to-do list for the day, a sales associate should NOT
    a. establish times for completing each task.
    b. save the least pleasant tasks for after lunch.
    c. transfer unfinished tasks from the previous day.
    d. make notes to include on tomorrow's list.

19. A customer who observes a sales associate covering his mouth while giving a listing presentation MOST likely would perceive that the sales associate
    a. has chapped lips.
    b. feels superior.
    c. is closed and defensive.
    d. may not be speaking honestly.

20. A productive sales associate should NOT
    a. stay out of the office as much as possible.
    b. employ a personal assistant.
    c. work with unqualified buyers.
    d. prioritize her time.

ACTION LIST

APPLY WHAT YOU'VE LEARNED!

The following actions will reinforce the material in "Section I: Laying the Foundation for a Successful Career":

❏ List the customer contacts you have had in the previous two weeks.

❏ Write a script that you could use with a seller for introducing and explaining the property condition disclosure statement.

❏ Select a federal law in this section. Go to the internet and find a site that includes the statutes. Print the statutes and then read the law, highlighting the important parts.

❏ List the personal characteristics that will be of most value to you in real estate, and then refine the list by showing which activities will best use those strengths.

❏ List the personal characteristics that you believe need improvement. Make one action plan focusing on ways to achieve those improvements and another focusing on ways to reduce the impact of those personal characteristics that are hard to change.

❏ At the next meeting of your board of REALTORS®, don't hesitate to give an opinion on the subject under discussion or to market your listing during the marketing time.

❏ Prepare a to-do list for tomorrow, arranged by priority.

❏ Set a goal of getting one new listing within the next seven days, and write out an action plan to achieve the goal.

❏ Prepare a short-term goal that includes the number of customer contacts you intend to make each day for the next 10 days.

OBTAINING LISTINGS THAT SELL

This section of the text leads the new associate through the activities to help reach the most important goal in real estate—obtaining salable listings. Listings generate sales leads. Those persons with a large inventory of salable listings will make the highest income because listers are the only sales associates who can be paid on both sides of the transaction.

Chapter 4 shows how to build a strong prospecting program to generate a substantial listing inventory. Power prospecting is hard work that separates the highly successful professional from the making-a-living licensees.

Chapter 5 shows how to make that listing salable by pricing it to sell.

Chapter 6 shows how to turn the hard work of prospecting into signed listing agreements through ef-fective listing presentations.

Chapter 7 describes the listing contract, showing licensees how to explain the agreement to the sellers. ▪

PROSPECTING FOR LISTINGS

LEARNING OBJECTIVES

When you finish reading this chapter, you will be able to:

- list the five principal sources of listings,
- describe at least three types of properties a licensee should not attempt to list,
- state the principal reason that listings expire, and
- list the five categories in a leads database.

KEY TERMS

farm	For Sale by Owner (FSBO)	power prospecting
For Rent by Owner (FRBO)	passive prospecting	targeted strangers

OVERVIEW

Listings are the lifeblood of the real estate industry. Without listings to advertise, a brokerage firm must expend more advertising dollars to get buyer prospects. This chapter describes some very effective methods for prospecting for listings, including how to work with FSBOs and FRBOs, how to communicate effectively with an owner whose listing has expired, how to organize a listing farm, and how to canvass for leads.

An important part of working with prospective sellers is the need to understand the situation and to tailor your presentation and problem-solving techniques to their particular needs.

Advanced prospecting techniques can be used to help you become a listing superstar. It will take a lot of work and a financial investment, but the results can be truly amazing.

At the end of the chapter is a discussion of using the internet and social media to get more customer leads and increase your income.

PROSPECTING OBJECTIVES

The main objective when prospecting for listings is to get an appointment to make a listing presentation. Because listings are the lifeblood of the real estate business, sales associates must know how to find sellers who need their professional services. In chapter 4, the new sales associate will learn the most productive sources of listings and how to effectively approach the sellers and obtain an appointment to make a listing presentation.

The most important sources of listings for a new sales associate (see Figure 4.1) are as follows:

- Sphere of influence
- Expired listing
- Farm
- For sale by owners (FSBOs) and For Rent by Owners (FRBOs)
- Canvass

F I G U R E 4.1 ■ The Listing Star

Notice that the discussion began with sources of listings for new sales associates. In two, three, or four years, the new sales associate who uses these sources will have the most powerful listing source of all: previous customers.

No matter which method a sales associate uses to locate prospective listings, he must prepare for listing appointments carefully. The comparative market analysis (CMA) is necessary to help price the listing. The sales associate also must understand what costs the seller can be expected to pay, how to complete and explain the listing agreement, and how to market and service the listing.

YOU DON'T WANT THEM ALL

When prospecting for listings, qualify the properties and prioritize your efforts. Be picky. Your time is limited, and there are only so many listings you can work to get. The amount of effort required for prospecting and making a listing presentation is the same for a good listing as for a poor one. Don't spend time working to get a listing if:

- the seller is not motivated;
- the seller suggests you break the law by nondisclosure or discriminatory practices;
- the listing is outside your target market, such as in an adjoining community or is a warehouse opportunity if you're a residential sales associate;
- the listing is outside your preferred price ranges;
- the property condition is so bad you would be embarrassed to show it; or
- the owners are so rude or demanding you don't want to work with them.

The secret is to prioritize your efforts and focus only on those listings that will sell within a reasonable time with reasonable effort on your part. For those you don't want, send a referral.

SPHERE OF INFLUENCE

For a new sales associate, the sphere of influence is the best source of new listings and sales. Your sphere of influence will include family, friends, past customers, and former co-workers.

Close Friends and Family

This category will be very small, probably having no more than 30–50 names, but it can be a powerful listing generator. Your close friends and members of your family will do business with you and send you referrals, but you may need to ask. The term "close friend" suggests a very strong, usually long-term relationship with mutual trust, care, and respect. Sometimes even close friends are reluctant to do business with friends for fear that the relationship could be affected. Your friends must be convinced of your professionalism and dedication. You must let them know that when you do business, you will wear your "professional hat." The contacts within this group are natural and frequent, and all requests for business will be low key.

Friends and Past Customers

Some people we know reasonably well, but they are not close friends. Perhaps we have had lunch together or worked on a committee together. The size of this category will grow with the number of years you are in real estate (past customers). This group is a significant source of new business and referrals. Work it diligently! Each person on the list should hear from you by mail or phone at least twice monthly.

You should start by making a contact list of your friends and acquaintances (see Figure 4.2). The number will vary depending on your social activities, but try to list at least 50 people. You should call your family members to ask for business. Because of the do-not-call registry rules, depending on your relationship, you should contact most of them with a handwritten note. Handwritten notes are much more personal than a typed letter. A sample note is included in Figure 4.3.

FIGURE 4.2 ■ **List of Friends and Acquaintances**

Name	Address	Phone	Date Mailed	Date Called
_____	_____	_____	_____	_____
_____	_____	_____	_____	_____
_____	_____	_____	_____	_____
_____	_____	_____	_____	_____

FIGURE 4.3 ■ **Sample Note to Your Friends**

Hi Sheryl,

Just a note to tell you hello, and to let you know I'm working full-time in real estate with Crystal Springs Realty.

If you should hear of anyone getting ready to buy or sell, I'd really appreciate your calling to let me know.

I hope Randy and the boys are all well. Let's have lunch soon!

(signed)

If your friend is not on the do-not-call registry, follow up in about a week with a phone call.

Current and former co-workers can be a very fertile prospecting area. Teachers, postal workers, firefighters, and state employees who work part time in real estate tend to do well because of their many contacts at work.

EXPIRED LISTINGS

Expired listings can be a profitable source of business for licensees if they understand why listings expire, how to locate them, and when and how to approach the owners of expired listings.

Why Listings Expire

Some listings don't sell during the listing period for a variety of reasons, including:

- market conditions (oversupply of homes available for sale),
- property condition,
- listing period too short,
- uncooperative owner or tenant,
- overpriced, or
- poor marketing effort.

Except for the uncooperative owner or tenant, the major reason listings expire is almost always price. If there is an oversupply of homes on the market, the price should have been reduced. If the property condition is poor, it was probably overpriced. A short listing period calls for a low price.

Finding Expired Listings

Listings expire from the multiple listing service (MLS) every day. They are shown in the change-of-status section where you can also find sales and price changes. Without the MLS, it is more difficult to work this market. An excellent way to find expired listings is to get a recommendation from sales associates who have a listing about to expire when the owner won't relist. You can either agree to have your broker pay a referral fee or have a cooperative arrangement to send your sellers to them at the end of a listing period.

How to Approach Owners of Expired Listings

The owner whose property did not sell may be disillusioned with brokers and not receptive to your approach. To effectively work expired listings, you must have empathy. The seller whose home was on the market for six months and didn't sell might:

- wonder why he bought a home that no one else likes,
- feel the broker did little or nothing to market the property, or
- believe the home was overpriced during the listing period.

Once you understand how the owner might feel, you will be better able to tailor your approach to the situation.

Using the same methods used with FSBOs or FRBOs, licensees can prospect for expired listings by:

- direct mail,
- telephone, or
- visit.

Direct mail may be too late because owners who want to sell often list with another broker immediately after the listing expires. A visit may not be as time-effective as first telephoning, but visiting the owner is more likely to result in getting the listing. When the owner answers the door, you might ask the questions in the telephone calling guide in Figure 4.4. Your objective is to be invited inside to view the home, getting an opportunity for a listing presentation.

F I G U R E 4.4 ■   Expired Listing Telephone Calling Guide

1. Check the do-not-call registry before calling.

2. Introduce yourself and your company, and say why you're calling.

3. Tell the sellers the listing has expired and ask if they still want to sell.

   - If the answer is yes, get an appointment.

   - If the answer is no, ask whether the sellers would like to know why the house didn't sell. Get an appointment, and make a CMA study.

   - If the answer is no, say thanks and place another call.

FARMING

Think of farming as the cultivation of listings, much like establishing an orange grove. You can't get rich planting one tree. The more trees you plant, the greater the harvest. The grove takes a lot of work for some time without any apparent return. But when the grove begins to produce, it can shower you with fruit for years to come. And as the trees grow larger, the size of the harvest increases and can make you rich.

The listing **farm** requires lots of hard work to get established and for a time may have no apparent return. Many listing farmers abandon the grove just before it produces. If you decide to farm an area, you must make a commitment to continue for at least three years.

What's the Payoff?

Farming is a disciplined approach to prospecting. It is intended to expand a sales associate's sphere of influence, thus increasing listings and sales. One suggestion is that farming should produce 20% of the listings in the farm area in the second year, 50% in the third year, and up to 75% of the listings after that.

Assume that owners in your farm area move once every six years and your farm has 800 houses. That means 133 homes will be listed this year (800 ÷ 6). If you're in the third year of your farm and get 50% of those listings, you'll get 67 listings, or 5.5 each month. Assuming further that the average sales price is $200,000, two-thirds of your listings sell, and your share is 1.5%, your listing commissions alone would be more than $134,000 ($200,000 × 67 × ⅔ × 1.5%).

How Many Homes Should Be in a Farm?

Because the farm may take six months before generating listings, a sales associate must also prospect using other methods. A new licensee should start a farm with no more than 200 homes but should select an area that allows for expansion of the farm. Many successful sales associates ultimately develop farms with 800 to 1,000 homes located in several neighborhoods.

How to Choose the Farm Area

You must carefully select your listing farm. It should have the following characteristics:

- Middle to upper price range
- High turnover
- Increasing property values
- Not currently being farmed by any other sales associate

The five steps to take are as follows:

1. Select at least six potential farm neighborhoods. Check the MLS or the tax appraiser's office for all sales during the previous year.

2. Of those sales, review the listing office and sales associate so you can see if one person is getting a large market share. This would indicate that person is farming the area.

3. Get the total number of homes in the area by looking at the subdivision plat map.

4. Divide the number of sales by the number of homes in the neighborhood to get the turnover index.

5. Select the neighborhood that is not currently being farmed that has the highest turnover index.

Figure 4.5 is an example of the evaluation process. Blackwater Farms and Green Valley are currently being farmed, so it's not worthwhile to try to compete if other good areas are available. Orangewood has a 25% turnover ratio, and the home prices are in the $200,000 range. Orangewood is our choice.

FIGURE 4.5 ■ Farm Area Evaluation

Neighborhood	Currently Farmed?	Home Prices	Sales Last Year	Homes in Neighborhood	Turnover Index
Rustling Woods	No	$175,000	88	521	17%
Blackwater Farms	Yes	$200,000	86	416	21%
Dolphin Downs	No	$150,000	145	740	20%
Glass Springs	No	$250,000	52	345	15%
Orangewood	No	$200,000	172	685	25%
Green Valley	Yes	$250,000	68	534	13%

Make Farm Contacts Now, Organize Over Time

Some sales associates spend too much time preparing to farm and too little time making contacts. While it's nice to have a wall map, a database of information about each homeowner, or prepared mailings for the next six months, that can be done later. It's tempting to "play office" rather than risk rejection by talking with prospective sellers.

One task that you should do up front, however, is to prepare a CMA for the neighborhood, showing listings and sales for at least three years. This will help you discuss prices and know what prospective sellers paid when they purchased. Preparation of a CMA is discussed in chapter 5.

How to Make Contacts in Your Farm Area

Contacts in your farm area should be a combination of direct mail, telephone, and a visit. Remember, direct mail is passive prospecting that works well as long as personal contact is part of the farming program. A multicolored newsletter with your name and company logo is inexpensive and can result in more business. You can also send a letter of introduction, a postcard, or any other mailing piece that keeps your name in front of the owners. Notice of listings and sales in the farm area can be one of the most effective and cost-efficient mailings but should be followed up with a phone call or a visit (see Figure 4.6).

Calling people in a farm area can be effective, but there should be a good reason for the call. Some of those reasons include telling about a new listing, a sale, or that you will be holding an open house. Remember to check the do-not-call registry.

The best way to cultivate your farm is by visiting owners in the neighborhood. Saturdays are wonderful visit days. A drive through the neighborhood will allow you to stop and meet people out walking or doing yard work. A cold canned drink is a good icebreaker.

F I G U R E 4.6 ■ **Notice of Sale Card**

We've done it again!

We have just participated in the sale of your neighbor's home located at

724 Oak Street.

Your neighborhood is very attractive and much in demand by buyers.
You might be pleasantly surprised when you learn the market value
of your home. I'd be glad to furnish information to you about
prices and marketability.

Please call me right away if you might be considering selling your home.

Hilda Cummings, Sales Associate
(312) 555-4300 • Floyd Realty, Inc.

Of course, just knocking on doors is one of the best activities. Give the homeowner a gift such as a calendar or yardstick with your name (and company name) imprinted on it. The owners may remember you when it's time to sell their homes.

Another great technique is to offer a private open house just for neighbors when you get a listing in the neighborhood. Not only does it give the sales associate a chance to get some referrals for business, but it also offers another opportunity to build relationships.

You should make at least one contact each month with everyone in your farm area. If you work 25 days each month and farm 500 homes, you must make at least 20 contacts each day. Rotating between mailings, phone calls, and visits may reduce your workload. After you become fairly well known, you can increase the mail contacts and reduce the personal contacts.

FOR SALE BY OWNER

The only potential prospect we know for sure who wants to sell his house is the **For Sale by Owner (FSBO)**. It is surprising that so few new sales associates use this outstanding source of listings in their daily plan. The myths many sales associates quote to avoid prospecting the FSBO market include the following:

■ It takes more organizational skills to make prospecting pay.

■ Sometimes FSBOs are not courteous to licensees who phone or visit (but remember, you can phone only if the owner is not on the National Do Not Call Registry).

■ They won't agree to add the commission to their price.

■ It takes significant selling skills to get a listing from a FSBO.

■ FSBO houses are overpriced already.

Sales associates who master the FSBO market by adapting to its unique characteristics are able to significantly increase their listing inventories.

WHY FSBOS ARE FSBOS

If you were an owner of a property, try to think why you might consider selling it yourself rather than listing it. Assume your home is worth $200,000. A broker's commission of 6% would result in your paying $12,000, a substantial amount. But if you further assume you bought the home two years ago for $185,000, with a 10% down payment, your equity is now approximately $35,000.

Calculation: $200,000 minus the original mortgage of $166,500 (.90 × $185,000) less some principal paid back.

Now, you see, the $12,000 is much greater than 6%. It's actually closer to 34% of the equity, perhaps explaining why a seller might want to try it alone. It also explains why you will need a good presentation to show them why they need you.

FSBO Characteristics

First, anyone in sales can be much more effective with a healthy supply of empathy. Empathy is the sensitivity to the thoughts and feelings of others. To be able to persuade an owner to list, the licensee must first understand the mindset of that owner.

Those of us who have sold a car directly, rather than trading it in, usually did it to make more money from the sale. Whether that savings occurs is not the point; the fact is we did it for that purpose.

It's fair to assume that of all the FSBOs out there, at least 90% are trying to sell without a broker in order to save the commission. It's also likely that only a certain set of circumstances will change that mindset. The FSBO may be ready to list if she is:

■ moving out of town right away,

■ concerned about personal security,

■ baffled by the home-selling process,

■ not available during normal hours to show the home,

■ uncomfortable negotiating with people, or

■ convinced that a buyer will reduce the price offered by at least the amount of the commission.

The sales associate who has made a positive contact with the sellers when those circumstances exist is most likely to get the listing. While the "moving out of town right away" item on the list is based on external conditions, the licensee may be able to change the sellers' minds on the others during the listing presentation (covered in chapter 6).

Finding and Tracking the FSBOs

An important part of the FSBO prospecting process is finding and tracking FSBOs. Most sellers use a yard sign, classified ad, or a note on a community bulletin board.

Most sales associates locate FSBOs in the classified ads or on a website like Craigslist. The licensee may assume that all ads that don't have the name of a brokerage firm are FSBOs. A broker's ad without the firm name is a blind ad, a violation of Chapter 475.

Landvoice provides a daily email service to subscribers in most cities, showing all new FSBOs advertised in the local newspapers that day. It includes the owner's name, phone number (with do-not-call registry status), address, and other advertised information. See Figure 4.7 for a sample of email data. Subscribers can also view complete data on the Landvoice website and search FSBOs by city area or price range.

F I G U R E 4.7 ■ For-Sale-by-Owner Email Service

From: Landvoice.com
Sent: Thursday, May 13, 2007 3:29 AM
To: AliceNewby@Hendricksrealty.com
Subject: May 13 2007 - FSBO Information

(1 of 2)
FL: Tallahassee (All) Source: TAL Newspapers A
First Advertised: 05/13/2007
850-555-0001 Do Not Call Registry

Sam Seller

5555 Main Rd., Tallahassee, FL 32310-4635
HOME in TALLAHASSEE $525,000
Bd: 3 Ba: 4 Style: Ga:
Sq. Ft.: 3645 Year Built: Lot Size:

A list of all FSBOs coming on the market for the previous week or month is also available with *Landvoice*, so it becomes easier to track time on the market.

WEBLINK

Visit Landvoice at www.landvoice.com.

Because not all FSBOs advertise in the newspaper, the licensee can find those properties by driving through neighborhoods and asking friends and family to call when they see a sign or notice on a bulletin board.

If you don't use a FSBO service such as the one shown, you should organize the FSBOs by phone number. Even though this is the age of technology, many sales associates keep index cards with the phone numbers prominently placed in the upper right corner of the card. If you use this system, you then sort the cards by the number. When going through the paper, look for the number, and then compare it with the cards. If it's not there, this is a new property. See Figure 4.8 for an example of the file card system. To find the owners' information, use a cross-reference directory as described later in this chapter.

F I G U R E 4.8 ■ FSBO Index Card

W. H. Lister (305) 555-4369
0123 Street Way
Miami, 33165

Contacts:
4/15   Phoned, said he did not want to list now.
4/20   Stopped by and gave him sample contracts. "Thanks!"
4/25   He got my "thanks" card. Called to ask me if I could give him an opinion of value.
4/26   Went over my CMA with him at the house.
4/27   He called me to come over and list his house at $220,000.

It's easier to sort the ads if the records are on your computer. A spreadsheet or a database program such as Access makes it easier. Even your word processor makes it simple to sort using the "table" function (see the sample of table function in Figure 4.9). Contact programs such as Top Producer or Act! are specifically designed for this purpose, have many more functions, and are more user-friendly.

FSBO Prospecting Techniques

Licensees who work the FSBO market must be persistent, organized, and disciplined (POD). The first approach to a FSBO can be done by:

- ■ direct mail,

- ■ telephone call, or

- ■ visit.

Direct mail is a low-risk exercise that is likely to have a low reward ratio. Direct mail is **passive prospecting**, which should always be followed by a phone call or a visit. When used in conjunction with one of the other methods, it can be an effective way to prospect. The objective of sending direct mail is to introduce yourself to the seller.

Before telephoning a FSBO, be certain to reread the section covering the National Do Not Call Registry in chapter 1. The liability for a violation of the law is quite substantial. If a FSBO's phone number is on the list, note it in all data (see Figure 4.9).

F I G U R E 4.9 ■   Sample Table for FSBO Information Sorted by Phone Number

Phone	Name / Address	Price	Contacts
(305) 555-2421 <DO NOT CALL LIST!>	Mary Mover 2222 Avenue Miami, 33134	$215,000	4/16 Stopped by. Told me she wasn't interested, but took sample contract.
(305) 555-2527	J. B. House 1111 Another St. Miami, 33185	$175,000	4/12 Phoned. Made listing appointment 4/13 Got listing at $175,000.
(305) 555-4369	W. H. Lister 0123 Street Way Miami, 33165	$220,000	4/15 Phoned, said he did not want to list now. 4/20 Stopped by and gave him sample contracts. "Thanks!" 4/25 He got my "thanks" card. Called to ask me if I could give him an opinion of value. 4/26 Went over my CMA with him at the house. 4/27 He called me to come over and list his house at $220,000.

The objective for the call is to get an appointment to give a listing presentation (see Figure 4.10).

F I G U R E 4.10 ■   FSBO Telephone Calling Guide

1 . Check the do-not-call registry before calling.

2 . Introduce yourself, your company, and say why you're calling.

3 . Ask to visit the home at a specific time.

4 . If the seller declines, you might ask whether the seller would agree to pay a commission if you bring a buyer.

5 . If the seller agrees to pay a commission, get an appointment to see the home.

6 . If the seller doesn't agree, ask whether he'd sell if the buyer agreed to pay the commission.

7 . If the seller says no, ask whether you can call again in the future.

The most effective way to get a listing is by visiting the house. Many licensees don't like to do this because of the risk of rejection. When you see a FSBO sign, just stop the car and walk to the door. You can also set up the visits by geographic area, using your FSBO data cards. Asking questions is the best approach. The objective for the visit is to get an appointment to give the sellers a listing presentation (see Figure 4.11).

F I G U R E 4.11 ■ So, You've Got a FSBO Appointment?

If an owner accepts your request to visit, set the appointment for a time when both parties will be home and available to talk. Ask that the sellers have several items ready for you, if possible:

- a copy of the paperwork when they purchased, especially the deed and title insurance documents;
- their homeowners insurance policy;
- a copy of the property survey, if available; and
- an extra set of front door keys.

Why do you need these items now?

1 . Because they will be helpful when you list the home
2 . Because when you get there and find all these items neatly stacked on the table, it's your signal that they are ready to list their home

---

In Practice

When the prospecting involves knocking on doors, several points should be considered:

■ The home may be in a gated community or apartment property that does not allow solicitation.

■ The home may be in a community with ordinances that do not allow solicitation.

■ Many owners dislike persons coming to their door and will be reluctant to enter into a conversation.

■ After sunset, sales associates should not make visits without an appointment.

■ After ringing the doorbell, stand at least three feet back from the door.

At the FSBO's Front Door

The following eight questions may help you build rapport with the sellers:

1. How much are you asking for the home?
2. How long has it been for sale?
3. Are you moving out of town?
4. Have you had any offers?
5. If I brought a buyer to you, would you pay commission?
6. Do you have a sales contract?
7. Would you like to see a market report on your neighborhood?
8. Have you used a real estate broker in the past to help you buy or sell real estate?

> **In Practice**
>
> Don't forget, sellers are also buyers. You have to find out what they intend to buy, and where, when this house is sold. If the seller tells you they are moving to another city, you have an opportunity to send a referral to a broker in that area. Referral commissions can be a significant part of your annual income if you always get the information about where people are moving.

FOR RENT BY OWNER

The most common way to find many **For Rent by Owners (FRBOs)** is by reading the classified ads in the newspaper or other classified-ad publication. Owners trying to rent a house are good prospects for a listing, a sale, or property management.

FRBO Characteristics

The following analysis demonstrates that while they are similar to FSBOs in some ways, FRBOs struggle with entirely different problems, requiring a more appropriate problem-solving approach by licensees who want to list their properties.

FRBO as Listing Prospect. Those who own rental homes experience difficulties such as vacancies, uncollectible rent, evictions, and damage to the property. When the home is currently for rent, the sales associate must understand that some or all of those problems may have occurred very recently.

FRBO as Buying Prospect. Sometimes investors have factored such problems into their business plan, understanding the characteristics of rental property. Those investors frequently plan to continue investing in rental property.

FRBO as Property Management Prospect. Persons who have their property for rent may be weary of the time and effort involved in managing their own property. They may have had difficulty showing the property because of other commitments, and sometimes rental prospects are "no-shows." Your call may come at the right moment and may turn into a management opportunity. If your company does not have a property management department, ask your broker to send a referral to a local company that will pay a referral fee for the business.

FRBO Prospecting Techniques

The first approach to an FRBO can be made by:

- direct mail,
- telephone, or
- visit

Because the phone number in the ad is that of the owner's home, not the rental, it's difficult to learn where the rental property is located. The first contact can be direct mail followed by a phone call. Before telephoning a FRBO, be certain to check the National Do Not Call Registry (see Figure 4.12).

F I G U R E 4.12 ■ FRBO Telephone Calling Guide

1 . Check the do-not-call registry before calling.

2 . Introduce yourself, your company, and say why you're calling.

3 . Ask whether the owner has considered selling rather than renting.
   - If the answer is yes, suggest you do a market report, and get an appointment.
   - If the answer is no, go to the next step.

4 . Ask whether the owner might consider buying other income property.
   - If the answer is yes, get an appointment to discuss other properties.
   - If the answer is no, go to the next step.

5 . Ask whether the owner has considered hiring a professional property manager.
   - If the answer is yes, get an appointment for your company's property manager.
   - If the answer is no, thank the owner for his or her time and say goodbye.

The objective for this call is to get an appointment to give a listing presentation. Remember, the advertised phone number matches the owner's address, not the rental property.

Another mailing, a phone call, or a visit should always follow direct mail. When used in connection with one of the other methods, it can be an effective way to prospect. The objective of sending direct mail is to get a call from the seller.

Because the owner does not live at the rental property, visiting is probably the least effective method.

CANVASSING

Every sales associate who aspires to attaining top producer status understands the power of canvassing. While this is the last prospecting tool mentioned as a listing source, it is likely the most important.

Canvassing is prospecting by mail, telephone, and in person, not necessarily in your farm. All **power prospecting** programs include canvassing.

Power Prospecting

Setting high income goals requires a commitment to prospect. The three keys to prospecting success are as follows:

1. Numbers

2. Consistency

3. Organization

Numbers. The difference between making a living and becoming a real estate sales superstar is numbers. Following these tips will help you become a successful prospector:

■ Follow all laws when prospecting, paying particular attention to the National Do Not Call Registry.

■ A cross-reference directory can give you information on area residents and businesses. Cross-reference directories are arranged by street addresses and numerically by phone number. Listings arranged by street addresses allow you to find all the residents and businesses on a particular street in sequence. Listings arranged by phone number allow you to find all the numbers and names for a particular area code and exchange. The product is available in print, online, or on CD. An annual subscription (costing from $150 to $400, depending on the location) will give current information, and can filter out phone numbers that appear on the National Do Not Call Registry.

WEBLINK

The Hill-Donnelly Corporation sells cross-reference directories for many market areas. Visit them online at www.hilldonn.com/hd/.

- Use a prospecting tool like "The Daily 100 Power Prospecting Points Chart" (see Figure 4.13). Note that this chart awards more weight to activities that are more likely to result in a listing or a sale. For example, sending a mailing to For Sale by Owners is worth one point, but visiting in person gives five points because it is a more productive activity.

- Work out of the office as much as possible. The only people you'll see there are other sales associates.

- Avoid time-wasting activities such as idle conversation, poor organization and planning, and uncontrolled interruptions. If you're worth $18.40 per hour, four hours per week of idle conversation with associates in the office costs you nearly $75!

It's all about prospecting. If a sales associate can just reduce wasted hours and hours spent on administrative "support" functions and shift them to A-level activities, talked about in chapter 3, income should show a dramatic rise.

For example, if a sales associate decides to make a commitment to do power prospecting, and is able to increase contacts, the income should show a dramatic increase. Figures 4.14 and 4.15 show what can happen to the income stream in seven months if a person goes from little or no prospecting to power prospecting. The amounts shown won't magically work for every sales associate, but they do depend on the following two assumptions:

1. The sales associate likes people and is articulate and organized.

2. The sales associate has finished training and knows how to:

    a.   prepare a CMA,

    b.   make an effective listing presentation,

    c.   show properties,

    d.   ask closing questions, and

    e.   ask for the order.

For example, John is a sales associate who has been "drifting" through his startup-training program. After he completes the program, he decides to work smarter and increase his prospecting time. The first month he works 20 days and gets 700 points (35 per day). He continues to work the program, becomes more focused, and is finally able to achieve a 2,500-point month. His business increases dramatically. He finally understands that "prospecting is the name of the game." While some licensees may be skeptical of the income levels shown, power prospectors know the numbers work.

Figure 4.15 is a graphic illustration of the results of the power prospecting program.

F I G U R E 4.13 ■ The Daily 100 Power Prospecting Points Chart—How to Survive and Make Money Selling Real Estate

Directions: Complete any combination of the activities listed below. If you consistently "earn" at least 100 Daily Power Prospecting points, your personal income will increase dramatically!

Name:_____ Week Beginning:_____ Goal for Wk:$_____

Suggested Activity	Points	Mon.	Tue.	Wed.	Thu.	Fri.	Sat.	Sun.	Total
Listings:									
FSBO (For Sale by Owner)—Mail	1								
FSBO—Phone	2								
FSBO—Visit	5								
Expired Listing—Mail	1								
Expired Listing—Phone	2								
Expired Listing—Visit	5								
Notice of Listing—Mail	1								
Notice of Listing—Phone	2								
Notice of Sale—Mail	1								
Notice of Sale—Phone	2								
FRBO (For Rent by Owner)—Mail	1								
FRBO—Phone	2								
Cold Call Completed	2								
Follow up on Listing Prospect	2								
Listing Presentation Made	10								
Listing Taken	20								
Servicing Listing by Mail	2								
Servicing Listing by Phone	3								
Servicing Listing by Visit	5								
Listing Price Change	5								
Listing Term Extended	5								
Contract on Listing Presented	10								
Listing Sold	20								
Sales:									
Office Caravan (per home seen)	3								
Previewing Listings	3								
Prospecting Calls to Renters	2								
Open House	10								
Name and Phone from Ad Call	5								
Follow up on Buying Prospect	2								
Property Shown to Buyer	5								
Contract Written	10								
Contract Accepted	20								
Sales Servicing Call	3								
Referral Requested from Buyer	2								
Referral Sent to Another City	5								
Closing Attended	10								

Source: O'Donnell, Edward J. *30-Day Track to Success*. Tallahassee: O'Donnell Publishing, 2013.

FIGURE 4.13 ■ **The Daily 100 Power Prospecting Points Chart—How to Survive and Make Money Selling Real Estate (continued)**

Suggested Activity	Points	Mon.	Tue.	Wed.	Thu.	Fri.	Sat.	Sun.	Total
Other:									
Attend Office Meeting	10								
Attend MLS Marketing Session	10								
Attend Education Meeting (hr)	10								
Past Customer Contacted	3								
Phone Friend about Real Estate	3								
Lunch with a Prospect	5								
Attend Civic Club Meeting	5								
Thank-You Card Mailed	3								
Personal Referral Received	5								
Newsletter Mailed	2								
Other Productive Activities	?								
Total Points									

FIGURE 4.14 ■ **Power Prospecting Program**

	Month 1	Month 2	Month 3	Month 4	Month 5	Month 6	Month 7
Points on Daily 100	**700**	**1,000**	**1,200**	**1,400**	**2,000**	**2,200**	**2,500**
Following month business results							
Listings taken	1	1	1	2	2	2	3
Sales made	0	0	1	1	2	2	3
Listings sold	0	1	1	2	2	3	4
Total transactions	1	2	3	5	6	7	10
Commissions: ($150,000 price with a 1.5% commission to sales assoc.)	$0	$2,250	$4,500	$6,750	$9,000	$11,250	$15,750

FIGURE 4.15 ■ **Income-to-Effort Ratios Using the Daily 100**

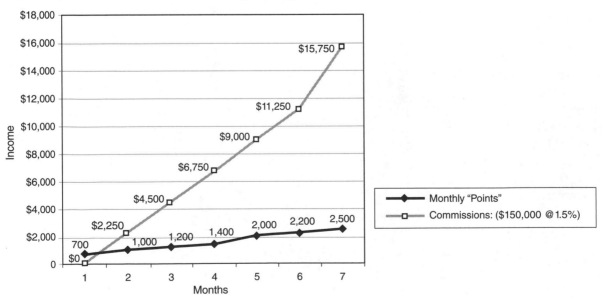

BECOMING A LISTING SUPERSTAR

This section is designed for sales associates who are not satisfied with the median net income but who want to be in the 90th percentile and above. The average licensee does some prospecting in small numbers, and the results are modest. The superstar prospects to a huge base of leads and harvests huge rewards. You should go back to your goals worksheet and "kick it up a notch"! Make the worksheet show you want gross income of $200,000.

Your Leads Database

First, set up a customer relationship manager (CRM) database. There are many programs available, including Microsoft Outlook, Salesforce, and Top Producer. Once you have selected the software, you can organize your potential leads into the following five database categories:

1. Close friends and family
2. Friends
3. Customers
4. Acquaintances
5. Targeted strangers

You need the different categories because your prospecting methods depend on your relationship. Your close friends and family relationships were discussed as your sphere of influence earlier in this chapter, and the next sections concern acquaintances and targeted strangers. Customers are an obvious self-explanatory category.

There is another category of persons called "others" who won't be put in our database. They make up the general population, strangers whom we don't consider prospects.

Acquaintances

These are people we've met or spoken to by phone but don't know well. We will develop this group into a powerhouse of direct and referral business. One of the major objectives of our prospecting efforts is to move as many targeted strangers to this category as possible. We should have a combination of contacts with this group using mail and telephone at least twice monthly.

Targeted Strangers

Your **targeted strangers** list contains persons we don't know but who are qualified by income, occupation, or residence address. This is by far the largest group in your database. The names might come from mailing list companies based on income levels; from cross-reference directories; or from lists of doctors, attorneys, accountants, and business owners. This list should be very large, starting with at least 5,000 names and addresses. In the beginning you should send this list as a direct mail piece (it could be a postcard or a newsletter) at least six times annually. Leads that are generated must be followed up immediately. If you generate one transaction for every 100 names (a modest goal), you will have an additional 50 transactions this year. If your average commission is $2,000 per sale, your income has increased by $100,000.

What Will It Cost? Postcards can be designed online using hundreds of templates. Five thousand glossy finish postcards, printed front and back, cost about $550 plus shipping. You can upload your photo and company logo. Send a different postcard each month. Your software will make label printing easy. Let's check the numbers:

Estimated gross income:		$100,000
Less prospecting costs:		
Postcards: $399 (for 5,000) for 12 months (12 × $399)	$4,788	
Estimated mailing costs:	$612	
Postage: 60,000 cards × .28	$16,800	
Labor: 6 hours × $8/hour × 12 months	$576	
Total Costs		$22,776
Net income generated		**$77,224**

Making Contacts

The following are seven important points to remember when you are prospecting:

1. *Success is in the numbers.* Be confident that this process will result in much higher income levels. You will discover a strong correlation between your prospecting and the number of transactions you make. When you discover what your personal ratios are, you will find it easy to better control your income levels by your daily prospecting. If you get $3,000 extra income, on average, from every 100 contacts you make, you should assume that by making 1,000 additional contacts (20 per week) you can increase your income by $30,000.

2. *Be consistent.* Set the same time every day to make your contacts. Stick to the schedule, but if a closing or an appointment is unavoidably scheduled, make sure the prospecting time is rescheduled for later in the day. It's like a diet; you might get off track, but success will come only if you get back to the plan.

3. *Call at your best time of day.* Some of us are great in the morning. Others are a little grumpy and should set a later prospecting time. Just be sure you have a high energy level. Because showing and listing appointments are usually set for afternoons or evenings, morning may be the best time for a prospecting routine.

4. *Make the first call!* The calls that follow will be easier. Think of the athletic slogan "Just do it!" The hardest call is the first call. Just think one call at a time.

5. *Don't leave a message.* They likely will not call back and may recognize your phone number and will probably avoid future calls when you call back.

6. *You'll get better.* As you make your daily calls, your contact skills will get better and your enthusiasm levels will increase.

7. *Remember the goal.* Before you make your calls, visualize what you want to happen as a result of the call. Put a sign above the phone that says "Get an appointment!" Another sign might read "Get a referral!"

Saturate and Remind

When you put a new entry into your "acquaintances" category, your strategy should be to "saturate and remind."

If you watch television, you have undoubtedly seen one or more companies start a major media campaign with saturation broadcasting. A three-hour sports program, for example, might have as many as ten 30-second commercials in the first two hours. For the next hour, the commercial is often abbreviated to 15 seconds, but because we know it well enough by then, the short ad is as effective as the longer one. This is saturate and remind.

When you meet a new qualified prospect by phone or in person, that person is now put in the saturate mode, with at least a weekly contact for six weeks. Now they know who you are and what you do. If your contacts have been skillful, they also like you, will do business with you, and will send you referrals.

After the saturation period, you can reduce the number of contacts to twice monthly, and you'll have a steady source of business.

GETTING LISTINGS USING SOCIAL MEDIA

Social media is the use of technology for people who want to create and share information in the virtual communities they join. Users of social media like Facebook and Twitter are spending more and more time in the sites, and for some people it's addictive. Businesses attempt to market to users of social media, but the marketing must be carefully done because participants resist direct marketing messages unless the marketer has earned their trust.

Most real estate professionals who use the internet for prospecting have found that it can be the most powerful of all lead generators. Social media is a new frontier for many real estate professionals. It can be a daunting task just to decide which media to use. Most experts say you should write a daily blog, have a strong presence on Facebook and Google+, use Twitter, place pay-per-click advertising, and use email marketing. That's a lot to do.

Facebook is by far the most popular of all social media sites with more than 1 billion users. But what about other social networking sites like LinkedIn, Pinterest, YouTube, and Foursquare? Perhaps the best course of action is to master a few of the more important media sites before trying to be expert in all of them.

Because technology changes quickly, some techniques described in this section are likely to change in the next six months or a year, but the basics remain the same: sales associates should use the available technology that generates customers who buy or sell real estate. In later chapters, we'll describe how the internet will generate many buyers.

Blogging

A blog is a contraction of two words—Web log. It's an article written by an individual or a group of individuals (like a company) that is posted on a website. Usually the latest post is at the top of the page with previous posts below. A real estate blog can attract buyers and sellers to your website. Blog sites include Tumblr, Blogger, Drupal, and Sharepoint, but probably the easiest platform to use in setting up your own website is WordPress.

The blogger must set aside a specific time for writing content that is relevant to real estate, the local scene, events in the area, schools, entertainment, et cetera. It's hard to think of fresh content, so the blogger should make notes as new ideas come to mind. Looking at feeds from other good real estate bloggers may generate ideas (but you can't plagiarize). You have to be authentic and write engaging articles, not tired boilerplate information.

In order to drive traffic to your site, there must be lots of content. It is not necessary that you write all of the content. A very simple way to keep your visitors informed with very little work on your part is by using syndicated news. Really simple syndication (RSS) lets you publish recent news from CNN, NAR, or other bloggers.

A microblog is different from a traditional blog because it is limited to small elements of content, such as short sentences. Twitter is one of the best-known microblogging sites and limits its text distribution to 140 characters in a "tweet." In September 2013, there were 190 million tweets each day.

SUMMARY

- The main objective of a licensee when prospecting is to get an appointment.
- The most important source of listings for new sales associates are:
  - spheres of influence,
  - expired listings,
  - farms,
  - For Sale by Owners (FSBOs), and
  - For Rent by Owners (FRBOs), and
  - canvassing.
- Licensees should avoid listing property if the:
  - seller is not motivated,
  - seller wants you to break the law by discrimination or nondisclosure of material defects,
  - property is out of your market area,
  - property is in poor condition, or
  - owners are rude.
- Most FSBOs try to sell direct in order to save the commission.
- Licensees who work the FSBO market must be persistent, organized, and disciplined (POD).
- Most FSBOs advertise in the classified ads or on Craigslist.
- Organize the FSBOs by telephone number.
- The most effective way to get a listing from an FSBO is to pay a visit.
- A sales associate who prospects FRBOs has a chance of three types of transactions: the FRBO might:
  - list the house,
  - buy another house, or
  - ask the licensee to manage the property.
- Farming is a prospecting activity with results that may not come until later. Persons who farm an area for several years may get up to 75% of the listings in a given neighborhood.
- The farm should be in a large area, but the associate should start with no more than 200 houses.

- The farm should be in a high-turnover neighborhood that is not currently being farmed.

- Canvassing is the process of contacting prospective customers by mail, by telephone, or in person.

- Licensees who want to engage in power prospecting must establish a leads database containing close friends and family, friends and past customers, acquaintances, and targeted strangers.

- Friends, past customers, and acquaintances should be contacted at least twice monthly.

- New persons in the acquaintances category should have a contact program of saturate and remind, meaning weekly contacts for at least six weeks, then twice monthly.

- Social media is the use of technology for people who want to create and share information in the virtual communities they join. Participants in social media tend to resist direct marketing messages from people they do not view as a trusted source.

- A blog is an article written by an individual or a group of individuals and posted on a website. Writing a daily blog is one of the most effective ways to get hits from Web searches. A microblog is limited to small elements of content, such as short sentences in a tweet.

REVIEW QUESTIONS

1. Which is NOT a prospecting source to find listings?
   a. For Sale by Owners
   b. Expired listings
   c. Buyer seminars
   d. Farming

2. The BEST listing source for new associates is
   a. referrals from previous customers.
   b. sphere of influence.
   c. farming.
   d. expired listings.

3. A sales associate who has limited time should NOT try to get a listing where the
   a. seller is motivated.
   b. property is in good condition.
   c. sellers don't need to sell.
   d. property is in the licensee's market area.

4. A sales associate is trying to list a FSBO house valued at $250,000 with a $220,000 mortgage. The seller says, "Your commission is too high!" The sales associate says, "But our listing commission is only 6%!" What is the commission as a percentage of the seller's equity?
   a. 6%
   b. 10%
   c. 25%
   d. 50%

5. It is more likely that a seller will list if she
   a. does not need to move right away.
   b. is available during normal hours to show the home.
   c. does not like meeting and negotiating with people.
   d. understands the home-selling process.

6. The three keys to prospecting success are
   a. numbers, consistency, and organization.
   b. FSBOs, FRBOs, and expired listings.
   c. technical, marketing, and product.
   d. oral skills, written skills, and listening skills.

7. Finding new FSBOs in the classifieds is easier if the prospect cards are arranged by
   a. addresses.
   b. sellers' names.
   c. telephone numbers.
   d. city area.

8. What type of prospecting is direct mail?
   a. High risk
   b. Passive
   c. Stand-alone
   d. Wasted

9. What must be consulted before making telephone canvassing calls?
   a. The broker
   b. The National Do Not Call Registry
   c. The national No Spam Directory
   d. Local ordinances

10. What is the MOST effective way to get a FSBO listing?
    a. Visit
    b. Telephone
    c. Direct mail
    d. Canvass

11. What is NOT a type of income transaction that can reasonably result from contacting a For Rent by Owner (FRBO)?
    a. Sale
    b. Listing
    c. Management contract
    d. Appraisal

12. When using direct mail as a prospecting tool for FSBOs, the mailing
    a. should stand alone as the principal activity.
    b. should be followed with a phone call or a visit.
    c. may be wasted time and effort.
    d. will generate many calls in response.

13. The MOST popular social media site is
    a. Facebook.
    b. Twitter.
    c. LinkedIn.
    d. WordPress.

14. The principal reason a listing expires is
    a. market conditions.
    b. an uncooperative owner.
    c. property condition.
    d. an unrealistic price.

15. The BEST source for finding expired listings is through
    a. classified ads.
    b. a multiple listing service.
    c. a sign on the property.
    d. friends and family.

16. Direct mail is NOT usually a good idea for prospecting expired listings because
    a. by the time it gets there, a motivated seller has already listed.
    b. no one reads mail.
    c. it's too expensive.
    d. it violates Federal Trade Commission rules.

17.   The principal drawback of a farm is
    a.   farms have proven to be time-wasters.
    b.   you may have to work for a long period before any returns are realized.
    c.   ordinances that prevent such activities.
    d.   too many sales associates are competing with you.

18.   Which characteristic should a listing farm NOT have?
    a.   Highly desirable area with low turnover
    b.   Middle to upper price range
    c.   Increasing property values
    d.   Not currently being farmed

19.   A neighborhood has 480 homes. Last year, 69 homes were listed and 60 were sold. What is the turnover rate?
    a.   7.2%
    b.   8.3%
    c.   12.5%
    d.   14%

20.   Which is NOT an important characteristic of a good blog post?
    a.   A "hook" in the title
    b.   Call to action
    c.   Maximum 140 text characters
    d.   Allowing reader comments

5

PRICING THE PROPERTY TO SELL

LEARNING OBJECTIVES

When you finish reading this chapter, you will be able to:

- explain the types of appraisals a real estate licensee may provide for a fee,

- differentiate between an appraisal and an opinion of value,

- describe the three categories of properties shown in a comparative market analysis, and

- explain the adjustment process and direction of the adjustment.

KEY TERMS

adjustments	federally related transaction	transactional characteristic
appraisal	opinion of value	*Uniform Standards of*
comparable property	property characteristic	*Professional Appraisal*
comparative market	reconciliation	*Practice (USPAP)*
analysis (CMA)	subject property	

OVERVIEW

Single agents and transaction brokers have the duties of skill, care, and diligence. Helping a seller set a realistic listing price or helping a buyer understand the market and set a realistic offering price are two of the most important services a sales associate can offer.

Because all real estate activity is related to value, a valid estimate of property value has a significant effect on marketing a listing.

Market value is the most important value in a real estate transaction. The market value of real estate is the most probable price a property should bring in an arm's-length transaction occurring in a competitive and open market.

Real estate licensees use the **appraisal** process to produce opinions of value, comparative market analyses (CMAs), and nonfederally related appraisals.

Licensees must be familiar with the valuation of real property. While most licensees do not prepare formal real estate appraisals, they will go through the appraisal process to some degree when listing properties. Licensees must have a good working knowledge of the market in which they operate to be able to use evaluation methods competently.

OPINION OF VALUE VERSUS CERTIFIED APPRAISAL

Real estate licensees may not refer to themselves as appraisers unless they are licensed or certified appraisers. All active licensees may be paid for providing appraisals or appraisal services as long as they do not represent themselves or their reports as being certified. The appraisal may not be used in a **federally related transaction**. However, the lack of state certification as an appraiser does not prevent a real estate licensee from appraising a property for compensation in a nonfederally related transaction. An appraisal must be professionally and competently completed, and it must comply with the *Uniform Standards of Professional Appraisal Practice (USPAP)*. Failure to do so leaves the licensee open to civil liability and disciplinary action. A licensee involved in the listing or sale of a property should not prepare an appraisal for that property.

A licensee may give an **opinion of value** when making a prospective sale or taking a listing. This opinion of value may not be called an appraisal or a certified appraisal because the licensee has a personal interest in the transaction. Chapter 5 focuses primarily on preparing opinions of value.

Basic Principles of Value

Many economic principles influence the value of real property. They are interrelated, and their relative importance varies, depending on local conditions. The following principles are important to licensees attempting to estimate market value:

- Substitution
- Highest and best use
- Law of supply and demand
- Conformity
- Contribution
- Law of increasing and diminishing returns
- Competition
- Change
- Anticipation

Substitution. This is probably the most important factor in pricing residential property in a neighborhood with an active market. The value of a given parcel of real property is determined by using the principle of substitution. The maximum worth of the real estate is influenced by the cost of acquiring a substitute or comparable property.

DISCUSSION EXERCISE 5.1

You have prepared a CMA for Savannah Cooley. Your opinion of value, based on sales of comparable homes, falls in a range between $192,000 and $203,000. Cooley needs $215,000 from the sale of her home to pay a number of obligations and requests that you list it at that price. Give four persuasive arguments for listing her property at market value.

Highest and Best Use. Of all the factors that influence market value, the primary consideration is the highest and best use of the real estate. A property's highest and best use is its most profitable legally and physically permitted use—that is, the use that provides the highest present value.

Law of Supply and Demand. As it does with any marketable commodity, the law of supply and demand affects real estate. Property values rise as demand increases or supply decreases. For example, when demand declined recently, the result was declines in property values throughout most of Florida.

Conformity. In neighborhoods of single-family houses, buildings normally should follow the principle of conformity; that is, they should be similar in design, construction, and age to other buildings in the neighborhood to realize their maximum value. An elaborate mansion on a large lot with a spacious lawn is worth more in a neighborhood of similar homes than it would be in a neighborhood of more modest homes on smaller lots. Subdivision restrictive covenants are designed to promote the principle of conformity to maintain and enhance values.

Contribution. Any improvement to a property, whether to vacant land or a building, is worth only what it adds to the property's market value. An improvement's contribution to the value of the entire property may be greater or smaller than its cost. A licensee's opinion should be determined by a feature's contribution to value, not its actual cost.

DISCUSSION EXERCISE 5.2

You have prepared a CMA for Phyllis, who lives in Scenic Heights, an area of $100,000 homes. Phyllis reviews the recent sales and sees that her house has a large swimming pool, a feature that is not present in the homes in the report. She produces the invoices for the cost of her pool, which total $25,000, and suggests a $125,000 list price. Sales data show that pools in the neighborhood add about $6,000 to the properties' list prices.

Do a role-playing exercise, with another person taking Phyllis's part, and discuss the pricing principles involved.

Law of Increasing and Diminishing Returns. Improvements to land and structures can reach a point at which they have no positive effect on property values. As long as money spent on such improvements produces a proportionate increase in income or value, the law of increasing returns is in effect. When additional improvements bring no corresponding increase in income or value, one can observe the law of diminishing returns.

Smaller homes in a neighborhood of larger homes may experience increasing returns when improved. Homes that are the same size or larger than surrounding homes should not be improved significantly until the owners have considered the economics of their decisions.

> ### DISCUSSION EXERCISE 5.3
>
> Sandy purchased a two-bedroom home in Betton Hills for $200,000. She builds an extra bedroom and bath and finds that the value has increased by much more than the cost of the improvements. She continues improving the property by adding two more bedrooms and a large family room with a fireplace. Sandy decides to sell, and she calls you to list the property. Your CMA shows that the value increase was much less than the construction cost. Sandy disagrees with your findings.
>
> Do a role-playing exercise, with another person playing the part of Sandy, while you explain to her why the value may not have increased as much as the cost of improvements.

Competition. All residential properties are susceptible to competition. The only house for sale in a nice, well-maintained neighborhood has a better chance of selling at or near market value than if several houses on the same street were for sale.

Change. All property is influenced by the principle of change. Because no physical or economic condition remains constant, licensees must be aware of market forces when preparing opinions of value.

Anticipation. Most buyers purchase real estate with the expectation that its value will increase, and they have been rewarded when the anticipation proves to be correct. In inflationary times, the anticipation of higher prices creates a multitude of buyers, driving prices higher than can be supported for long periods. In Florida, the prices for oceanfront properties have increased dramatically.

But when the market begins to top out, the anticipation of a price recession can cause investors to dump property on the market, forcing prices lower. Anticipation also is important to prices of property in times of decreasing interest rates, when builders rush to fill the expected demand. Licensees must be aware of the importance of anticipation when valuing property for sale.

COMPARATIVE MARKET ANALYSIS

Most licensees use a **comparative market analysis (CMA)** for arriving at an opinion of value. A CMA is a process of gathering and analyzing the **property characteristics** of homes currently for sale, homes recently sold, and homes listed that did not sell. It may range in form from a simple list of recent sales with no adjustments to a detailed adjustment grid. Whether taking a simple or a complex approach, licensees need to ensure that they have met all the conditions for selecting comparables.

Gathering CMA Data

First, the sales associate must have knowledge of the **subject property**. If it is a standard-floor-plan subdivision home, it may be possible to complete a market analysis without a property inspection. However, if the seller has made many improvements or if the home has other amenities not typical of the market, it may be difficult to make adjustments during the CMA's presentation phase. The truly professional approach is to inspect the property before completing the CMA.

Once the property inspection has been completed, the licensee should select the best properties for comparison. The following three categories of comparison help sellers and buyers better understand the market:

- Properties that have sold
- Properties that are now on the market
- Property listings that have expired

The CMA will be a good indication of value only when comparables exist in a reasonably active market and where sufficient, reliable market sales information is available.

A **comparable property** should meet the following four conditions before it is used in a CMA:

- It should be similar to the subject property.
- If this is a sale, it should have sold recently—within the past year.
- It should be located in the same market area as the subject property.
- It should have changed owners as a result of an arm's-length transaction.

Reviewing actual sales prices of comparable properties helps buyers and sellers see what buyers actually pay in the marketplace. Comparable sales data are important when new financing is necessary because an appraiser relies on the data to estimate market value. Many sales are contingent on financing the purchase price, so it is of no value to overprice a property only to lose the sale when the lender and the buyer receive the appraisal report.

Reviewing the prices of comparable properties now on the market shows the seller what owners of properties with similar characteristics are asking. These properties will compete with the seller's. The principle of substitution means that a buyer will select the property with the best price, all other things being equal. A seller who wishes to position the property in the most effective price window values it just above recent sales and just below competing properties. A properly priced listing should result in a reasonably quick sale at the optimum price.

The listing prices of properties that do not sell demonstrate the resistance level of buyers to overpriced listings. In almost every case, the expired listing has been priced too high for the amenities offered.

The best sources for gathering CMA information include:

- multiple listing service (MLS) records,
- company files,
- public records,
- other licensees, and
- data service companies.

MLS records are the most convenient and comprehensive method of getting listings and sales information. MLS computer records can be searched by address and subdivision for ease in finding comparable sales. The information can be retrieved for sold, current, or expired property listings.

Company files are limited in scope but may be more complete as to property descriptions and financing used in purchases.

The public records include information recorded in the clerk's office and information on file with the tax appraiser. Except for verification of sales data and identities of the parties, the information from the clerk's office is not as important as the information available at the tax appraiser's office. While the information from the property appraiser's records is sometimes outdated, the records are still a useful source of data. Because the "sold" section of the CMA should include for-sale-by-owner properties, the appraiser's office is often the best information source for such sales.

Licensees often know of properties that have just closed. The information given should be verified and added to the report to include current sales.

Data service companies compile property sales data and sell the information to interested parties. Because this information does not give complete property descriptions, it is best used as a checklist to ensure that all sales have been considered.

Selecting Comparable Properties

A licensee preparing a CMA has two choices when selecting properties to compare. The first choice is to report every sale and every listing in the neighborhood, together with features and prices. The other choice is to analyze only the properties that are comparable.

Reporting all properties gives the seller an overview of the entire neighborhood market. Some sellers believe a list is incomplete if they know of a neighbor's home that sold recently that is not on the list; therefore, a complete list may make sellers more comfortable. However, problems sometimes arise with this all-inclusive list. Properties that are not comparable may mislead a seller concerning values. When making CMA adjustments, the sales associate should not use those that have significant differences in construction quality or size. The sales associate should exclude properties sold to relatives because the price may not reflect the fair value.

Listing only three or four comparable properties makes a clearer presentation for a seller and reduces the chance for confusion about values. Appraisers use this approach.

Perhaps the best approach for the licensee is to prepare a comprehensive list of all properties that have sold, are listed currently, or have expired and then select the most comparable properties from that list for analysis. This method satisfies the needs of completeness and clarity. The characteristics for comparison are described next.

Common Elements of Comparison

Clearly, the accuracy of the comparable sales approach relies on the elements of comparison selected for adjustment. The elements listed on the CMA chart in Figure 5.1 are some of the most common and significant factors that affect value in standard residential appraisals. In any given analysis, it may be necessary to include other adjustments. The easiest way to fill out the CMA is to list all the details of the subject property, then evaluate each comparable with the data that have been gathered.

F I G U R E 5.1 ■ Sample Property Characteristics*

Location	Number of bedrooms
Size and shape of lot	Number of bathrooms
Landscaping	Kitchen characteristics
Style	Condition of exterior
Construction quality	Condition of interior
Design	Garage
Age	Other improvements
Square feet of gross living area	General condition
Number of rooms	

*These are selected examples only; more or fewer characteristics may be applicable.

Location. What are the three most important determinants of property value? The old expression "location, location, location" is the best answer. Location is so important that only in very unusual circumstances would a licensee use a property outside the subject's neighborhood as a comparable sale. In such a case, the comparable should come from a similar neighborhood. Even within the same neighborhood, locations can result in significant variances. A property across the street from a park is more valuable than one across the street from a commercial area.

D I S C U S S I O N   E X E R C I S E   5 . 4

Sara wants a For Sale by Owner to list with her, but the FSBO says that the commission added to his price would make the property overpriced. Sara really wants the listing, so she finds several homes the same size as the FSBO's property and prepares a CMA. However, the comparables she uses are located in another, more upscale neighborhood. The owner looks at the CMA and lists with Sara.

Has Sara prepared an acceptable CMA? Why or why not?

Has Sara violated any ethical or legal code? Why or why not?

Size and Shape of Lot. Irregularities can make portions of a site unusable for building, impair privacy, or restrict on-site parking, which could require major adjustments. Street frontage and total square footage of the lot are other important considerations.

Landscaping. The sales associate should evaluate the maturity, quantity, and quality of trees, plantings, and other types of landscaping.

Construction Quality. The sales associate will make a major adjustment if construction quality of a comparable is not equivalent to that of the subject property and may disqualify the property as a comparable if the difference is too pronounced.

Style. Generally, the style of a house follows the rule of conformity (a house should not be the only one of its type in the neighborhood). An important aspect of style is the number of floors of the residence. A one-story ranch house probably could be compared to a split-level, with some adjustment made. A three-story house is not comparable to a one-story ranch house, however.

1   **Design.** Design must be viewed from both functional and aesthetic standpoints. Func-
2   tional aspects include the existing traffic patterns in a house, placement of doors and win-
3   dows, room-to-room relationships, and the usefulness of rooms. Aesthetic aspects focus on
4   how pleasant and attractive an interior appears to an observer.

5   **Age.** Because most subdivisions are built within a relatively short period of time, there
6   may not be significant age differences among comparables. A new home is likely valued
7   by the builder according to actual costs, overhead, and profit. While overall upkeep is
8   important, the home's age may alert the licensee to outmoded design and fixtures or to
9   needed repairs.

10 **Square Feet of Gross Living Area.** This is one of the most common areas for making
11 adjustments because size differences among homes can be calculated easily. If licensees
12 make adjustments for square footage, they also must be careful when adjusting for num-
13 ber of rooms or bedrooms because this could lead to double counting. Adjustments for
14 gross living area can be misleading if all properties are not comparable. For instance, a
15 small house normally sells for more per square foot than a large house in the same area. A
16 one-story house has a higher cost per square foot than a two-story house. Be sure that all
17 properties used are comparable to the subject property. Appraisers normally do not count
18 any floor area that is below grade as gross living area, so do not use such properties unless
19 the subject also has below-grade area.

DISCUSSION EXERCISE 5.5

Silas Dean is trying to set a price for a 1,500-square-foot home in Green
Hills. He finds the following comparable sales:

Price	Square Feet	Price per Square Foot
$49,500	980	$50.51
51,000	1,025	49.76
50,000	1,000	50.00
61,500	1,500	41.00

The average price per square foot for these properties is $47.82. Sam Wil-
liamson, who owns the home, asks, "What is it worth?" Dean replies, "Houses
sell for $47.82 per square foot in this neighborhood. Based on that, your property
should sell for about $71,700." Williamson agrees and lists at $71,500.

Do you agree with Dean's analysis? Why?

---

20 **Measuring Practice.** Measurement of a house is extremely important. An error could
21 cause problems in pricing the property if the home's square footage is given to buyers.
22 Calculate the square footage of gross living area of the house shown in Figure 5.2.

FIGURE 5.2 ■ **Measuring a House**

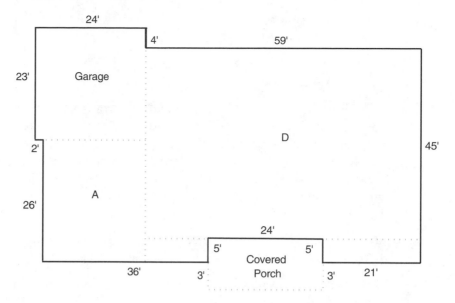

DISCUSSION EXERCISE 5.6

You have done a market report for the Meadows at Woodrun subdivision. Your analysis of property value, based on several 1,200-square-foot homes, indicates that homes sell at prices averaging $50 per square foot. When talking by phone with a prospective seller, you quote that figure after setting the listing appointment.

When you arrive at the property with your listing information in hand, the seller proudly shows you the 500-square-foot two-car garage that has been converted into a heated and cooled family room. He indicates that the price at which you should list the home is $85,000, based on 1,700 square feet times your $50-per-square-foot figure. Role-play this situation, and explain why it may be difficult to market this home at $85,000. Also discuss some methods of arriving at a more realistic price.

Number of Rooms. The total number of rooms in a house does not include the foyer or bathrooms and generally does not include basement rooms. Don't double count when adjusting for square feet and number of bedrooms.

Number of Bedrooms. The sales associate would make a major adjustment if the subject property has two bedrooms and the comparables have at least three, or vice versa. Don't double count when adjusting for square feet.

Number of Baths. Full baths (lavatory, toilet, and tub, with or without shower), three-quarter baths (lavatory, toilet, and shower), and half baths (lavatory and toilet) comprise this category. Modern plumbing is assumed, so an adjustment must be made for out-of-date fixtures, if different from the subject property.

Kitchen. Licensees should focus on certain key factors, as follows:

- Location
- Counter space and storage
- Service triangle
- Appliances

The location of the kitchen is an important factor, based on its convenience to dining areas and accessibility for unloading groceries. Usually the market will not accept a kitchen with inadequate counter and storage space. The sales associate calculates the food service triangle by drawing straight lines connecting refrigerator, range, and sink. Most consumer polls show that the total length of the three lines combined should be greater than 12 feet but should not exceed 22 feet. Appliances represent a sizable portion of the home's cost, and their age and condition are important.

Other Space. Unfinished attic, porch, utility room, Florida room, or any other room not part of the primary house area is included in this category.

Condition of Exterior. Make an adjustment for any needed repair work.

Condition of Interior. Make an adjustment for needed repairs. Luxurious finishing such as real wood paneling, adds to a home's value.

Garage. If the subject does not have one, any garage on a comparable property requires an adjustment. Compare garages on the subject and comparable properties for type of construction and size.

Other Improvements. Adjust for differences between the subject property and the comparable. Adjust for landscaping, driveways, trees, and pools based on their contribution to value.

Adjusting for Differences

Ideally, the licensee wants to find comparable sales that are identical in characteristics to the subject property. In the real world, this doesn't always happen. While the CMA is not an appraisal, it is often necessary to make **adjustments** for some of the major differences that have been discussed. A major difference between the subject property and comparable property, such as a pool, could make an opinion of value very misleading if no adjustment is made for the pool. Many licensees recognize the difficulty in doing a CMA because when they look at a sold property, they see it as it is today, not how it looked when it went under contract. The important consideration in adjusting the comparable sale is how it looked at the time of sale.

> **EXAMPLE:** Whitney Cooley, a licensed sales associate, is preparing a CMA for Brian Edwards' three-bedroom, two-bath home in Eastgate. One of the comparable properties with the same floor plan sold recently for $73,000. The only difference between the properties is that the comparable property has a swimming pool. Whitney has done CMAs in Eastgate before and estimates that a pool contributes about $4,000 to value. The subject property doesn't have a pool, so Whitney makes a minus adjustment of $4,000 to the comparable's sales price. This indicates a value of $69,000 for the subject.
>
> How did Whitney determine that a pool contributes $4,000 to value in that neighborhood? The matched pair technique helped her make the estimate. She examined two recent sales in which the only difference was the fact that one

property had a pool. The property with the pool sold for $4,000 more than the home without the pool. Because the pool was the only difference, the $4,000 must be attributable to that amenity. It would be better to make the comparison with several matched pairs to support the conclusion, but the technique is valid. The cost to build the pool is not added, just the value that buyers and sellers place on the pool.

Adjustments are always made to the comparable property, never to the subject. Adjustments are subtracted from the comparable property if the comparable is bigger or better. Adjustments are added if the comparable is smaller or less desirable. An easy way to remember is "CIA, CBS":

- If the Comparable is Inferior, Add
- If the Comparable is Better, Subtract

Adjustments should be made for sold properties, listed properties, and expired properties; then each category should be reconciled.

Reconciliation

Reconciliation is the resolution of several adjusted values on CMAs into a single estimate of value. Although an appraiser reports a single-market value amount, a licensee making an opinion of value may prefer to report a range of values, from lowest to highest adjusted value of the comparables. Presenting a range rather than a single estimate of value allows a seller to price the property somewhat higher than the sold properties would indicate. The seller should understand that the home will likely sell at some price other than the list price and should consider all offers within the range of values.

Reconciliation enables the licensee to set the range differently. The first step is to estimate the value for each section of the report (sold properties, listed properties, and expired listings). Reconciliation is not simply the averaging of these values. The process requires the licensee to examine carefully the similarity of each comparable property to the subject property. If one comparable is nearly identical to the subject, including all relevant **transactional characteristics**, the sales price of that comparable might be the subject's estimated market value. When the comparables vary in their degree of similarity to the subject, the comparable property judged most similar is assigned the greatest weight in the reconciliation process.

The estimates for each section should be rounded. The range would then be calculated from the reconciled value of sold properties and the reconciled value of properties listed currently.

Another method for setting a range of values is to reconcile the sold properties to a value estimate, then check to see what properties sell for as a percentage of list price, then divide the value estimate by that amount. The two values comprise the range high and low.

DISCUSSION EXERCISE 5.7

You have just completed a CMA for Tim Palmer's home at 1112 Bristol Court. The reconciled market value of his home is $127,500. MLS statistics indicate that homes sell at approximately 95% of list price.

What is the range of value you quote to Tim?

A Visual Aid to the CMA

"A picture is worth a thousand words" is a timeworn expression because it is true. Sellers who review CMAs with licensees often have difficulty visualizing the comparable properties. The licensee who provides visual data can make a clearer presentation, and that may result in more realistic pricing. Owners who are motivated to sell do not set out to overprice their properties. Overpricing is usually the result of an inadequate understanding of the market, and that responsibility belongs to the listing sales associate.

Valuable visual aids include plat maps of the subdivision and pictures of the comparable properties. The plat map should be color-coded to show which properties were sold, which properties are now for sale, and which listings have expired (see Figure 5.3). Photographs can be printed from the MLS computer system or taken with a digital camera. The licensee should also include a photo of the seller's home. The seller will appreciate your personal touch and the extra photo for her scrapbook. Leaving a family home of some years can be a sentimental experience, and the seller will remember a licensee who is sensitive to those feelings.

FIGURE 5.3 ■ Plat Map of Neighborhood

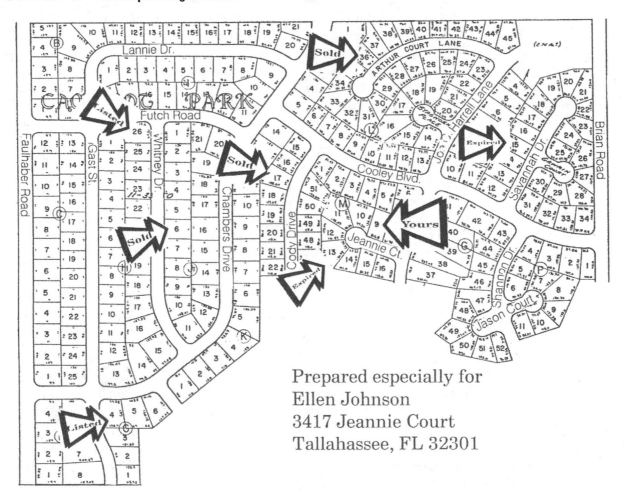

Prepared especially for
Ellen Johnson
3417 Jeannie Court
Tallahassee, FL 32301

COMPARATIVE MARKET ANALYSIS

Your CMA will require getting information from the owner, gathering information from the tax rolls through the MLS system, and analyzing the value contributed to the property by amenities.

Getting Information from the Owner

You have just received a request from John Halliburton to discuss listing his family's home. Halliburton gives you some basic information:

- The full names of all persons on the deed: *John Halliburton and Susan C. Halliburton, HW*
- The property address: *4316 Landtowne Drive, Orlando*
- The owner's home and office phone numbers: *407-555-3557; 407-555-3917*
- The number of bedrooms and baths in the home: *Four bedrooms, two baths*
- A description of extras in the home: *1,920 square feet of gross living area, two-car garage*
- A convenient time for an appointment: *This is the time to decide whether to do a pre-presentation inspection of the property (two appointments required: one to inspect the property, one to present the CMA). You decide to have one appointment at 6:20 this evening and will inspect the property at that time.*

Gathering Information from the Online Tax Rolls

The tax rolls for Orange County show the following information for the property:

- Legal description: *Lot 14, Block H, Landover Hills, Unit 2 - Orange County*
- Property tax appraisal: *$149,300*
- Annual taxes: *$2,986.45*
- Year built: *1989*
- Base area: *1,920 square feet (later verified by physical measurement)*
- Total area: *2,420 square feet (includes attached 2-car garage)*
- Last sale: *1996*
- Last sale price: *$128,000*
- Mortgage: *Sun Title Bank*

A search of the tax records shows seven sales in the subdivision within the previous year, ranging from $168,000 to $174,800. Six of the seven sales were reported in the MLS. The sales are shown in the first section of the CMA in Figure 5.4.

Four properties are currently listed for sale in the MLS, shown in the second section of the CMA, and three listings have expired within the last 12 months, shown in the third section.

FIGURE 5.4 ■ Comparative Market Analysis

Comparative Market Analysis

Prepared for:
Property Address: _____
Date: June 8, 201___
Description: _____

Properties sold within the previous 12 months

Property Address	Sales Price	List Price	Days on mkt	Living Area	Features	Estimated Adjustment	Adjusted Sales Price	Comments
1816 Hibiscus	172,800	180,000	120	1820	Pool, FP, Screen Porch			
2412 Nasturtium	169,900	177,900	71	1920	FP			
1763 Camellia	173,500	182,000	45	1900	Pool			
1421 Azalea	168,900	175,000	52	2000	Screen Porch			
1640 Clover	171,200	179,500	61	2000	1 Car Garage			
2210 Hibiscus	168,000	175,900	32	1900				
1240 Camellia	174,800	182,500	70	1920	Screen Porch, FP			

Median $ _____

Percent sales price/list price _____

Properties currently on the market

Property Address	List Price	Days on Mkt.	Living Area	Features	Estimated Adjustment	As Adjusted	Comments
1818 Azalea	191,000	75	2100	Pool			
1740 Hibiscus	178,800	120	1900	FP			
2210 Clover	185,000	38	1820	Screen Porch, Pool			
1604 Magnolia	177,000	45	1920	Screen Porch			

Median $ _____

Properties which were listed but failed to sell during the previous 12 months

Property Address	List Price	Days on Mkt.	Living Area	Features	Estimated Adjustment	As Adjusted
2212 Camellia	192,800	180	1900	Pool, FP, Screen Porch		
1812 Hibiscus	185,500	240	2000	Screen Porch		
2211 Azalea	186,600	140	1800	FP		

Median $ _____

The suggested marketing range is $ _____ to $ _____

This information is believed to be accurate, but is not warranted.

Analysis of Value Contributed to the Property by Amenities

When reviewing historic data on sold properties, we can estimate what a pool, a garage, an extra bedroom, or a fireplace contributes to value. The matched-pair technique would compare similar houses with and without a particular feature. The difference in price would tend to show what the feature contributes in value.

For purposes of this CMA, we shall assume that sold properties in the neighborhood have shown the following value contributions over time:

- The contribution of a pool is $7,000.
- The contribution of a fireplace is $1,800.
- The contribution of an extra garage stall (2 cars, rather than 1) is $2,800.
- The contribution of extra square footage differences is $50 per square foot.
- The contribution of a screened porch is $2,000.

The CMA has been filled in with the exception of the adjustments shown above. Please compare the subject property with the comparable properties and adjust the comparable properties. Then complete the analysis and estimate the marketing range for the property. Presenting this CMA to the sellers will be discussed in chapter 6.

CMAs Using Comparable Sales and Listings (No Adjustments)

Licensees commonly use a no-adjustments CMA method in pricing property. It involves listing properties for sale now, properties sold in the previous year, and expired listings, without making adjustments. Its simplicity is appealing to licensees and sellers alike because it provides an overview of the market. However, if properties on the chart are not comparable and the subject property is priced from an average of sales prices or square-foot calculations, the pricing method can be misleading.

DISCUSSION EXERCISE 5.8

In this role-playing session, assume the CMA has been explained, but the seller is attempting to set an unreasonably high listing price. Discuss as many persuasive points as possible to encourage the seller to price the property in the range suggested.

Computer-Generated CMAs

Most MLS services make the preparation of a CMA much easier. Many of these programs are formatted to print out an entire listing presentation to the sellers, tailored to their specific needs. In many cases, the time required is less than that of handwriting the old CMA grids. Most of the programs provide raw sales data without adjustment, although the sales associate, by selecting only comparable properties, is able to come quite close to market value.

SUMMARY

- A real estate licensee may prepare an appraisal in a transaction that is not federally related.

- F.S. 475 requires that appraisals be made in conformity with the *Uniform Standards of Professional Appraisal Practice*.

- Normally, when listing or selling property, licensees prepare a comparative market analysis (CMA) and give their opinion of value. The opinion of value may not be called an appraisal.

- Many important principles of value exist, including highest and best use, substitution, supply and demand, contribution, and conformity.

- The comparable sales approach to estimating value is usually the most common method used by appraisers to value homes and vacant sites.

- The comparative market analysis is the method most licensees use to prepare an opinion of value.

- The three sections of a CMA are:

  - properties that have sold recently,
  - properties for sale now, and
  - properties that did not sell during the listing periods.

- Data for the CMA are gathered primarily from the MLS and county property appraiser's records.

- Only comparable properties should be used in the analysis.

- A range of values is provided to the seller because it is more meaningful than a single value.

R E V I E W   Q U E S T I O N S

1. An appraisal of real property is
    a. an accurate determination of its value.
    b. a process of arriving at its value.
    c. an estimate of its value.
    d. a reconciled statement of just value.

2. Of all the factors that influence market value, the MOST important is the
    a. principle of substitution.
    b. highest and best use.
    c. law of increasing and diminishing returns.
    d. principle of conformity.

3. A married couple lives in a 2,100-square-foot home. Home sizes in the area range from 1,200 square feet to 2,100 square feet. A sales associate found seven comparable sales from different sized homes. He calculated the sales price per square foot for each home, averaged all the prices, and applied it to the square feet in the subject home. In preparing the CMA, the sales associate
    a. has prepared the CMA properly.
    b. should have asked the couple how they wanted him to do it so they could get the best price for their home.
    c. has violated Chapter 475 because he did not follow the *USPAP*.
    d. should have used only the sales prices of similar-size homes.

4. The MOST profitable legally and physically permitted use of real property is called its
    a. market value.
    b. appraised value.
    c. location.
    d. highest and best use.

5. A comparative market analysis would be LEAST effective when trying to establish value for a
    a. residential property.
    b. duplex.
    c. public school property.
    d. vacant property.

6. Which is designed to promote the principle of conformity to maintain and enhance value in a subdivision?
    a. Restrictive covenants
    b. Zoning codes
    c. Comprehensive plans
    d. Land use codes

7.   When a man added a family room to his house, which was already too large for the area, he did not see the value increase as much as the cost of the addition. What principle was demonstrated?
      a.   Highest and best use of the land
      b.   Increase in value at least equal to the cost of construction
      c.   Law of increasing returns
      d.   Law of diminishing returns

8.   When listing a property in the ordinary course of business, any active real estate licensee in Florida is authorized to prepare an
      a.   opinion of value.
      b.   appraisal report.
      c.   appraisal assignment report.
      d.   analysis assignment report.

9.   A mansion in a neighborhood of smaller, average homes would violate the principle of
      a.   change.
      b.   conformity.
      c.   competition.
      d.   contribution.

10.   In a neighborhood of three-bedroom, two-bath homes, an owner added a second bathroom at a cost of $1,600. An appraiser adjusted the value of the home upward by $2,000 due to the improvement. This is an example of the principle of
      a.   change.
      b.   conformity.
      c.   competition.
      d.   contribution.

11.   A woman is preparing a CMA for property located in Arbor Hills. She finds three homes that sold recently: a four-bedroom home with a pool that sold for $90,000; a three-bedroom home with no pool that sold for $81,000; and a three-bedroom home with a pool that sold for $85,000. Based solely on this information, what does a swimming pool contribute to value in Arbor Hills?
      a. $0
      b. $4,000
      c. $5,000
      d. $9,000

12.   The ideal kitchen service triangle should be from
      a.   9 to 25 feet.
      b.   12 to 22 feet.
      c.   120 square feet.
      d.   12 by 24 feet.

13.   The comparable sales approach to value is based primarily on what principle of valuation?
      a.   Conformity
      b.   Substitution
      c.   Supply and demand
      d.   Highest and best use

14.   Which is NOT important in comparing properties using the comparable sales approach?
a.   Date of sale
b.   Size of house
c.   Original cost of improvements
d.   General condition and appearance

15.   You are preparing a CMA and want to be certain that it reflects comparable sales of properties sold directly by owners. The BEST place to find the information is in
a.   either the clerk's office or the tax appraiser's office.
b.   city hall.
c.   the MLS records.
d.   the tax collector's office.

16.   When the term *recently* is used to describe a comparable sale, it is generally understood to mean that the property sold within the past how many months?
a.   12
b.   8–15
c.   12–18
d.   18

17.   Which is NOT a condition that a licensee must meet when selecting comparable properties using the comparable sales approach to value?
a.   Similar
b.   Sold recently
c.   Same market area
d.   Same floor plan

18.   Which is correct if a broker charges a $400 fee for preparing an appraisal that will NOT be used in a federally related transaction?
a.   The broker may prepare an appraisal but not charge a fee.
b.   The broker must follow the *Uniform Standards of Professional Appraisal Practice*.
c.   The broker has violated Chapter 475, F.S.
d.   The broker must call the appraisal an opinion of value.

19.   You are estimating the value of a vacant lot zoned for single-family residence use. One year ago, a comparable lot sold for $25,000. Your analysis of market conditions and property characteristics produced the following needed adjustments: subject lot, $2,000 inferior; subject site location, $3,000 superior. These adjustments result in an estimated market value for the subject lot of
a. $23,000.
b. $24,000.
c. $26,000.
d. $27,000.

20.   A home has dimensions of 35 feet by 57 feet that include an attached 24-foot by 22-foot garage and a 200-square-foot screen porch. How many square feet of gross living area does the home have?
a.   1,267
b.   1,467
c.   1,995
d.   2,354

MAKING THE LISTING PRESENTATION

LEARNING OBJECTIVES

When you finish reading this chapter, you will be able to:

- enumerate at least four requirements for a proper listing presentation,
- list the five major steps in a listing presentation,
- list the three major sections in a seller's net proceeds form, and
- prepare a seller's net proceeds form.

KEY TERMS

equity   net proceeds

OVERVIEW

As a licensee's ability to deliver an effective listing presentation increases, the "close" rate for listing appointments will be higher. Prospecting is a numbers game. It may take up to 50 calls to get one listing appointment. What a shame it would be to have all that effort rendered worthless by failing to prepare carefully before sitting down with the sellers.

REQUIREMENTS FOR THE LISTING PRESENTATION

This presentation is a "sit down at the dining room table" discussion when all owners are present. It will be successful only if you:

- know all the parties who need to sign your listing are available;
- are fully prepared to list the property, meaning you must have all the forms ready for signature when the parties agree to list;
- know this presentation thoroughly;
- know about the house you are trying to list by using the information you gathered from the tax appraiser's office, the plat books, or from your own personal inspection;
- have prepared a comparative market analysis (CMA) to help you show the sellers a fair value for their house and to protect you from the overpriced listing, a nemesis that will cost you time and aggravation, and make for unhappy customers;
- have your information organized in a businesslike fashion and your mind organized as well;
- are properly dressed and professional in appearance and manner; and
- are on time for the appointment.

THE FIVE MAJOR SEGMENTS OF THE PRESENTATION

A listing presentation consists of the following five major segments:

1. Building rapport with the sellers
2. Explaining the pricing process (going over the CMA)
3. Estimating the seller's proceeds (the seller's net proceeds form)
4. Discussing the reason most FSBOs don't sell their homes
5. Asking for the listing

Building Rapport with the Sellers

The following six strategies, if followed conscientiously at a listing presentation, will help almost any real estate salesperson build rapport with sellers:

1. Greet the sellers at the door with a smile, and be yourself. Thank them for the opportunity to visit their home and, after some initial small talk, begin taking control of the interview. If you are offered a beverage (non-alcoholic) or a snack, offer thanks and accept it.

2. If you haven't already made a preliminary visit to the property, ask the sellers to give you a tour. Tour the outside first before dark, if possible. Ask permission to make notes for each room. Ask questions about the house while on the tour. If you see any features that indicate the sellers' hobbies, awards, or family photos, try to acknowledge them. Show the owners that you've done your homework by confirming some of the information you've gotten from the tax appraiser.

3. Inspect the property boundaries; make notes of exterior features, then ask the sellers to help you measure the exterior of the house. Confirm that total with the information you have from the tax appraiser.

4. After returning indoors, arrange to have all parties sit at a dining or kitchen table. Suggest that the TV be turned down (or off) so that you can hear them well.

5. Find out why they are selling. If they are moving to a new town, find out how they feel (not think) about the move. Is it scary? Has he or she met the new boss? How do they feel about the new job? Let them know you care about them as individuals.

6. Discuss the sale process. Go over the home-selling process time line in Figure 6.1.

F I G U R E 6.1 ■ Home-Selling Process Time Line

1 . At first meeting:
   * Get acquainted and see the property inside and outside
   * Describe the reasons for selling and timing needs:
      * Have you purchased another home in the area, or do you intend to purchase?
      * If you are leaving town, can we help in getting housing information for the new city?
2 . Determining the best price for the property:
   * A review of current market conditions
   * Review the comparative market analysis
   * Discuss the reasons for pricing the property to make it competitive
   * Decide on the best price for the market conditions
3 . Review the potential net proceeds from the sale:
   * The price of the property, less mortgages and closing costs
   * Remember that it's not how much you need from the sale—it's the amount you likely will get.
4 . Discuss the marketing plan for the property
5 . Review and sign the listing agreement
6 . Showings
   * Discuss present condition of the property
   * Plan for suggested changes—bright, clean, and neat
   * What the sellers should do when prospective buyers come to the property with the sales associate
      * Turn on all the lights
      * Do a last-minute walk-through to remove any clutter
      * Make it smell good
      * Lock up the pets
      * Leave the house during the showing, if possible
      * Try to not get into discussions with the buyers
7 . When buyers make an offer to purchase
   * Request a preapproval offer from the buyers' lender
   * We will discuss all aspects of the offer and I'll prepare a statement of your net proceeds from this offer
   * Seller can decide what to do with the offer
8 . After reviewing the offer, you may
   * Accept the offer—you have a contract
   * Decline the offer—you do not have a contract
      * The buyers can raise their offer
      * The buyers can decide to keep looking for another house
   * Counteroffer
      * If you don't like some part of the offer (price, closing date, etc.) you can change it.
      * The buyers can accept your counteroffer—you have a contract
      * The buyers can reject the your counteroffer and look for another house
9 . When you have a signed contract, refer to Figure 13.1, The Road to Closing

Explaining the Pricing Process

The presentation should provide information the sellers need to fully understand the listing process. Agents who give a value without first going over the CMA may lose the opportunity for realistic pricing if the sellers are surprised and offended at the value. A proper presentation should proceed in the following 11-step sequence:

1. Help the sellers understand the current market conditions. You can get this information from MLS statistics or from your broker. Provide statistics for the overall market. The CMA will help show the neighborhood statistics. For example, tell the sellers the:

    - number of houses currently listed,
    - number of homes sold last month, and
    - month's supply of homes on the market (divide listed homes by sales).

2. Give the sellers your analysis of the market:

    - Is it a buyers' or a sellers' market?
    - Are prices rising or falling?
    - What is likely to happen if interest rates rise (or fall)?

3. Explain the importance of pricing the property within the selling range. Use the pricing pyramid in Figure 6.2.

4. Inform the sellers that the purpose of the CMA is to determine the best list price for the property.

5. Explain the report and how you researched the material in it. If your conclusions of market value are less than the sellers' desired price, you may have a problem. Do not state your conclusions at this time. Wait to see what the sellers conclude from the comparable sales. (Often, sellers will quickly realize that their price is too high and, if motivated to sell, will agree to reduce the price.)

6. Explain how each section of the CMA is important in the decision-making process by giving the sellers an overview of the following:

    - Sold listings prove what selling prices have been and what bank appraisals might show.
    - Homes now for sale illustrate the importance of competitive pricing.
    - Expired listings demonstrate the futility of pricing property at an unrealistically high price.

7. Review individual properties on the report while referring to visual aids such as a subdivision map and photos.

8. Ask the sellers for questions or comments.

9. Give the sellers time to arrive at a range of values independently.

10. If the sellers want to price the property too high, discuss the reasons why that approach is unproductive.

11. When a realistic listing price has been agreed upon, complete the seller's net proceeds form.

F I G U R E 6.2   ■   The Pricing Pyramid

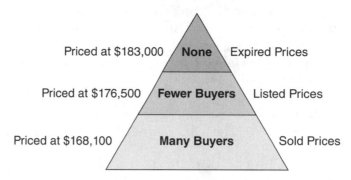

The Number of Potential Buyers Is
Related to Your Home's Price

Priced at $183,000   **None**   Expired Prices

Priced at $176,500   **Fewer Buyers**   Listed Prices

Priced at $168,100   **Many Buyers**   Sold Prices

This chart helps sellers to visualize the effect pricing
may have on the activity level the house will experience.
The lower the price, the more buyers will be attracted.

C A S E   S T U D Y

PRESENTATION OF A CMA

Assumptions

Use the CMA from chapter 5.

You visited the house yesterday when Mrs. Halliburton was home to measure it, evaluate its features, and take some digital photos for the presentation this evening. This allowed you to prepare a CMA with confidence that there would be no surprises.

Cast:

Sales associate: Alice Newby
Sellers: John Halliburton, Susan Halliburton

Alice: Mr. and Mrs. Halliburton, thanks for inviting me into your home. Helping you get the most dollars for your home in a reasonable time is one of my most important responsibilities in my real estate practice. One of the ways I can really be helpful is by carefully preparing a market report. It's called a comparative market analysis. Have you seen one of these before? [Hand them a copy of the CMA.]

John: No, we haven't. But this is our first home.

Alice: OK, it will take us a few minutes to go over it, but it's well worth the time. The decisions we make based on this analysis are going to be very important to you as we go forward.

You can see I've put your names and addresses here at the top.

You can see that the report is broken into three main sections [pointing]: Here are the sales in your neighborhood for the last 12 months. The sold properties section will tell us what homes appraisers can use and will give us an idea of the value for a homebuyer's bank appraisal. The section on properties that are now listed shows your competitors. And here are the properties that failed to sell, usually because they were overpriced. All of these properties are going to help us to decide at what price we should offer your home. Here's a map of the neighborhood so you can see where each of these homes is located. Do you have any questions so far?

Susan: Well, I don't see one of our neighbor's homes on your list, and I know he sold his house last May. The address is 4425 Landtowne Drive.

Alice: Right. Let me see [looks at another list of every sale in the area]. Yes, you're right. Here it is on this list [shows list]. As you can see, his house had only 1,500 square feet, while yours has more than 1,900. I didn't use it in our pricing guide because it's just not comparable, don't you agree?

Susan: Yes, I see.

Alice: On each of the homes included on our list, I've made some adjustments based on major differences from your house. For example, the house at 1640 Clover has only a one-car garage, and yours has a two-car garage. The price difference for that feature is about $2,800, so your house should sell for about $2,800 more.

John: OK, that makes sense.

Alice: You can see that in the first section, sold properties, the median sales price of properties—and what yours will probably appraise for—is about $168,100. In the second section, your competition has a median listed price of $176,500. Now our best chance at a sale within a reasonable period is to price your home somewhere above the sold properties and below the competing properties. Does that make sense?

John: Sure does.

Alice: Here are the properties that were overpriced and stayed on the market a long time. They didn't sell. You can see they had a median price of $183,000. We want to avoid being in this group, don't you agree? Let me show you the pricing pyramid. [Shows them the pyramid (such as the one illustrated in Figure 6.2).] As you can see, if you price the home at the median of the sold homes in your area, you'll attract the most buyers. If you price at what the other homes are listed for, you'll get some activity, but not as much. And if you price it too high, you won't see many buyers at all. The more buyers we can get to look, the better the chance of a sale.

John: Yes, we'd like to get it sold within the next few months.

Alice: Great. Based on what you've seen here, what do you think would be the best listing price for us to put it on the market?

Susan: Well, I think we've got to be somewhere in between the sold ones and the listed ones. Do you think we could list it at the higher end, like $176,500?

Alice: What do you think, John?

John: I'd like to get as much as possible, Susan, but two of the homes for sale now are at $175,000. I think maybe $174,500 might get it sold faster.

Susan: Yes, that's true. I'm cool with $174,500.

Alice: I wholeheartedly agree. Could we schedule your home for our office inspection next Monday, or will the following week give you more time to get it ready?

Susan: Well, we may not be quite ready to do anything yet. Can we think about it and let you know?

Alice: Absolutely. Maybe it would be helpful if I showed you what you are likely to clear from the sale after paying off the mortgage and all your expenses. Would that be helpful?

John: Sure would.

DISCUSSION EXERCISE 6.1

Using the CMA report in Figure 5.4, role-play the complete presentation of a CMA without referring to the script above. The instructor might assign several persons to present the different sections of the material. Assign a classmate to represent a "reasonably motivated" seller who is kind to the agent.

ESTIMATING THE SELLER'S PROCEEDS

A seller generally is reluctant to enter into a listing agreement until she understands what expenses she must pay at closing. The **net proceeds** after paying off the mortgage and expenses of a sale are of primary interest to the seller and are often a factor in setting a list price. It is extremely important that a licensee use skill, care, and diligence in estimating the seller's proceeds from the sale. The following is a discussion of the seller's net proceeds form (see Figure 6.3).

F I G U R E 6.3 ■ **Seller's Net Proceeds Form**

Seller's Name: _____

Property Address: _____

Selling Price	$	$

Less:
1st mortgage
2nd mortgage
Other

Seller's Equity	$	$

Less: Expenses

Doc stamps on deed

Termite Inspection and treatment

Title insurance

Homeowner's warranty

Buyer's closing costs
Buyer's origination fee
Buyer's discount points

Repairs and replacements

Seller's attorney fee

Brokerage fee

Other miscellaneous costs

Other

Total Expenses	$	$

Less: Prorations

Property taxes

Interest

Homeowners assn. dues

Rents and deposits

Total Prorations	$	$

Net Proceeds to Seller	$	$

These figures are estimates and intended only as a guide. They will vary at closing because of prorations, the mortgage balance, and unforeseen costs. An exact itemization will be provided to you at closing. Please read this and all other documents relating to this sale carefully. If you require further explanation, please consult an attorney.

Date: _____ Prepared by: _____

Seller: _____ Seller: _____

Seller's Net Proceeds Form

A section for the seller's name and the property address should be completed. The left side of the form itemizes income and expenses related to the sale. Two columns are provided for calculations:

- *When listing the property.* The licensee might use column 1 when calculating an estimate based on a recommended price; the licensee would use column 2 if the seller wanted to know how much a different list price would net.

- *When giving the seller a range of values.* The sales associate could provide for the seller a high-end list price and a low-end list price.

- *At the time of listing.* Column 1 could be used for showing the net proceeds if customary seller's expenses were paid; column 2 could be used if the seller were asked to pay the buyer's loan closing costs. This is much like a best-case, worst-case scenario.

- *For estimates given at the time of listing.* Column 1 is for listing proceeds; column 2 could be used when an offer is submitted.

- *At the time an offer is submitted.* Column 1 shows the seller's net if the offer was accepted; column 2 shows the seller's net if a counteroffer was accepted.

Seller's Equity Section. The seller's **equity** section consists of the sales price, less mortgage balances and other encumbrances. Special assessment liens and construction liens would be shown in the space provided for other encumbrances. All items should be rounded because this is an estimate. An exact mortgage balance is unnecessary because of the closing date's uncertainty. Uneven dollars and cents amounts should not be included. Exact amounts imply an accuracy that does not exist in the estimate.

Expenses Section. Any expenses that the seller might be required to pay should be listed. It is better to overestimate than to underestimate the expenses. Sellers will not be unhappy if they receive more at the time of closing than they had expected, but they likely will be upset if expenses have been underestimated. Even though the bottom of the form provides a disclaimer, the licensee must be careful to avoid errors. Some expenses that should be discussed follow:

- Documentary stamps on deed are $.70 per $100 or fraction thereof of the sales price. The seller normally pays the cost of these stamps.

- Termite inspection (treatment and repairs) could be a substantial expense to the seller but is not known at the time of listing or contract. A conservative approach would be to show the cost of both in this section. A licensee should stay current on the costs of inspection and treatment in the property's market area. In many areas, the inspection is the buyer's expense.

- When making the seller's statement, the licensee would include the typical charge a seller might be expected to pay for title insurance and related costs based on local practice.

- Homeowners warranty costs often are associated with the seller's need to assure the buyer that the home is in good condition and will be warranted against many defects by an independent home warranty company. Depending on the company, these costs may range from $300 to $500.

- Buyer's closing costs, the origination fee, and discount points can be very substantial expenses to the seller if the seller agrees to pay them. When taking a listing, a sales associate should include these items if the custom in the market area dictates.

When preparing this estimate at the time of contract, the sales associate should take extra care if the seller will pay the buyer's costs. The licensee should use the lender's loan estimate, with a maximum amount agreed to in the contract. Leaving this open-ended in a contract can be problem if the discount points or other costs increase between the time of acceptance and the time of closing.

■ Repairs and replacements usually are those that a lender might require. They also could be the result of wood-destroying organisms or nonfunctioning appliances. The licensee should overestimate somewhat as a cushion for such contingencies.

■ The seller's attorney fee is an expense left to the seller to decide. The licensee should list the normal closing review fee for the seller in his market area.

■ The brokerage fee is the commission the brokerage firm charges.

■ Other miscellaneous costs include items like express mail fees for mortgage payoffs and recording mortgage satisfactions. The licensee should overestimate somewhat as a cushion here to allow for contingencies. A seller on a tight budget cannot afford unpleasant surprises. This line also could be used to round uneven expense amounts into even amounts. For example, if the expenses were $8,945.60, the miscellaneous costs could be estimated at $54.40, resulting in total estimated expenses of $9,000.

Prorations Section. This section, if not carefully estimated, could result in an unpleasant surprise for the seller because most prorations are debits (charges) to the seller. Because the closing date is not certain, it is not necessary to do exact prorations; approximations are satisfactory if amounts are rounded higher. The statement offers no provision for insurance prorations or proceeds from a lender's escrow account. Insurance should not be prorated; the buyer should purchase her own policy, and the seller should get a cancellation refund. Because the insurance refund and escrow refund from loans paid off are not received at closing, the net proceeds statement does not include these items (if the mortgage is to be assumed, the prorations could be offset by the amounts held in escrow because the buyer will be expected to reimburse the seller for those amounts).

■ Property taxes should be estimated for the year if tax information is not available. An assumed closing date is used to estimate prorations. If the closing were anticipated for June 28, for example, the licensee would show a charge to the seller for half the year's taxes.

■ Interest prorations can be difficult to calculate. The amount depends on the time of month for the closing. Most interest is paid in arrears, but not all loans have that feature. The safest policy, if the loan is current, is to show a charge for a full month's interest.

■ Homeowners association dues can be substantial in some areas, particularly with condominiums and other properties having substantial common maintenance areas. The dues may be paid in advance but often are paid in arrears. The homeowner should be asked about the status of the dues.

■ Rents and deposits can be major charges to the seller of an income property. If the seller has collected rent in advance, the buyer is entitled to the rent for the part of the month after the closing. The buyer also should be paid the security deposits.

Net Proceeds to Seller. The net proceeds equal the seller's equity less expenses and prorations. The amount of the seller's proceeds should be rounded to the next lowest $100.

Exercise: Estimating Net Proceeds to Seller

Estimating the seller's net proceeds properly is extremely important. This exercise should be completed carefully using the seller's net proceeds form found in Figure 6.3. Round up on expenses, prorations, and mortgages, and do not use cents. The final estimate should be rounded to the lowest hundred, using the following information:

Seller's name	Cindy Lewis
Property address	1947 Oldfield Circle
Prepared by	Janice Brown
Estimated closing date	August 26
Sales price	$93,800.00
Existing first mortgage (8.5%)	47,425.67
Home equity loan (11%)	14,659.42
Brokerage fee	7%
Termite inspection and treatment	400.00
Buyer's title insurance	650.00
Repairs and replacements	450.00
Seller's attorney fee	350.00
Homeowner's warranty	375.00
Discount points	2,100.00
Annual taxes	1,325.00
Interest	?
Annual homeowners assn. dues	150.00

DISCUSSION EXERCISE 6.2

Using the seller's net proceeds form from Figure 6.3, role-play the presentation of the form to the seller. The instructor might assign several persons to present the different sections of the material. Assign a reasonably motivated seller who is kind to the agent. The licensee should ask a closing question when showing the net proceeds from the sale.

Ask for the Order

Show the sellers the net amount to be received and ask, "Can you live with this figure?" If the answer is yes, follow up with "Do you have any objections to my making the property available to all the licensees in the city through the multiple listing service?" If the answer is no, ask for the current mortgage information, and proceed to fill out the listing forms. You have obtained the listing!

If the answer is "We are not ready to list at this time," say, "I understand," and then go to the next step.

DISCUSS THE REASONS MOST FSBOS DON'T SELL THEIR HOMES

During any listing presentation, be prepared if necessary to carefully explain to your potential clients that FSBOs usually don't sell their homes for a variety of reasons, the most serious of which are discussed here.

The Problem of Showing the Property

FSBOs must be made aware of the following three reasons why showing their home themselves is extremely difficult, annoying, and exasperating:

1. Explain that the sign in front of the home invites any passersby to come to the front door and ask to be let inside. Normally, a resident of a home would never allow the person access, but it's now more difficult to say no. Talk for a moment about the family's security and that trained real estate professionals will escort all buyers after they are qualified.

2. Remind the owners that a buyer cannot know everything about their property by simply looking at the front of the house. This is a very important point, especially if the home has only average curb appeal but the inside is far nicer than average. Without knowing about the good features, a buyer might drive right by. You should explain that when their home is shown, trained real estate professionals will escort qualified buyers inside, the only place they can truly evaluate this home.

3. You can remind the sellers that if they are not home all day and on the evenings and weekends to show the home, the buyer may not call back. Every time they go shopping or to work, their property is "off the market." Explain that when they list with you, the property will be on the market 24 hours a day because they can reach a licensee who will have the information the buyer wants.

The Problem of Financing

Because the buyers will likely need new financing on the property, you could explain that they may want assistance in deciding where to go for a home mortgage and may not understand the process. Because of that reason, many buyers ask for the help of a real estate professional.

The Problem of Oral Negotiations

Discuss with the sellers the disadvantage of direct negotiations with a buyer. Many buyers buy direct because their negotiation skills give them an advantage. Buyers will ask questions about the reason for selling and about how much lower the sellers might go. If the sellers remain firm, explain that the buyers may leave. But the sellers should also know that if they give a buyer a lower figure, that buyer may later try to negotiate even lower.

The sellers should be told that when a buyer wants to make an offer, the licensee will put it in writing and ask for a good-faith deposit so that if the price offered by the buyer is acceptable, all the sellers need to do is sign it.

The Problem of Writing a Purchase Contract

You can ask sellers whether they have a contract form and whether they feel comfortable filling it in for the buyers to sign. If the sellers have a contract form and think they can fill it in, let them know about the education process most licensees undergo so they can write one that will not end up in court.

If the sellers say they have an attorney to write the contract, suggest that it's important for the attorney to be qualified in real estate practice. You might also raise the question of how quickly a good, but busy, attorney could get a contract written when a buyer is ready to buy.

The Major Problem: FSBOs Want to Save the Commission

In this last part of your discussion, you want to get the sellers' agreement that they are willing to try to overcome these obstacles in order to save the commission. When they agree, you must answer their objection to listing with you by letting them see that their efforts won't save a commission. Ask the sellers why they believe a buyer would be willing to take the time and make the effort to buy a house directly from a seller when the buyer could get much more help from a licensee. Then explain to them that the reason is that the buyer is also buying direct solely to save the commission and that it won't be possible for both parties to save the full commission. In the unlikely event that both seller and buyer complete the transaction without help from a licensee, why couldn't both parties save the full commission?

ASKING FOR THE LISTING

A closing question such as "Can you see how most persons who try to sell their homes turn to a real estate professional?" might generate a positive answer. You can then ask whether they'd like you to try to get the home into the MLS as soon as possible, or bring your office staff over on Monday morning to see it, or whether they would like you to hold an open house next Sunday. If their response is positive, you can begin filling out listing paperwork.

In many cases, the sellers won't be ready to list with your company. You should ask for the reason, and if they want to think about it, you should tell them why, when they decide to list the property, the listing person should be you.

Show the seller why the licensee should be you. Tell the sellers about you and your brokerage firm. For example, explain that you:

- have an office in a high-traffic location;
- went through a rigorous training program that makes all your associates more professional and successful;
- generate more sales through your office listing caravans;
- will put their home into the MLS immediately;
- will be advertising the home;
- pride yourself on holding successful open houses;
- are a member of an out-of-town referral agency;
- offer a warranty program, explaining how that will help to sell the property;
- will call them each week to tell them of your progress; and
- will give them your special seven-step service program.

SEVEN-STEP SERVICE

A seller wants to know what the brokerage firm will do to earn the commission, and a chart similar to the one shown in Figure 6.4 may be helpful. While the chart itself is rather sparse, for easy understanding, the sales associate might tell the seller about each step in more detail. After you have finished your presentation, you should clearly and directly ask for the order. "Mr. and Mrs. Halliburton, may I help you sell your property?"

If the answer is no, you should review every point of the presentation point-by-point, then ask for the order again. In many cases, the presentation will result in a listing. If for any reason you do not get a listing, arrange to visit again in three days. You may never get the listing, but it won't be because you gave up too soon.

F I G U R E 6.4 ■ Seven-Step Service Chart

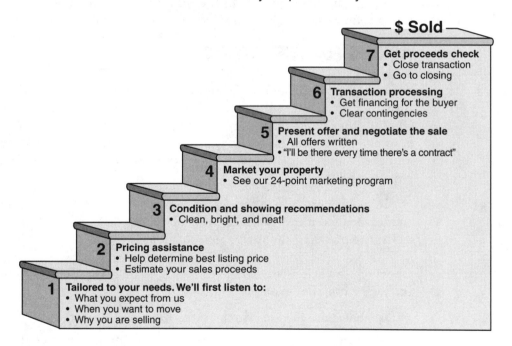

SUMMARY

- Making an effective listing presentation will result in a much higher close rate for listing appointments. Several conditions must be met in order to succeed:

  - All parties on the deed must be present.
  - All forms must be ready for the seller's signature.
  - The licensee must know each step of the presentation.
  - The licensee must have complete information about the property to be listed.
  - A comparative market analysis must be prepared.
  - The licensee must be organized, have a professional appearance, and be on time.

- A listing presentation has five major parts:

  1. Building rapport with the sellers
  2. Explaining the pricing process (going over the CMA)
  3. Estimating the seller's proceeds (the seller's net proceeds form)
  4. Discussing the reason most FSBOs don't sell their homes
  5. Asking for the listing

- A seller usually is more interested in the net proceeds from the sale of his property than the home's actual sales price.

- The seller's net proceeds form is a financial disclosure to the seller and consists of three major sections:

  1. The seller's equity section provides the sales price less mortgage balances, with the difference being the seller's equity.
  2. The expenses section shows expenses the seller must pay at closing.
  3. The prorations section includes taxes, interest, rents, and homeowners association dues.

R E V I E W   Q U E S T I O N S

1. When presenting a CMA, a licensee should NOT
   a. discuss current market conditions for the overall market, only for the sellers' neighborhood.
   b. recommend a price for the property before going over the data in the CMA.
   c. give the seller a range of values rather than a single value.
   d. ask for the order after the explanation.

2. Where is the BEST place in the house to make the listing presentation?
   a. Living room sofa
   b. On the deck outside
   c. At the dining room table
   d. In front of the TV

3. The reason for eliminating cents and rounding to the nearest $100 on the seller's net proceeds form is to
   a. avoid giving the impression that the figures will be exactly as shown at closing.
   b. make the statement easier to understand.
   c. provide a cushion in the estimate.
   d. do all of these.

4. The components of the seller's equity section of the seller's net proceeds form include
   a. seller's equity, expenses, and seller's net proceeds.
   b. sales price, prorations, and expenses.
   c. seller's equity, prorations, and seller's net proceeds.
   d. sales price, mortgages, and seller's equity.

5. What is the proper order for a complete listing presentation?
   a. CMA, sellers' net, building rapport with the sellers, reasons for listing with your brokerage firm, and ask for the order
   b. Ask for the order, CMA, sellers' net, building rapport with the sellers, and reasons for listing with your brokerage firm
   c. Building rapport with the sellers, ask for the order, CMA, sellers' net, and reasons for listing with your brokerage firm
   d. Building rapport with the sellers, CMA, sellers' net, reasons for listing with your brokerage firm, and ask for the order

6. When explaining the current market conditions to the seller, one piece of information that would NOT normally be included is the
   a. aggregate square footage of all listed homes.
   b. number of houses currently listed.
   c. month's supply of homes on the market.
   d. number of homes sold last month.

7. Which part of the CMA would indicate overpriced listings?
   a. Sold houses
   b. Houses currently for sale
   c. Expired listings
   d. Withdrawn listings

8. The preferable approach to setting the listing price is to
    a. list at the price the seller wants.
    b. go over the CMA carefully and to help the seller to arrive at an appropriate range of values.
    c. tell the seller the maximum price at which you will list the house at the beginning of the meeting.
    d. find out what the seller needs from the sale and add your commission.

Use the following information to answer questions 9 through 12.

A broker is compiling a seller's net proceeds form for a seller. The figures she gathers are as follows:

Brokerage fee	7%
Title insurance	$ 780.00
Termite inspection and treatment	300.00
Sales price	127,500.00
Existing first mortgage @ 10%	98,601.60
Documentary stamps on deed	?
Property taxes for the year	1,745.60
Interest proration (paid in arrears)	?
Closing date	June 30

9. What is the seller's equity, rounded to the nearest $100?
    a. $16,300
    b. $20,000
    c. $28,900
    d. $29,000

10. What are the total expenses, rounded to the next highest $100?
    a. $10,100
    b. $10,800
    c. $10,900
    d. $11,800

11. What are the total prorations, rounded to the nearest $100, and will the prorations be added or subtracted from the equity?
    a. $2,600 added
    b. $900 subtracted
    c. $1,300 subtracted
    d. $1,700 subtracted

12. What are the seller's net proceeds, rounded to the nearest $100?
    a. $14,500
    b. $15,400
    c. $16,300
    d. $17,100

13.   A broker is making a listing presentation to a FSBO. She completes the CMA and gets the sellers to accept the net amount on the seller's net proceeds form. She should be able to take the listing now primarily because
a.   she has completed all steps of the listing presentation.
b.   the commission is included on the seller's net proceeds form, and the sellers have agreed to the amounts shown.
c.   the FSBOs should know they would not be able to sell the property themselves.
d.   she has not gone over the reasons the sellers should list with her firm.

14.   The reason it is NOT practical for a licensee to determine the exact prorations on the seller's net proceeds form when taking a listing is that
a.   it takes too long.
b.   a mistake will likely lose the listing.
c.   most sellers refuse to list when they see the prorations.
d.   the exact closing date is unknown.

15.   When preparing the interest proration on a seller's net proceeds form, the best policy is to enter
a.   zero on the line, with a note that it can't be determined at this time.
b.   a full month of interest.
c.   one-half month of interest.
d.   two months' interest.

16.   Which is NOT one of the three major problems in showing the property a FSBO should be told to expect?
a.   The risk to personal safety exists because of letting all prospective buyers into the house.
b.   The fact is that most new buyers will need financing.
c.   It is hard to get prospective buyers inside if the exterior of the house is not particularly attractive
d.   The house is off the market when the seller is away from home.

17.   The reason most FSBOs won't be able to save the commission is that
a.   they may not understand how to help the buyer get financing.
b.   they may show the house to an unqualified buyer.
c.   the prospective buyer is buying direct to save the same commission.
d.   the seller may not know how to write a binding contract.

18.   The final step in the listing presentation is
a.   explaining to the sellers why they should list with your brokerage firm.
b.   asking for the order.
c.   delivering the CMA.
d.   putting the listing into the MLS.

19.   If the sellers want to list the property before you have completed the listing presentation, you should
a.   politely request a little more time to cover the presentation.
b.   suggest they may wish to think about it overnight, and leave the paperwork for them to sign later.
c.   ignore the interruption and continue with your presentation.
d.   take the listing.

20.   On the seller's net proceeds form, which proration should NOT be included?
  a.   Property taxes
  b.   Insurance
  c.   Interest
  d.   Rents, if this is a rental property

LISTING CONTRACTS

LEARNING OBJECTIVES

When you finish reading this chapter, you will be able to:

- state the legally required elements in a listing contract;

- explain the distinguishing characteristics of each of the following types of listings: open, exclusive agency, and exclusive right of sale;

- explain each paragraph of the listing agreement that applies to your market area; and

- design a listing servicing program for your personal listings.

KEY TERMS

exclusive-agency listing
exclusive-right-of-sale
   listing

open listing
servicing the listing

warranty of owner clause

OVERVIEW

A listing contract is an agreement between a real estate broker and a property owner. The listing contract specifies the duties of both the broker and the owner in the sale of the owner's real property. Without listing contracts, there would be little or no inventory to sell, exchange, lease, rent, or auction. It is important to understand that a listing agreement is a personal services (employment) contract requiring the broker to perform one or more professional services to fulfill the agreement. The broker may seek assistance from other licensees, but the primary responsibility remains with the listing broker. The listing contract is a broker's employment contract, and all listings should be in writing. If litigation should result from some misunderstanding, default, or breach, it is much easier to resolve by showing the terms of a written contract than by obtaining testimony to prove the terms or conditions of an oral listing. Because listing contracts need not be written, oral listing contracts are enforceable with the proper amount of evidence and testimony.

TYPES OF LISTING CONTRACTS

In this chapter, three types of listing contracts are identified. The exclusive-right-of-sale listing contract is emphasized because of its predominance in residential property transactions.

Open Listing

An **open listing** is a contract in which an owner reserves the right to employ any number of brokers. Brokers may work simultaneously, but the first broker who produces a ready, willing, and able buyer at the terms accepted by the seller is the only one who earns a commission. If the owner himself sells the property without the aid of any of the brokers, he is not obligated to pay any commission; but if a broker can prove she was the procuring cause of the transaction, she may be entitled to a commission. While most residential brokers will not accept open listings, commercial and agricultural property brokers sometimes work with sellers with this type of listing.

Any listing contract normally creates an open listing unless the contract is worded in a manner that specifically provides for a different type of listing. While open listings may be either oral or implied, a contract does not exist until terms are negotiated. For example, a for-sale-by-owner sign that indicates "brokers protected" or in some other way invites offers from brokers does not create a listing contract.

Either or all parties may terminate an open listing at will, and in the absence of formal notification, an open listing may terminate after a reasonable time. The owner principal is not obligated to notify any of the brokers that the property has been sold.

Exclusive-Agency Listing (Exclusive Listing)

The **exclusive-agency listing** is the preferred listing agreement of an owner who has selected one particular broker as his or her exclusive agent, for a specified period, to sell real property according to the owner's stated terms. In an exclusive-agency listing, the owner appoints the broker but reserves the right to sell the property without paying a commission to the broker if the broker has not introduced or identified the buyer. If the broker performs by selling the property before the owner can do so, the broker is entitled to a commission. Exclusive-agency residential listings are less common than exclusive-right-of-sale listings.

A common problem with exclusive-agency and open listings is the exposure to lawsuits for procuring cause between the broker and the seller.

DISCUSSION EXERCISE 7.1

   Arthur Cody lists Donald Wilson's home under an exclusive-agency listing agreement. Arthur shows the property to William Farkas. William notices
that the seller has a sign on the property saying For Sale by Owner—555-1145.
Arthur drops William off and writes a letter to Donald, registering William as a
prospect. Immediately after Arthur drops him off, William calls Donald directly.
Donald does not know that Arthur has shown the property and agrees to a
reduced price because no commission is involved. Donald and William enter
into a contract for sale. It is only after the contract is signed that Donald gets
Arthur's prospect registration letter. When the sale closes, Arthur sues for a commission as the procuring cause of the sale.
   Role-play the court argument: Arthur, arguing for a commission on the sale,
and Donald, explaining why no commission is due.

---

1   In the discussion exercise, Donald, whom we assume to be an honest person, was sued
2   because of the buyer's actions, not his own. How can a broker prevent this type of mis-
3   understanding? Registration is not enough because the notification may come after the
4   parties have entered into a contract.

In Practice

Protect your sellers by suggesting that when they sell directly, they should put
these words in the contract:

   *This property is listed with a broker under an agreement that the broker will be
   paid a commission for procuring a buyer for the property. Buyer warrants to seller that
   he or she was not shown or made aware of this property by any real estate broker or
   sales associate. Buyer agrees that if a broker claiming a commission provides information to the contrary, buyer will reimburse seller for commissions due to said real estate
   broker as well as legal fees.*

5   A buyer who has seen the property with a broker will refuse to sign such a statement,
6   putting the seller on notice that the buyer is trying to save the commission by excluding
7   the broker.

8   Two other problems can arise from an exclusive-agency agreement. First, a broker
9   is reluctant to show property to a buyer if the owner's phone number is displayed promi-
10 nently on a sign in front of the property. The sign invites the buyer to exclude the broker
11 to get a better price. If the broker takes the listing under an exclusive agency, the broker
12 should get the owner's agreement to remove the sign.

13 Another problem the broker faces is the possibility of the owner's advertising a lower
14 price (broker's price less commission). The broker likely will lose the buyer if the buyer
15 sees the owner's ad. The broker and the owner should quote the same price.

Exclusive-Right-of-Sale Listing

The **exclusive-right-of-sale listing** is the most advantageous listing from the broker's viewpoint and the most common type of listing. The listing is given to a selected broker, who then becomes the exclusive broker for the sale of the property. The broker is due a commission regardless of who sells the property. That is, if the owner sells the property during the contract period, the broker still earns a commission. Also, if the owner sells the property within a designated period after the listing contract has expired to a buyer originally introduced to the property by the broker, the owner usually is liable for a sales commission to the broker.

To be enforceable, this type of listing contract should be in writing and include valuable consideration. The listing brokers may enter only exclusive-right-of-sale and exclusive-agency listings into the MLS.

Florida Laws Regulating Listing Agreements

Florida law recognizes written, oral, or implied listings, assuming evidence is available to support a claim for compensation. If a listing is written, it must include a definite expiration date, a description of the property, the price and terms acceptable to the sellers, the amount of commission due upon the broker's performance, and the signature of the parties. A written listing agreement may not have wording that makes it self-renewing, or the listing will be void. The broker, or the broker's authorized representative, must deliver to the sellers a copy of the listing agreement within 24 hours of signature.

Warranties by the Owner

If the listing broker is a single agent for the seller, both the broker and the seller have obligations under the listing agreement. The principal has legal obligations to the broker, including performance of all promises made in the contract, as well as the obligation to engage in honest, straightforward dealing. The actions and misrepresentations of a seller can become a liability to the agent. For example, if a seller tells a sales associate that the plumbing pipes are copper and the sales associate passes along that information to a buyer without qualification, both the seller and the brokerage firm may be liable for damages if the buyer later discovers the plumbing pipes are polybutylene. Litigation may result in damages assessed against both the seller and the broker.

THE EXCLUSIVE-RIGHT-OF-SALE AGREEMENT

The sales associate should complete as much of the paperwork as possible before the listing appointment. Because the task can be done in a controlled environment without distractions, it is more likely to be correct. The advance preparation also results in a more efficient process once the sales associate is with the seller. The sales associate should explain that the paperwork was prepared in advance to save the owner's time.

Understanding the Exclusive-Right-of-Sale Listing Agreement

The real estate licensee is expected to be knowledgeable about the listing contract and able to explain the provisions clearly and completely. Sellers lose confidence in a sales associate who stumbles through an explanation of the agreement or who doesn't know the meaning of a clause.

**Forms
To Go**

Florida REALTORS® distributes the Exclusive Right of Sale Listing Agreement (see Appendix B). If you use a different form, the clauses in your listing agreement probably are very similar. The numbered paragraphs that follow correspond to the 13 paragraphs in the agreement.

The parties are the owner(s) of the property and the brokerage firm, not the sales associate. All persons owning an interest in the property should be included here. The licensee should check the seller's deed to ensure that all persons on the deed sign the listing. Corporations, partnerships, trusts, and estates require special treatment. See the broker or an attorney for advice.

1. *Authority to sell property.* This paragraph gives the broker an exclusive right to sell the property. The listing term also is shown here. Many brokerage firms have policies for the listing term, depending on the type of property. A typical residential period is six months. The licensee should examine that policy carefully, however, in light of the best marketing period. For instance, in many areas of Florida, the best sales period is May through August. If that is the case, a six-month listing taken on January 2 expires July 2, with two months remaining in the best selling period. A far better approach is a minimum of six months, provided all listings remain active at least through August 31. A contract written during the listing period extends the listing until the closing. The seller agrees to offer the property without unlawful discrimination. The seller warrants that he can convey the property legally.

2. *Description of property.*

   a. *Real property street address.* The property address is entered here. The legal description should be taken from the public records or from the owner's deed, if available. If it is a metes-and-bounds description, it should be attached. A description taken from the tax records or from former listing information is not satisfactory because these sources are not always reliable.

   b. *Personal property.* Fixtures as well as other personal property must be listed here. Often a seller agrees to leave a refrigerator, drapes, or a washer/dryer; however, the licensee should discuss with the seller the possibility of holding back the offer of these items, using them as negotiating tools when an offer is made (for example, "The seller says that if you can increase your offer by $1,000, she will give you her washer-dryer.").

   Some items are not included as part of the agreement. The licensee should ask the seller an important question: "Is any item attached to the property that you do not want to be included with the sale?" The agreement does not provide a section for this exclusion, but the licensee should be certain to include any such items on an addendum. If possible, the fixture should be removed before the home is shown.

   c. *Occupancy.* This section covers the seller's representation about occupancy rights by another party. If a third party is in possession of the property, the buyer's rights are subject to those of the tenant.

3. *Price and terms.*

   a. *Price.* Here the licensee records the price at which the property will be offered.

   b. *Financing terms.* The terms are important to the seller and the listing broker, particularly in the way the property is marketed. If the seller agrees to seller financing, the terms of such financing are stated here. If there is an existing mortgage on the property, the seller is asked whether it can be assumed with or without lender approval. The seller is warned about liability in case of an assumption. The seller also agrees that the loan is current in case of assumption.

   c. *Seller expenses.* This section limits the amount the seller agrees to pay for discount points and other closing costs as a percentage of the sales price. The licensee should take care to ensure that the amount shown is enough to pay typical costs of sale, including a commission. Of course, the seller could agree to pay more when signing a contract for sale. The licensee should disclose anticipated seller's costs on the seller's net proceeds form before presenting the listing agreement and each time an offer is presented to the seller.

4. *Broker obligations and authority.* The broker makes promises in this section (the consideration is what makes this a bilateral contract) that include working diligently to sell the property. The seller authorizes the broker to take the following steps:

   a. Advertise the property as the broker deems advisable, place an appropriate sign on the property, and use the seller's name in marketing the property. This section also allows the seller to opt out of displaying the property on the internet.

   b. Place appropriate signs on the property, including For Sale and Sold signs.

   c. Obtain information about the mortgage (usually a signed request from the seller for a status letter).

   d. Place the property in the MLS. Some brokers hold a listing out for an extended period, during which time the broker attempts to sell the property himself. If the licensee is a single agent, this could be considered as subordinating the principal's interests to the broker's personal interests, a clear violation of fiduciary duties.

   e. Provide a CMA to potential buyers.

   f. Place a lockbox on the property if the seller specifically authorizes it. The seller is asked to relieve the broker, staff, and board of REALTORS® from liability due to loss. The seller may request that the broker withhold oral offers and all offers once the seller accepts a contract.

   g. Act as a transaction broker.

   h. Virtual office websites that allow automated estimates of value or comments or reviews about the property. This section allows the seller to opt out of the value estimates or comments.

5. *Seller obligations.* The seller agrees to:

   a. cooperate with the broker to obtain a sale and refer all inquiries to the broker;

   b. give keys to the broker and make property available for showing during reasonable times;

   c. inform the broker before leasing or mortgaging the property;

   d. hold the broker harmless because of (1) the seller's negligence or misrepresentations, (2) losses from the use of a lockbox, (3) the existence of undisclosed facts about the property, or (4) arbitration or lawsuits against the broker by another broker (this serves as a warranty that the seller's statements to the broker are true and that indemnifies the broker against representations made by the seller that the broker passes on to a buyer; the warranty against seller misrepresentations is commonly called the **warranty of owner clause**);

e.   comply with the Foreign Investment in Real Property Tax Act (FIRPTA) requirements in case the seller is a foreign national (This could require that the buyer withhold 10% of the sales proceeds and forward the funds to the IRS.);

f.   make legally required disclosures affecting the property's value. This usually involves the seller completing the Seller's Property Disclosure—Residential (see Appendix B). The sales associate should not complete this form for the seller. This is often called a latent defects addendum; and

g.   consult with qualified professionals for legal, tax, and other matters, the intent of which is to reduce the licensee's liability.

6. *Compensation*. This is an agreement to find a purchaser who is ready, willing, and able to buy, either at the list price or at any other price agreeable to the seller. It is not dependent on a closing (as in a listing "to effect a sale").

a.   This paragraph sets the commission as a percentage of the price or as a dollar amount. The commission is due no later than closing but may be due whether or not a closing occurs.

b.   In case the seller and a buyer agree to an option contract, this paragraph sets the commission as a percentage of the option amount or as a dollar amount. The commission is due at the time the option is created. The total commission, less the commission received from the option, is due when the option is exercised.

c.   In case a lease agreement is created, this paragraph sets the commission as a percentage of the price or as a dollar amount. The commission is due when the seller enters into an agreement to lease. An exception occurs if the seller employs another broker under an exclusive-right-to-lease agreement.

d.   Broker's fee. This paragraph describes when the broker's fee is due:

i.   if any interest in the property is transferred, whether by sale, lease, exchange, government action (e.g., eminent domain), or bankruptcy, no matter who finds the buyer;

ii.   if the seller refuses to sign an offer at full price and terms, defaults on a contract, or agrees with a buyer to cancel an executed sales contract; or

iii.   if, after the listing's expiration, a prospect who learned about the property through a broker buys the property within the protection period. An exception occurs if another broker has subsequently listed the property.

e.   Retained deposits. This paragraph entitles the broker to a specified percentage of all deposits that the seller retains as liquidated damages for a buyer's default. The amount cannot exceed the total commission as shown in paragraph 6(a).

7. *Cooperation and compensation with other brokers*. This section states that the broker's policy is to cooperate with all other brokers except when it would not be in the seller's best interests. It authorizes the listing broker to offer commission splits with other brokers. The seller checks her approval for splits with (1) buyers' agents, (2) nonrepresentatives, (3) transaction brokers, or (4) none of the

above. If the seller checks "none of the above," the listing broker may not put the listing into the MLS, because the MLS requires an offer of compensation to a cooperating broker.

8. *Brokerage relationship.* As described in chapter 1, brokers may work with buyers or sellers as nonrepresentatives, single agents, or transaction brokers. The listing contract includes the disclosure forms for single agent or transaction broker. The seller should sign the forms, or, if the seller declines to do so, the licensee should so indicate on the listing contract form. If the broker is starting as a single agent and may become a transaction broker, the transition notice must be signed.

9. *Conditional termination.* If the seller decides not to sell the property, the broker may agree to terminate the contract. The seller must sign a withdrawal agreement, and then pay the broker's direct expenses and a specified cancellation fee. If the seller contracts to transfer the property during the protection period, the broker may cancel the termination and collect the balance of the commission due.

10. *Dispute resolution.* This paragraph requires that conflicts be submitted to a mediator agreed to by the parties. If the mediation is not successful, and unless the parties agree in advance to arbitration, either party may sue. The prevailing party is entitled to recover attorney's fees and costs.

11. *Arbitration.* This section allows the parties (seller, listing associate, and listing broker) to agree to settle disputes by binding arbitration in the county where the property is located. The parties agree to split the costs equally. The inclusion of the listing associate in the contract is curious because the listing agreement is between the seller and the broker, and only the broker is authorized to take action for a commission. If the intent was to protect the broker from the sales associate's later claims for a commission if arbitration was unsuccessful, that might be better handled in the employment agreement. The agreement suggests that the costs will be split among the three parties.

12. *Miscellaneous.* The agreement may be assigned to another listing office, which is a departure from the former practice. Fax communications are enforceable.

13. *Information and signature section.* This section provides space for additional terms and personal information, including tax ID numbers as well as signature lines. Note that the listing sales associate may be authorized to sign the listing for the broker. This facilitates giving the seller a copy of the agreement immediately, satisfying the 24-hour requirement. The box at the bottom of the contract indicates when the seller's copy was legally delivered.

Explaining the Agreement to the Seller

The presentation of the listing agreement to the seller needs to be thorough to ensure that the seller fully understands. Sales associates sometimes take a casual approach to explaining the listing agreement or offer no explanation at all to the seller. A sales associate may say, "Don't worry, it's the standard agreement. Sign here." Or the sales associates might try an explanation even though they don't understand the agreement themselves. This misleads the seller and is not acceptable. The licensee's job is to give the seller an understanding of the important provisions the agreement contains.

New sales associates should understand the agreement totally and explain each paragraph clearly. If a seller asks, "What happens during the listing period if I decide I want to lease the property to a tenant?" the sales associate should answer, "If you'll look at paragraph 6(c), you'll see that the property can be leased. You agree to pay my company a fee of X%, but the fee does not include management."

The professional sales associate explains the listing agreement in language that the seller easily understands. Role-playing is an excellent method of learning this skill. When the role-playing results in wording that sounds appropriate, the sales associate should write it down so she can then refer to the written explanation during the listing appointment.

The following scenario might result from a licensee's role-playing exercise:

"Mr. Jones, this is the standard agreement all brokers use for homes listed in the MLS system. Let's go over it together, paragraph by paragraph.

"This top section shows your name as the seller and Sunrise Realty as the broker. Do I have your names spelled correctly?

"Section 1 shows that you give my company the authority to sell your property starting today and ending on September 4, 2014. You understand that I can't guarantee a sale of the property. I must offer property without violating any fair housing laws. And you agree that you can legally sell the property.

"Section 2 shows that the address of the property is 125 Creekmont Court. And the legal description of the property taken from your deed is shown here."

The sales associate continues to explain sections 3 through 11 of the listing contract in a similar manner. She refers to the checklist in Figure 7.1 to be certain she has completed all the necessary documents and taken all the necessary actions concerning the listing.

DISCUSSION EXERCISE 7.2

Using the listing agreement for your market area, paraphrase the legal words in everyday language that will help a seller understand the agreement better. In a group situation, each person should be assigned a paragraph. The person then explains the paragraph to the group in lay language, and the group provides constructive criticism. Because each person would explain each paragraph differently, every sales associate should prepare his own written text for use in presentations.

The sales associate should preface the explanations with a statement like "this is not legal advice, and you may wish to consult with an attorney." The listing packet could also include a disclaimer that the owner is not relying on the broker or the sales associate for legal advice on any of the documents presented. This would also be appropriate when presenting an offer to the owner later.

F I G U R E 7.1 ■ Listing Procedure Checklist

You must complete brokerage relationship disclosures in accordance with Chapter 475, F.S. This form should accompany all listings.

Property Address: _____

Listing Associate: _____

Listing Packet Contents (bold print indicates seller's signature is required):
- Comparative market analysis
- Brokerage relationship disclosures
- **Exclusive right of sale listing agreement**
- MLS profile sheet
- **Mortgage status request**
- **Property condition disclosure statement**
- **Home warranty agreement**
- **Seller's net proceeds form**
- Survey, if available
- Copy of mortgage and note
- Copy of deed restrictions
- Title insurance policy
- Key to property
- Floor plan, if available
- Copy of seller or buyer referral sent out
- Three ads
- Sign installation form
- Lockbox installation form
- Client contact sheet
- Copy of computer printout

Office Action:
- Get office manager's approval on listing forms.
- Enter listing data into computer.
- Put copy of printout into floor duty book.
- Distribute copies of printout to all sales associates.
- Turn in listing packet to secretary.

Follow-Up Action:
- Return all original documents to seller.
- Send seller copy of the MLS listing book photo and information.
- Contact seller weekly.
- Send seller copy of mortgage status letter when received.
- Send copies of all ads to seller.

Many sales associates have the seller sign all forms at the same time rather than sign each as they are presented. Others request a signature when the document is presented. A sample discussion of the conversation is shown in Figure 7.2.

F I G U R E 7.2 ■ Getting Signatures on Listing Documents

Mr. and Mrs. Jackson, I've prepared this letter to your mortgage company to send us the current balance and payoff amount. We'll use this when we have your house sold. They'll send it to me, and I'll give a copy to you for your records. They require your approval, so I'll need your signatures right here, please. [When they sign the form, put it back in your stack.]

Now, we agreed to market the property at $175,000. Based on that, you remember we went over the statement showing your expenses of the sale and what you would receive as proceeds. Here's a copy for your records, and I need you to OK this form for our records. [After they sign the form, put it back in your stack.]

OK, you completed the disclosure statement that we'll give to buyers when they are interested in the home. This will protect you from later claims that you held back important information. I need your signatures here, please. [After they sign the form, put it back in your stack.]

Great. We've gone over the agreement for us to market your home. I need your OK right here. [After they sign the form, put it back in your stack.]

I appreciate your confidence, and I'll start marketing your home right away. I'm going to try to get back to the office and prepare information to put the property into MLS. Before I leave, do you have any questions?

Marketing the Listing

The seller employs the listing broker to market the property. Many sellers believe that the licensee has not done her job unless the listing broker actually sells the listing. The licensee should discuss this misconception with the seller during the listing presentation. The seller should understand that if the licensee does her job properly, the house will sell through the licensee's marketing efforts—both to potential buyers and to other licensees, who will show the property to their buyers.

The broker has been hired to get the best price in the shortest time and with the least inconvenience to the seller. This requires the licensee to market the property in ways other than just showing it herself. Some of these activities include:

- educating the sellers on what to do when the house is going to be shown, such as turning on the lights, remove clutter, remove or lock up the pets, and leave the property if possible;

- disseminating the property information to all agents in the company;

- putting the sign on the property;

- putting an MLS lockbox on the property (if approved by the seller and available in the market area);

- arranging for all company sales associates to inspect the listing on caravan day;

- getting the information into the MLS as soon as possible (it is unethical and self-serving to withhold the information from other brokers and sales associates while the agent attempts to sell the property herself);

- announcing the listing at company sales meetings and at the board of REALTORS® marketing meetings;

- preparing a brochure to place in the home for prospective buyers and cooperating licensees;

- scheduling an open house, if appropriate, for the listing;
- writing at least three good ads to generate potential buyers;
- putting listing on websites (personal page, company page, and other advertiser's pages);
- using email autoresponders to get immediate feedback for customers who ask for information from a website;
- preparing web advertising and virtual tour;
- preparing mail-outs to send to potential buyers;
- telling 20 neighbors about the listing by mail;
- calling the neighbors to ask for help in finding buyers;
- holding a REALTORS® luncheon at the property to increase activity; and
- reviewing sales and listing activity in the neighborhood. Update the CMA at least once a month.

A detailed marketing program such as this could be the basis for a "Satisfaction Guarantee" or "Steps to a Successful Sale" listing presentation.

DISCUSSION EXERCISE 7.3

In small groups, prepare a 30-point marketing plan for a brochure you use in your listing presentation. Brainstorm to come up with different marketing ideas.

Staging the Home

Chefs say the first taste of a meal is with our eyes. Presentation is extremely important! That wisdom is true also when we market a home. Home presentation, or staging, can make your listing stand out from comparable homes and is especially effective in a buyer's market. Many of the cable channels have very popular programs showing house makeovers, and many of the ideas presented will be helpful in marketing your listing.

Sometimes when buyers are shown a property, the sales associate will have to say, "Try to look past the clutter and you'll see how much potential there is here." When there are many homes for sale in the area, it's unlikely that the potential buyer will want to look past the clutter.

Steps to get the house ready to sell include the following:

- *Get it clean.* After living in the home for years, owners tend to overlook some of the surface buildup and strange odors. Kitchens and baths must be spotless. One way to help them be more objective about the condition of the house is to suggest you take them to see other houses on the market in their price range. When they see how spotless many of the homes are, it may convince them to use some elbow grease on those frayed areas.
- *Get it light.* When you get it clean, light it up! When the home is shown, every light in the house should be on and drapes open. Cut back bushes around windows. Kitchens and baths should be bright. It's fine to use candles, but fire safety is an important concern.

- *Decorating is not staging.* Many homeowners have pretty homes, and they have decorated them to match their personalities. Red flocked wallpaper may be nice for some, but anathema for others. Take "personality" out of the house, and stage it so that it will appeal to the largest number of people.

- *Staging is cosmetic.* When you look at an appraisal report, there are two categories of depreciation: curable and incurable. Curable depreciation, when the problem is fixed, adds more to the property value than the cost to fix it. That's the object of staging: to make only those cash outlays that are returned in the sale price. That can include painting, wallpapering, decluttering, and focusing on dramatic, cosmetic transformations.

- *Go for the model home look.* Warm and cozy without your "personality." Get the kids' toys packed up after they use them; remove the family pictures that cover the wall in the hallway; take down Dad's electric train layout in the family room.

- *Remove excess furniture and accessories.* Make the space seem larger by having less clutter. In some model homes, smaller than normal beds are used. While you don't want to do that, you can probably get rid of 50% of the contents of a room. Take the excess furniture to mini-storage.

- *Get rid of the old stuff.* Remove furniture and paintings more than 10 years old unless they are true antiques. Accessories should be used to give the house an updated look.

- *Have appropriate furniture in rooms.* A computer station in the dining room simply may not feel right to a buyer, so relocate it.

- *Highlight with color.* For years, real estate professionals suggested to paint it all beige. A great home stager can work wonders with dramatic accent walls. Owners should be careful if not trained in staging skills because bad choices can ruin the effect.

- *Pet odors can kill a sale.* Get the odors out. Because you are used to the odor, ask a friend to give an unbiased opinion.

- *It should smell and sound luscious.* We all know the trick of freshly baked cookies in the home (you can buy a spray product that saves the trouble of baking). But don't forget that when a buyer will be escorted through the home, soft music often sets the stage.

- *Use healthy houseplants and throws on the sofa.* Make the house livable so your buyers can picture themselves enjoying the home. Set the dining table as though for company and put a book next to the easy chair.

- *The best stage is empty.* When an agent is showing the house, the owners should leave (and take the dogs). Let the buyers have emotional possession, ask questions, sit on the sofa, and make themselves at home!

Servicing the Listing

Servicing the listing is often more important than acquiring it. "I never hear from him!" is probably the complaint sellers make most often about their sales associates. A seller who does not hear from the listing sales associate perceives that the agent is not doing her job.

DISCUSSION EXERCISE 7.4

You are a real estate sales associate who is quite busy and disorganized. You have had a listing for six months that is about to expire, and you wish to renew it. Despite your best intentions, you have failed to contact your clients, Harold and Deidra, for more than two months. As the time progressed, it became even harder for you to make the call. You set an appointment to visit the home at 7:30 pm. Because you are caught in traffic, you are 20 minutes late when you walk up to the house. You are surprised to see that a competitor has listed the property next door. Even worse, it has a "contract pending" sign attached. Harold answers the door, nods his head seriously, and says, "Well, stranger. Long time no see!"

Role-play this situation. Try your best to reestablish the trust and rapport you had at the beginning of the listing period. It may be instructive enough that you will never allow this situation to happen in your career.

Those professional licensees who are successful consistently do not accomplish this on the strength of salesmanship alone. The licensees are successful because they provide service to their clients and customers. Often, a family's home is the largest asset it will ever have, so a sales associate never must take the marketing of the home lightly. Failure to maintain regular contact with a seller is a detriment to a sales associate's future success.

In Practice

Select one evening each week, such as Thursday night, to service your listings.

Contact every seller in person, by phone, or if personal contact is not successful, by mail or email. If you call and the seller does not answer, write a card immediately to let them know you called.

Clip every ad from every paper and homes magazine, then paste it on a note card and mail it with a note that says, "Thought you'd like to see a recent ad on your home. Regards."

Ask every seller to call immediately if another licensee shows the property. Then follow up to help make the sale.

Call the seller after talking to a cooperating broker and give feedback about the showing.

Often sales associates lose touch with sellers because they don't know what to talk about and feel that they sound like broken records because they repeatedly say the same things.

Each sales associate should prepare a listing servicing schedule, which provides a basic format for the servicing of every listing. A sample form is shown in Figure 7.3.

FIGURE 7.3 ■ **Listing Servicing Schedule**

Property Address_____ H Phone: _____ W Phone: _____
Sellers' Names _____ Children: _____

First Day:
- Verify tax information and legal description.
- Send out mortgage status request.
- Write three ads.
- Place listing on webpage.
- Send thank-you card to seller.
- Enter listing information in computer.
- Put copies of listing information in floor book.
- Distribute copies of listing information to all sales associates.
- Put sign and lockbox on property.

Second Day:
- Mail out notice of listing cards to at least 20 neighbors.
- Call or email seller to tell of above steps.

End of First Week:
- Send letter to seller signed by broker.

Day after Caravan:
- Collect caravan comment sheets.
- Visit with seller to evaluate results of caravan and comments.

Second Week:
- Clip ads of property. Send to seller in postcard format.
- Check MLS information on computer, verify information, and then email to seller.
- Call seller to tell of progress. Ask seller to call when house is shown.

Third Week:
- Clip ads of property. Send to seller in postcard format.
- Run MLS computer check for new listings and listings under contract, and then email information to seller.
- Call or email seller to find out who has seen home.
- Check with sales associates who have shown home; give feedback to seller.

Fourth Week:
- Clip ads of property. Send to seller in postcard format.
- Run MLS computer check for new listings and listings under contract, and then email information to seller.
- Call or email seller to find out about who has seen home.
- Check with sales associates who have shown home; give feedback to seller.

Fifth Week:
- Clip ads of property. Send to seller in postcard format.
- Run MLS computer check for new listings and listings under contract, and then email information to seller.
- Visit seller in the home, and go over CMA. Get price reduction if appropriate.
- Walk through property again. Point out areas needing attention.

F I G U R E 7.3 ■   Listing Servicing Schedule (continued)

Sixth Week:
- Clip ads of property. Send to seller in postcard format.
- Run MLS computer check for new listings and listings under contract, then email information to seller.
- Call or email seller to find out who has seen home.
- Check with sales associates who have shown home; give feedback to seller.
- Schedule open house for the property, if appropriate.
- Send notice of open house to at least 20 neighbors.

Seventh Week:
- Run open house, and leave a note for seller on results. Call later.
- Clip ads of property. Send to seller in postcard format.
- Run MLS computer check for new listings and listings under contract, then email information to seller.
- Call or email seller to find out who has seen home.
- Check with sales associates who have shown home; give feedback to seller.
- Send out notice of listing to additional 20 homes in neighborhood.

Eighth Week:
- Clip ads of property. Send to seller in postcard format.
- Run MLS computer check for new listings and listings under contract, and then email information to seller.
- Call or email seller to find out who has seen home.
- Check with sales associates who have shown home; give feedback to seller.

Ninth Week:
- Clip ads of property. Send to seller in postcard format.
- Run MLS computer check for new listings and listings under contract; then email information to seller.
- Call or email seller to find out who has seen home.
- Check with sales associates who have shown home; give feedback to seller.
- Do another CMA. Visit with seller, and get price reduction and extension.
- Schedule luncheon for sales agents.

10th Week:
- Clip ads of property. Send to seller in postcard format.
- Run MLS computer check for new listings and listings under contract, and then email information to seller.
- Call or email seller to find out who has seen home.
- Check with sales associates who have shown home; give feedback to seller.

Continue this pattern until listing has been sold.

WHEN LISTINGS DON'T SELL

Occasionally, sales associates feel that they are wasting their time listing property. "I make more money working with buyers. I have 10 listings and haven't earned a dime!" they say.

Sales associates who feel that way may need to evaluate their listing inventory using a listing quality report, as illustrated in Figure 7.4.

F I G U R E 7.4 ■ Listing Quality Report

	123 Main St.		412 First St.		821 Jones St.	
	Yes	**No**	**Yes**	**No**	**Yes**	**No**
Listed at recommended CMA price?		✓		✓		✓
House in good condition?	✓			✓		✓
Seller motivated?	✓		✓			✓
Yard sign?	✓		✓		✓	
Easy showing access? (Lockbox, etc.)	✓		✓		✓	
Good curb appeal?		✓	✓			✓
Recommend price reduction	$10,000		$15,000		$17,500	

A. Address	B. Time Left	C. List Price	D. Chance of Sale During Term	E. Quality Volume [C × D]	F. Recommended Price Change
123 Main St.	3 months	$205,000	25%	$51,250	$10,000
412 First St.	1 month	$178,200	10%	$17,820	$15,000
821 Jones St.	2 months	$312,500	40%	$125,000	$17,500
1250 Sipa Rd.	4 months	$285,000	60%	$171,000	$10,000
116 Third St.	5 months	$180,000	30%	$54,000	$10,000
TOTAL	**Avg. 3 mo.**	**$1,160,700**	**1.65 listings**	**$419,070**	**$62,500**

Notice that the bottom part of the listing evaluation indicates that sales associates who think he has five listings has the equivalent of only 1.65 listings (adding the percentages of chance of sale). The associate may boast of a listing volume of $1,160,700 (average of $232,140) but really has the equivalent of only $419,070 (average of $83,814) when considering the chance of sale.

Overpriced listings result in frustration for the sales associate and resentment by the owner, who may become more demanding and tell friends of the lack of effort on the part of the sales associate. Sometimes, if the seller will not price the property appropriately, it may be best for the sales associate to give the listing back to the seller. A comment such as "We value our relationship with you and don't want you to feel we are not being productive. I feel you may be mad at us later on if we didn't give you the opportunity to talk with other agencies."

If the sales associate internalizes this evaluation and mentally reviews it when taking a listing, it is more likely that only salable listings would be taken thereafter.

SUMMARY

- The three major types of listing agreements are:
  - open listings, in which the first broker to produce a buyer is paid;
  - exclusive-agency listings, which allow the seller to sell without paying a commission, but if any broker sells the property, the listing broker is paid; and
  - exclusive-right-of-sale listings, which are the most advantageous listing from the broker's viewpoint. The broker is due a commission regardless of who sells the property.
- Written listings may not be self-renewing.
- The broker must deliver to the sellers a copy of the listing agreement within 24 hours of signature.
- An owner's warranty in a listing indemnifies the broker from false statements the owner makes to the broker.
- A latent defects addendum to a contract holds the owner accountable for failing to disclose existing defects to the property that are known or should have been known.
- Licensees should review and understand the listing contracts.
- A licensee should be able to explain clearly to a seller the important provisions of a listing agreement.
- A licensee must market property with skill, care, and diligence.
- Home presentation, or staging, can make your listing stand out from comparable homes, and is especially effective in a buyer's market.
- A major part of the licensee's professional duties, in addition to listing and selling, is servicing listings and keeping in touch with sellers on a regular basis.

R E V I E W   Q U E S T I O N S

1. If an owner reserves the right to sell the property himself, but allows many brokers to work simultaneously, he has given the brokers
    a. exclusive-agency listings.
    b. no listings.
    c. exclusive-right-to-sell listings.
    d. open listings.

2. An open listing is created by
    a. written document only.
    b. a sign that says "brokers protected."
    c. negotiation.
    d. a broker putting a sign on property.

3. A broker just listed a house for six months. The listing will automatically renew for an additional three months unless canceled in writing by either party. This type of agreement
    a. is advantageous to the seller and is endorsed by the National Association of REALTORS®.
    b. is a violation of the license law.
    c. is permissible, provided full disclosure is made to the seller of its self-renewing provision.
    d. may be used only by single agents and is not available to transaction brokers.

4. What clause in a listing contract contains a promise by the owner certifying that all the information related to the property is true and accurate?
    a. Property owner's
    b. Property condition
    c. Warranty of owner
    d. Owner's certification

5. What addendum to a listing contract states that the owner has a duty to disclose any facts materially affecting the property's value?
    a. Caveat emptor
    b. Latent defects
    c. Special clauses
    d. Hold harmless

6. What type of listing is used when an owner selects one brokerage firm to sell his property but reserves the right to sell the property personally and not pay a commission?
    a. Exclusive right of sale
    b. Exclusive-agency
    c. Open
    d. Option contract

7.   A seller refuses to allow the listing broker to split commissions with buyers' brokers, transaction brokers, or nonrepresentation brokers. Based on this information, which statement is TRUE?
    a.   The seller's viewpoints are perfectly acceptable and understandable; the broker may take the listing and enter it in the MLS.
    b.   The broker may not take the listing under these circumstances.
    c.   The broker may take the listing but may not enter it in the MLS.
    d.   The listing may be placed into MLS only if it is an exclusive-right-of-sale listing.

8.   A seller tells a sales associate that she intends to take the ceiling fan when she moves, so he should be sure the listing information shows that it is not part of the sale. In this case, what should the sales associate do?
    a.   Tell the seller that the ceiling fan is a fixture and must stay with the property.
    b.   Tell the seller, "Let's wait and see if it's mentioned in the purchase contract; if it is not specifically itemized, you can take it."
    c.   Strongly urge the seller to leave the fan.
    d.   Tell the seller to remove the fan before the property is shown.

9.   The legal description entered into the listing agreement and into MLS
    a.   should be taken from the owners' deed or the public records.
    b.   is usually omitted in listing and sales contracts.
    c.   should be either the lot and block number or the seller's mailing address.
    d.   is not a significant piece of information for listing or sales contracts.

10.   If sellers, when listing the property, offer to leave a washer/dryer combination, the sales associate should
    a.   warn them of the sales tax liability.
    b.   tell them not to leave it.
    c.   suggest it not be included until an offer is received.
    d.   disregard the offer without discussing it with the sellers.

11.   The section of the Florida REALTORS® listing agreement titled "Cooperation and Compensation with Other Brokers" indicates that the
    a.   broker need not cooperate with other brokers.
    b.   broker's policy is to cooperate with other brokers except when it would not be in the seller's best interests.
    c.   broker pays the cooperating broker at least 50% of the total listing commission.
    d.   broker may not cooperate with any other broker without prior written approval.

12.   The Florida REALTORS® listing agreement has a dispute resolution clause that
    a.   requires the parties to seek redress in a court of law.
    b.   allows only the broker and the seller to settle disputes by binding arbitration.
    c.   allows the broker, the sales associate, and the seller to settle disputes by binding arbitration.
    d.   requires the parties to seek resolution at a hearing before the Florida Real Estate Commission.

13.   A broker lists a large townhome in Pebble Creek. The broker has to give the seller a signed copy of the agreement
    a.   before leaving the seller's presence.
    b.   within 24 hours.
    c.   within 48 hours.
    d.   within 7 days.

14. A broker is talking with a man about listing his home. If the man says that he is ready to list but has two people he wants to exclude from the listing for three weeks, the broker should
    a. wait three weeks, then come and get the listing.
    b. have the man sign an open listing.
    c. have the man sign an exclusive-right-of-sale listing.
    d. have the man sign an exclusive-right-of-sale listing with an addendum that excludes the two prospective buyers.

15. Two problems faced by a licensee who has taken an exclusive-agency listing result from
    a. a dishonest seller and a dishonest broker.
    b. other brokers and other sales associates.
    c. an owner's sign on the property and the owner advertising a different price.
    d. a buyer going to another broker and the other broker failing to disclose his brokerage relationship.

16. The maximum period between a listing sales associate's calls to the seller should be
    a. 1 day.
    b. 7 days.
    c. 10 days.
    d. 14 days.

17. An open listing
    a. may be terminated at will.
    b. must be written to be enforceable.
    c. may be given to only one broker at a time.
    d. requires the owner to notify the broker if the property is sold.

18. On June 18, a broker listed a couple's house for six months. On August 16, the couple terminated the listing, paying the broker a cancellation fee of $250. In September, the couple listed their house with another realty company. They accepted a contract in October, which closed on November 28. Based on the conditional termination clause of the Florida REALTORS® listing agreement, the couple
    a. is liable to the broker for the full commission.
    b. has acted in violation of state law.
    c. has terminated the original listing and need pay only the new realty company.
    d. may owe the broker up to 1% of the sales price of the home.

19. The parties to a listing agreement are the
    a. seller and buyer.
    b. seller and sales associate.
    c. sales associate and broker.
    d. seller and broker.

20.   A seller lists property with a multimillion-dollar broker. The broker's agreement calls for him to enter the listing into the MLS within three working days. On the second day, the broker shows the property to a prospective buyer, who loves it. The buyer is leaving town the next day but will be back in one week to purchase it if it is still on the market. The broker wants to double his commission by selling his own listing, so he withholds the information from the MLS for 10 days. Based on this information, the broker

a.   is following a legal, time-honored tradition in real estate by working to sell his own listing.

b.   may be liable to the seller for violating duties required by the listing agreement.

c.   will not be disciplined by FREC if he does in fact sell the property.

d.   is likely to be more successful in real estate.

A C T I O N   L I S T

APPLY WHAT YOU'VE LEARNED

The following actions will reinforce the material in "Section II—Obtaining Listings That Sell":

❏ Set up your power prospecting database. Start with your close friends and family, and then list all the friends and past customers you can think of. After that, try to think of anyone, even vaguely familiar, that you have met and get the names down. You can get the addresses and contact information later.

❏ If you own a home, estimate its current value, then prepare a CMA. If you do not own your home, do this exercise for a friend. Does the CMA support the value you guessed?

❏ Based on the CMA you did on your own house, or your friend's house, prepare a seller's net proceeds statement.

❏ Complete a listing agreement for your home, along with other forms required by your broker. Ask your broker to review them.

❏ Write three practice ads to market your home.

❏ Pick a large neighborhood in your city with lots of sales activity. Find as many sales as possible for the previous 12 months. Using the matched pair technique, identify the dollar contribution from:

 ■ a swimming pool,

 ■ an extra bedroom,

 ■ an enclosed garage, and

 ■ a corner lot.

❏ Using the same analysis, calculate the percentage difference between listing price and selling price.

❏ Using MLS data, divide the number of houses on the market by the number of house sales last week to find how many weeks' supply of homes are on the market. Do this at least once a month. It's an excellent indicator of market activity.

❏ Write a script for the explanation of a CMA to a prospective seller. Record your presentation on audiotape to hear how it sounds. Edit as necessary until it sounds just right.

❏ Record your explanation of the listing agreement used in your office. Edit your remarks until you are satisfied.

SELLING REAL PROPERTY

A sales associate must understand the buyer's needs and financial abilities. Licensees should understand how to find buyers and live up to the buyers' expectations. Buyers expect licensees to have broad knowledge about properties on the market and market values. They also want to know how much they can afford to pay for a house, based on their income.

The sales associate must be able to estimate the buyer's costs so that the buyer who contracts for a property is aware of the cash requirements expected at closing.

Knowledge of contracts is extremely important to sales associates. Not only do licensees need to know how to prepare purchase agreements, they must be able to explain the basic terms of the agreements so that buyers and sellers are aware of their rights and responsibilities.

Once a licensee shows the right property, the licensee must be ready to write the offer. Chapter 8 has a case study on writing and presenting the offer that will help the new licensee understand the process of presenting offers and negotiating counteroffers. ▪

WORKING WITH BUYERS

LEARNING OBJECTIVES

When you finish reading this chapter, you will be able to:

- list four methods that will enhance your product knowledge,

- list at least five sources of buyers,

- list two important reasons for qualifying a buyer, and

- describe the benefits of using IDX in your website.

KEY TERMS

buyer brokerage agreement	fallback list	previewing properties
canvassing	key safe	qualifying

OVERVIEW

Working with buyers is an important function of the professional real estate sales associate. Buyers are interested in working with knowledgeable, caring sales associates, and they generally are reluctant to make appointments without evaluating the sales associate's skills. A sales associate be adept at handling telephone inquiries, know the inventory, and stay current with available financing plans. Above all, the sales associate must understand and observe the laws with respect to required disclosures and fair housing.

PRODUCT KNOWLEDGE

A buyer usually benefits from working with a licensee, regardless of the brokerage relationship, because of the licensee's product knowledge. It is hard work to acquire the extensive product knowledge that buyers expect. To become proficient, sales associates should accomplish the following goals:

- Spend most of the first few weeks in real estate looking at property.

- See at least 30 new properties each week.

- Keep a record of listings they have viewed by using a contact program like Top Producer or Act! or even by using index cards grouped by price range and outstanding features. Sales associates may use the cards like flash cards to remember five good listings in each price range or five with pools or five fixer-uppers. With practice, sales associates can remember more than five listings.

- Constantly practice matching neighborhoods with price ranges or house sizes.

- Prepare a five-star home list showing a best-buys-on-the-market sheet for each price range (for instance, $175,000 to $200,000). See a sample list in Figure 8.1.

F I G U R E 8.1 ■ Five-Star Homes List

★★★★★
FIVE-STAR Homes
(BEST BUYS ON THE MARKET)
Price Range: $175,000–$200,000

Price	Address	MLS #	Comments
$176,900	116 Belmont Rd.	15432	Great deck, vaulted ceiling
$179,500	1272 Scenic Rd.	16523	Brick, large oak in front
$185,000	784 Wilson Ave.	16132	Wood frame colonial
$185,000	1216 Kara Dr.	15478	Huge back yard with hot tub
$188,500	8754 Skate Dr.	15843	Heavily wooded, secluded
$199,900	124 E. Call St.	16021	Downtown, arched doorways

If a buyer calls to ask for an address of one of the sales associate's listings, the sales associate may provide the information to the caller and, before the caller hangs up, suggest that the caller hear about "my five favorite homes on the market in your price range" to get an appointment with the buyer.

DISCUSSION EXERCISE 8.1

If you actively sell residential properties, try to name from memory the location of at least three single-story, four-bedroom listings. Try to name the location for four listed homes with swimming pools.

FINDING BUYERS

Some good sources of buyers include:

- calls resulting from advertising (both print and online),
- calls resulting from signs,
- past customers and clients,
- friends and family,
- open house visitors,
- canvassing prospects,
- buyer seminar attendees, and
- a buyer farm.

It's very important that the response to customers requesting is quick and thorough. Once the customer has been impressed by your professionalism, that customer is more likely to use you for all property searches and to contact you for property showings.

DISCUSSION EXERCISE 8.2

Carol is on floor duty when she receives a call from a buyer who says, "I'm looking for a four-bedroom home with a pool, northeast, but it's got to have a large workshop. Do you have anything like that listed in the $150,000 range?"

"No, I don't have any listings like that," she says, "but I can show you another company's listing that may be just right for you. I saw it last week. It's very spacious, in an elegant setting with a great view. I believe it's priced at $148,500. I'm available to show it to you this afternoon at 4:30, or I have another time available at 6:15. Which is better for you?"

Is Carol likely to get an appointment to show the property? Why or why not? Is there something she said that you would say differently?

Calls Resulting From Advertising

Licensees who want their personal name to appear in a brokerage firm's ad must include their last name at least once in the ad. The brokerage firm's name must be included to avoid charges of blind advertising. For example, Joseph J. Perkins, a sales associate, could place an advertisement with "call Joe for more information," provided the ad includes the brokerage firm's name and Joe's last name somewhere in the ad (61J2-10.025(2)).

When advertising online, the brokerage firm name must be placed adjacent to or immediately above or below the point of contact information. Point of contact information refers to any means for contacting the brokerage firm or individual licensee, including mailing address, physical street address, email address, telephone number, or facsimile telephone number (61J2-10.025(3)(a)).

Advertisement calls are an extremely important source of buyers. A buyer calls for more information to determine whether a house is right for him. A buyer seldom calls to make an appointment with a sales associate, but the sales associate's objective is always to get the appointment with the buyer. The sales associate must remember two important points when answering buyer advertisement calls:

1. It is difficult for the sales associate to talk intelligently about properties that she has not seen. For this reason, the sales associate should see every company listing before answering calls on ads or signs.

2. The sales associate should review all company advertising in newspapers and homes magazines. The licensee should clip each ad and paste it on a separate piece of notebook paper or index card. A **fallback list**, sometimes called a switch list or pivot list, should be prepared for each ad. A fallback list comprises three to five properties that are similar to the property being advertised. The list can consist of the sales associate's personal listings, the brokerage firm's listings, or other brokers' listings. If a caller isn't satisfied after learning more about the property in question, the sales associate can refer to the fallback list of other properties that might be suitable. The fallback list becomes invaluable in getting the appointment and helping the buyer find the right property. A sample fallback list is shown in Figure 8.2.

F I G U R E 8.2 ■ Fallback List

FALLBACK LIST FOR 3415 MONITOR LANE

Address	MLS #	Price	Comments
1546 Merrimac Dr.	16546	$189,500	Large workshop, lots of trees, 2 streets over
1247 Thresher Ln.	16478	$194,500	20' × 30' deck, screened pool area, spotless
1687 Woodgate Way	16521	$195,000	2 stories, 4 bedrooms, close to town
1856 Hoffman Dr.	16493	$185,000	Huge oak in front, lots of azaleas, big kitchen
1260 Dunston Ct.	16470	$192,500	Quiet street off Meridian, very clean, bright

---

D I S C U S S I O N   E X E R C I S E   8 . 3

Have a class member role-play calling on an ad for 3415 Monitor Lane. Try to get an appointment using one of the methods discussed.

Often, a caller wants a property's address but is unwilling to give her name or phone number. "I just want to ride by to see whether I like it," the caller says. The sales associate will not get the appointment unless the caller feels she will benefit by meeting with the sales associate. The best-buys sheet and the fallback list may come in handy to get the appointment. Most buyers would feel that the sales associate had market information that would make it worthwhile to make an appointment.

> **In Practice**
>
> If a buyer resists giving a name and phone number, try this approach:
>
> "I understand your feelings. You know, many properties that come on the market are sold before they are even advertised because they have a sales associate who watches the market and calls immediately. Would you like to have the first opportunity to see these prime properties right away?" This question will often get their contact information.

When a caller is adamant about wanting an address but will not make an appointment, some sales associates do not give the address because they will lose the call. It is not worthwhile, however, to generate ill will with the consumer. Perhaps a better approach is to be helpful in every way. Ask how many property ads the caller has circled in the newspaper or homes magazine. Tell the caller you will give him an address and information on each listing advertisement, even though other real estate companies hold the listings. You should have a copy of the classified ad section and a homes magazine handy. Follow along with the caller, mark each ad, and set a time that you can get together. Prepare a list with addresses, prices, square footage, and other property features. What is the attraction to the buyer? One call gets it all because the consumer sees a benefit to meeting with the licensee. The attraction to the sales associate? The buyer places no calls to the competition, and an appointment has been set.

Once the sales associate makes an appointment, it is time to evaluate the buyer's needs and financial capabilities. This is called **qualifying** the buyer.

Often the first visit with the buyer is simply a get-acquainted visit, meant for making required disclosures and for qualifying. After this is completed, a second appointment is set to show properties.

Calls Resulting From Signs

Another source of buyers is calls on property signs. Callers on real estate ads generally want the properties' addresses. Callers on signs generally want the prices because they already know the locations. A sales associate should handle a sign call like an ad call, with the exception of the information provided.

Past Customers and Clients

One of the best sources of buyers is past customers and clients because they already have enjoyed the benefits of the sales associate's services. Agency representation may be a problem, however. If the sales associate listed a client's property in a prior relationship, the person may feel that the same agency relationship exists in the purchase of a new home. The sales associate must give the buyer the appropriate brokerage relationship disclosures.

Friends and Family

Among the sales associate's first sources of buyers when he starts in real estate are friends and family. The agent should write to everyone he knows and stay in contact for news of potential customers. When working with a friend or family member, the sales associate must evaluate the loyalty issue to decide whether being a single agent for the buyer is more appropriate than being a transaction broker.

Co-workers

Current and former co-workers can be a wonderful source of buyers. Remember to let them know that you are in real estate and that if they need to buy or sell property, you'd like to help.

Open House Visitors

Holding open houses is a good way to find prospective buyers. The primary objective of an open house is not to make the seller happy (a sale makes the seller happy) but to get buyer prospects. If the buyer purchases the home on display, so much the better. The sales associate should prepare a brochure for the home with the sales associate's name and picture prominently placed.

Usually, open house visitors are just looking. The sales associate should tell them that they are welcome to walk through the home but that she wants to point out a few features that are not readily apparent. If this home is not right for the visitors, the licensee should have her list of the five best homes in the price range ready, as well as a fallback list, and then set an appointment to talk.

Canvassing Prospects

Canvassing is an excellent method of finding buyers and is discussed in detail in chapter 4. The same canvassing call can be a source of either buyers or sellers. The sales associate might ask, "Do you know someone who may be getting ready to buy or sell real estate?" Often the answer is yes, and the sales associate can set an appointment. Remember, you may not call anyone on the national or state do-not-call registry.

Buyer Seminar Attendees

Many sales associates and brokers consider buyer seminars to be outstanding prospecting tools and offer them to the public to attract large numbers of buyers at one time. Some real estate companies have impressive materials and workbooks for attendees of the classes, which run over two or three evenings. Often attendees pay a nominal fee to cover the cost of books. Most seminars entitle an attendee to schedule a one-hour consultation with the seminar leader about a specific real estate problem or need. This can benefit both the consumer and the licensee if a business relationship results. Remember that the appropriate brokerage relationship disclosures must be made.

Buyer Farm

Buyer farms are organized in much the same way as listing farms, requiring good selection techniques, strong organizational skills, and periodic, effective communications. The farmer could contact renters or buyers who might want to trade up.

Renters. One source of buyers is contacting occupants in rental properties, but the success of farming tenants will depend on local market conditions. In some areas of the state rent prices are now substantially below the monthly mortgage payments of similar properties, so convincing tenants to become owners is more difficult. Additionally, the subprime loan fallout has greatly reduced the chances for marginal buyers to get loans. That said, many tenants continue to buy homes, and a consistent approach to contacting tenants may result in many sales.

Because most apartment properties will not allow door-to-door solicitation, a licensee can phone renters who are not on the do-not-call registry or send direct mail. The materials mailed to the tenants could be as simple as a postcard showing listings available in an appropriate price range or as robust as a company folder with brochures, information about financing available, and photos of current listings.

Buyers Who Might Want to Trade Up. Perhaps a better source is an owner of a house who wants to trade up to a larger home. This buyer will likely have enough equity in the current home to make a down payment on a new home, and because the home has appreciated recently, won't feel the price "sticker shock" as keenly. This person can be found in first-time-buyer neighborhoods that have a large turnover of homes. Farming an area like this can result in many listings, as well as buyers.

Using the Internet to Attract Buyers

In chapter 4, we discussed the benefits of using social media and blogging to generate listing prospects. Another way to leverage online content to find buyers is to use an internet data exchange (IDX). An IDX is a way for brokers to share their MLS listings with one another in a way that gives them control over which listings are displayed and how they are displayed. These listings may be the most important content you feature online to generate buyer traffic.

Homebuyers want photos and details of properties for sale. There are many online tools that will help answer homebuyers' questions, including:

- mortgage and affordability calculators;
- closing costs estimators;
- lists of schools within a selected area, sorted by type, grade level, school district, and ZIP code;
- live mortgage rates;
- market trends and statistical graphs/charts;
- Google Maps, which can display grocery stores, restaurants, gas stations, banks, golf courses, hospitals, and more; and
- reviews of local businesses and restaurants.

QUALIFYING THE BUYER

It is a waste of time to show properties the buyer does not like or cannot afford. So, before showing properties, the sales associate must get the answers to two important questions: (1) What are the buyers' housing objectives? (2) What can the buyer afford to pay?

What Are the Buyers' Housing Objectives?

Some of the information the sales associate should get from the buyers includes the following:

- What features do they want in the home?
- How quickly do they need to move?
- Must the buyers sell their current home?

- If they're leasing now, when does the lease expire?
- Have the buyers already spoken to a lender and been preapproved?
- Is there a specific area they want?

Desired Features. The sales associate should ask the buyers what features the home must have and what features would be nice to have (see Figure 8.3). The "must have" might include features such as a particular area of town, four bedrooms, and a two-car garage. The "nice to have" might be features such as high ceilings, a heat pump, or a wood deck.

F I G U R E 8.3 ■ 20 Questions for Prospective Buyers

1. What part of town do you want to live in? _____

2. What price range would you consider? $_____ to $_____

3. How soon do you need to move? _____ months

4. Have you been preapproved for a mortgage loan? ☐ yes ☐ no

5. Do you have a home you need to sell first? ☐ yes ☐ no

6. Are you leasing? ☐ yes ☐ no   If yes, when is your lease up? _____

7. Do you want a specific school? _____

8. Do you want ☐ an older home or ☐ a newer home (less than 3 years old)?

9. What kind of houses would you be willing to look at?
   ☐ 1 story   ☐ 2 story   ☐ town house or condo   ☐ mobile home

10. What style house appeals to you most?
    ☐ contemporary   ☐ traditional   ☐ Spanish   ☐ no preference

11. How much fixing up would you be willing to do? ☐ a lot   ☐ a little   ☐ none

12. Do you have to be close to public transportation? ☐ yes ☐ no

13. Do you have any physical needs, such as wheelchair access? ☐ yes ☐ no

14. The site:

	Must have	Would like to have
Large yard (¼ acre or more)	☐	☐
Small yard (less than ¼ acre)	☐	☐
Fenced yard	☐	☐
Garage	☐	☐
Carport	☐	☐
Patio/deck	☐	☐
Pool	☐	☐
Extra parking	☐	☐
Other buildings (barn, shed, etc.)	☐	☐

The Interior:

15. How many bedrooms must you have? _____ How many would you like to have? _____

16. How many bathrooms do you want? _____

17. How big would you like your house to be (square feet)? From _____ to _____ sq. ft.

F I G U R E 8.3 ■ 20 Questions for Prospective Buyers (continued)

1 8 . Features	Must have	Would like to have
Air-conditioning	☐	☐
Wall-to-wall carpet	☐	☐
Ceramic tile	☐	☐
Hardwood floors	☐	☐
Eat-in kitchen	☐	☐
Separate dining room	☐	☐
Formal living room	☐	☐
Family room	☐	☐
Separate den or library	☐	☐
Separate laundry room	☐	☐
Fireplace	☐	☐
Workshop	☐	☐
No interior steps	☐	☐
"In-law" apartment	☐	☐

Community Features

1 9 . Neighborhood amenities	Must have	Would like to have
Community pool	☐	☐
Golf course	☐	☐
Basketball court	☐	☐
Tennis courts	☐	☐
Gated community or doorman	☐	☐
Clubhouse/activities	☐	☐

2 0 . Other special features _____

Urgency Level. The sales associate also needs to know the buyer's urgency level. Each buyer should be classified based on urgency and motivation to purchase (see Figure 8.4). A person needing to move within the next 30 days, for example, is a Priority 1 buyer, needing immediate attention. A person who doesn't have an immediate need, but who should not be ignored, is classified as Priority 2. A buyer who either will not or cannot purchase immediately is Priority 3 and should be contacted regularly for showings. If a buyer relocating to the city is in town just for the weekend to purchase a home, the sales associate knows this is a Priority 1 buyer. After financial qualifying shows the buyer to be capable of making a purchase, the sales associate might say, "It sounds like your situation needs my full attention. If you approve, I'll clear my calendar so we can find the right home for you." A buyer whose present lease expires in six months has less urgency to purchase now and is classified as Priority 3.

F I G U R E 8.4 ■ Prioritizing Your Buyers

Buyer's Situation	Priority Level
Needs to move within 30 days or in town for the weekend to find a house	1
Wants to buy a house within the next three to six months	2
Can't buy right now but is just starting to look; perhaps on a lease expiring next year	3

Current Housing Situation. If the buyers currently own a home that must be sold, one of the first actions should be to look at their home and make a listing presentation. After their home is listed, the best way to motivate the buyers-sellers to price their present home competitively is to show homes they might want to purchase during that listing period. When they see the right home, they will be prepared to sell their own quickly.

If the buyers are currently leasing, the licensee must determine when the lease expires. That will help in prioritizing the buyer.

Buyer's Family Helping in the Decision. The sales associate must also find out whether someone other than the buyers will be involved in making the final purchasing decision. If the buyers' uncle will evaluate the final choice, the sales associate should try to get the uncle to see each property along with the buyers. Why? The uncle may have a better grasp of the market and of property values and may help the buyers reach a decision sooner.

Best Times to See Property. The licensee must find out what times are most convenient for the buyers to look at properties. Are they available during the day? Can they come immediately to see a property if the right one comes on the market? Or does their job situation require that they see property only in the evenings after work or on weekends?

Describing the Buying Process to the Buyer

At the first meeting with the buyer, the sales associate should provide, in addition to the agency disclosure form, a clear picture of the entire process, from the time of this first meeting right up until the day the buyer moves into his new home. The buyer who understands the process is less likely to become uneasy or reluctant to purchase when he finds the right property. The buyer should be given a copy of the purchase agreement, and the sales associate should explain important provisions in the agreement. A buyer's cost disclosure should be prepared for the home the buyer desires. This also helps in the financial qualifying process. Figure 8.5 is a sample time line to give to the buyers.

Financial Qualification

Financial qualification is the key to a successful sale. If the buyer contracts for a home and applies for a loan that is later denied, the seller, buyer, and sales associate have wasted time and effort. In addition, loan application fees ranging from $250 to $500, depending on the lender, could be lost. Licensees should explain both issues to their customers to help them understand the importance of financial qualifying.

Financial qualification helps to determine how much money the buyer can borrow for the purchase of property.

Lender Prequalifying Versus Preapproval. Having a lender preapprove the buyer is the best approach and should be used whenever possible, but certainly before the buyer actually contracts for property. Preapproval means the buyer has been interviewed and the buyer's credit report has been reviewed and the income verified.

A lender's preapproval letter makes the buyer's offer much stronger in the eyes of a seller and will result in more contracts.

Most lenders adhere to the Fannie Mae/Freddie Mac standards in reviewing loan applicants. Those agencies recommend the maximum housing expense ratio (front) of 28% and the maximum total obligations ratio (back) of 36% for qualifying potential buyers for first mortgage (conforming) loans. The FHA's maximum housing expense ratio is 31%, and the maximum total obligations ratio is 43%. These figures are guidelines only. Some lenders will vary from these guidelines, so a prospective buyer who does not meet the guidelines may still be able to talk with a lender that will make the loan.

F I G U R E 8.5 ■ **Homebuying Process Time Line**

1 . Initial meeting
- Discuss brokerage relationship
- Discuss housing objectives—features needs and wants, area of the city, etc.
- Discuss time desired for moving in to the new home
- What is the buyers' present housing situation—need to sell, currently leasing, etc.

2 . Become familiar with the sales contract

3 . Review and sign the Buyer Brokerage Agreement

4 . Financial qualification
- Buyer to talk with a lender and get a preapproval letter for loan amount
- Review cash required for closing, closing costs, and monthly payments

5 . Begin the property search
- Number of houses seen in one appointment
- The importance of feedback about likes and dislikes

6 . When you find the right house
- Tell your sales associate that this is the one you want
- Sales associate will complete the contract form and review it with you
- You will sign the contract form and give a good-faith deposit

7 . Sales associate presents your offer to the seller. The seller may:
- Accept your offer—you have a contract
- Decline your offer—you do not have a contract
  - You can raise your offer.
  - You can decide to keep looking for another house.
- Counteroffer
  - You can accept the sellers' counteroffer—you have a contract.
  - You can counter the sellers' counteroffer—you don't have a contract.
  - You can reject the sellers' counteroffer and keep looking for another house.

8 . When you have a signed contract, refer to Figure 13.1, "The Road to Closing."

The common reason buyers don't qualify under the Fannie Mae/Freddie Mac standards is usually the back ratio: total obligations. If that's too high, perhaps a creative lender can still help by increasing the qualifying income or suggesting prepaying some installment debt to less than 10 months so that it's no longer counted. A very high credit score could also help get the loan. Other compensating factors include:

■ having a good record of promotions and raises;

■ having little or no installment debt if housing expense ratio is too high;

■ making a down payment greater than 20%;

■ having saved money while making rent payments higher than the mortgage payments of the new mortgage; and

■ having a job with great benefits, such as a company car, free health plan, and high company contributions to a 401(k) plan.

> ### DISCUSSION EXERCISE 8.4
>
> The following role-playing skit is designed to highlight mistakes some sales associates make in their first meetings with prospective buyers and allows both spectators and participants to learn from the process. Three actors are needed—a sales associate and two buyers. The persons in the skit should be enthusiastic and as realistic as possible. During the presentation, if the sales associate says something that may violate the law or ethics, group members should shout "zap!" to signify their disapproval. At the end of the skit, group members should be able to itemize the sales associate's errors and recommend responses to the buyers' questions.

1 ## SKIT

2 ### Buyers' First Meeting with a Licensee

3 Buyers walk in and are greeted by sales associate.

4 **Licensee:** Hello, may I help you?

5 **Husband:** Yes, we are here to see Lee Wilson.

6 **Licensee:** I'm Lee. You must be Mr. and Mrs. Camp?

7 **Wife:** Yes, we are. Very nice to meet you.

8 **Licensee:** Great. Please sit down. [*Pause while they sit.*]

9 **Husband:** Our mutual friends, the Joneses, recommended we get in touch with you.

10 **Licensee:** Yeah, the Joneses send me lots of people. By the way, if you send me anyone
11 who buys a house, I'll give you $50.

12 **Wife:** That's what they told us. I hope you can find us a good deal, too.

13 **Licensee:** I love working with buyers, Mrs. Camp, and because I'm a transaction bro-
14 ker, I can work harder on your behalf.

15 **Wife:** Well, do you have any distress sales of houses in the $200,000 range that we
16 could take advantage of?

17 **Licensee:** As a matter of fact, my company just listed one. The listing sales associate
18 suggested that I look at it. Confidentially, the owners' business is in trouble, and
19 they need to sell quickly. The listing sales associate says they are desperate and
20 probably would come off the price as much as $20,000, but we should start even
21 lower to get the best counteroffer.

22 **Husband:** Tell us about it.

23 **Licensee:** Well, it's in Bent Tree Estates, close to Lake Jackson. It's got three bedrooms,
24 two baths, a large lot, and a two-car garage. It's in absolutely perfect condition.

25 **Wife:** The newspaper ran an article last week suggesting that buyers get a home inspec-
26 tion. Is that a good idea?

Licensee: It is if you want to spend $300 for nothing. I've looked over the house, and it's just perfect. No problems whatsoever.

Husband: I need to tell you that we may have a problem qualifying for a new loan. I had some credit problems last year, and we got turned down on another house we tried to buy. We really need to get an assumable loan with no qualifying.

Licensee: If you like this house, maybe we can structure a wraparound loan to beat the due-on-sale clause with the seller carrying some of the financing. Can you work with $20,000 down?

Husband: I think we can come up with that much, if we can get the price right. Can we put some kind of contingency in the contract in case I can't get the money?

Licensee: Hey! I can write up a contract with contingencies that will let you out at any time with no risk. Don't worry about that. But let's go see it.

Husband: Should we have an attorney?

Licensee: You know what's wrong with five attorneys up to their necks in sand?

Husband: [*Smiles*] No, what?

Licensee: Not enough sand. [*He laughs.*] Seriously, folks, you don't need an attorney. I can help you with anything an attorney can.

Wife: Can we ask you some more questions first?

Licensee: Sure. Go ahead.

Wife: Is it a good neighborhood?

Licensee: Oh, yeah, there are hardly any minorities living there!

Wife: Well, I didn't mean that. I meant is it pleasant and well maintained?

Licensee: Uh, sorry. Yes, it's really nice.

Husband: Well, let's go looking. I hope it works out.

Licensee: I'll do everything I can for you. [*The Camps leave*] [*To an associate in the office*] Hey, Jim! I'll be back in a while. I've got some flakes with no money again, but I'm going to show a house!

Is it possible to learn from mistakes? The mistakes made in this skit may seem ridiculous, but these statements are actually made—although probably not all in a single transaction. Sales associates must be alert in their presentations and when answering questions to avoid these mistakes.

After qualifying the buyer, the sales associate should prepare the customer to buy.

PREPARING THE CUSTOMER TO BUY

The successful sales associate will prepare the customer for signing the contract long before the right property is found. After qualifying the buyer's needs, the sales associate should give the buyer a copy of the contract for purchase and sale and explain the more important paragraphs to the buyer.

This explanation of the contract serves two important functions:

1. If the buyer receives important information from the sales associate at their first meeting, this works to cement the buyer's loyalty to the associate.

2. Because the buyer is given a copy of the contract along with an explanation, the contract becomes the buyer's property. When the buyer becomes interested in a particular property, she is not startled when the sales associate pulls out a contract form.

> **In Practice**
>
> Keep a contract on a clipboard, along with the MLS information on the property. It's always in sight so the buyer can see it. If the buyer asks questions like "Can the seller leave the draperies?" you would ask, "Shall I put that in the agreement?" while writing on the contract.

BUYER BROKERAGE AGREEMENT

While licensees nearly always require a written agreement from sellers, they often work with buyers on an open-listing basis. A licensee may give the customer valuable information on the market and other ideas on purchasing a home but may end up working for nothing. Many successful licensees are requesting that buyers also enter into a written **buyer brokerage agreement** for representation by the licensee, either as a single agent or as a transaction broker.

Some prospective buyers will be reluctant to sign such an agreement because they may be required to pay a commission. They may not be aware that the agreement calls for the broker to offset the commission from monies received from a seller if the property is listed with a cooperating broker. A buyer who understands the benefits will be more likely to sign the agreement. When the buyer agrees to pay a commission, the broker can show the buyer unlisted property (FSBOs, properties being foreclosed, real estate owned by banks, etc.). Buyers would not be shown these properties unless a commission agreement was in place.

Forms To Go

The real estate licensee should understand the Exclusive Buyer Brokerage Agreement (see Appendix B) and be able to explain its provisions clearly and concisely. The numbered paragraphs following the form correspond with the 14 sections of the agreement.

1. *Parties*. The parties are the buyer and the broker. This paragraph also explains that the terms "acquire" or "acquisition" include "purchase, option, exchange, lease, or other acquisition or ownership or equity interest in real property."

2. *Term*. This paragraph sets forth the dates the agreement will be effective. Notice that if a contract is pending on the expiration date of the agreement, the agreement is extended until the contract is closed or terminated.

3. *Property*. This section shows the following:

   a. *Type of property*—for example, residential, agricultural, office, et cetera.

   b. *Location* would normally be used to describe a city or county, or another geographic area.

    c. *Price range* would set the minimum and maximum limits the broker should use in selecting properties to show. This section also discloses that the buyer may have already been preapproved for a mortgage.

    d. *Preferred terms and conditions* sets out the buyers' preferences, such as owner financing, small down payment, lease-purchase, and so forth.

4. *Broker's Obligations.*

    a. *Broker assistance:* The broker agrees to cooperate with seller's brokers to complete a transaction. It also states that even if the broker is paid a commission split from the seller's broker, the broker's duties to the buyer are not reduced.

    b. *Other buyers:* This section discloses to the buyer that the broker may work with another buyer interested in the same property but must maintain confidentiality as to the terms of any offers.

    c. *Fair housing:* Broker states he will not participate in unlawful discrimination.

    d. *Service providers:* Broker will not be responsible for acts of a third party recommended by the broker, such as a home inspector or title insurance company.

5. *Buyer's Obligations.* In this section, the buyer agrees to tell sellers or other brokers that he is working under contract with a broker, to conduct all negotiations through the broker, to give the broker personal financial information and allow the broker to run a credit check, to hold the broker harmless for any damages, and to consult an appropriate professional for tax, legal, and other services.

6. *Retainer.* Many licensees ask prospective buyers for a nonrefundable retainer at the time this contract is signed. It has an option for the retainer to be credited to the total compensation.

7. *Compensation.* This obligates the buyer to pay a commission to the broker, offset by any commissions the broker may receive from a seller or a broker working with the seller. The broker is entitled to a commission if the customer purchases, leases, or options the property. The commission may be stated as a percentage of the sale, lease, or option, or it can be a fixed fee. The broker is also entitled to a commission if the buyer defaults on any contract.

8. *Protection Period.* If the broker has shown property to the buyer and the buyer purchases the property within the agreement period, the buyer will owe the commission unless the buyer has entered into a buyer brokerage agreement with another broker after the termination date.

9. *Early Termination.* The buyer may terminate the agreement, but if the buyer buys property that she learned about during the contract term, the buyer owes the commission. The broker may terminate the agreement at any time by giving written notice.

10. *Dispute Resolution.* Disputes must be mediated first. If mediation is not successful, the parties must agree to submit the dispute to binding arbitration.

11. *Assignment; Persons Bound.* The broker is allowed to assign the agreement to another broker.

12. *Brokerage Relationship.* This section has several checkboxes for the parties to indicate what type of broker relationship they will have. Note that a box being checked does not discharge the broker from giving the buyer the prescribed brokerage relationship notice before showing a property or entering into this agreement.

13. *Special Clauses*. This gives the parties additional space to add other provisions to the agreement.

14. *Acknowledgment; Modifications*. Indicates the buyer has read and understands the agreement. There are spaces for signatures of the buyer(s), sales associate, and broker.

SHOWING THE PROPERTY

Once the buyer has been qualified, it is time to show properties that meet the buyer's needs. The sales associate should use the following sequence in the showing and contracting process:

1. Setting the appointment
2. Previewing the properties
3. Planning the route
4. Entering and showing the properties
5. Evaluating the buyer's level of interest
6. Estimating the buyer's costs and making required disclosures
7. Writing the contract

Steps 1 through 5 are discussed in the following sections. Step 7, writing the contract, is the subject of chapter 9. Step 6, estimating the buyer's costs and making required disclosures, is covered in chapter 10.

Setting the Appointment

This step is important not only for the obvious reason (nothing can happen until a meeting occurs) but also from a timing standpoint. Many times a sales associate will not set an appointment until he has previewed homes and is confident that good choices are available to show. The advantage of this method is that the sales associate can describe properties that meet the buyer's needs. Two disadvantages in this approach follow:

1. The sales associate might spend a lot of time looking at properties, only to find that the buyer is working with another licensee.
2. If the sales associate can't find anything just right and puts the buyer off, the buyer might decide to work with another licensee.

> **In Practice**
>
> Set the appointment—you'll find the properties. Showing homes helps the buyer focus on likes and dislikes and showing homes that are not quite right is better than not showing homes at all.

It is important to keep in contact with the buyer regularly, based on priority status. At least weekly, the sales associate should match the buyer's profile with new listings, and then call the buyer for an appointment. If the sales associate wants a Saturday showing appointment, the appointment must be made far enough in advance that the buyer can make the necessary arrangements. Saturday morning is too late to make the call. Early in the week is the best time to call for weekend showing appointments.

The best way to match a buyer with property is to use a contact program like Top Producer or Act! A separate card may be printed for each property. Match-ups between buyers and properties also are possible using some of the MLS system software. If the sales associate does not have access to a computer, it is simple to enter the buyer information on prospect cards. Spread out the cards on a tabletop and group them by price range when reviewing new listings. Listings should be matched to the buyer, and the sales associate should call the buyer about the properties. The more frequently the sales associate makes the buyer aware that the sales associate is continually searching for the right property for the buyer, the more likely it is that the buyer will call about properties he has seen.

Previewing the Properties

The sales associate should preview properties before actually showing them to the buyers. If possible, the sales associate should visit the properties, but if time did not permit, the properties can be previewed via the internet. The sales associate would be surprised and embarrassed if, after telling the buyers, "I think you'll like this next one!" she takes them to a property in terrible condition.

Each time the sales associate sees a new property, whether on a showing appointment, a preview day, or an office caravan of new listings, she should match that property with a buyer, taking careful notes before contacting the appropriate buyer.

In Practice

Being prepared is one of the most important factors in "closing the sale." That means having the objective firmly in mind that today you will write the contract. So before showing property, you should have the following items in your file folder:

- A copy of the lender's loan estimate for the top price the buyer can qualify for so you're ready to write the buyer's estimated cost disclosure

- All the necessary forms, including the cost disclosure estimate sheet and the contract for sale and purchase.

Planning the Route

Normally, the sales associate should show no more than five properties in one tour. However, if a Priority 1 buyer is in town for the weekend in order to buy a home, the sales associate must continue to show homes or risk losing the buyer.

When setting the appointment to show properties, the sales associate must consider in which order the homes will be shown. Buyers go through a continual evaluation process during the inspection tour, and the sales associate should help that process. Many sales associates like to schedule the home they consider just the right property as the last on the tour. While there are good arguments for this procedure, there are also disadvantages. The biggest problem is that if the houses get better between numbers one and five, and five is the best, the buyer wants to see house number six. Most brokers recommend showing the best house early in the tour. This sets a standard against which all other homes are measured. It usually makes the tour faster because the buyer can decide quickly that the home shown earlier was more to his liking.

Once the route has been decided, the sales associate should make appointments for the showings with the property owners. The time scheduled for each showing should not be fixed but should fall in a range because it is often difficult for the sales associate to judge how long the buyer will stay in each home on the tour. The seller should be asked to prepare the home for showing by opening the drapes and turning on all the lights so that the house will be bright and pleasant. The sales associate should ask the seller to vacate the property during the showing so that the buyer can have emotional possession of the property. If the sales associate has a cell phone, she should call the seller when leaving the previous house on the tour. If the seller owns a dog, the sales associate should ask that the seller arrange to contain the pet. If the sales associate will be later than scheduled or must cancel, common courtesy as a professional dictates calling the seller to explain the circumstances. Nothing is more disappointing to a seller than to needlessly prepare the home for a showing.

The route taken on the way to each property also is important. A trip past a beautiful park nearby makes the home site more interesting to the buyer, as does a trip past the shopping areas and schools closest to the home. While the initial route might avoid unsightly areas, they should be shown on the way out. Failure to show such surroundings is misrepresentation.

In Practice

■ If the property has negative features, discuss those features by phone before the appointment or, at the latest, on the way to the property—for example: "When I previewed the home yesterday, the housekeeping was not up to its usual standard because the kids are out of school this week. I hope that's all right." This reduces the shock the buyer might feel when entering. Often, the buyer defends the property: "Considering everything, the house is surprisingly clean!"

■ Avoid exaggerating a home's positive aspects to the buyer. This may create an expectation that the house will not meet. Let the buyer be pleasantly surprised when discovering the features.

Entering and Showing the Properties

This process depends on a property's general appearance. If the home's exterior is outstanding, the presentation should give the buyer time to appreciate this feature. Many sales associates park across the street so that a buyer's walk to a house is as pleasant as possible.

When highlighting a property's features, the sales associate must remember the most important words in any sales presentation:

■ Fact

■ Bridge

■ Benefit

■ Picture

The sales associate often points out facts that she believes to be important to the buyer and expects the buyer to be able to translate each fact into a benefit. "This house is on a cul-de-sac" might be a typical comment when driving up to the property. The sales associate believes this is important information to the buyer. The buyer might be thinking, "Yes, that's quite obvious. So what?" The full presentation should include fact, bridge, benefit, and picture.

The *fact* is that the property is on the cul-de-sac. The *bridge* might be "What that means to you, Mr. and Mrs. Jones, . . ." The *benefit* is the rest of the sentence: "is that because there is no through-traffic, automobiles travel very slowly, resulting in greater safety to your children." The *picture* is a word picture: "Imagine being out here on the street while your children roller-skate safely."

DISCUSSION EXERCISE 8.5

Picture a house that you have been in recently. Try to think of as many features of the house as you can, then express those features to represent fact, bridge, benefit, and picture statements.

Set up a group contest to see who can come up with the most fact-bridge-benefit-picture statements about a house that is familiar to all of you.

The sales associate should practice this technique whenever she can: when driving in the car alone, when **previewing properties**, or when on the office caravan of listings. Once this technique becomes a habit, buyers will find the sales associate's statements clearer and more interesting, and the sales associate will make more sales.

Many times, the listing office gives out the key to the back door, or the back door key may be the only key provided in the lockbox, or **key safe**, at the house. Although the sales associate must go in through the door for which she has a key, the buyer should always enter through the front door.

In Practice

Don't over show a property (overshowing is walking through a property making statements such as "This is the dining room."). Let the buyer discover some of the best features on his own.

Making the Buyers' Decision Easier

Normally, a sales associate will only show five to seven homes during a showing appointment. This is usually recommended so the buyer can have an opportunity to give feedback and not become confused by a huge number of homes. In some cases, however, many homes are shown to a buyer during one appointment. This might happen if the buyer is making a trip from out-of-town and needs to find the right house during this trip.

If a buyer sees 20 to 30 homes in a tour, the buyer will certainly be confused about which home had what feature. To make it easier, an experienced associate will have the buyer make a decision after seeing each home. You say, "Which home do you like best—this house or the house on Hibiscus Lane?" If the answer is "Hibiscus Lane," you say, "OK, forget all the other homes." At the last home on the tour, it is then easy to close with the question, "Well, which home do you want to buy, this one or the one on Hibiscus Lane?"

If you show more homes tomorrow, and the buyer liked Hibiscus Lane best, start the tour by taking the buyer back to Hibiscus Lane, with a comment like "OK, so this is the house we're ready to buy if we don't find one better today, right?"

Evaluating the Buyer's Level of Interest

Buyers usually know they are not interested shortly after entering the house. The sales associate should stop showing the property and proceed to the next. Because this is not the right house, it would be pointless to answer any of the buyer's objections. If the seller is at home, the sales associate should explain tactfully that the house does not satisfy the buyer's needs.

Handling Objections

Here are some important points to remember about buyers' objections:

- An objection can be an opportunity to make the sale. Many objections can be turned into immediate selling points. "The house needs paint" might provoke an argument from an unprofessional sales associate. The empathetic sales associate simply asks, "Would you paint it yourself, or would you hire someone to paint it for you?" With a positive response from the buyer, both parties are happy.

- Be certain you understand the objection; restate it. For example, a buyer may say, "This house costs too much money!" You may follow with a question like, "If I understand you, you feel that the house is overpriced?" The buyer may answer, "No, I'm just not certain I want to buy a house at this price level." By clarifying with a question, you avoid being argumentative.

Don't answer an objection until you have isolated it; if there are many more objections, this is not a suitable property. "If it were not for the problem about the house price, would you buy this house?" A yes answer tells you this: "Satisfy me regarding this problem, and I'll buy."

If you don't feel you can answer an objection to the buyer's satisfaction, especially if the objection is valid and you believe it is a deal-breaker, you shouldn't. You should agree with the buyer and go to the next property.

Make a list of as many objections as you can think of, and then write out at least two plausible answers to the objection. Try them in your office sales meetings and practice them regularly.

Chapter 9 covers the legal document called a Contract for Sale and Purchase. It is very important for licensees to understand the wording of the agreement they will ask buyers and sellers to sign. Chapter 10 discusses writing and presenting an offer.

SUMMARY

- Extensive product knowledge is necessary if a sales associate is to provide the best service to a consumer.
- The sales associate has many ways to acquire product knowledge, but all consist of looking at properties.

- Index cards or client contact software helps the licensee remember properties, and a best-buys-on-the-market list helps the sales associate better exhibit her product knowledge.

- Sales associates draw buyers from a number of sources:

  - Calls on ads, website, or signs
  - Past customers
  - Friends and family
  - Co-workers
  - Open house visitors
  - Canvassing
  - Buyer seminars

- When handling an ad or a sign call, a licensee's primary objective is to get an appointment.

- Sales associates should prepare carefully for ad calls, know the properties advertised, and have fallback lists.

- An internet data exchange (IDX) is a way for brokers to share their MLS listings with each other in a way that gives you control over which listings you will display, and how they will be displayed.

- A sales associate should qualify a buyer's housing objectives and have the buyers preapproved for a loan, as well as prioritize buyers based on the immediacy of their needs.

- Sales associates should request that buyers enter into a written buyer brokerage agreement.

- When showing properties, the sales associate should describe benefits and be careful not to over show the properties.

- The sales associate can help reduce buyer confusion by helping buyers decide which house they favor, or like best, after showing each house.

R E V I E W   Q U E S T I O N S

1. MOST brokers recommend showing the best house
   a. last.
   b. early in the tour.
   c. second to last.
   d. whenever—it doesn't matter.

2. Before showing properties to a buyer, a sales associate should NOT
   a. qualify the buyer's financial abilities and housing needs.
   b. preview the homes to be shown.
   c. make the required brokerage relationship disclosures.
   d. find out what church they would like to live near.

3. A Priority 1 buyer is one who
   a. has an immediate need to buy.
   b. is important but not as important as Priority 3.
   c. will not buy right away but should be contacted regularly.
   d. is not highly motivated.

4. Normally, the prospective buyer calling about a property with a For Sale sign wants information from the sales associate about the property's
   a. location.
   b. lot size.
   c. price.
   d. address.

5. According to the Florida REALTORS® Exclusive Buyer Brokerage Agreement, if there is a dispute between the buyer and the broker that they are unable to resolve, the parties
   a. must submit to a decision of the local board of REALTORS® professional standards committee.
   b. must submit first to binding arbitration.
   c. have the option of arbitration or litigation.
   d. must first submit to mediation, and if that is not successful, to arbitration.

6. A broker entered into an agreement with a prospective buyer, using the Florida REALTORS® Exclusive Buyer Brokerage Agreement. The broker showed the buyer a property, but the buyer said he really didn't care for it. After their agreement expired, the buyer signed a similar agreement with a second broker. About one month later, the second broker showed the buyer the same property and the buyer bought it. Which is TRUE?
   a. The second broker committed a violation of Chapter 475 by interfering with a previous contract.
   b. According to the terms of the contract, the first broker is entitled to the commission as the procuring cause of the sale.
   c. According to the terms of the contract, the second broker is entitled to the commission as the procuring cause of the sale.
   d. The buyer is not liable to either party.

7. Which is FALSE about an IDX?
   a. It is probably the most important piece of online content to generate buyers.
   b. It is a way for brokers to share their listings on the internet.
   c. It is a website that allows licensees to post a daily blog.
   d. It is the acronym for internet data exchange.

8. Because of high prices, high property taxes, and high insurance rates, the BEST buyer farms are likely to be in areas
   a. of high-priced houses.
   b. where the occupants need subprime loans.
   c. of owner-occupants who are ready to trade up to a larger house.
   d. owned by elderly people.

9. How does a buyer benefit by agreeing to pay a brokerage commission to her broker?
   a. The commission will be lower than if the seller has to pay a commission.
   b. The broker will automatically be the buyer's single agent.
   c. The broker will be able to work harder on the buyer's financing alternatives.
   d. The broker can show the buyer unlisted properties such as FSBOs and foreclosures.

10. For a buyer to decide to work with a licensee, the MOST important factor probably is the licensee's
    a. low fee.
    b. product knowledge.
    c. dress code.
    d. automobile make and model.

11. When making an appointment with a seller to show her property, a sales associate should NOT
    a. set the time as a range rather than a specific time.
    b. tell the seller to turn on the lights.
    c. tell the seller to leave the home during the showing.
    d. fail to call if it looks like the visit will be much later than the time specified.

12. A sales associate's primary objective when answering a sign call or an ad call is to
    a. give out the information requested.
    b. make a friend.
    c. make an appointment.
    d. get a name.

13. A fallback list consists of
    a. past customers.
    b. answers to objections.
    c. places to find part-time employment.
    d. properties similar to those advertised.

14. If a property is particularly attractive from the front, the BEST way to show it is by
    a. parking in the garage.
    b. parking at the street.
    c. sending a photo to the buyer.
    d. driving up and down the street first.

15.   Before a buyer begins seeing properties, the sales associate should NOT
   a.   give the buyer a brokerage relationship notice.
   b.   qualify the buyer.
   c.   ask the buyer about his feelings about having minorities living in the neighborhood.
   d.   find out what area of town the buyer would prefer.

16.   A sales associate asks a seller to vacate the property while it is being shown because the
   a.   seller can't hear what the sales associate is saying about the property.
   b.   buyer can take emotional possession of the property during the showing.
   c.   children of the buyer can use the bathroom if necessary.
   d.   buyer can inspect the structure for defects without interruption.

17.   Generally, the only features a sales associate should discuss with a buyer on the way to viewing a property are the
   a.   home's most outstanding attributes.
   b.   negative features if any.
   c.   beautiful Jacuzzi and huge master suite.
   d.   features previously discussed.

18.   One way to find many buyers at one time is
   a.   calling friends.
   b.   calling past customers.
   c.   canvassing.
   d.   conducting buyer seminars.

19.   A sales associate's statement that "the house is built of brick" should be followed immediately by the
   a.   fact.
   b.   bridge.
   c.   benefit.
   d.   picture.

20.   The safest way for a sales associate to determine whether a buyer is qualified is to use
   a.   the services of a lender to do it.
   b.   national mortgage market guidelines.
   c.   Fannie Mae/Freddie Mac underwriting guidelines.
   d.   any of these methods.

9 SALES AND OPTION CONTRACTS

LEARNING OBJECTIVES

When you finish reading this chapter, you will be able to:

- explain the exceptions to the statute of frauds that are recognized as valid real estate transactions,
- list at least three transactions that are not suitable for using the Florida REALTORS®/Florida Bar Residential Contract for Sale and Purchase,
- describe the legal test for the sufficiency of a legal description, and
- list the requirements for completing an option contract.

KEY TERMS

contract	sales contract	title insurance
exercised	statute of frauds	voidable contract
option contract	time is of the essence	

OVERVIEW

Contracts are part of our everyday lives. When a person orders telephone service, buys a refrigerator, or pays for an airline ticket, a contract has been formed.

Licensees regularly work with many different kinds of contracts. The broker's employment agreement, listing contracts, buyer brokerage agreements, leases, options, and sales contracts are just a few. Understanding the information in a contract and being able to correctly explain it to sellers and buyers is an important function of a sales associate. Licensees may legally prepare listing contracts, sales contracts, and option contracts. Preparing notes, mortgages, or deeds is unauthorized practice of law.

ANALYSIS OF REAL ESTATE CONTRACTS

A **contract** is a promise or set of promises that must be performed. Once the promise is given, the law recognizes performance of that promise as a duty. If the promise is broken or breached, the law provides a legal remedy for the injured party. However, one promise, standing alone, does not constitute a contract. Some specific act by the party to whom the promise is made, or a mutual promise from that party, is required to conclude a contract. For example, if you promise to fix your neighbor's roof and the neighbor thanks you, no contract exists because you asked for nothing in return for your promise. If your neighbor promises to give you $1,000 to fix her roof and you promise to do it, mutual promises have been exchanged, and a contract has been made.

DISCUSSION EXERCISE 9.1

You are a sales associate who has listed John Wilson's home in Foxcroft. Wilson would rather not repair several property defects (such as a cracked foundation). He suggests the use of an "as is" clause in the contract so that a buyer can do any inspection desired. "Based on this clause," Wilson tells you, "we have no need to disclose."

Does the use of an "as is" clause in a sales contract excuse a broker from disclosing material facts regarding a property? Explain.

Statute of Frauds

Before the enactment of the **statute of frauds**, it was not uncommon for a person to pay so-called witnesses to falsify testimony to support a nonexistent oral contract for the sale of real property. The law commonly called the statute of frauds requires that certain types of contracts, in order to be enforceable, be in writing and be signed by the party against whom enforcement is sought. Contracts that must be in writing and signed are of two general types: those that will not be performed fully within a short period and those that deal with specific subjects.

In Florida, an agreement or a promise that cannot be performed by both parties within one year after the contract date must be evidenced by a written document. Also, an agreement to sell or the actual sale of any interest in real property is subject to the statute of frauds and must be in writing and signed by all parties bound by the contract to be enforceable. Witnesses are not required.

Two common exceptions to the statute of frauds are recognized:

1. *Executed contracts.* Performance of the promise made proves the contract existed; therefore, the function of the statute of frauds has been accomplished, and a written form is not required.

2. *Partial performance.* Usually, the statute of frauds does not apply to partially performed contracts as long as two conditions have been met: (1) partial or full payment has been made, and (2) the buyer has either taken physical possession of or made improvements to the subject property. For example, if a buyer has evidence of a $500 payment toward the purchase of a parcel of land, then moves onto the property and plants a crop of tomatoes, the statute's function has been

accomplished. The payment and possession are regarded as evidence that a valid contract exists.

In Practice

When a buyer or a seller wants to change anything in a contract, such as moving the closing date beyond that required in the contract, be sure to get a written addendum to the contract signed by both buyer and seller. An oral agreement isn't worth the paper it's not written on.

Forms To Go

SALES CONTRACTS

A **sales contract**, also called a purchase and sale contract or a contract for sale and purchase, is a written agreement setting forth the terms for the transfer of real property from seller to buyer, with both signing the document. The Residential Contract for Sale and Purchase (see Appendix B) is the standard contract for sale and purchase and was developed by the Florida Association of REALTORS® and The Florida Bar. It is the most widely used preprinted sales contract form in the state. This section of the chapter presents specific instructions for the correct preparation of that contract, providing licensees with hands-on practice in preparing contracts to increase their professional skills. If licensees in your area use a different sales contract form, substitute that form for the Florida REALTORS®/Florida Bar contract. The discussion that follows applies to your contract form as well.

Online Contracts for REALTORS®

Florida REALTORS® members have access to the Form Simplicity website, which allows users to:

- fill in forms such as listing and sales contracts;
- save forms as internal data or flat PDF files;
- print forms;
- email forms to customers;
- link common information between forms, providing the quick processing of contract-related forms;
- create a Form Transaction, managing forms as a group and for the auto-filling in of information common to the deal such as names and addresses;
- save their own special clauses to insert into contracts;
- use their contact list information on customers, cooperating licensees, title companies, and loan institutions to automatically populate their contracts; and
- set up a brokerage office database account so the broker can review all contracts.

WEBLINK
@

Visit the Form Simplicity website at www.floridarealtors.org/ToolsAndSupport/FormSimplicity/.

Whether to Use a Printed Form

No two real estate transactions are exactly alike. Even two nearly identical houses located adjacent to one another may require different contractual handling. The earnest money deposits, mortgage sources, and prices, as well as many other items, must be considered. Even the tried-and-proven clauses in a standard form may need to be adapted to the requirements of a particular transaction. Therefore, licensees should use printed form contracts cautiously. This text will describe the features of the Florida REALTORS®/Florida Bar contract. Both contracts are similar and are intended for use in routine transactions involving the sale of single-family dwellings or unimproved real property. If a licensee is involved in any one of the following types of transactions, the contracts are not suitable:

- Business purchase or sale
- Construction or improvements contract
- Contract for deed (installment contract, agreement for deed)
- Exchange agreement (contract for exchange of real property)
- Lease with option to buy
- Option contract (to be described later in this chapter)
- Unique or complex transactions

If vacant land, other than a single-family vacant lot, is involved in a transaction, special provisions should be included in the contract concerning the concurrency status of the property for development purposes, as well as suitability for its intended use relative to the area's comprehensive plan.

Responsibility for Preparation

The sales contract is the most important instrument for closing a real estate transaction. Because it is the final agreement after all the offers and negotiations that have taken place, a licensee must be very careful when preparing it. Any time a licensee is not certain whether an attorney is required in preparing any special clause or type of contract, the best course of action is to advise the buyer and the seller to consult an experienced real estate attorney.

The sales associate and his employer may be held financially responsible for any mistakes in the agreement. If any errors, omissions, or ambiguities exist regarding material terms, the courts will not go outside the contents of the contract to determine intent. The licensee who prepared the contract will not be allowed to explain later intent that was not indicated in the contract contents. If the contract is vague and unenforceable, the result could be no transaction at all, loss of commission, and a possible civil lawsuit against the licensee.

"Time Is of the Essence" Provision

"Time is of the essence for all provisions of this Contract," a single sentence in Paragraph 18-F, has important legal effects. If a party fails to perform the duties or promises made within the exact time limits in the contract, an automatic default occurs. This default then creates a right of cancellation on the part of the other party (**voidable contract**).

In Practice

Because of the importance of meeting requirements with dates and times, licensees should:

- use realistic time periods,

- check that the time periods complement and are consistent with times in other blank spaces, and

- set up calendar deadlines in the file to monitor performance by the parties to the sales contract once it has been signed (see Figure 9.1).

FIGURE 9.1 ■ Stated Performance Dates

Some important contract performance dates and deadlines are in the following paragraphs:
- 2(b)   Additional deposit
- 3(a)   Time for acceptance
- 4   Closing date
- 8(b)   Financing period: time for buyer to qualify for and obtain financing
- 8(b)   Buyer to apply for financing
- 9(c)   Delivery of title evidence
- 10(d)   Buyer cancellation period for flood zone floor level problems
- 12(a)   Inspection period
- 12(c)(ii) WDO Inspection
- 12(e)   Walk-through inspection
- 16   Dispute resolution
- 18F   Effective date definitions
- Signature: Offer, counteroffer, and effective date of contract

Gathering Contract Data

Collecting the information required to complete all the entry blanks in the Florida REAL-TORS®/Florida Bar contract is a sizable task. Information may become available or should be obtained as the real estate licensee helps negotiate the contract. Once the licensee gathers the information, she must verify it for accuracy and currency. Including obsolete information in a contract may be more harmful to a successful closing than having insufficient information to complete the contract. The licensee should pay particular attention to and be sure to verify the following two categories of data:

1. *The owner/seller's name and address and the property's legal description.* MLS data, property appraiser information, and even listing agreements have been in error on occasion. Place more reliance on an existing or a prior **title insurance** policy, a deed, or a survey for the information.

2. *Financial information.* Financial data tend to change frequently and require last minute updating. Check with local lenders to make certain that times allowed for obtaining financial commitments are realistic and that the rates and terms contemplated actually are available.

PREPARING SALES CONTRACTS

While the following guidelines are provided as an aid in understanding and preparing each element in the Florida REALTORS®/Florida Bar Residential Contract for Sale and Purchase (see Appendix B), these instructions are generic in description and should apply to most other sales contracts. Each specific provision of the form is described separately to help licensees examine the contract thoroughly. Paragraph numbers in this section refer to contract paragraph numbers.

Residential Contract for Sale and Purchase

1. Parties

Seller: Seller's name(s) should be shown in the manner in which title is held, showing the marital status of each seller. You can get this information from the seller's title insurance policy or a copy of the recorded deed.

Residence: If a married person owns the property individually, you should obtain the signature of the spouse to avoid possible future litigation.

Joint Ownership: If the property is jointly owned, obtain the signatures of all joint owners. If a residence is located on the property, obtain the signatures of joint owners and their spouses.

Corporations, Partnerships, Estates, Trusts, and Use of Powers of Attorney: Each requires special attention and instructions. Seek broker or legal counsel, as appropriate.

Buyer: Buyer's name(s) should be shown in the same manner as the buyer wishes title to be taken at closing. Other points to consider include the following:

- Each buyer shown on the contract must execute the contract.
- If the buyer later desires to take title in some other manner and this is permitted by the contract, an appropriate assignment or amendment to the contract should be obtained at closing.
- Buyers often seek advice as to the manner in which they should take title to property—for example, tenancy by the entireties, tenants in common, and so on. If the buyer asks how title should be taken, advise him to see his attorney. Under no circumstances express an opinion.
- *Non–U.S. Corporations, U.S. Corporations, Partnerships, et cetera:* Seek broker or legal counsel, as appropriate.
- *Addresses and Telephone Numbers:* Include complete information concerning these items to make handling the transaction easier for all involved.
- *Address:* If the street address, city, and ZIP code are available, insert them. This may render an otherwise insufficient legal description legally sufficient.

1.   *Property Description:*

Material Term: The legal description of the property to be sold is an essential provision of the contract. A defective legal description can render the contract unenforceable.

Sufficiency Test: The classic test of the sufficiency of a legal description is whether a surveyor can locate the property by reference to the description used.

Reliable Information: Do not rely on tax roll descriptions. The tax rolls are filled with errors and abbreviated descriptions that could be regarded as legally insufficient. Also, do not rely on descriptions contained in MLS listing sheets because they may only repeat errors others have made. Instead, rely on copies of prior deeds, prior title insurance policies, or prior surveys.

Description Not Known at Time of Contract: If any question remains as to the property's exact location, size, or description, and if the question cannot be resolved before the execution of the contract, agreement must be reached as to the survey of the property and as to who will bear the expense of the survey. Furthermore, agreement must reflect that the contract will be amended to conform to the legal description. The buyer also should have the right to terminate the contract if the property location and size are not substantially as represented.

Easements, Other Interests: The legal description should include any interest in the property being conveyed—for example, private right-of-way or common elements. This information usually is found on the deed or title insurance policy.

Quantity: From the seller's point of view, references to exact acreage in the legal description should be avoided. This could give rise to a right on the part of the buyer either to cancel the contract or to reduce the purchase price should the actual acreage prove to be materially different.

Minimum Description Requirements—Platted Subdivision:

- County in which property is located
- Lot and block numbers
- Name of subdivision (include phase or unit if applicable)
- Plat book and page number of recorded plat

Minimum Description Requirements—Condominium:

- County in which property is located
- Condominium unit or parcel number
- Name of condominium complex
- Identification of common elements—for example, parking spaces and storage spaces, if applicable
- Recording information (official record book and page number) of original declaration of condominium and any amendments
- Reference to ground lease or recreational lease and recording information if applicable

Minimum Description Requirements—Unplatted Property:

- County in which property is located
- Legal description provided by survey or prior deed(s)
- Reference to section, township, and range

Improvements and Attachments: The contract includes all improvements and attached items, and further describes fixtures, built-in furnishings, built-in appliances, ceiling fans, light fixtures, attached wall-to-wall carpeting, rods, draperies, and other window coverings, refrigerators, ranges and ovens, storm shutters, and smoke detectors (unless any of these items are specifically excluded). It has a section to add other items of personal property. If personal property is to be included, you should prepare an accurate description. Because personal property may be regarded as a material term of the contract, inaccurate, incomplete, or insufficient descriptions can render the contract voidable or unenforceable. To reduce appraisal problems and potential sales tax liability, the contract has these words: "Personal property listed in this contract is included in the purchase price, has no contributory value, and shall be left for the buyer."

What to Include: In the normal residential transaction, a detailed inventory of all personal property (with defects disclosed if applicable) should be prepared and attached to the contract. The list should include all kitchen equipment and appliances, plus other equipment and appliances, such as outside television antennas and satellite dishes, pool equipment, lawn furniture, and other easily removable fixtures. Quantify items where applicable. Failure to provide an accurate and complete inventory of all property included in the sale can lead to closing day problems, and the broker may have to make up any difference to close the transaction.

Florida Sales Tax on Personal Property: The Florida Department of Revenue has made several rulings on the tax liability of personal property included in the sale of real property. If itemized in the sales contract, with a separately stated value for each item, sales tax must be paid. No sales tax is due if the contract simply lists the property, such as a "refrigerator, range, microwave, and washer/dryer combination."

2. Purchase Price:

Fixed Purchase Price: The format of the preprinted contract calls for a fixed purchase price to be expressed in monetary terms using U.S. dollars.

Variable Price: If the full purchase price cannot be expressed in monetary terms, the manner in which it might be determined accurately should be stated in the contract in an addendum. For example, if acreage is involved and the parties agree on a price per acre, that price per acre should be set forth in an addendum (under "Special Clauses," check "Addendum is attached") together with a provision for an accurate survey determination. Whenever an addendum is used, it should have the date of the original contract, the complete names of the parties, and a complete legal description. It also must be dated and signed by the parties.

Method of Payment: The subparagraphs set forth the manner in which the purchase price is to be paid. The sum total of the monetary amounts set forth in these subparagraphs should equal the purchase price.

DISCUSSION EXERCISE 9.2

You are writing a contract for the purchase of a tract of land that is to be subdivided. The parties mark on the actual property lines where the division is to be made but can only estimate the size of the property at about 24 acres. Both parties agree on a price of $12,500 per acre.

Write a special clause that will set forth the parties' agreement and be legally binding.

Deposit Received:

2(a): With the amount of the deposit, the date, and the escrow agent. The deposit is subject to collection, which means the funds have been fully deposited into the account of the escrow agent.

1   *2(b):* This line is used when the payment of the deposit is split between the initial
2   deposit and an additional deposit. Typically, the second deposit is much larger than the
3   initial deposit. The amount of the additional deposit and the date or the number of days
4   within which it must be made should be inserted. The contract allows the seller to recover
5   not only the initial deposit but also any unpaid deposit. If the buyer defaults by failing to
6   make the additional deposit, the seller is faced with having to initiate litigation to recover
7   the balance. While the seller has an alternate remedy of specific performance, the seller's
8   best remedy in the event of buyer default is a forfeiture of the deposit.

9   *2(c):* Enter the amount of total financing in this line. It can be shown as a dollar
10   amount or as a percentage, but a dollar amount is usually better to determine whether the
11   balance to close is correctly added.

12   *2(d):* This line can be used for items that are not cash or financing. For example, it
13   might be a boat taken as part of the purchase price.

14   *2(e):* State the balance of the cash to be paid after deducting from the purchase price
15   the cash deposit, financing, and other payments. Note that this figure does not include
16   closing costs, prepaid items, or prorations. The contract requires that the funds be by wire
17   or by other collected funds. "Collected" means any checks, including deposits, must have
18   become actually and finally collected and deposited in the account of escrow agent or
19   closing agent.

3. Time for Acceptance of Offer and Counteroffers; Effective Date:

21   *(a):* If the contract is not signed and delivered to all parties by the date entered in the
22   offer, the offer is void and the deposit is to be returned to the buyer. If a date is not
23   inserted, counteroffers will be void if not signed within two days.

24   *(b):* The effective date of the contract is the date that the last of the parties initialed or
25   signed the latest offer.

4. Closing Date:

27   The closing date should be set for a reasonable period after any conditions have been
28   satisfied and the title evidence delivered.

DISCUSSION EXERCISE 9.3

You are writing a contract for the sale of a 160-acre farm and home. All parties have agreed that the buyer should have 40 days from the contract date to
produce a written commitment for financing the purchase.

What would be an optimum time for the contract closing date?

---

5. Extension of Closing Date:

30   *(a):* Closing date may be extended up to seven days to satisfy Truth in Lending Act (TILA)
31   requirements.

32   *(b):* If extreme weather or other "Force Majeure" disrupts closing, or if insurance cover-
33   age is not available, closing may be delayed up to three days after these items become
34   available.

6. Occupancy and Possession:

(a) Seller must deliver occupancy and possession free of tenants, occupants, and future tenancies. Seller must have removed all trash and shall deliver all keys, garage door openers, access devices, and codes to buyer.

(b) If the property is subject to a lease, the seller must deliver a copy of the lease within five days of the effective date. Buyer has five days to review the lease terms, and may cancel the contract during that period.

7. Assignability:

The contract allows three options for assignability:

1. Buyer may assign the contract and be released from liability.
2. Buyer may assign the contract but will not be released from liability.
3. Buyer may not assign the contract. It's a bad idea to let the buyer assign the contract and be released from liability, in effect walking away from the contract.

In Practice

If the buyer assigns the contract without liability

It's a bad idea to let the buyer assign the contract and be released from liability, in effect walking away from the contract. Make the buyer keep "skin in the game."

8. Financing:

There are several options that can be selected in this section:

(a) A cash transaction with no financing contingency

(b) A financing commitment no later than the date specified or the closing date, whichever is sooner, by a new loan (fill in the amount or percentage of value) with a contingency of getting a specific rate, if that is inserted into the blank

(c) Assumption of an existing loan

(d) Seller financing

In Practice

Filling in a specific interest rate may cause some problems.

First, a small upward fluctuation in rates may give the buyer a free out. Second, if the buyer wants out based on the rate, the seller might cry, "You can pay points and get that rate! I won't give back the earnest money!" What'll you do then?

Prompt Application: The number of days the buyer will have to make an application is inserted. Except under unusual circumstances, it should be possible for the buyer to make an application for the mortgage almost immediately. The broker or sales associate should ensure that the buyer proceeds diligently to make a loan application. Keep in mind that paragraph 11 of the contract makes time of the essence, and failure to make a timely application may be a default.

In Practice

Monitor the buyer.

You should make sure the buyer applies on time, or the seller may declare a default and require the buyer to forfeit the deposit. If additional time is needed to obtain a loan commitment and the parties agree, get a written amendment, signed by the parties, to extend the time.

Financing Contingency: If the buyer cannot qualify for the loan in time after making all necessary good-faith efforts, if the buyer is turned down, or if the appraisal is too low to get the financing, the buyer may elect not to proceed, return all seller's documents, and, after all interested parties agree, get the deposit back.

Know the Mortgage Market: All active licensees should have current information on the local mortgage market, including data on available interest rates (fixed and adjustable), points, time for processing applications, and so on.

Contingency Should Be Broad: Whether the buyer or the seller is the principal, make certain that the financing contingency clause describes a mortgage that is obtainable by the buyer.

Time to Get Commitment: The number of days the buyer has to obtain a loan commitment is sometimes based on how much time the seller will give the buyer to find financing. In any event, the broker or sales associate should know approximately how long local institutions take to process loan applications. Then a reasonable period should be inserted.

Type of Mortgage: A mortgage loan can be obtained based on either a fixed rate or an adjustable rate, and the appropriate box should be checked. If the buyer has not decided, the third block should be checked, indicating that the buyer will seek a commitment for either a fixed-rate or an adjustable-rate loan. If the buyer seeks a different type of mortgage, address this in an addendum.

Principal Amount: The principal amount of the third-party mortgage that the buyer seeks is inserted. Licensees should have a working knowledge of what is available in the local financial market.

9. Closing Costs

(a) **Costs to be Paid by Seller:** This section shows the expenses to be paid by the seller, including taxes on the deed; documentary stamps on the deed; and repairs up to 1.5% for repairs on warranted items, wood-destroying organism treatment, and costs associated with permits.

(b) **Costs to be Paid by Buyer:** Buyer agrees to pay taxes on notes and mortgages and recording fees on deed and financing statements. Buyer also agrees to pay for lender's title insurance, inspections, survey, and flood insurance.

(c) **Title Evidence and Insurance:** This section lets the parties determine what type of title evidence is appropriate and who will pay for title insurance.

(d) **Survey:** Buyer may have property surveyed at buyer's expense.

(e) **Home Warranty:** The parties may agree on a homeowners' warranty and who will pay for it.

(f) **Special Assessments**

10. Disclosures:

This section covers disclosures such as radon gas, permits, mold, flood zones, energy disclosure, lead-based paint, homeowner's association, ad valorem taxes, and FIRPTA withholding. The sellers must also disclose all known defects that materially affect the value of the property other than those that are readily observable.

11. Property Maintenance:

This section requires the seller to keep the property in the same condition until closing except required repairs.

12. Property Inspection and Repair:

(a) **Inspection Period:** Inspections must be completed within 15 days or at least five days before closing. If the property sale does not close, Buyer shall repair property damaged by the inspections and give Seller paid receipts for all work done.

(b) **General Property Inspection and Repair:**

(i) **General Inspection:** Buyer shall notify seller of any items not functioning correctly as noted by a licensed home inspector.

(ii) **Property Condition:** Ceiling, roof, exterior and interior walls, doors windows, and foundation shall be free of leaks, water damage, or structural damage. Pool equipment, major appliances, heating and cooling, mechanical, electrical, security, sprinkler, septic and plumbing systems must be in working order. Torn screens, fogged windows, and missing roof tiles shall be repaired or replaced by seller. Seller need not repair cosmetic items.

(iii) **General Property Repairs:** The seller is to pay for repairs up to the general repairs limit as shown in the contract. If the amount is higher, the seller may elect to pay the excess; or the buyer can designate which repairs are to be done so that the total does not exceed the contractual limit; or if neither parties delivers written notice to the other, then either party may terminate the contract.

(c) **Wood Destroying Organism (WDO) Inspection and Repair:**

(i) Property may be inspected by a licensed WDO inspector. If infestation or damage is found, the buyer must notify the seller within the contract's time limits.

(ii) Seller is to pay for repairs up to the general repairs limit as shown in the contract. If the amount is higher, the seller may elect to pay the excess; or the buyer can designate which repairs are to be done so that the total does not exceed the contractual limit; or if neither parties delivers written notice to the other, then either party may terminate the contract.

(d) **Inspection and Close-Out of Building Permits**

(e) **Walk-Through Inspection/Re-Inspection:** The buyer may perform a walk-through inspection solely to confirm that all items of personal property are on the property, to verify that seller has maintained the property as required, and has made required repairs.

13. Escrow Agent:

This paragraph authorizes the escrow agent to accept and disburse funds and releases the escrow agent from liability unless there has been willful breach of the contract or gross negligence. If the escrow agent has to interplead the subject matter with a court, the court costs and attorney's fees may be paid from the deposit.

14. Professional Advice; Broker Liability:

This section advises the buyer to get legal and other professional advice. The buyer agrees to look solely to the seller for property condition, square footage, and other facts that affect property value. If the buyer or the seller makes misstatements, the broker is entitled to collect court costs and attorney's fees to defend against damage claims.

15. Default:

(a) Buyer Default: If the buyer defaults, the seller can collect the deposits as liquidated damages, agreeing to pay the broker 50% of the deposits up to the full brokerage fee.

(b) Seller Default: If the seller defaults, buyer can either get the binder back and cancel the contract or seek damages, or can sue for specific performance. Seller will also owe the broker a commission.

16. Dispute Resolution:

(a) In case of disputes over the escrow deposits, the buyer and the seller have 10 days to resolve the dispute.

(b) In disputes other than over escrow deposits, the parties will attempt to settle the dispute by mediation, after which they must seek a resolution in the courts.

17. Attorney Fees; Costs: The parties will split the mediator's fee and pay their own costs, expenses and attorney fees. In any litigation, the winning party is entitled to collect all costs and fees from the other party.

18. Standards:

Some of the more important standards are shown here.

Effective Date; Time:

This paragraph makes the effective date the date that the last of the parties initialed or signed the latest offer. It also has the wording that "time is of the essence." Time periods do not include Saturdays, Sundays, or holidays, and the periods end at 5 pm.

Notices:

Notices may be made by mail, personal delivery, or electronic media. The paragraph emphasizes that if the buyer does not make the required notices about contingencies to the seller on time, the contingency will no longer exist.

Complete Agreement:

Except for brokerage agreements, this is the only agreement between the parties. Handwritten portions of the agreement supersede preprinted portions if the two conflict. This sentence protects the contract if a licensee fails to delete an inconsistent provision covered in handwritten clauses or to protect any riders or addenda that are designed to show the parties' true intent. To know whether it is necessary to revoke, amend, or replace a printed provision, a licensee must know the content of the printed provisions.

19. Addenda:

Licensee should check the appropriate boxes for addenda that apply to this agreement. The Comprehensive Addendum to the Residential Sale and Purchase Contract has many of the most common clauses. Various laws and regulations require that some riders be attached to the contract and that other riders expand and clarify contract terms. All of the riders listed are available as preprinted forms.

20. Additional Terms:

This is the area for special clauses specific to the needs of this particular transaction.

Brokers:

Parties agree in this paragraph that the listing and cooperating brokers are the only brokers entitled to compensation. The seller and the buyer direct the closing agent to disburse brokerage fees according to the brokerage agreements and the cooperating broker arrangements for commission splits.

Practicing with the Residential Contract for Sale and Purchase

This discussion was meant to familiarize the student with some of the contract language. In chapter 10, the student will have an opportunity to complete another Florida REALTORS®/Florida Bar Residential Contract for Sale and Purchase, along with a cost disclosure statement, and prepare a counteroffer.

OPTION CONTRACTS

An **option contract** is a contract between a property owner (optionor) and another (optionee) in which the optionee, for a consideration, has the right (not the obligation) to purchase or lease the property at a specified price during a designated period. To be enforceable in Florida, an option must contain all of the essential elements of a contract.

Strictly speaking, it is important to distinguish between an option contract and an option (in actual practice, the terms are often used interchangeably). If you offer to sell your house to a friend for $100,000 and your friend says she wants to think about the offer for a day or so, your friend might have an option, but she does not have an option contract. Therefore, you could revoke your offer to sell and no breach of contract would occur because no contract exists when there is a lack of consideration (exchange of promises). Had your friend paid you $1,000 in consideration of a 30-day or 60-day period to decide about your offer and you agreed to those terms, an option contract would have been concluded. The consideration given legally may be applied as part of the purchase price in the event the option is **exercised**.

An option creates a contractual right; it does not create an estate in the optioned property. When first written and executed, an option contract is unilateral. The owner/optionor is obligated to sell if given proper notice by the buyer/optionee, but the buyer/optionee is not obligated to purchase and may allow the option to expire. Options frequently are used to give a developer or a buyer time to resolve problems related to financing, zoning, title, or feasibility before committing to purchase or lease. Options also are useful instruments in the land assemblage process.

In addition to the required information in an option contract, other provisions should or may be included. For example, a statement of the method of notice required to exercise the option normally is provided. Also, some provision should be included concerning the option money (the consideration) if the option is not exercised. Unless expressly prohibited by the wording of the terms, an option normally is assignable.

Option contracts often are written with less care and attention than they deserve. Keep in mind that an option contract is converted into a sales contract when the option is exercised. However, if the option fails to include all the terms material to the transaction and leaves some terms or decisions for future agreement, the option contract normally is not enforceable. For example, if the option calls for a purchase money mortgage as part of the method of payment and does not include the mortgage interest rate or the duration, courts normally would refuse to enforce the contract. Generally, having a competent real estate attorney construct the option agreement reduces the broker's liability.

DISCUSSION EXERCISE 9.4

Oscar paid Silvio $2,000 for a 30-day option to buy Silvio's house for $160,000. Two weeks later, Silvio sold his house to Benny for $175,000.

Can Oscar enforce his option and require that the property be sold to him? Why or why not?

The optionee may wish to record the option. This establishes the optionee's rights back to the option date and gives priority over subsequent rights of third parties. Good title practice requires that a release of option be recorded later in the event a recorded option is not exercised. Otherwise, the expired option may create a cloud on the title. Many times, an option is constructed to include a defeasance clause stating that the recorded option will automatically cease to be a lien on the property upon expiration of the exercise date.

SUMMARY

- A contract is a legally enforceable agreement that can be classified in a number of ways, such as bilateral, unilateral, express, implied, executory, executed, quasi, voidable, and void.

- Each classification has specific legal effects in a court of law.

- The statute of frauds requires that an agreement for the sale of real property or an agreement that cannot be performed by both parties within one year after the contract date must be evidenced by a written document. Two common exceptions are:

  - executed contracts, and
  - partial performance. If partial payment has been made and the buyer has
    - taken possession, or
    - made improvements.

- The licensee is permitted to "prepare" three types of real estate contracts:

  - Listing
  - Sales
  - Option contracts

- A sales contract is an agreement for the sale and purchase of real property.

- The various provisions and standards contained in a sales contract include

  - information on the parties to the agreement,
  - a legal description of the property,
  - the purchase price and method of payment,
  - deadline times and dates,
  - information about financing, and
  - other contract riders and disclosures.

- If the term "time is of the essence" is in the contract, all parties must perform within the time limits of the agreement, or will be in default.

- An option contract is a contract between a property owner and another person (optionee) in which the optionee, for a consideration, has the right (not the obligation) to purchase or lease the property at a specified price during a designated period.

REVIEW QUESTIONS

1. Your neighbor promises to paint your house while you are on vacation. You tell the neighbor you would like him to paint it white. At that point, you and your neighbor have
   a. an implied contract.
   b. no contractual agreement.
   c. an employment contract.
   d. an option contract.

2. A good practice when writing an offer to purchase a house owned separately by the wife is to
   a. have a title search performed before allowing the seller to accept the offer.
   b. require that the seller's signature be notarized.
   c. insist that two witnesses sign the contract.
   d. have both the wife and her spouse sign the contract.

3. The Florida REALTORS®/Florida Bar Residential Contract for Sale and Purchase is LEAST suitable for transactions involving the sale of a
   a. single-family home.
   b. condominium dwelling unit.
   c. vacant residential site.
   d. business.

4. A man is trying to close on his new home. The required closing date was August 26. The previous day, a hurricane in the Caribbean caused insurance underwriters to suspend writing new policies. If the man fails to close on the 26th, what effect will this have on his Florida REALTORS®/Florida Bar contract?
   a. His contract will be void.
   b. His contract will be voidable by the seller.
   c. He has three days to close after the suspension is lifted.
   d. He has five days to close after the suspension is lifted.

5. When "time is of the essence," failure of any party to perform within established time limits can result in automatic
   a. cancellation of the contract.
   b. liability for damages.
   c. default by the tardy party.
   d. forfeiture of all contractual rights and deposits.

6. When a licensee verifies contract information, one of the preferred sources regarding the owner/seller and the legal description is
   a. the MLS databank.
   b. a previous title insurance policy.
   c. the listing agreement.
   d. the latest appraisal report.

7. Which statement is FALSE regarding a violation of the statute of frauds?
   a. It may not constitute an illegal act, but it invalidates a sales contract.
   b. It carries with it prescribed times for enforcement.
   c. It questions the contract's validity.
   d. It normally has to do with whether a contract is in writing.

8. What is FALSE about a valid real estate sales contract?
    a. It is legally enforceable in a court of law.
    b. It has five essential elements.
    c. It requires witnessing.
    d. It deals with the transfer of an interest in real property.

9. Sales tax liability is due on a real estate purchase contract when personal property is
    a. described in a contract.
    b. itemized and a separate value for each item is placed in the contract.
    c. said to add value.
    d. said to be left for the convenience of the parties.

10. The Florida REALTORS®/Florida Bar Residential Contract for Sale and Purchase requires that the initial deposit is to be
    a. paid either in U.S. currency or Euros.
    b. held in escrow subject to collection.
    c. held in escrow subject to clearance.
    d. made within five days of effective date of contract.

11. A prospective buyer signs a sale and purchase contract form offering to pay the seller $175,000. The seller counteroffers for the full list price of $190,000. The buyer refuses the counteroffer. Later, the seller signs the original $175,000 offer. Which is correct?
    a. No enforceable contract exists because the counteroffer terminated the original offer.
    b. The contract is enforceable.
    c. The seller owes the broker a commission.
    d. The buyer owes the broker a commission.

12. A sales associate wrote a special clause into paragraph 20 of the Florida REALTORS®/Florida Bar Residential Contract for Sale and Purchase that contradicted one of the preprinted clauses in Paragraph 4. The special clause as written
    a. has no effect.
    b. has no effect because she failed to cross out the preprinted clause.
    c. is valid and binding.
    d. was improper and is considered unauthorized practice of law.

13. What is the classic test of the sufficiency of a legal description?
    a. It is the one used on the property tax bill.
    b. It is the one recorded in the clerk's office.
    c. It includes the address as shown by the U.S. Postal Service.
    d. A surveyor can locate the property by reference to the description.

14. Under the Florida REALTORS®/Florida Bar Residential Contract for Sale and Purchase, the party responsible for a property tax increase because of a change in ownership is the
    a. buyer.
    b. seller.
    c. both parties equally.
    d. broker, if the broker did not specifically write the provision into the contract.

15.   The minimum description requirement in a contract for a platted subdivision does
       NOT include the
       a.   lot and block number.
       b.   number of acres in the parcel.
       c.   plat book and page number of recorded plats.
       d.   county in which the property is located.

16.   The effective date of the Florida REALTORS®/Florida Bar contract is the date
       a.   the buyer signs the contract and gives the earnest money deposit.
       b.   the seller signs the contract.
       c.   the transaction will close.
       d.   that the most recent of the buyer or the seller signs the contract and communi-
            cates it to the other.

17.   If the buyer asks to have occupancy of a house before closing, the BEST suggestion
       from the sales associate to the seller would be
       a.   "Let's put the early occupancy in the contract so that if the sale falls through,
            the buyer easily can be required to vacate."
       b.   "We should require that the buyer give an additional deposit of up to $1,000."
       c.   "Don't let them move in if you can avoid it."
       d.   "Because I know the buyers, I'm sure it will be OK."

18.   An option contract is
       a.   bilateral and binds the optionor.
       b.   bilateral and binds the optionee.
       c.   unilateral and binds the optionor.
       d.   unilateral and binds the optionee.

19.   A sales associate drafts a six-month option agreement for a buyer on a commer-
       cial property. The buyer pays $2,000 option money. The sales associate writes,
       "Terms of owner financing will be negotiated when this option is exercised." When
       the buyer later exercises the option, the seller wants a higher interest rate and a
       shorter loan term than the buyer will accept. In this case, which is correct?
       a.   The buyer can sue and the court will force the seller to a lower interest rate.
       b.   If the buyer sues, the court probably will decide that the option contract is not
            enforceable because it is too vague.
       c.   The seller can sue the buyer and force him to close at the higher interest rate.
       d.   The parties must go to binding arbitration.

20.   A man purchases an option on property. He requires that the option contract be
       acknowledged and recorded. The seller asks his agent about the best way to pro-
       ceed. How should the agent answer?
       a.   Option contracts cannot be recorded under Florida law.
       b.   Don't ever sell an option because they never close.
       c.   The option should include a defeasance clause stating that the recorded option
            will automatically cease to be a lien on the property upon expiration of the
            exercise date.
       d.   Option contracts are illegal in Florida.

10

WRITING AND PRESENTING THE OFFER

LEARNING OBJECTIVES

When you finish reading this chapter, you will be able to:

- ■ describe the different parts of the Loan Estimate,
- ■ list the steps involved in presenting an offer,
- ■ list the three possible seller responses to an offer, and
- ■ describe the process involved when a seller makes a counteroffer.

KEY TERMS

counteroffer

OVERVIEW

Licensees hope that at the end of the showing process, the buyers will have found the right house. Sometimes, the buyers will tell the licensee, "This is the house; we'd like to make an offer." More often, a buyer will say, "This is our favorite so far, but we'd like to think it over." The professional licensee can help the buyer make the decision by ensuring that the buyer has been preapproved by a lender and by describing the process of making an offer. Chapter 10 will help sales associates become familiar with that decision-making process.

HELPING THE BUYER TO DECIDE TO MAKE AN OFFER

A buyer who feels information is lacking may be reluctant to make an offer. What if I don't have enough cash? What if the lender turns me down? Could I lose my deposit?

A professional sales associate can ensure that the buyer will have this information before showing properties. The steps are to:

- get the buyer preapproved by a lender, and get a Loan Estimate,
- show the buyer the important financial aspects of the purchase, and
- describe the sales process to the buyer.

Settlement Statement (HUD-1) and Good Faith Estimate (GFE) Have Gone Away

**Forms
To Go**

For more than 30 years, lenders were required to give the Truth in Lending Act (TILA) disclosure and the Good Faith Estimate (GFE) disclosure to consumers when they applied for a mortgage. For the closing, the title closing agent would prepare the TILA and the Settlement Statement (HUD-1). Two different federal agencies developed these forms separately, under two federal statutes. The information on the forms was overlapping, inconsistent, and confusing.

As directed by the Dodd-Frank Act, the Consumer Financial Protection Bureau combined the four forms into two. The GFE was combined with the TILA and is now called the Loan Estimate (see Appendix B). The Loan Estimate must be given to the borrower within three days of the loan application. The HUD-1 was combined with the TILA and is now called the Closing Disclosure. It must be given to the borrower at least three days before the closing.

The changes were effective for loan applications made on or after October 3, 2015, significantly changing the way real estate professionals prepare for closings.

The Closing Disclosure will be discussed in Chapter 13.

CASE STUDY

WRITING THE REAL ESTATE CONTRACT

You are a sales associate for Sunny Hills Realty, Inc. In March of this year, a past customer referred Bob and Sandy Smith to you. At your request, they visited Security Atlantic Mortgage Company, which preapproved them for a mortgage loan of up to $200,000. They have shown you a copy of the Loan Estimate the lender gave them (see Figure 10.1). They tell you they have enough cash for a 20% down payment (80% loan) in addition to their settlement costs, so you can show them homes in the $250,000 range ($200,000 ÷ 80%).

FIGURE 10.1 ■ Case Study Loan Estimate

Save this Loan Estimate to compare with your Closing Disclosure.

Loan Estimate

DATE ISSUED February 18, 201_
APPLICANTS Robert Smith and Sandy Smith
A married couple

PROPERTY 1854 West Chancery Ct. Destin FL 32541
SALE PRICE $250,000.00

LOAN TERM 30 Years
PURPOSE Purchase
PRODUCT Fixed Rate
LOAN TYPE ☑Conventional ☐FHA ☐VA ☐_____
LOAN ID # 1234567
RATE LOCK ☐NO ☑YES, until April 18, 201_

Before closing, your interest rate, points, and lender credits can change unless you lock the interest rate. All other estimated closing costs expire on March 1, 201_

Loan Terms

		Can this amount increase after closing?
Loan Amount	$200,000	**NO**
Interest Rate	4.5%	**NO**
Monthly Principal & Interest *See Projected Payments below for your Estimated Total Monthly Payment*	$1,013.37	**NO**
		Does the loan have these features?
Prepayment Penalty		**NO**
Balloon Payment		**NO**

Projected Payments

Payment Calculation

Principal & Interest	$1,013.37
Mortgage Insurance	+ $0
Estimated Escrow *Amount can increase over time*	+ $654.16
Estimated Total Monthly Payment	$1,667.53

Estimated Taxes, Insurance & Assessments *Amount can increase over time*	$654.16 a month	**This estimate includes** ☑Property Taxes ☑Homeowner's Insurance ☐Other:	**In escrow?** YES YES

See Section G on page 2 for escrowed property costs. You must pay for other property costs separately.

Costs at Closing

Estimated Closing Costs	$10,864	Includes $3,150 in Loan Costs + $5,664 in Other Costs − $0 in Lender Credits. *See page 2 for details.*
Estimated Cash to Close	$55,864	Includes Closing Costs. *See Calculating Cash to Close on page 2 for details.*

Visit **www.consumerfinance.gov/mortgage-estimate** for general information and tools.

FIGURE 10.1 ■ **Case Study Loan Estimate (continued)**

Closing Cost Details

Loan Costs

A. Origination Charges	$2,000
1 % of Loan Amount (Points)	$2,000

B. Services You Cannot Shop For	$100
Appraisal Fee	$55
Credit Report Fee	$25
Courier Fee	$20

C. Services You Can Shop For	$1,050
Survey	$350
Title Services	$700

D. TOTAL LOAN COSTS (A + B + C)	$3,150

Other Costs

E. Taxes and Other Government Fees	$1,153
Recording Fees and Other Taxes	$53
Transfer Taxes	$1,100

F. Prepaids	$2,469
Homeowner's Insurance Premium (12 months)	$2,050
Mortgage Insurance Premium (months)	
Prepaid Interest ($24.66 per day for 17 days @ *)	$419
Property Taxes (months)	

* Assuming settlement on 3/15

G. Initial Escrow Payment at Closing			$3,242
Homeowner's Insurance	$170.83	per month for 2 mo.	$342
Mortgage Insurance	$0	per month for 0 mo.	
Property Taxes	$483.33	per month for 6 mo.	$2,900

H. Other	$850
Owner's Title Policy (optional)	$850

I. TOTAL OTHER COSTS (E + F + G + H)	$7,714

J. TOTAL CLOSING COSTS	10,864
D + I	
Lender Credits	

Calculating Cash to Close

Total Closing Costs (J)	$10,864
Closing Costs Financed (Paid from your Loan Amount)	
Down Payment/Funds from Borrower	$50,000
Deposit	($5,000)
Funds for Borrower	
Seller Credits	
Adjustments and Other Credits	
Estimated Cash to Close	**$55,864**

FIGURE 10.1 ■ **Case Study Loan Estimate (continued)**

Additional Information About This Loan

LENDER	Security Atlantic Savings Association	**MORTGAGE BROKER**	N/A
NMLS/___ LICENSE ID	12345	**NMLS/___ LICENSE ID**	
LOAN OFFICER	Jess Linder	**LOAN OFFICER**	
NMLS/___ LICENSE ID	76543	**NMLS/___ LICENSE ID**	
EMAIL	JessLinder@xyzlender.com	**EMAIL**	
PHONE	850 555 4543	**PHONE**	

Comparisons

Use these measures to compare this loan with other loans.

In 5 Years	$62,802	Total you will have paid in principal, interest, mortgage insurance, and loan costs.
	$17,684	Principal you will have paid off.
Annual Percentage Rate (APR)	4.594%	Your costs over the loan term expressed as a rate. This is not your interest rate.
Total Interest Percentage (TIP)	82.4%	The total amount of interest that you will pay over the loan term as a percentage of your loan amount.

Other Considerations

Appraisal
We may order an appraisal to determine the property's value and charge you for this appraisal. We will promptly give you a copy of any appraisal, even if your loan does not close. You can pay for an additional appraisal for your own use at your own cost.

Assumption
If you sell or transfer this property to another person, we
☐ will allow, under certain conditions, this person to assume this loan on the original terms.
☑ will not allow assumption of this loan on the original terms.

Homeowner's Insurance
This loan requires homeowner's insurance on the property, which you may obtain from a company of your choice that we find acceptable.

Late Payment
If your payment is more than _15_ days late, we will charge a late fee of _5% of the_ _monthly principal and interest payment_

Refinance
Refinancing this loan will depend on your future financial situation, the property value, and market conditions. You may not be able to refinance this loan.

Servicing
We intend
☐ to service your loan. If so, you will make your payments to us.
☑ to transfer servicing of your loan.

Confirm Receipt

By signing, you are only confirming that you have received this form. You do not have to accept this loan because you have signed or received this form.

_____   _____
Applicant Signature   Date   Co-Applicant Signature   Date

LOAN ESTIMATE   PAGE 3 OF 3 • LOAN ID #

You learned that they wanted a three- or four-bedroom home with two baths and a two-car garage. They wanted a home in the northeast less than five miles from the regional hospital, where Bob is a pharmacist.

You described the entire process of buying a home, from showing homes through moving into their new home using the homebuying process timeline in Figure 8.5.

You discussed the important clauses in the purchase agreement, and gave them copies of the paperwork along with a transaction broker notice.

Finding the Right Home

You set a showing appointment for Saturday and begin previewing homes that might satisfy your customers' requirements. You find five houses that seem like real possibilities; one of them is perfect. It is located at 816 Harrison Court, a quiet street in a well-kept neighborhood, just two miles from the hospital. The owners have kept it in wonderful condition. And it has great "curb appeal." It was listed by Blue Sky Realty, Inc., and is priced at $255,000. Perfect! You make appointments with the sellers to show the homes.

On Saturday morning, you show the Smiths your favorite home first. They love everything about it. You give them a copy of the sellers' disclosure statement that was available on the kitchen counter. It has no apparent problems. After entering each house after that, it doesn't take long to walk through, because they love the first home. You suggest a return visit and clear it with the sellers. The sellers tell you they are going out for several hours and the house will be available most of the day. After returning to the home, you stay unobtrusive and let the Smiths discover more features of the home. They want to think it over.

Writing the Offer

You suggest that, even if they end up "sleeping" on the decision, it might be helpful to have the contract filled out. Bob says to make the paperwork out as though they were paying $245,000. Because Bob wants to see the backyard again, you suggest Bob and Sandy look around the property some more while you complete the paperwork.

You will ask the buyers to give you a good-faith deposit of $5,000. Based on previous conversations, the Smiths will want to be in the home in 20 days. Because the sellers are in town and because the market is so active, you will give them until 10 pm tonight to accept or reject the offer.

In Practice

Make the acceptance time short. The seller is more likely to decide quickly and not "shop" the offer.

You pull out the MLS data from the house that shows the following information:

Sellers' names: Larry and Wilma Palmer

Street address: 816 Harrison Court, Sunny Hills, FL

Legal description: Lot 18, Block C, Old Hills as recorded in book 126, page 368, Houser County.

Personal property included: range, draperies, rods, and window treatments (as shown by the MLS information). The Smiths also want to include the washer, dryer, and the riding lawn mower. You explain that these items are not included in the sale, but they want to try for them anyway.

Forms To Go

PRACTICE EXERCISE 10.1

Preparing the Florida REALTORS® Residential Sale and Purchase Contract.   Complete the Residential Sale and Purchase Contract (see Appendix B) with the information you have been given so far.

Just as you are finishing the contract, Sandy and Bob return to the kitchen. You ask if there is anything they want to do to the home after they buy it, and Bob says he wants to pour a concrete patio. At your request, they write a short note to the sellers about why they want to buy this house, and then both sign it.

You go over the cost-disclosure statement and attach it to the lender's loan estimate. Then you go over the contract form carefully. Sandy says it all looks good. You say, "You could go home and worry about this tonight, or I could take this to the seller and you might have great news to celebrate tonight. Wouldn't it be better if we went ahead?" Wait for the answer, because in many cases, the buyer will agree.

If the Smiths agree, ask them to:

1. approve the cost disclosure first,

2. sign a receipt for the sellers' property disclosure statement, and

3. approve the agreement with their signatures.

Ask for the good-faith deposit and clip all the paperwork together. To prepare them for a counteroffer, ask that they not be too disappointed if the seller does not accept the offer at $245,000. After dropping them off, you should immediately contact the listing agent, Hillary Jenkins.

Presenting the Offer

Hillary answers her mobile phone right away. After you tell her that you have an offer that expires at 10 pm, she asks whether you'd like to fax it to her office. Because you want to present the offer with her, you arrange to meet at her office 45 minutes before her appointment with the Palmers. You ask whether there are any other offers to be presented, and she says there are not. You request that you be called if that situation changes, and she agrees. In some cases, especially if you are a buyers' agent, the listing sales associate will be reluctant to let you present your offer. Explain that you will not stay during the discussions, but that it may be helpful if you tell them about the buyer, present the offer, and see whether they have any questions about the flexibility of the buyers, for example, on the closing date.

Hillary calls back and says she has an appointment with the Palmers at 7 pm and will see you at her office at 6:15 pm. Following are some suggestions that will prove helpful in presenting an offer to purchase:

- Present it with the listing agent. You are the only one who can answer questions about the buyers and give the buyers a "face" to the sellers. But this is top priority time and your buyer's dreams and lots of your money is riding on your performance.

- ■ If you are the listing associate, have the selling associate help you present. It also stops second-guessing about the quality of your presentation if the offer is not accepted.

- ■ If the other associate is a buyers' single agent, you should tell your sellers not to show reactions that may affect their negotiating position.

In Practice

Go with your offer. Teamwork will get it through.

If you are the listing sales associate, prepare your sellers for a low offer before the cooperating sales associate arrives to present the offer. If a seller has raised expectations, a low offer may insult the sellers and make it very difficult to put a transaction together.

If the parties are far apart on the offered price, try to keep the buyers and sellers from taking it personally. It is your job to be sure personalities are not a factor in the negotiations.

Going to the Sellers' House

You make extra copies of the offer, gather all the documents, and arrive at the Blue Sky Realty office at 6:15 pm. You show Hillary the bank's preapproval letter and give her a copy of the offer. If she has no questions about the offer, you ask if she'd like you to present it to the sellers and she agrees. She also suggests that after presenting the contract, if the sellers have no questions, that you might excuse yourself so they have time to discuss the offer. This is very gracious on her part because she will not ask to you leave; it will be your idea.

You go in separate cars to the house. Hillary waits outside so you can go in together.

In Practice

If it's a good offer, bring a Sold sign on top of your folder.

At the door, Hillary introduces you to the seller and takes charge, asking whether everyone can sit at the kitchen table. The sellers agree.

In Practice

While you're presenting, be sure to do the following:

- Be courteous to the cooperating sales associate—always. Nothing can derail the presentation of an offer more than distrust and dissension between the licensees.

- Don't give the offer out to the sellers until you have summarized the important parts. It is hard to maintain control if the parties are looking at all different parts of the contract, interrupting by asking questions.

- Cover all points of the agreement, making price last. Have all the buyers' requirements depend on "getting the price right."

- Make enough copies for everyone so they don't have to read over your shoulder.

- Give copies, never the original offer, so it isn't marked.

Hillary starts the presentation by complimenting you. You look at her with gratitude and admiration, understanding why she is successful.

She continues: "I'm going to let _____ tell you a little about the prospective buyers and go over the offer with you, if that's all right." The sellers nod in agreement and look in your direction.

In Practice

Following are tips in how to handle low offers carefully:

- If you are the listing associate and the selling associate brings in a very low offer, have the cooperating associate present the offer to your sellers.

- If the offer is low and the sellers are angry, let them vent their frustration before starting to work on a counteroffer.

"Hi, Mr. and Mrs. Palmer," you say. "I'd like to say how pleased I am to be working with Hillary again. You made a great choice when you listed your home with her. Before I go over the offer, I'd like to tell you a little about the buyers. Their names are Robert and Sandy Smith. Robert is a pharmacist at Sunny Hills Regional Hospital. They have two children, Mary, who's three, and Brett, who's one.

"They have owned a condominium since they've been married, so this is their first home. They have been approved for financing by the bank to buy your home. And they love it! They have written you a note about your house and why they want to buy it." Hand them the note (see Figure 10.2).

F I G U R E 10.2 ■ Handwritten Note

Dear Mr. and Mrs. Palmer,

We just want to tell you how much we love your home. We can tell that you love it too, by the way you keep it so beautiful.

We can't think of a home that would be better to raise our two young children in. Their names are Mary and Brett.

We hope you will let us have it.

And we hope you'll be happy in your new home, too.

Sandy Smith
Bob Smith

Mr. Palmer says, "They sound like pretty nice people, but let's see what they're willing to pay."

And you present the contract. Save the offered price until last. Ask whether they will let you cover the highlights before starting a discussion on any one item, and that you'll give them copies of the agreement in a moment. Then cover the contingencies first before talking about price.

"The buyers need to close and move in 20 days. I've spoken with the lender who says they can close it on time. They're including your refrigerator, range, washer and dryer, riding mower, and the window treatments. They're getting new financing and have been preapproved for their loan."

Now tell them the offer is $245,000. Reassure the sellers that the buyers' offer is not meant to insult them, but they can qualify to buy a $250,000 home and are hoping to keep $5,000 to build a concrete patio. Give statistics about sales: "Listings sell at 94% of list price," et cetera, so this offer is right on target.

In Practice

If the parties are far apart on the offered price, try to keep the buyers and the sellers from taking it personally. It is your job to be sure personalities are not a factor in the negotiations.

Tell the sellers that if they have no questions for you about the buyers or the offer, you'd like to excuse yourself to give them an opportunity to discuss the offer with Hillary. You can tell them you have some calls to make anyway and will do it from your car, so you'll be close by if any other questions arise.

Sellers' Responses to an Offer

Sellers who receive an offer on their home have the following three possible responses:

- Acceptance
- Rejection
- Counteroffer

Acceptance. Obviously, the selling sales associate hopes the response will be an acceptance. The offer is signed and becomes a contract between the buyer and the seller.

Rejection. If the price offered is very low, and is obviously a "fishing expedition," the seller may be advised to reject the offer outright. A better approach might be to reject the offer with an invitation to come back with a more serious offer. The market is currently a strong buyers' market in Florida, so sellers should be cautious in rejecting offers, and even when making counteroffers. Many sellers have refused to accept low offers and later regretted missing the opportunity to sell. As their counselor, be certain that the sellers are aware of market conditions.

Counteroffer. If the offer is not acceptable but is close enough to be considered serious, a **counteroffer** form should be used. A counteroffer keeps the parties "at the table," making continued negotiations easier.

Keep notes when the sellers are discussing the pros and cons of the offer. When the sellers reach a decision on the terms of the counteroffer, use a counteroffer form rather than marking on the contract. This is a good idea for legibility and enforceability purposes.

In 15 minutes, Hillary comes to the door and motions you inside. Back at the table, Hillary says, "Mr. and Mrs. Palmer want the Smiths to have this home, but they want to make several changes. First, they feel the house is worth the asking price of $255,000, but they will split the difference with the buyers at a price of $250,000. They will include the range and window treatments but want to take the other items of personal property. Also, because they cannot get into their new home, the closing date will have to be 30 days from now. Do you think you can help me prepare several copies of the counteroffer? "

Forms To Go

PRACTICE EXERCISE 10.2

Preparing the Counteroffer.   Enter the following information in paragraph 2 of the Florida REALTORS® Counter Offer form (see Appendix B).

Clause	Counteroffer Terms
1.	Washer, dryer, and riding lawn mower are not included in the sale.
2.	Price shall be $250,000.
3.	Closing date shall be 30 days from the date of this contract.

In paragraph 3 of the counteroffer, check that the counteroffer must be delivered to the seller or the seller's licensee within 24 hours from 11 pm on October 18.

After the counteroffer has been prepared and signed by the sellers, all it will take to make the counteroffer into a contract will be the buyers' signatures on the counteroffer.

You say to the sellers, "Thank you all so much for your courtesy. I'll do everything I can to sell your home. Hillary, I'll call you as soon as I've spoken with the buyers."

In Practice

Work the contract until it's either accepted or dead. Don't stop working it because it's nearly midnight. Sellers want to sell and buyers want to buy, and they respect professionals who work hard. Working late brings an urgency that gets many offers accepted.

When you arrive at the Smiths' house, tell them you have great news. "The sellers came off their price by $5,000! Let's go over their counteroffer."

They agree to all the terms of the counteroffer. You change the cost disclosure statement to reflect the new price and have them sign the counteroffer. Call Hillary and tell her you'll take the counteroffer to her office or her house, and she should get it to the sellers. She agrees.

You have sold the house and made several people very happy.

In Practice

If you are the listing associate and there are multiple offers from both your company and other companies, get your broker involved. If your company has an offer to present, tell the other associates not to fax their offers. You don't want to know what they have so you won't be suspected of "shopping" the offer. The broker should meet with all the associates before the presentation to establish the ground rules. The broker should arrange for the selling associates to present their individual offers in the order received. Everything should be scrupulously fair and transparent.

SUMMARY

- A licensee should practice preparing offers on different types of properties with a variety of financing programs. Once the practice offer is written, you should role-play the explanation of the offer. Practice will give you the skills to help you get more transactions to the closing table.
- A sales associate should:
  - get the buyer preapproved by a lender and get a Loan Estimate,
  - show the buyer the important financial aspects of the purchase, and
  - describe the sales process to the buyer.
- If the buyer finds the right house but wants to delay making a decision, suggest that you prepare an "as if" contract form. They may decide to go ahead after reviewing the paperwork.

- After writing the offer, take the buyers back to their car, then call the listing agent for an appointment.
- Go with the listing agent to present the offer.
- A seller has three possible responses to a counteroffer:
    - Acceptance
    - Rejection
    - Counteroffer
- To counteroffer, the seller makes the appropriate changes, initials each change, and then signs the offer.
- To accept the counteroffer, a buyer need only initial the changes.

R E V I E W   Q U E S T I O N S

1. A sales associate is preparing a buyer's cost disclosure statement. Because he wants to protect himself from later problems, he should
    a. use a disclosure form for a similar house from the office closed-sales files.
    b. talk to several licensees in the firm to get their ideas on current costs.
    c. ask his broker for the information on closing costs for a new loan.
    d. get the information from the lender's Loan Estimate.

2. The buyers have been prequalified for a $160,000 mortgage. If the buyers have enough cash for a 20% down payment, they can get a house priced at
    a. $200,000.
    b. $220,000.
    c. $240,000.
    d. $320,000.

3. According to the text, the sales associate who is presenting the offer should normally give copies of the offer
    a. before starting to present the information.
    b. only after summarizing the important parts of the offer.
    c. just before asking for a signature.
    d. to the listing sales associate by fax as soon as the associate is notified of the offer.

4. When presenting an offer, a sales associate should NOT
    a. give the seller the offer with the original signatures.
    b. make copies for all the parties who are present.
    c. work the offer until it's accepted or dead.
    d. present all terms of the offer before discussing the price.

5. When the seller wants to make a counteroffer,
    a. it should be made orally.
    b. the seller should initial the changes but should not sign the offer.
    c. the seller should initial the changes and sign the offer.
    d. the sales associate should strongly object and try to get the original offer accepted.

6. If you are the listing sales associate and there are multiple offers to be presented, both from your company and other companies, you should
    a. present your company's offers first.
    b. tell the sales associates in your company the details of the other offers.
    c. get your broker involved.
    d. get the associates from the other companies to fax their offers.

7. When presenting an offer to the sellers, it is helpful to
    a. tell them first what price is being offered.
    b. make only one copy of the offer in order to keep better control of the presentation.
    c. get them to like the buyers.
    d. tell them nothing about the buyers.

8.   If you have an offer to present to a seller, and you are not the listing sales associate, you should
    a.   excuse yourself after making the presentation, making sure the sellers have no further questions for you.
    b.   require that the listing broker be present in case there is a problem during the presentation.
    c.   not attend or present your offer but, instead, let the listing agent do so.
    d.   first give the good-faith deposit to the listing agent for deposit, if the offer is accepted.

9.   When buyers just want to "sleep on the decision," and you want them to make an offer on a home they love, the best way to help them make the decision is to
    a.   tell them there are three other buyers interested, whether or not that's true.
    b.   prepare the paperwork, and then explain the sales agreement and the offer process.
    c.   tell them you'll be out of town for the rest of the week.
    d.   offer to pay their closing costs.

10.   Principal and interest on a new loan is $1,564.90. Annual taxes are estimated to be $3,575, and insurance is estimated to be $1,289 annually. What is the monthly payment?
    a. $1,862.82
    b. $1,970.24
    c. $5,139.90
    d. $6,428.90

ACTION LIST

APPLY WHAT YOU'VE LEARNED!

The following actions will reinforce the material in "Section III—Selling Real Property":

- ❏ Preview at least five homes in your favorite price range. Try to see five each day for the next five days. Use a tape recorder to describe each home thoroughly, and try to match it with a prospective buyer or type of buyer.

- ❏ From your preview visits, list the best homes on the market. Pick your favorite home from that list.

- ❏ Describe every characteristic of *your* favorite home from your preview trips as though you were writing a book on the house. Try to remember colors, room sizes and arrangements, and garage size. Describe each room in as much detail as possible. If you can't do it, go back to the house again and make careful notes. Try to increase your observation powers every time you preview homes.

- ❏ When you visit a vacant home, thoroughly describe each room aloud as though your buyer were sight-impaired.

- ❏ Keep a tape recorder near your phone. The next time you answer a call from a prospective buyer, turn on the recorder. (You must observe the law, however; record only your side of the conversation.) When you have completed the call, listen to the tape. Make written notes about what you would change about your side of the conversation.

- ❏ Ride through a neighborhood you have not yet explored, describing into your tape recorder the details you see. Then do the same thing in the surrounding area to find shopping areas, libraries, car washes, schools, and churches.

- ❏ Write the features you think some close friends would like in a home. From memory, list the properties you would show them and give reasons for your decisions. Make a buyer's cost statement based on a 90% conventional loan.

- ❏ Call your friends and tell them about the previous exercise. Ask whether they will let you show them the homes that you chose for them. How well did you judge their tastes?

FINANCING AND CLOSING REAL ESTATE TRANSACTIONS

Licensees often are asked for advice by buyers about the most appropriate type of loan to secure. The advice licensees provide requires an understanding of the advantages and disadvantages of each mortgage type and the situations that make certain mortgages more suitable.

Sales associates must understand the loan application and underwriting process completely to effectively assist a buyer in dealing with lenders. This section will give licensees a better idea of the steps required to take a loan from application to closing.

The closing is often the most troublesome part of a real estate sale. This section is intended to give licensees information on how to reduce stress levels at closings and to make the licensees more efficient and professional. Many problems result from communication failures between cooperating brokers and sales associates. This section explores methods of tracking the necessary components of the closing to ensure that everything is completed on time.

Sales associates are expected to oversee closings and to review the closing documents, particularly the closing statement. A sales associate must understand each part of the statement. This section provides hands-on practice for the sales associate in preparing closing statements.

11

EXPLORING MORTGAGE ALTERNATIVES

LEARNING OBJECTIVES

When you finish reading this chapter, you will be able to:

- calculate the PITI payment for a borrower,
- compare the interest savings on a 15-year fixed-rate mortgage versus a 30-year fixed-rate mortgage,
- explain the five components of an ARM, and
- calculate the interest rate adjustments on an ARM loan.

KEY TERMS

adjustable-rate mortgage (ARM)	calculated interest rate	margin
	cap	negative amortization
annual percentage rate (APR)	fixed-rate mortgage	PITI payment
	index	refinance
biweekly mortgage		

1 OVERVIEW

Between 2003 and 2006, the United States experienced the biggest housing boom in its history, a boom that began to deflate in 2007, causing a meltdown in the credit markets. The fault belongs everywhere in the system, but perhaps the great engine of the catastrophe was Wall Street. Large banks, hedge funds, and investment firms had losses of a magnitude never imagined, eroding their capital bases, and requiring large infusions of capital to avoid a systemic failure. The Federal Reserve worked to hold the system together to prevent catastrophic failure of the credit system.

In September 2008, Fannie Mae and Freddie Mac were placed under the conservatorship of the Federal Housing Finance Agency, one of the most sweeping government interventions in private financial markets in many years.

In the years since then, the market has begun to claw its way back, and some areas are experiencing a shortage of housing inventory. One of the factors that retarded the recovery has been the inability of buyers to find financing.

Twenty years ago, commercial banks and savings associations originated more than 80% of home mortgages. That share has dropped sharply, and today mortgage companies are the dominant factor in the market, originating more than 50% of all home loans. Driven by market forces, lenders offer a wide variety of mortgage products tailored to the needs of consumers. Experts expect the changes in the mortgage industry to accelerate in the future.

A general knowledge of these changes can enhance the opportunities available to the real estate professional. Developing strong relationships with lenders who preapprove loans for prospective buyers saves licensees' time and can significantly increase their income.

STEPS BEFORE LOAN APPLICATION

Before buyers begin looking at houses, they should have a good understanding of their own financial capabilities and housing objectives. Licensees should explain both issues to their customers to help them understand the importance of being preapproved. This is important because if the lender denies the application, the applicant may lose the opportunity to buy the home. In addition, some expense is involved in applying for a loan. Fees may range from $150 to $500, depending on the property and circumstances.

Mortgage Shopping

Licensees should advise buyers to look for competitive rates and a lender with a reputation for integrity and good service.

Surveys show that mortgage interest rates and closing costs vary in metropolitan markets for the same mortgage product. Comparing prices obviously is important, but it is not an easy task. Lenders charge a variety of fees. Discount points are a significant item, almost like prepaid interest (pay more points to get a lower interest rate). Points vary from lender to lender in the same market area. The new GFE provides alternatives to a borrower who can better decide whether to pay extra points to get a lower interest rate.

Licensees must learn which lenders act quickly with good service to borrowers. Licensees should recommend those lenders that provide good service.

Seller-Paid Closing Costs

A buyer must have the necessary income and debt ratios to afford a mortgage payment. Coming up with enough cash to close is another big hurdle. The closing costs and prepayments on a typical mortgage loan for $120,000 can reach $5,000 in addition to the down payment. Many qualified buyers are forced to rent in order to save enough funds to buy. Licensees who know lender standards on seller-paid closing costs are able to sell to these buyers much sooner. The seller can pay part of the closing costs for conventional, FHA, and VA mortgage loans. Figure 11.1 shows the current allowed percentages.

FIGURE 11.1 ■ **Maximum Seller-Paid Closing Costs That Can Be Applied to Buyer's Closing Costs, Prepaid Items, and Reserves, Expressed as a Percentage of the Purchase Price**

Type of Loan	Percent
Conventional	
Less than 10% down payment	3
19% or greater down payment	6
FHA	6
VA	6

A seller who could pay only 3% of the buyer's closing costs on a house that sells for $120,000 would contribute $3,600. If a two-income family is saving $300 per month, the family could purchase the home 12 months sooner.

DISCUSSION EXERCISE 11.1

Do you think most licensees guide potential borrowers to lenders with which they have built relationships or to lenders that have the best mortgage rates on a given day?

Annual Percentage Rate (APR)

The Truth in Lending Act (TILA) requires that mortgage lenders disclose their annual percentage rates to potential borrowers. The **annual percentage rate (APR)** is a standard expression of credit costs designed to give potential borrowers an easy method of comparing lenders' total finance charges. These financing costs include points and any other prepaid interest or fees charged to obtain the loan in addition to the contract interest cost. The APR must be, by law, the relationship of the total financing charge to the total amount financed, and it must be computed to the nearest one-eighth of 1 percent. Perhaps the best and most accurate definition of the APR is that it is the effective interest rate for a mortgage loan repaid over its full term.

The law allows a lender three days after loan application to inform the applicant of the APR. The lender is required to notify the borrower within three days if the APR changes by more than one-eighth of 1 percent.

Regulation Z of TILA was amended by the Federal Reserve Board because of the losses sustained during the recent housing bubble. The amendment:

■ requires that fee appraisers be paid reasonable and customary compensation,

■ prohibits coercion of appraisers for both permanent mortgages and home equity loans,

■ prohibits appraisers and appraisal management companies from having financial or other interests in the properties being appraised, and

■ requires creditors and closing agents that have information about appraiser misconduct to file reports to the appropriate state licensing authorities.

Another feature of this act is that it assumes that borrowers will keep their loans for the full number of years for which the loans are written. Records of mortgage lending, however, show that most borrowers either sell or refinance their homes in less than 12 years. The actual (effective) interest rate paid depends on the number of years a loan is kept.

EXAMPLE: If the borrower expects to keep the loan for longer than 12 years, divide the points by 8 and add the result to the note interest rate. For example, if a lender has offered a first mortgage for 30 years at 5% and 3 points, the effective interest rate would be 5.375%, computed as follows:

$$\text{note rate} + (\text{points} \div 8) = \text{effective interest rate}$$
$$5\% + (.03 \div 8) = 5\% + .375\% = 5.375\%$$

When the lender gives a prospective borrower a rate quote, the borrower is often undecided about whether to pay discount points. Discount points can be considered prepaid interest that will reduce the interest rate on the note. In effect, a borrower has a "menu" of interest rates based on the amount paid as discount points. Figure 11.2 shows a sample market quote for a 30-year fixed-rate loan. Fluctuations in the market cause differences from day to day in the differential of discount points and yield.

FIGURE 11.2 ■ **$100,000 30-Year Fixed-Rate Mortgage Comparison of Rates and Discount Points**

A. Interest Rate	B. Discount Points	C. Principal and Interest Payment	D. Payment Difference from 5% Rate	E. Amount Paid in Discount Points	F. Months at Lower Rate for Points Payback (E ÷ D)
5.000	0	$536.82	—	$0	0
4.875	0.5	529.21	$7.61	500	65.7
4.750	1.2	521.65	15.17	1,200	79.1
4.625	1.7	514.14	22.68	1,700	75.0
4.500	2.3	506.69	30.13	2,300	76.3

From the example, it's obvious that a person who intends to occupy the property for three years should avoid paying points because it will take almost six years to break even. In some cases, a borrower should ask the lender to raise the interest rate not only to avoid discount points but also to avoid paying an origination fee.

If a person expects to remain in the property for the full 30-year period and will not be refinancing or making an early loan payoff, the savings could be worth paying points. At line 5, for instance, the borrower breaks even at 76 months. The difference in payments of $30.13 for the remaining 284 months would total $8,557, well worth paying the points.

Of course, the better way to analyze points is by considering the time value of money. Using the 4.5% rate on line 5, the borrower pays $2,300 in today's dollars (that could be invested to return some interest) to get a savings sometime in the future. The financial calculator approach below shows the payback period is longer (91 months versus 76.3 months).

%I	PMT	PV	FV	Solve for N
.3750	30.13	2,300	0	91 months

Where: % = monthly market interest rate: 4.5% ÷ 12 months = .375

PMT = savings per monthly payment = $30.13

PV = dollars paid in points = $2,300

FV = input zero for this problem = 0

Solve for: N = number of months to pay back points

Solution is 91 months

DISCUSSION EXERCISE 11.2

John is moving to Miami and expects to stay for about three years before being transferred again. He needs to borrow $200,000 for his new home. With no points, he can get a 5% fixed-rate mortgage with principal and interest payments of $1,073.64. The lender offers him a 4.6% mortgage (payments of $1,025.29) with two points.

Should John take the lower interest rate mortgage?

Using simple math, how many months will it take John to break even by paying the points if he takes the lower interest rate?

PITI Payment

Customers often ask licensees to calculate the monthly mortgage payment for a possible purchase or sale. Most lenders require an amount each month that includes principal and interest plus escrow items—property taxes, homeowners insurance, and possibly mortgage insurance or homeowners/condominium association dues. This entire package of payments commonly is referred to as the **PITI payment**.

Principal and interest payments on the mortgage are the largest part of the monthly PITI payment. Using the mortgage payment factors shown in Figure 11.3, multiply the loan amount by the appropriate factor to get the principal and interest portion of the payment.

For example, the payment factor for a 30-year mortgage at 5% is 5.37. To calculate the monthly principal and interest for a 30-year loan of $198,000 at 5%, use the following equation:

$$\$198,000 \div \$1,000 \times 5.37 = \$1,063.26$$

While the factor table has been included in this text so that all students can calculate the monthly payment, most real estate licensees use a financial calculator to obtain the monthly mortgage payment of principal and interest.

Assume that annual taxes are $2,400 and annual insurance is $1,200. To find the PITI payment, divide the taxes and insurance by 12 months ($2,400 + $1,200 ÷ 12 = $300) and add that to the principal and interest payment. The total payment will be $1,363.26.

FIGURE 11.3

Mortgage Factor Chart

How To Use This Chart

To use this chart, start by finding the appropriate interest rate. Then follow that row over to the column for the appropriate loan term. This number is the *interest rate factor* required each month to amortize a $1,000 loan.

To calculate the principal and interest (PI) payment, multiply the interest rate factor by the number of 1,000s in the total loan. For example, if the interest rate is 4 percent for a term of 30 years, the interest rate factor is 4.78. If the total loan is $100,000, the loan contains 100 1,000s. Therefore, 100 × 4.78 = $478 PI only.

To estimate a mortgage loan amount using the amortization chart, divide the PI payment by the appropriate interest rate factor. Using the same facts as in the first example:

$478 ÷ 4.78 = $100 1,000s or $100,000

Rate	Term 10 Years	Term 15 Years	Term 20 Years	Term 25 Years	Term 30 Years
3	9.66	6.91	5.55	4.74	4.22
3⅛	9.71	6.97	5.61	4.81	4.28
3¼	9.77	7.03	5.67	4.87	4.35
3⅜	9.83	7.09	5.74	4.94	4.42
3½	9.89	7.15	5.80	5.01	4.49
3⅝	9.95	7.21	5.86	5.07	4.56
3¾	10.01	7.27	5.93	5.14	4.63
3⅞	10.07	7.33	5.99	5.21	4.70
4	10.13	7.40	6.06	5.28	4.78
4⅛	10.19	7.46	6.13	5.35	4.85
4¼	10.25	7.53	6.20	5.42	4.92
4⅜	10.31	7.59	6.26	5.49	5.00
4½	10.37	7.65	6.33	5.56	5.07
4⅝	10.43	7.72	6.40	5.63	5.15
4¾	10.49	7.78	6.47	5.71	5.22
4⅞	10.55	7.85	6.54	5.78	5.30
5	10.61	7.91	6.60	5.85	5.37
5⅛	10.67	7.98	6.67	5.92	5.45
5¼	10.73	8.04	6.74	6.00	5.53
5⅜	10.80	8.11	6.81	6.07	5.60
5½	10.86	8.18	6.88	6.15	5.68
5⅝	10.92	8.24	6.95	6.22	5.76
5¾	10.98	8.31	7.03	6.30	5.84
5⅞	11.04	8.38	7.10	6.37	5.92
6	11.10	8.44	7.16	6.44	6.00
6⅛	11.16	8.51	7.24	6.52	6.08
6¼	11.23	8.57	7.31	6.60	6.16
6⅜	11.29	8.64	7.38	6.67	6.24
6½	11.35	8.71	7.46	6.75	6.32
6⅝	11.42	8.78	7.53	6.83	6.40
6¾	11.48	8.85	7.60	6.91	6.49
6⅞	11.55	8.92	7.68	6.99	6.57
7	11.61	8.98	7.75	7.06	6.65
7⅛	11.68	9.06	7.83	7.15	6.74
7¼	11.74	9.12	7.90	7.22	6.82
7⅜	11.81	9.20	7.98	7.31	6.91
7½	11.87	9.27	8.05	7.38	6.99
7⅝	11.94	9.34	8.13	7.47	7.08
7¾	12.00	9.41	8.20	7.55	7.16
7⅞	12.07	9.48	8.29	7.64	7.25
8	12.14	9.56	8.37	7.72	7.34

In the example on the previous page, the licensee with a financial calculator would solve the problem as shown below:

N	%I	PV	FV	Solve for: PMT
360	.4167	198,000	0	$1,062.90

Where: N = number of monthly periods in loan term
         %I = interest rate (5% ÷ 12 months = .4167)
         PV = loan amount
         FV = input zero when solving for present value

Solve for: PMT = monthly mortgage payment

Note that the small difference in payment between the equation above and the calculator method is due to rounding the mortgage factor; the calculator method is more accurate.

FIXED-RATE MORTGAGES

Any mortgage written to preclude change in the interest rate throughout the entire duration of the loan is a **fixed-rate mortgage**. The term includes the traditional 30-year mortgage, the 15-year mortgage, and the biweekly mortgage. The use of a due-on-sale clause in a fixed-rate mortgage reserves the lender's right to make an interest rate change if a transfer of ownership takes place. Practically all conventional mortgages issued since the early 1980s contain a due-on-sale clause.

Traditional 30-Year Mortgage

The fixed-rate, fully amortizing mortgage loan has been the standard of the real estate finance industry for the past 50 years. A 30-year term provides a reasonably low payment for the amount borrowed, while the interest rate, payment amount, and repayment schedule are set permanently at the beginning of the loan period. Fixed-rate loans often are sold in the secondary market because they appeal to pension funds and other investors searching for a relatively safe investment with a known interest rate and a long duration.

Advantages of a 30-Year Mortgage. Monthly payments on the loan are spread over 30 years, offering the borrower protection against future increases in interest rates and inflation rates while providing for the orderly repayment of the amount borrowed. Household budgets are easier to manage when the borrower does not have to plan for changing payment amounts or interest rates.

Disadvantages of a 30-Year Mortgage. If overall interest rates drop, as they did in years 2000–2001, the rate on a fixed-rate mortgage will not go down with them. To take advantage of lower interest rates, the original loan must be **refinanced**, requiring the borrower to pay substantial closing costs on the new loan.

15-Year Mortgage

The 15-year fixed-rate mortgage has become popular with both lenders and borrowers in recent years. It is just like a traditional 30-year loan, except that its monthly payment is higher, its interest rate typically is slightly lower, and it is paid off in 15 years. The 15-year mortgage saves the borrower thousands of dollars in interest payments.

The popular press sometimes compares the two mortgage plans, showing dramatic savings from the 15-year plan. The gross savings, however, usually are overstated. The higher payments on the 15-year plan have an opportunity cost. If the difference were invested, the return on the investment would reduce the net cost of the 30-year mortgage. The tax savings from mortgage interest deductions also would reduce the savings.

For many borrowers, the 15-year mortgage may be the best way to finance a home because in addition to the overall savings in total cost, it forces a monthly saving in the form of extra equity and allows a person who needs it a sense of confidence that her home will be paid off in 15 years. This is true for those planning for retirement. Also, many in the baby boomer generation are in their 40s, with a growing number eager to end their mortgage payments and own their homes free and clear.

Licensees should point out, however, that the 15-year mortgage robs the borrower of some flexibility. A 15-year mortgage cannot be extended to 30 years, but a 30-year mortgage can be paid off in 15 years if the borrower accelerates monthly payments to create a 15-year loan or remits a lump-sum payment on principal each year. The borrower retains the right to decide when, or if, he will make extra payments. Borrowers must evaluate the benefits of the 15-year mortgage based on their personal situations.

Advantages of a 15-Year Mortgage. Because lenders get their money back sooner than they do with traditional 30-year mortgages, they charge slightly lower rates for 15-year loans. Also, the loans are paid off faster, less money is borrowed for less time, and less total interest is paid over the lives of the loans—more than 50% less. As with a 30-year, fixed-rate loan, the interest rate on a 15-year mortgage does not change, and the monthly principal and interest payment does not go up. Finally, the higher monthly payment results in forced savings in the form of faster equity buildup.

Disadvantages of a 15-Year Mortgage. The monthly payment on a 15-year loan is higher, and the borrower forgoes investment opportunities voluntarily for the extra dollars paid on the loan each month. Some income tax advantages related to home mortgages and investment opportunities are lost. The mortgage payment is not flexible, and any future increase in income tax rates could increase the 15-year mortgage's net costs.

Biweekly Mortgage

The development of computer programs to service biweekly mortgages properly, the creation of a secondary market (Fannie Mae), increased familiarity with the product, and growing consumer demand all are combining to bring about a comeback for the biweekly mortgage. The **biweekly mortgage** alternative is a fixed-rate loan, amortized over a 30-year period, with payments made every two weeks instead of every month. Borrowers pay half the normal monthly payment every two weeks, which means 26 payments each year, or the equivalent of 13 monthly payments. The extra month's payment each year reduces the principal faster and results in considerable savings in interest, as well as a reduction in the duration of the loan to between 19 and 21 years.

Normally, interest rates for biweekly mortgages are comparable to the rates charged for traditional 30-year mortgages. Most biweekly loans are scheduled to mature in 30 years even though the actual number of years to maturity depends on the interest rate. The higher the interest rate, the larger the monthly payment, and the more that is applied to reducing mortgage principal. A biweekly mortgage with a 7% interest rate, for example, would be paid off in approximately 23 years, 9 months.

Figure 11.4 compares the results of making scheduled payments on a traditional 30-year mortgage, of adding different amounts of additional principal payments each month, and of making scheduled payments on a biweekly mortgage amortized over 30 years. The table shows that a borrower who uses a biweekly loan saves nearly $17,000 in interest over a 30-year fixed-rate mortgage ($93,255 – $76,345 = $16,910).

FIGURE 11.4 ■ Comparison of Interest Costs for Various Mortgage Plans for a $100,000 Loan at 5% Interest

Payment Pattern	Regular Payment Amount	Total Paid Each Year	Time Until Paid Off	Total Interest Paid
30-year mortgage	$536.82	$6,441.84	30 years	$93,255
Added $25/month	561.82	6,742.00	27 yrs. + 2 mos.	83,153
Added $100/month	636.82	7,642.00	20 yrs. + 2 mos.	63,026
Biweekly mortgage	268.41	6,979.00	25 yrs. + 3 mos.	76,345
15-year mortgage	$790.79	$9,489.00	15 years	$42,342

Advantages of a Biweekly Mortgage. A biweekly mortgage combines the benefits of the 30-year loan and the 15-year loan without the increased payments of the 15-year loan. It offers borrowers the affordability of the 30-year loan because the two biweekly payments come within a few pennies of the one monthly payment on a 30-year loan.

Also, Fannie Mae requires that payments be deducted automatically from a borrower's checking or savings account every two weeks. Because more than half of the nation's workforce is paid on a biweekly basis, it is compatible with a large number of paychecks. Some lenders include a conversion clause that permits a borrower to change a biweekly mortgage to a traditional 30-year, fixed-rate amortized mortgage at little or no cost with only 30 days' advance notice.

Disadvantages of a Biweekly Mortgage. The biweekly mortgage has the same disadvantages as other fixed-rate mortgages. In addition, the biweekly loan threatens those borrowers who do not maintain stable checking or savings account balances. The biweekly mortgage also locks borrowers into payment plans that they could set up themselves, at their own discretion, with a traditional 30-year loan. Some lenders also charge a set-up fee.

DISCUSSION EXERCISE 11.3

If the biweekly mortgage combines the good features of both the traditional 30-year fixed-rate mortgage and the 15-year fixed-rate mortgage, why is it so seldom used, comparatively speaking, to finance residential purchases?

ADJUSTABLE-RATE MORTGAGES

The **adjustable-rate mortgage (ARM)** is an alternative to the traditional 30-year, fixed-rate, level-payment mortgage. The popularity of ARMs increases when interest rates rise, and they lose favor when interest rates are low. An adjustable-rate mortgage is, as the term implies, a financing instrument that allows the lender to increase or decrease the interest rate based on the rise or fall of a specified index.

Components of Adjustable-Rate Mortgages

The primary elements in determining the acceptability of an ARM from the borrower's viewpoint are the index, the lender's margin, the calculated interest rate, the initial interest rate, and the interest rate caps.

Lending institutions can link the interest rate of a conventional ARM to any recognized **index** (indicator of cost or value) that is not controlled by the lender and is verifiable by the borrower. The **margin**, also called the spread, is a percentage added to the index. The margin usually remains constant over the life of the loan, while the selected index may move up or down with fluctuations in the nation's economy. The calculated (or actual) interest rate is calculated by adding the selected index to the lender's margin (index plus margin equals calculated interest rate). This calculated interest rate may be discounted during the initial payment period, but it is the rate to which all future adjustments and caps apply.

To be competitive, lenders sometimes reduce the first year's earnings by discounting the calculated interest rate, thus creating a lower initial interest rate. This helps to qualify potential buyers at artificially low interest rates, which may or may not be a service to the borrowers, and establishes the amount of the monthly loan payment during the first loan adjustment period. Be aware that many lenders now use the second year's interest rate rather than the discounted rate as the qualifier. Both Fannie Mae and Freddie Mac require borrowers with less than a 20% down payment on one-year, adjustable-rate loans to be qualified at the initial interest rate plus 2%.

The main appeal of ARM loans is the lower-than-market initial interest rates offered as inducements (teasers). But without some type of protection from unacceptable increases in interest rates, borrowers would be in danger of being unable to make future mortgage payments. To prevent this, most lenders and all federal housing agencies have established standards calling for ceilings on increases. Three types of **caps** (ceilings) limit increases in the calculated interest rates of ARM loans:

1. Amount of increase that can be applied at the time of the first adjustment (for example, cap of 1% or 2% per adjustment period)

2. Amount of increase that can be applied during any one adjustment interval (for example, no more than 2% during any one-year period)

3. Total amount the interest rate may be increased over the life of the loan (for example, no more than 6%)

Borrowers should be cautious when payments are capped and interest rates are not because of the probability that **negative amortization** will be involved in the loan. Negative amortization occurs when the monthly payment is not enough to pay the interest on the loan. The shortfall is added to the mortgage balance.

1 Lenders must provide potential borrowers with a worst-case example at loan applica-
2 tion. If conditions should warrant maximum interest rate increases, this disclosure must
3 show the maximum possible payment increases at the earliest opportunities.

Conventional ARM

5 To help you better understand adjustable-rate versus fixed-rate mortgages, Figure 11.5
6 compares two approaches to a $100,000 conventional mortgage using a worst-case sce-
7 nario for interest rate increases.

FIGURE 11.5 ■ $100,000 Mortgage Loan, 30-Year Term, 8% Fixed-Rate Versus 5.5% Adjustable-Rate Mortgage (Annual Cap 2%, Lifetime Cap 6%)

	Fixed Rate			Adjustable Rate		ARM Savings (Loss)	
Year	Payment	Rate		Payment	Rate	Monthly	Accumulated
1	$734	8%		$568	5.5%	$166	$1,992
2	734	8		699	7.5	35	2,412
3	734	8		841	9.5	(107)	1,128
4*	734	8		990	11.5	(256)	(1,944)

*ARM savings exhausted in fifth month of year 4.

8 In this example, all monthly payment amounts are for principal and interest, and the
9 amounts are rounded to the nearest dollar. The up-front costs of points and fees will be
10 discussed later.

11 ARM loans have lower initial rates than fixed-rate mortgages primarily because lend-
12 ers can avoid the risk of market interest changes for the full 30 years of the loan period.
13 ARM loans reduce the risk, so lenders don't need as much cushion for contingencies.
14 New ARM products combine the ARM features of lower initial interest rate with a longer
15 fixed-rate period between adjustments. For example, 3-year, 5-year, or 10-year ARMs are
16 available at slightly higher initial rates than 1-year ARMs, but at lower rates than 30-year
17 fixed mortgages.

DISCUSSION EXERCISE 11.4

In your opinion, do the lower initial rates offered on ARM loans cause borrowers to take on more mortgage debt than they can afford? Why or why not?

---

18 **Interest Rates and Recognized Indexes.** The index to which a conventional ARM is tied
19 can increase or decrease the volatility of interest rate changes. Four principal indexes are
20 used for residential mortgages:

21 1. The London Interbank Offered Rate (LIBOR) index is the base interest rate paid
22 on deposits between banks in the Eurodollar market.

23 2. The Monthly Treasury Bill Average (MTA) is a stable, slow-moving index. It is a
24 12-month moving average of the U.S. one-year Treasury bill.

3. The 11th District Cost of Funds Index (COFI) is another stable, slow-moving index, consisting of the weighted average of deposits and borrowings between banks in the Federal Home Loan Bank District of San Francisco.

4. Prime rate is the rate charged to most favored customers by major banks. This rate is commonly used for adjustments to home equity or second mortgages and can be quite volatile.

Lenders must provide consumers with details on conventional ARMs to assist them in comparison shopping. Potential borrowers must be informed of the index used, how often the loan will be adjusted, and the maximum amount of loan payment increase allowed.

When helping prospective borrowers sort through the many factors to be considered in selecting a conventional adjustable-rate loan, licensees should make sure the borrowers know:

- what rate will be used when interest rate caps are applied to an ARM loan;
- that the margin is one of the most important benchmarks in comparing lenders (most other ARM features are relatively similar, but the margins can vary considerably);
- to seek another lender if the one they are considering has policies that call for ARM increases exceeding the 2% annual cap or the 6% lifetime cap;
- not to consider loans that call for negative amortization;
- to compare up-front costs, such as underwriting fees, points, and origination fees, because some lenders offer lower interest rates but make up for it with inflated up-front costs; and
- not to stretch their borrowing to the limit, as they could with a fixed-rate loan, because the payments remain fixed and income should increase. Borrowing to the limit can become a disaster when an ARM is involved. Prospective borrowers should calculate their first-year payments at the initial interest rate plus 2%; otherwise, the first adjustment could hurt them financially.

Advantages of the ARM Loan. The ARM's low initial interest rate and the borrower's ability to qualify for a larger mortgage top the list of advantages of adjustable-rate mortgages. ARMs are most appropriate for those who plan to hold the mortgage loans for no more than four years. Also, any time the interest rate gap between a fixed-rate loan and an adjustable-rate loan reaches 3% in favor of the ARM, an ARM loan with interest rate caps and a one-year Treasury bill constant maturity index should make sense to homebuyers. Many ARMs are now written with conversion privileges, allowing the mortgagors to convert to fixed-rate loans for a modest fee during a specified period. This enables borrowers to take advantage of falling interest rates if they desire to do so. One of the standard features of ARMs is no prepayment penalty.

Longer Adjustment Periods Are Available. Many borrowers prefer an ARM loan that won't adjust for several years. For example, the low initial rate may last for three, five, or seven years, then adjust once each year. Such loans would be called 3/1, 5/1, or 7/1 ARMs. Other options would be for loans that had an initial rate that lasted five years, and then went to a fixed-rate loan at the prevailing rates available for the fifth year. This would be called a 5/25. There are 3/27s, 5/25s, 7/23s, or 10/30s. No one program is better for everyone, so each borrower must evaluate the possibilities based on his or her personal situation.

Disadvantages of the ARM Loan. ARM borrowers bet against the lenders that interest rates will not rise to the extent that the maximum interest rate caps will be needed. The main disadvantages of the ARM loan are the uncertain amounts of future mortgage payments and the difficulty in calculating adjustments in interest rates as they occur. Lenders, of course, do the actual calculation of adjustments, but they have been known to make mistakes, and such mistakes can be expensive to the borrowers. Calculation details are spelled out in each loan document, but they are somewhat complicated and require the use of either a financial calculator or a handbook of ARM payment tables. For a borrower who wants to audit a lender's ARM adjustments without going to the trouble of research and math calculations, Loantech LLC (800-888-6781), a mortgage consulting firm, will perform a complete individual ARM adjustment review for a fee based on the terms of the loan document submitted.

FHA Adjustable-Rate Mortgage

Section 251 of the National Housing Act authorizes the Federal Housing Administration (FHA) to insure adjustable-rate mortgages on single-family properties. The interest rate is the sum of the index and the margin. The index changes, but the margin will remain the same over the life of the loan. The initial interest rate may be a result of combining the current one-year Treasury bill index with the margin at the time the loan is closed. This combination of components produces what is often called the **calculated interest rate**. Each FHA-approved lender is allowed to discount the calculated interest rate to a lower amount if local competition requires it, or the calculated interest rate may become the initial interest rate. The initial interest rate cannot be a rate higher than the current index plus margin.

Once the initial interest rate is set, annual adjustments to FHA ARMs must be calculated. The first interest rate adjustment may not occur sooner than 12 months from the due date of the first monthly payment or later than 18 months from that first designated payment date. In other words, the first adjustment must be made during a six-month period or it is forfeited. This period permits lenders to complete the collection or pooling of many mortgages for sale to secondary market institutions. Whatever date is designated as the initial interest rate adjustment date, all subsequent rate adjustments must be made on the anniversary of that first adjustment date.

Unlike the conventional ARM choice of index, all FHA ARMs must use the published one-year constant maturity Treasury security index, using the most recently available figure that applied exactly 30 calendar days before the designated change date. The new current index plus the constant margin rounded to the nearest one-eighth of one percentage point is the new calculated interest rate. It is then compared with the existing interest rate. If it is the same as the existing interest rate, no change is made to the existing rate. If it is up to 1% higher or lower than the existing interest rate, the new calculated interest rate becomes the new adjusted interest rate. If it is more than 1% higher or lower than the existing interest rate, the new adjusted interest rate is limited to a 1% increase or decrease of the existing interest rate.

The new adjusted interest rate becomes effective on the designated change date and is regarded as the existing interest rate until the next allowable change date. In no event may any future combination of interest rate adjustments exceed five percentage points higher or lower than the initial interest rate.

The FHA considers interest payable on the first day of the month following the month in which the interest accrued. Therefore, adjusted monthly mortgage payments resulting from the adjusted interest rate are not due until 30 days after the designated change date. No negative amortization is allowed with FHA ARMs. The FHA requires that payments be recalculated each year to provide for complete amortization of the outstanding principal balance over the remaining term of the loan at the new adjusted interest rate. Lenders must give borrowers at least 30 days' notice of any increase or decrease in the monthly mortgage payment amount. The adjustment notice must contain the date the adjustment notice is given, the ARM change date, the new existing interest rate, the amount of the new monthly mortgage payment, the current index used, the method of calculating the adjustment, and any other information that may be required to clarify the adjustment.

FHA Required Disclosure Statement. All approved lenders making FHA adjustable-rate loans must provide each borrower with a mortgage loan information statement that includes a worst-case example form. The borrower must receive this statement and be given an opportunity to read the informative explanation before signing the borrower's certification on the loan application. Licensees are urged to obtain personal copies of the FHA adjustable-rate mortgage disclosure statement to use when counseling clients or advising customers.

Advantages of the FHA ARM. An FHA ARM has several advantages over a conventional ARM. Often, an FHA ARM bears a slightly lower interest rate because of the government insurance provided the lender. In addition, the FHA commonly uses more lenient qualification formulas. The down payment (required investment) also is lower in many cases, and the interest rate increase each year is limited to 1%, with a lifetime cap of 5% (conventional caps usually are 2% per year, with a 6% lifetime cap). FHA loans continue to be easier to assume than conventional loans, although the FHA has increased the requirements for assumption of FHA loans. The FHA now requires a review of the credit-worthiness of each person seeking to assume an FHA-insured loan.

Disadvantages of the FHA ARM. The FHA imposes a maximum loan amount that differs from region to region, depending on the cost of living in each region. Also, the FHA requires an up-front mortgage insurance premium (UFMIP) of 2.25%, although this cost may be financed along with the mortgage. If FHA loans are repaid early, mortgagors may apply for partial refunds of the mortgage insurance premiums.

Bond Money for First-Time Homebuyers

States, counties, and cities can offer below-market mortgage financing by selling tax-free bonds. These loans are available to first-time homebuyers (who haven't owned a home for the previous three years). Sometimes divorced persons who want to buy their own home also qualify. These programs come and go, so check with local lenders for availability.

MORTGAGE INSURANCE

Conventional lenders usually require that the borrower pay for private mortgage insurance (PMI). PMI protects the lender if the borrower defaults on the loan. The Homeowners Protection Act of 1998 established rules for automatic termination and borrower cancellation of PMI on home mortgages. These protections apply to certain home mortgages signed on or after July 29, 1999. These protections do not apply to government-insured FHA- or VA-guaranteed loans or to loans with lender-paid PMI.

For conventional home mortgages signed on or after July 29, 1999, PMI must, with certain exceptions, be terminated automatically when the borrower has achieved 22% equity in the home based on the purchase price, if the mortgage payments are current. PMI also can be canceled when the borrower requests it—with certain exceptions—when the borrower achieves 20% equity in the home based on the original property value, if the mortgage payments are current.

There are three exceptions for which the PMI may continue:

1. If the loan is "high risk"
2. If the borrower has not been current on the payments within the year prior to the time for termination or cancellation
3. If the borrower has other liens on the property

The FHA 203(b) loan requires that borrowers pay a UFMIP. In 1913, the amount was 1.75% of the loan amount on a 30-year mortgage. In addition, FHA charges an annual mortgage insurance premium (MIP) of 1.25% of the loan amount, broken into monthly installments. The MIP is canceled for borrowers who have achieved 22% equity in their house and after five years have elapsed, based on the lower of the purchase price or the appraisal.

WEBLINK

Visit Fannie Mae online at www.fanniemae.com.

The Freddie Mac website is www.freddiemac.com.

Information on the Federal Housing Administration (FHA) is available at http://portal.hud.gov/hudportal/HUD?src=/program_offices/housing/fhahistory/.

Information on the Federal Reserve System is available at www.federalreserve.gov.

The U.S. Department of Veterans Affairs maintains a website at www.va.gov.

SUMMARY

- Buyers should be preapproved before looking at houses.
- The Truth in Lending Act requires that lenders disclose the annual percentage rate to potential borrowers.
- The APR is the effective interest rate for a mortgage loan repaid over its full term.
- When considering whether to pay discount points, divide the difference in monthly payments into the total dollar amount of points to determine how many months it will take to break even.
- PITI stands for principal, interest, taxes, and insurance.
- The standard mortgage loan is the 30-year fixed-rate mortgage.
- Many borrowers prefer the 15-year fixed-rate mortgage because of the savings in interest over the life of the loan, but payments are substantially higher.
- The biweekly mortgage alternative is a fixed-rate loan, amortized over a 30-year period, with payments made every two weeks instead of every month. Borrowers pay half the normal monthly payment every two weeks, which means 26 payments each year, or the equivalent of 13 monthly payments.

- The primary elements in determining the acceptability of an ARM from the borrower's viewpoint are the index, the lender's margin, the calculated interest rate, the initial interest rate, and the interest rate caps.

- The interest rate is calculated by adding the selected index to the lender's margin.

- ARMs are most appropriate for those who plan to hold the mortgage loans for no more than four years.

- FHA ARMs have an advantage over conventional ARMs because the interest rate increase each year is limited to 1%, with a lifetime cap of 5% (conventional caps usually are 2% per year, with a 6% lifetime cap).

- Private mortgage insurance must be terminated automatically when the borrower has achieved 22% equity in the home based on the purchase price, if the mortgage payments are current. PMI also can be canceled when the borrower requests it upon achieving 20% equity in the home based on the original property value.

- FHA charges an up-front mortgage insurance premium and a monthly mortgage insurance premium.

- The monthly MIP is canceled for borrowers who have achieved 22% equity in their house and after five years have elapsed, based on the lower of the purchase price or the appraisal.

R E V I E W   Q U E S T I O N S

1. Disclosure of the annual percentage rate on a mortgage loan is required by the
    a. Real Estate Settlement Procedures Act (RESPA).
    b. Truth in Lending Act (TILA).
    c. Equal Credit Opportunity Act (ECOA).
    d. Cost of Funds Index (COFI).

2. The interest rate that major banks charge to MOST favored customers and that is commonly used for home equity loans is the
    a. London Interbank Offered Rate (LIBOR).
    b. prime rate
    c. Monthly Treasury Bill Average (MTA).
    d. 11th District Cost of Funds Index (COFI).

3. Of the recognized indexes used on ARM loans, which is MOST volatile?
    a. Prime rate charged by money center banks
    b. One-year Treasury bill index
    c. LIBOR index
    d. Cost-of-funds index of the Federal Home Loan Bank, 11th District

4. Total interest rate increases on an FHA adjustable-rate loan may NOT exceed what percentage over the life of the loan?
    a. 1%
    b. 2%
    c. 3%
    d. 5%

5. On January 10, the one-year Treasury bill index was 4%. A mortgage company used that index to write a new one-year adjustable-rate with a 2.5% margin. What is the calculated interest rate?
    a. 4%
    b. 6%
    c. 6.5%
    d. 8%

6. The MOST common type of real estate mortgage is the
    a. biweekly mortgage.
    b. 30-year fixed-rate mortgage.
    c. adjustable-rate mortgage.
    d. 15-year fixed-rate mortgage.

7. A $127,000, 30-year fixed-rate mortgage with a 5.5% rate has a mortgage payment factor of .0056779. Annual payments for property taxes are $2,400. The annual insurance premium is $600. What will be the monthly PITI payments?
    a. $721.09
    b. $771.09
    c. $921.09
    d. $971.09

8. The component of an adjustable-rate mortgage that does NOT usually change is the
   a. margin.
   b. index.
   c. points.
   d. calculated rate.

9. A man purchased a new home at the FHA appraisal amount of $100,000 and financed it with an FHA mortgage loan. To what amount must he reduce the outstanding loan balance before he no longer has to pay the .5% annual mortgage insurance premium?
   a. $78,000
   b. $80,000
   c. $85,000
   d. $90,000

10. What is the index measuring the base interest rate paid on deposits between banks in the Eurodollar market that is used in many adjustable-rate mortgages?
    a. COFI
    b. MTA
    c. PRIME
    d. LIBOR

11. The FHA adjustable rate mortgage limits increases on interest rates to
    a. no more than 2% annually.
    b. no greater than 4% over the life of the loan.
    c. no greater than 2% in the first five years.
    d. 1% annually.

12. What is the maximum amount of a buyer's closing costs that can be paid by the seller under conventional lending standards when the borrower is making a 5% down payment?
    a. 3% of the purchase price
    b. 4% of the purchase price
    c. 5% of the loan amount
    d. 6% of the loan amount

13. Which is FALSE about the annual percentage rate (APR) disclosure?
    a. The rate must be calculated to the nearest one-eighth of 1%.
    b. The effective rate of interest is not affected by the number of years the mortgage loan stays in force.
    c. The lender has a maximum of three days after loan application to make the disclosure.
    d. The definition is the effective interest rate for a loan repaid over its full term.

14.   A woman is shopping for a new $150,000 mortgage. She expects to live in her new home for about four years. She can get a 30-year, 4.75% fixed-rate mortgage with principal and interest payments of $1,074.62 with no points. She can also get a 4.25% mortgage loan (payments of $1,023.26) with three points. How many months will it take the woman to break even on the points if she takes the lower interest rate loan, using simple arithmetic?
   a. 48.5
   b. 58.6
   c. 87.6
   d. 101

15.   ARM loans are more popular
   a. than fixed-rate mortgages in most markets.
   b. when interest rates are low.
   c. for people who are risk-averse.
   d. when interest rates are high.

16.   A man is shopping for a new loan and has narrowed the field to two choices. One is a 30-year fixed-rate loan that has principal and interest payments of $940 per month. The other is a biweekly mortgage. What is the difference in the annual payments based on this information?
   a. $470
   b. $940
   c. No difference in payments but a big difference in interest saved
   d. No difference in payments and no difference in interest saved

17.   When compared with a 30-year mortgage, a 15-year mortgage has
   a. more flexibility in repayment possibilities.
   b. slightly higher interest rates.
   c. slightly lower interest rates.
   d. lower monthly payments.

18.   Popular literature shows dramatic interest savings on a 15-year loan versus a 30-year loan. What is TRUE about most of these analyses?
   a. Amounts saved are even more because income tax effects are not considered.
   b. They are false because a borrower with a 30-year loan saves more in interest costs.
   c. They usually show that the amounts of interest saved are not substantial.
   d. Amounts saved usually are less because opportunity costs of the additional payments required are not considered.

19.   Disclosure of the annual percentage rate of interest need NOT
   a. be given to the borrower within three days of loan application.
   b. be computed to the nearest one-eighth of 1%.
   c. show the total financing cost in relation to the amount financed.
   d. be given to a prospective buyer of a single-family home who is paying all cash.

20.   Which is TRUE about a loan's effective interest rate?
   a.   Each point equals a .5% increase in the lender's yield.
   b.   Origination fees should be added to the points charged in making the calculation.
   c.   Each point equals a one-eighth of 1% increase in the lender's yield, even if the loan is in force for less than five years.
   d.   Origination fees should not be considered on an ARM based on index changes.

12

ACQUIRING FINANCING FOR THE PROPERTY

LEARNING OBJECTIVES

When you finish reading this chapter, you will be able to:

- list the four basic loan processing procedures,

- differentiate between qualifying the borrower and qualifying the property,

- itemize at least three sources of income that will be counted when qualifying a buyer,

- list the components of a full title report, and

- describe the differences between an owner's title insurance policy and a lender's title insurance policy.

KEY TERMS

credit scoring	loan processing procedure	quality of income
FICO score	loan underwriting	quantity of income

OVERVIEW

The regulatory overhaul following the financial crisis is resulting in big changes in how buyers obtain a mortgage. There are more protections against risky or complex mortgages. There are fewer choices of loans available, and the loans might be a little more expensive. Fewer borrowers will qualify. Lending standards are tighter today than at any time during the past 20 years.

The origination of a home mortgage is subject to a number of federal statutes, particularly the Equal Credit Opportunity Act (ECOA), the Consumer Credit Protection Act (Title I: Truth in Lending Act), and the Real Estate Settlement Procedures Act (RESPA). Together, these laws control the information a lender may obtain and consider in qualifying consumer mortgage loan applicants. They also dictate both the content and the form of information lenders must present to borrowers, the procedure for closing mortgage loan agreements, the documents to be used in closings, and the fees that may be charged.

Because of increasing concern about protection of consumer rights, most mortgage lenders have developed specific guidelines for loan underwriters to follow to ensure compliance with federal laws affecting consumer mortgage lending. Although the guidelines are protective of consumers' rights, they do not interfere with the analysis of an applicant's credit standing. The purpose of such guidelines is to prevent homebuyers from being victimized, not to guarantee that a loan will be approved. In the final analysis, good underwriting policies and practices by a lender combine compliance with the continual search for financial safety and streamlined processing. Licensees can serve themselves and their customers well by becoming knowledgeable about residential mortgage loan processing and closing.

Most lenders follow loan processing procedures that reflect a combined concern for the borrower's credit ability and the collateral's value. Some loan transactions require an emphasis of one factor over the other, but generally both borrower credit and collateral value are essential determinants in the real estate finance loan processing equation.

TRENDS IN THE MORTGAGE MARKET

Lending standards tightened because of the financial crisis and plummeting housing values. New regulations require:

- lenders to retain at least 5% of the loans that are securitized, except for those fully documented fixed-rate loans that are considered "safe";
- stricter limits on prepayment penalties or fees that lenders charge when a loan is paid off early;
- borrowers to show they can pay the loan, and lenders will have to require much more documentation—self-employed borrowers may have more problems getting a loan; and
- creation of management companies to facilitate the ordering of appraisals by lenders and act as insulators from lender pressure in arriving at market value.

These changes were the result of loose regulation during the bubble years of real estate lending. Wall Street was responsible for many of the problems, with pressure to securitize more and more mortgages. The result was many fraudulent mortgages.

Mortgage Fraud

For years, Florida has had the dubious distinction of having more mortgage fraud cases than any other state. Mortgage brokers, appraisers, real estate licensees, sellers, buyers, builders, and others have been found guilty of financial fraud, identity theft, mail fraud, and other crimes, carrying sentences of up to 30 years in prison. Florida laws regulating mortgage brokers were changed to help reduce the incidence of fraud.

CHANGES TO LAWS REGULATING MORTGAGE BROKERS AND APPRAISERS

Loan Originators and Mortgage Brokers

The Florida Office of Financial Regulation oversees loan originators and mortgage brokers under the provisions of Chapter 494, F.S.

Persons who engage in loan modification activities must be licensed under Chapter 494.

Loan originators working as employees of lenders are no longer exempt from licensing. Loan modification activities require the borrower's written consent. The modifier may charge fees only after performing all services under the agreement and only if the modification results in material benefit to the borrower.

Mortgage broker license applicants and licensees must submit filings on uniform forms via the Nationwide Mortgage Licensing System and Registry (NMLS). The application review will include not only a criminal background check but also a review of the applicant's credit history. Applicants who have had a bankruptcy or who have charge-offs must provide a satisfactory explanation.

A Mortgage Broker Guaranty Trust Fund, somewhat like the Real Estate Recovery Fund, was established, with payments into the fund by applicants and licensees. Payment from the fund in settlement of a claim against a licensee will result in revocation of the license.

All licenses issued under Chapter 494 must be renewed annually by December 31 through the NMLS. A criminal background check and a credit report are required for each renewal.

The principal loan originator or branch manager must sign and date the mortgage broker agreement, and include the loan originator's unique NMLS identifier. Fees received by the business (mortgage broker) from a borrower must be identified as a loan origination fee, with the exception of application and third-party fees. Fees must be disclosed in dollar amounts.

The office may summarily suspend a license if there is reason to believe that a licensee poses an immediate, serious danger to the public's health, safety, or welfare; if the licensee has been arrested for any felony crime or any crime involving fraud, dishonesty, breach of trust, money laundering; or any other act of moral turpitude.

Mortgage lenders must meet specific net worth requirements, depending on the activities of the lender, and provide financial statements to the office.

The law added penalties for the following:

- Attempting to manipulate or influence an appraiser's evaluation of a property
- Being convicted of, or entering a plea of guilty or nolo contendere to, regardless of adjudication, any felony
- Having a loan originator, mortgage broker, or mortgage lender license, or the equivalent of such license, revoked in any jurisdiction
- Engaging in unfair, deceptive, or misleading advertising

Maximum fines for violations of Chapter 494 were increased to $25,000 for each count or separate offense. Persons who are guilty of unlicensed activity may be fined up to $1,000 per day to a maximum $25,000. The Office of Financial Regulation must report disciplinary actions to the NMLS.

Some penalties carry lifetime bans from licensure.

Appraisers and Appraisal Management Companies

The appraisal profession in Florida is regulated by the Florida Real Estate Appraisal Board (FREAB). The FREAB also regulates appraisal management companies. These companies retain appraisers to perform appraisal services for clients or act as intermediaries between clients and appraisers to facilitate the clients' contracting with appraisers.

Appraisal management companies must be registered with the DBPR. Owners, direc-tors, officers, or partners, depending on the type of entity, must be registered with the department and pass a criminal background check. They must sign a pledge to comply with the *Uniform Standards of Professional Appraisal Practice (USPAP)*. These persons may not have had a registration or license to practice any profession denied or revoked.

For example, if Bayfront National Bank has taken a loan application, the bank may contact XYZ Appraisal Managers, Inc. to arrange for a property appraisal. XYZ will then assign one or more appraisers from its appraisal panel to prepare the appraisal report. XYZ Appraisal Managers, Inc., would violate the law if it:

- instructs an appraiser to violate the *USPAP*;
- accepts an appraisal assignment if the fee is contingent on a predetermined result;
- contracts with an appraiser whose license has been suspended or revoked; or
- attempts to influence the appraisal by:
    - withholding payment or future business,
    - promising future business,
    - conditioning a request for service based on a preliminary estimate from the appraiser,
    - requesting a preliminary valuation from the appraiser,
    - providing to the appraiser a desired value for a subject property,
    - allowing the removal of an appraiser from an appraiser panel without prior written notice, or
    - paying for a second appraisal without cause.

In Practice

Refuse to get involved in questionable practices involving mortgage loans. State and federal authorities vigorously enforce the law.

Equal Credit Opportunity

Lenders are required by the civil rights acts to refrain from discriminating against con-sumer mortgage loan applicants based on race, color, national origin, religion, sex, age, or marital status. Borrowers' rights have been enhanced since passage of the Equal Credit Opportunity Act (ECOA) and the Federal Reserve Board of Governor's Regulation B, which implemented the act. The ECOA requires fair consideration of consumer loan applications from women, minority races, part-time employees, and others who may have suffered prejudicial treatment in the past. Additionally, lenders may not discriminate based on the fact that all or part of the applicant's income comes from any public assis-tance program or on the fact that the applicant has exercised any right under any federal consumer credit protection law.

QUALIFYING THE BORROWER

The framework for current real estate financing is the 30-year amortization schedule and regular monthly payments of principal and interest. In addition, mortgagees currently can lend up to 100% of a property's value. High loan-to-value ratios combined with long-term loan amortization payment schedules require that a lender look to the credit of the borrower as the primary protection.

Even though lenders using insured or guaranteed programs of real estate finance do not bear the risks of default directly, they still must follow the directions of their guaranteeing agencies and carefully screen loan applicants to derive some reasonable estimate of borrowers' ability to pay and their inclinations to meet their contractual obligations responsibly. Thus, a great effort is made to check and evaluate thoroughly a potential mortgagor's credit history and current financial status to predict her future economic stability.

To accomplish the financial safety goals of government agencies and originating lenders, the following four basic **loan processing procedures** have been developed:

1. Determining a borrower's ability to repay the loan
2. Estimating the value of the property being pledged as collateral to guarantee this repayment
3. Researching and analyzing the marketability of the collateral's title
4. Preparing the documents necessary to close the loan transaction

Loan underwriting is the evaluation of the risks involved when issuing a new mortgage. This process involves qualifying the borrower and the property to determine whether they meet the minimum requirements established by the lender, investor, or secondary market in which the loan probably will be sold.

Loan Application

**Forms
To Go**

When a licensee works with a buyer, one of the services the licensee can offer is that of helping the buyer obtain financing. Before the buyer goes to the lender to make an application, the licensee should provide a list of items the buyer will need (see the mortgage loan application checklist in Appendix B).

Data Verification. The loan processor will verify the information included in the application by actually checking with the various references given, the banks where deposits are held, and the applicant's employer.

Deposits. The borrower must sign a separate deposit verification form for each bank account, authorizing the bank to reveal to the lender the current balance in the borrower's account. Under the Federal Right to Privacy Act of 1974 (FERPA), the bank cannot release such confidential information without a verification form. The knowledge that the loan processor can verify account amounts usually is enough incentive for the borrower to be truthful in reporting financial information. When the deposit balances are verified, the appropriate entries are made in the applicant's file.

Employment. The applicant also is required to sign an employment verification form authorizing the employer to reveal confidential information concerning the applicant's job status. Not only will the applicant's wages or salary and length of employment be verified but the employer also will be requested to offer an opinion of the applicant's job attitude and give a prognosis for continued employment and prospects for advancement. Employment may be checked again before closing.

Credit Report. Simultaneously with the gathering of financial and employment information, the loan processor sends a formal request for the borrower's credit report to a local company offering this service. The credit report is a central part of the loan approval process, and the lender relies on it heavily. Of the two types of credit reports, consumer credit and mortgage credit, this discussion centers on the latter.

A credit report is the result of the compilation of information accumulated from a thorough check of the creditors indicated on the loan application, as well as a check of the public records to discover whether any lawsuits are pending against the applicant. When completed, the credit search company sends the loan processor a confidential report of its findings.

This report usually states the applicant's (and co-applicant's) age, address, status as a tenant or owner, and length of residency at his or her current address and includes a brief employment history and credit profile, both past and present. The credit profile itemizes the status of current and past accounts, usually identified by industry, such as banks, department and specialty stores, and finance companies. In addition, it indicates the quality and dates of the payments made and their regularity; delinquency and any outstanding balances also are reported. This payment history is the most important part of the report because it indicates how well the applicant has managed debt over time. Underwriters view a person's past behavior as the best indicator of future attitude toward debt repayment. Research tends to reinforce these opinions, indicating that slow and erratic payers generally retain those attitudes when securing new loans and that prompt and steady payers also are consistent in meeting their future obligations. As a result, lenders pay careful attention to the last section of a credit report, which indicates an applicant's attitude toward debt and the payment pattern.

When a credit report is returned revealing a series of erratic and delinquent payments, the loan is usually denied at this point and the file closed. An applicant who is denied a loan because of adverse information in a credit report has the right to inspect a summary of that report, to challenge inaccuracies, and to require corrections to be made (see the most current RESPA-required brochure, *Shopping for Your Home Loan*). If one or two unusual entries stand out in a group of otherwise satisfactory transactions, the applicant will be asked to explain these deviations.

As with many standardized procedures, credit reporting has become computerized, dramatically shortening the time needed for completing a check. In exchange for time efficiency, however, credit-reporting bureaus risk sacrificing the borrower's confidentiality. The fraudulent use of credit reports is increasing now that information is so easily accessed. Credit reports should be used only by the persons or institutions requesting the information and only for the purposes stated. Because of increased seller financing, credit bureaus are receiving more requests from agents and sellers to check the credit of potential purchasers. To protect a buyer's confidentiality, most credit agencies insist on receiving the buyer's written permission before issuing any information.

After the deposit and employment verifications are returned with acceptable information and a favorable credit report is obtained, the lending officer makes a thorough credit evaluation of the data collected before continuing with the loan process.

Evaluation of Credit Ability

Despite the standardization of the detailed guidelines used in the lending process, the one area allowing for the greatest amount of latitude in interpretation is the analysis and evaluation of a borrower's credit ability. A degree of subjective personal involvement may be introduced into an otherwise strongly objective and structured format by an evaluator's unintentional bias or by a loan company's changing policies.

In addition, credit standards are altered periodically to reflect a lender's changing monetary position. When money is scarce, standards are more stringent; when money is plentiful, standards are lowered. An applicant who qualifies for a loan at one time may not at another. Thus, although a credit analyst is governed by guidelines, rules, and regulations, the criteria fluctuate with the analyst's discretionary powers. In the long run, a lender's success is demonstrated by a low rate of default on approved loans and by the fact that no discrimination complaints have been filed.

Credit Scoring

One of the most significant changes in mortgage lending has been the use of credit scores to better evaluate a borrower's ability to repay.

Credit scoring uses statistical samples to predict how likely it is that a borrower will pay back a loan. To develop a model, the lender selects a large random sample of its borrowers, analyzing characteristics that relate to creditworthiness. Each of the characteristics is assigned a weight based on how strong a predictor it is. Credit scores treat each person objectively because the same standards apply to everyone. Credit scores are blind to demographic or cultural differences among people.

The most commonly used credit score today is known as a **FICO score**, named after the company that developed it, Fair, Isaac, & Co. FICO scores range from 300 to 850. The lower the score, the greater the risk of default.

Freddie Mac has found that borrowers with credit scores above 660 are more likely to repay the mortgage, and underwriters can do a basic review of the file for completeness. For applicants with scores between 620 and 660, the underwriter is required to do a comprehensive review. A very cautious review would be made for persons with credit scores below 620.

Is Credit Scoring Valid? With credit scoring, lenders can evaluate millions of applicants consistently and impartially on many different characteristics. To be statistically valid, the system must be based on a big enough sample. When properly designed, the system promotes fast, impartial decisions.

In 2009, Fair, Isaac, & Co. launched NextGen®, designed to more precisely define the risk of borrowers because it analyzes more criteria than the old model. Using the new model, lenders can evaluate credit profiles of high-risk borrowers in terms of degrees, rather than lumping them into the same category.

What Information Does Credit Scoring Use? The scoring models use the following information when evaluating a score:

- Of the score, 35% is determined by payment history with higher weight for recent history. If late payments, collections, and/or a bankruptcy appear in the credit report, they are subtracted from the score.
- Outstanding debt is very close in importance to payment history—30% of the total score. Many scoring models evaluate the amount of debt compared with the credit limits. If the amount owed is close to the credit limit, it affects the score negatively.
- Of the score, 15% is the result of credit history. A long history is better if payments are always on time.

1 ■ The score assigns 10% to very recent history and "inquiries" for new credit. If the
2 applicant has applied for credit in many places recently, it will negatively affect
3 the score. This problem occurs when a person goes car shopping. Sales associates
4 at each car lot will ask for the consumer's Social Security number in order to pull
5 a credit report (at "no charge"). The shopper has no idea that as more reports are
6 ordered, the shopper's credit rating declines.

7 ■ Finally, 10% is based on the mix of credit, including car loans, credit cards, and
8 mortgages. Too many credit cards will hurt a person's credit score. In some mod-
9 els, loans from finance companies or title loan companies will also hurt the score.

10 To improve the credit score, persons should pay bills on time, pay down outstanding
11 balances, and not take on new debt. It may take a long time to improve the score sig-
12 nificantly. See Figure 12.1 for examples of the effects on the FICO credit score caused by
13 actions a potential borrower might take.

F I G U R E 12.1 ■ Results on FICO Score From Certain Financial Decisions

Assume that your current FICO score is 707 (very good).

This table shows the likely effect on your score based on the following actions:

Action	New FICO Range
Currently have a combined revolving balance of $2,230 and you pay down $750 on the balance	
Paying your bills on time is a substantial factor affecting your FICO score. If you have no negative items on your file, your score will remain stable as you continue to pay your bills on time.	
If you have some history of late payments, how recently they occurred is important. The more recently they happened, the more impact they will likely have on your score. As they age, their impact on your score will gradually lessen.	707–727
Max out your credit cards	
Carrying extremely high balances on all of your revolving accounts makes you look "maxed out" on your available credit. It is often considered a high-risk trait by lenders and the FICO score.	
In this simulation, the impact to your FICO score will depend on how high your current balances are on your revolving accounts. If you already carry high balances, the impact will probably be minimal. The impact will be more noticeable if you currently have a low or medium balance.	637–687
Apply for and receive a new credit card with a credit limit of $3,000	
Consumers seeking and obtaining new credit are generally riskier than consumers who are not. The impact on your FICO score will vary, depending on your current credit profile. The score takes into consideration the level of your existing credit history (recently opened files versus more mature files, for example), the amount of recently opened credit you currently have on file, and other factors.	
This simulation is based on your applying for and receiving a new credit card with a limit of at least $3,000.	697–717
Miss payments on all accounts with a payment due	
FICO scores evaluate late payment information in a variety of ways, including the frequency of missed payments, the recency of the missed payments, and the level of delinquency (how late the payment is).	
In this simulation, the impact on your score of missing a payment will depend on your status and the level of the delinquency. For example, the impact will probably be more substantial if you miss a payment this month, and you currently have a spotless or relatively clean credit report. There will be less impact on the score if you currently have multiple negative items on your credit report.	582–632

Source: Fair, Isaac & Co.

Getting a Mortgage Loan Is More Difficult for Some People. During the years 2002 through 2006, the capital markets, particularly hedge funds, purchased from lenders what are called subprime mortgages. These were mortgages made to people who ordinarily would not have qualified for financing. In many cases, little or no documentation was required. Lending standards are now much stricter, and persons with poor credit find it very difficult to get financing for a house purchase.

Because of the default rate, many lenders that made mortgage loans to self-employed persons have gone out of business. Lenders that still offer the loans have made it tough. The self-employed will need the following:

- *More documentation.* Now, small-business owners will need more documentation, including two years of tax returns, profit-and-loss statements, bank statements, and proof that they've been in business for at least two years.

- *More money down.* They'll also need a bigger down payment. It may take 20% down to qualify.

- *Great credit.* A credit score lower than 700 probably will result in a turndown.

WEBLINK

The following are useful financial links:

Fannie Mae: www.fanniemae.com

Federal Housing Administration: http://portal.hud.gov/hudportal/HUD?src=/federal_housing_administration

Federal Reserve System: www.federalreserve.gov

Fair, Isaac & Co.: www.fico.com

Freddie Mac Home Page: www.freddiemac.com

HSH.com: www.hsh.com

U.S. Department of Veterans Affairs: www.va.gov

The quantity and quality of an applicant's income are the two major considerations in determining ability to support a family and make the required monthly loan payments. Analysts consider the **quantity of income**—the total income—when they review a loan application. Not only is the regular salary of a family's primary supporter basic to the analysis but also the inclusion of a spouse's full income. Extra sources of income also may be included in the analysis if circumstances warrant it.

Any bonuses will be accepted as income only if they are received on a regular basis. If commissions are a large part of an applicant's income base, the history of past earnings will be scrutinized to estimate the stability of this income as a regular source for an extended time. Overtime wages are not included in the analysis unless they have been—and will be—earned consistently. Pensions, interest, and dividends are treated as full income, although it is recognized that interest and dividends fluctuate over time and could stop if an investment were cashed out.

A second job is accepted as part of the regular monthly income if it can be established that the job has existed for approximately two years and there is good reason to believe it will continue. Child support also can be included in the determination of monthly income, but only if it is the result of a court order and has a proven track record. Government entitlement funds must also be considered.

In addition to its total quantity, a loan analyst pays careful attention to the **quality of income**. An applicant's employer will be asked for an opinion of job stability and possible advancement. Length of time on the job no longer carries the importance it once did. Applicants whose employment records show frequent shifts in job situations that result in upward mobility each time will be given full consideration. Lenders will, however, be wary of an applicant who drifts from one job classification to another and cannot seem to become established in any specific type of work.

When the accumulated data strongly support a positive or negative decision, the loan underwriter's decision is easy, and minimal use of discretion is needed. However, numerous borderline cases make it difficult for a loan officer to form objective judgments. In such a case, the loan officer schedules an in-depth personal interview with the applicant during which questions regarding data appearing on the credit report are clarified or mistakes in bank balances can be explained. More often, however, the loan officer merely wishes to visit with the applicant to observe and probe her attitudes regarding the purchase of the property and the repayment of the prospective loan. Thus, although a person's credit history can be measured objectively, personal character is subject to interpretation.

After reviewing all the information provided in the application. as well as the other data collected, the loan officer decides to either approve or disapprove the loan application. If the officer judges a loan application to be unacceptable, he states the reasons for the rejection, the parties to the loan are informed, and the file is closed.

QUALIFYING THE COLLATERAL

Despite the trend toward emphasizing a borrower's financial ability as the loan-granting criterion, real estate lenders and guarantors are practical and fully understand that life is filled with events beyond one's control. Death is a possibility that can abruptly eliminate a family's wage earner. Economic conditions can exert devastating financial impact. Corporate downsizing and layoffs have resulted in hardship for many families. Honest mistakes in personal decisions can result in bankruptcies, often damaging or destroying credit.

To reduce the risk of loss, real estate lenders look to the value of the collateral (the real property) as the basic underlying assurance for recovery of their investments in a default situation. The recent drop in home values has made the valuation process more difficult. The old definition of market value that excluded comparables when the sale was under duress has been modified so that some foreclosed properties are used as comparable sales.

DISCUSSION EXERCISE 12.1

Which do you consider the more important factor in granting or denying a mortgage application: the borrower's ability to make the required payments or the value of the collateral? Why?

ANALYZING THE TITLE

The assurance of good title is as essential to a loan's completion as are the borrower's credit and the collateral's value. In anticipation of issuing a loan, the loan officer secures a title report on the collateral property. The components of a full title report are a survey, a physical inspection of the collateral, and a search of the records to determine all the interests in a property. Normally, property interests are perfected through the appropriate filing and recording of standard notices. A recorded deed notifies the world that a grantee has the legal fee simple title to the property. A recorded construction lien, for example, is notice of another's interest in the property.

In Florida, two methods have been used to obtain assurance of good title: (1) the abstract and attorney's opinion of title and (2) title insurance. Title insurance is preferred. If title is later found to be bad, and an attorney's opinion was used, the buyer or the lender would have to sue the attorney to recover, but the attorney may not have the financial strength to reimburse for the loss. Lenders prefer title insurance, but whichever method is used, the title report should provide the loan officer and the lender's attorney with all available information relevant to the legal status of the subject property, as well as any interests revealed by constructive notice. This title search requirement represents another effort by the lender to protect the loan investment. Because title insurance is most lenders' and buyers' method of choice, it is discussed here.

Title Insurance

Title insurance companies combine the abstracting process with a program of insurance that guarantees the validity and accuracy of the title search. A purchaser of title insurance can rely on the insurance company's assets to back up its guarantee of a property's marketable title. This guarantee is evidenced by a policy of title insurance. Most financial institutions now require that a title policy be issued to them for the face amount of a loan. Insurance is defined simply as coverage against loss.

When a title insurance policy is issued to a lender, it is usually on the American Land Title Association (ALTA) form. While a standard title policy insures against losses overlooked in the search of the recorded chain of title, an ALTA policy expands this standard coverage to include many unusual risks, such as forgeries, incompetency of parties involved in issuing documents pertaining to the transfer of ownership, legal status of parties involved in the specific loan negotiations, surveying errors, and other possible off-record defects. Some additional risks can be and usually are covered by special endorsements to an insurance policy. These could include protection against any unrecorded easements or liens, rights of parties in possession of the subject property, mining claims, water rights, and additional negotiated special items pertinent to the property involved. Participants in the secondary mortgage market (Fannie Mae, Freddie Mac, and Ginnie Mae) generally require the expanded ALTA policy for the added protection it provides. Many lenders use the phrase "an ALTA policy" when describing an extended-coverage policy.

Surveys

Whether the abstract and opinion of title method or the title insurance policy method is used, a property's title is searched by an experienced abstractor who prepares a report of those recorded documents that clearly affect the quality of ownership. In addition, lenders usually require a survey of the collateral property as a condition for a new loan. Although many properties are part of subdivisions that have been engineered and described by licensed and registered surveyors and engineers, some owners might have enlarged their homes or made additions to the improvements since the original survey. These might not meet the various setback restrictions set forth in the local zoning laws. Some properties might have been resubdivided, while others now might have encroachment problems.

An ALTA survey is a boundary survey prepared in a way that meets minimum standards adopted by the American Land Title Association/American Congress on Surveying and Mapping (ALTA/ACSM). It's much more than just a boundary survey of the land with flags at the corners. An ALTA survey shows improvements, easements, rights-of-way, and other encumbrances that affect land ownership.

The surveyor must have a current title commitment. The title commitment includes the legal description of the property and legal descriptions of any easements and encumbrances. The surveyor works closely with the title insurance company because they depend on the others' work. The surveyor must show any encroachments, including pertinent information. The certification language of the ALTA survey includes the names of the parties, including buyer, seller, title company, and lender.

Defects

If a defect is found, sometimes called a cloud on the title, the loan process does not continue until the cloud is cleared to the lender's satisfaction. Such a cloud might be an unsatisfied construction lien, an income tax lien, a property tax lien, an easement infraction, an encroachment, or a zoning violation. Sometimes a borrower's name is not correct on the deed, an error exists in the legal description, or the deed has a faulty acknowledgment or lacks the appropriate signatures. Because of the many complexities in a real estate transaction, possibilities exist for defects to appear in a title search and property survey. It is the abstractor's responsibility to discover and report them.

In certain instances where clouds are difficult to remove by ordinary means, they must be cleared by filing suits to quiet title. After appropriate evidence is submitted, a judge removes or modifies an otherwise damaging defect in a title. The loan process can continue when a clear chain of title is shown on the public records.

SUMMARY

- The housing and financial crisis has resulted in tighter loan processing guidelines.

- Florida remains the number one state in mortgage fraud cases.

- The Florida Office of Financial Regulation oversees loan originators, mortgage brokers, and persons who engage in loan modification activities.

- Mortgage broker license applicants and licensees must submit filings on uniform forms via the Nationwide Mortgage Licensing System and Registry (NMLS).

- Real estate licensees and mortgage loan originators are prohibited from attempting to manipulate an appraiser's evaluation of property.

- Fines for violations of the law carry penalties of $25,000 and lifetime bans from licensure.

- Appraisal management companies must be registered with the DBPR.

- The various civil rights acts prohibit lenders from discriminating against consumer mortgage loan applicants based on race, color, national origin, religion, sex, age, or marital status.

- The Equal Credit Opportunity Act requires fair consideration of consumer loan applications from women, minority races, part-time employees, and others who may have suffered prejudicial treatment in the past.

- The process of obtaining a real estate loan includes four steps: qualifying a borrower, evaluating the collateral, analyzing the title, and closing the loan transaction.

- Loan underwriting is the evaluation of the risks involved in making a mortgage loan.

- Credit scoring uses statistical samples to predict how likely it is that a borrower will pay back a loan.

- The evaluation of the collateral is made by a certified appraiser giving an opinion of the subject property's value.

- In Florida, two methods have been used to obtain assurance of good title: (1) the abstract and attorney's opinion of title and (2) title insurance.

- Lenders generally require title insurance to guarantee the title search. When a title insurance policy is issued to a lender, it is usually on the American Land Title Association (ALTA) form.

R E V I E W   Q U E S T I O N S

1. Qualifying the buyer has to do with income and assets. Qualifying the property has to do with the
   a. income, credit report, and appraisal.
   b. appraisal, survey, and title report.
   c. appraisal, title report, and credit report.
   d. survey, title report, and income.

2. A lender, interested in evaluating an applicant's willingness to pay, reviews
   a. income.
   b. assets.
   c. the credit report.
   d. all of these.

3. Which is NOT one of the basic loan processing procedures?
   a. Determining a borrower's ability to repay the loan
   b. Researching and analyzing the marketability of the property's title
   c. Use of an appraisal management company
   d. Preparing the documents necessary to close the loan transaction

4. A man has a FICO credit score of 725. He pays an additional $1,000 down on his installment debt. His FICO score will MOST likely
   a. decline because he has less debt.
   b. increase because he has less debt.
   c. decline because he has less credit.
   d. be unaffected unless he does this for at least three consecutive months.

5. What is given greatest weight in calculating the FICO credit score?
   a. Outstanding debt
   b. Credit history
   c. Payment history, with higher weight for recent history
   d. Recent "inquiries" for new credit

6. Which federal law requires fair consideration of loan applications from women, minority races, part-time employees and others who may have been discriminated against in the past?
   a. Equal Credit Opportunity Act
   b. Real Estate Settlement Procedures Act
   c. Truth in Lending Act
   d. Consumer Credit Protection Act

7. The maximum fine for each violation that can be levied against a Florida mortgage loan originator or mortgage broker under Chapter 494 was increased to
   a. $5,000.
   b. $10,000.
   c. $25,000.
   d. $75,000.

8.   A woman earns $1,000 per week. Based on Fannie Mae's 28% housing expense ratio guidelines, for what monthly payment would she qualify?
     a. $867.33
     b. $1,000.00
     c. $1,120.00
     d. $1,213.33

9.   Bonuses are acceptable as income on a loan application, provided that they
     a. are actually collected.
     b. are regular occurrences.
     c. exceed $2,000 per year.
     d. total less than $2,000 per year.

10. A second job will NOT be counted as a source of income on a loan application if it
     a. pays less than $2,000 per year.
     b. is likely to continue.
     c. has been held for at least two years.
     d. is temporary.

11. The guidelines for loan underwriting are tightly structured. The one facet that allows the MOST subjectivity on the part of the lender's evaluation is the
     a. credit profile.
     b. amount of debt.
     c. asset valuation.
     d. income quantity.

12. The primary assurance to the lender if the borrower defaults on the loan is the
     a. borrower's income.
     b. borrower's assets.
     c. borrower's net worth.
     d. property value.

13. A title policy offering coverage over and above the standard coverage is which type of policies?
     a. Mortgagor's
     b. Fannie Mae
     c. Owner's
     d. ALTA

14. Because of the financial crisis, lender standards have become more
     a. lenient.
     b. strict.
     c. relaxed in the evaluation of credit.
     d. relaxed in the evaluation of income.

15. When a loan officer evaluates a credit report, the MOST important part of the report is the
     a. employment history.
     b. payment history.
     c. public records section.
     d. applicant's current address.

16. The employment verification is a NOT a check on the applicant's
    a. length of employment.
    b. salary.
    c. prognosis for continued employment.
    d. assets.

17. The components that together make a title report complete are a physical inspection of the collateral property, a search of the public records, and
    a. an abstract of title.
    b. a title insurance policy.
    c. a satisfaction of previous mortgage document.
    d. a survey of the property.

18. Which action will NOT negatively affect a FICO score?
    a. Applying for credit in several places
    b. Slow payment history
    c. High balances on credit cards
    d. Paying down debt

19. If a cloud on title cannot be easily removed by ordinary means, a court case is often the result. The legal action is called a suit
    a. for certiorari.
    b. to quiet title.
    c. for partition.
    d. for declaratory judgment.

20. The MOST common credit scoring used by lenders today was developed by
    a. Fanning and Investors Company.
    b. ING Investments.
    c. Fannie Mae.
    d. Fair, Isaac & Co.

13

CLOSING REAL ESTATE TRANSACTIONS

LEARNING OBJECTIVES

When you finish reading this chapter, you will be able to:

■ list at least four objectives of a preclosing inspection,

■ describe the reasons a real estate sales associate should provide closing documents to the buyer and seller at least one day in advance of a closing,

■ calculate prorations of taxes and prepaid interest on a new loan, and

■ review a Closing Disclosure before a closing.

KEY TERMS

certified check	intangible tax	preclosing walk-through
contingency	mortgage insurance	inspection
documentary stamp taxes	premium (MIP)	private mortgage insurance
funding fee		(PMI)

OVERVIEW

Once the real estate contract has been signed, the licensee's work has just begun. The parties to a transaction expect their sales associate to personally monitor and coordinate all the details of their closing. While the licensee may believe he has "passed the torch" to the next group of professionals (lenders and closing agents), the buyer and the seller continue to look to their sales associate to coordinate all the details of the transaction. These details are outlined in Figure 13.1.

A sales associate must be familiar with the documents that will be presented to the parties at the closing table. One of the most important documents, the Closing Disclosure, relates to the financial side of the transaction. A closing disclosure is, in effect, the purchase and sales agreement reduced to numbers. The sales associate must understand each number in the disclosure and be able to explain it clearly to the buyer or the seller. Chapter 13 is designed to make the process easier.

FIGURE 13.1 ■ The Road to Closing

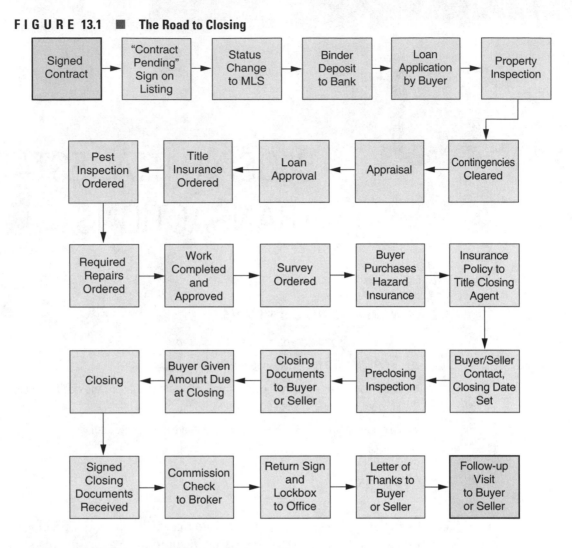

TEN STEPS TO A SUCCESSFUL CLOSING

Sales associates can avoid closing problems by following each of these 10 steps:

1. Disclose everything to all parties that will affect their decisions before the buyer and the seller sign the contract. Surprises after a contract is signed almost certainly will result in one party wanting to get out of the contract.

2. Write the contract carefully and properly explain it to the parties.

3. Recommend that buyers and sellers select lenders and title closing agents who are organized professionals able to meet deadlines.

4. Tell the loan officer and closing agent what the licensee expects in the way of communication and performance.

5. Prepare a Property Sale Information Sheet (see Appendix B).

6. Give the closing agent a copy of the prior title insurance policy, if possible.

7. Provide a complete legal description of the property to the closing agent.

8. Ask a lender and a title agent to communicate by email, speeding the process while also giving written documentation of the transaction.

**Forms
To Go**

**Forms
To Go**

**Forms
To Go**

9. Use a checklist of duties such as the Closing Progress Chart (see Appendix B).

10. Ask the closing agent to close the buyer's and the seller's sides separately to reduce confusion during the closing.

THE SALES INFORMATION SHEET

To organize the work program, the sales associate needs to complete the Property Sale Information Sheet (see Appendix B). It provides necessary data about the sale, the cooperating agent, the lender, the title company, and more. This form should be clipped inside the closing file and referred to as necessary when servicing the sale.

Establishing a Plan of Action

One of the first steps after both the buyer and the seller sign the contract is to set up a plan for closing. This step is even more important if another sales associate is involved because miscommunication often delays closings and causes unnecessary problems. Organization and attention to detail are keys to a successful closing.

THE CLOSING PROGRESS CHART

The Closing Progress Chart will help the licensee organize the details of the closing. If there is a cooperating licensee, the chart should be a joint effort so that licensees agree about which licensee will handle certain duties and when the tasks should be completed. Once the associates agree, each sales associate should place a copy of the chart in the closing file. Additionally, each date scheduled should be transferred to the sales associate's appointment book. As each task is completed, the sales associate should place a check mark in the appropriate row. An "X" in the chart indicates that comments have been made on the back of the form. A discussion of each item follows.

Preclosing Duties

Sold or Sale Pending Sign on Listed Property. Placing a Sold or Sale Pending sign on the listed property is a function of the listing sales associate. Some sellers prefer a Sold sign so that prospective buyers are no longer escorted through the property, while others do not want to discourage activity until at least after the buyer's loan approval and prefer a Sale Pending sign.

Notice of Under Contract to MLS. Multiple listing services (MLSs) require that all offices be notified of a listed property's status. Failure to change the status to "under contract" can result in agents from other offices appearing at the property with customers or clients. This wastes both the sales associate's and the prospective buyers' time and reflects poorly on the listing office.

Binder Deposited in Bank. A sales associate must give the earnest money deposit to the broker no later than the end of the next business day. FREC rules require that the buyer's good-faith deposit be placed in a bank no later than three business days after receipt of the funds. The broker might deposit the funds immediately or wait until the seller accepts the contract (in no case, however, may the broker wait longer than three days). If a title-closing agent will hold the deposit, the broker must deliver the deposit to the title-closing agent within the same periods allowed by FREC for depositing the funds in a brokerage account. The broker should get a receipt for the funds.

Get a Receipt if the Title Closing Agent Is Holding the Deposit. If an attorney or title insurance company will hold the buyer's deposit, you must indicate the name and address of the entity, and get a written receipt proving you delivered the deposit on time.

Additional Binder Received, if Required. If the contract requires that the buyer put up additional funds as a good-faith deposit, it is the sales associate's responsibility to ensure that the funds are received and deposited according to FREC requirements. The buyer's failure to comply with contract requirements is a default. The seller must be notified and the seller's instructions followed.

Loan Application Made by Buyer. The Florida REALTORS® contract requires that the buyer make application for the loan by a certain date. The buyer's failure to comply with contract terms is a default, and the seller must be notified.

Contingencies Cleared in Writing. Sales associates must ensure that contingencies are satisfied as soon as possible. Some normal contingencies include a home inspection, a soil test, a roof inspection, and financing. If a problem arises with one of the contingencies, sales associates should do everything within their power to correct the problem, and all parties should be made aware of the situation.

Appraisal. The appraisal normally is ordered and paid for at the time of loan application. The sales associate wants to be certain that the appraiser selected by the financial institution has complete cooperation, particularly with respect to access to the property. Failure to provide access wastes the appraiser's time and may delay the closing.

Loan Approval. The Florida REALTORS® contract requires a loan commitment within a certain number of days from the contract's effective date. The licensee must monitor the lender's progress and provide to the lender immediately any information or documents requested. The lender's failure to provide the commitment within the required time may allow the buyer or the seller to void the contract.

Title Insurance Ordered. Many lenders permit the sales associate to select the title-closing agent, provided the company is on the lender's approved list. The seller or the buyer also may have a preference in making the decision, based on who will pay for the policy. Many title companies prefer that the agent deliver the contract and financing information even before loan approval is obtained so that the title search can begin. Often little time is available from loan approval to closing, and the companies like a head start. If that is the case, the licensee must verify that the title company agrees to take the risk of a failed closing and that it will not charge a fee if the sale does not close.

The licensee should give the title-closing agent the following items when a title insurance order is placed:

- A signed and dated sales contract
- A previous title insurance policy on the property, if available
- Enough information about the sellers, the buyers, the property, and the lender to process and close the transaction, including:
    - the sellers' and the buyers' marital status;
    - a complete legal description—for example, lot, block, subdivision name, phase or unit, recording information, and county;
    - street address, including ZIP code;
    - terms of any purchase-money mortgage the title company must prepare;

- ■ closing date and information about whether all parties will attend; and
- ■ information on commission to broker and commission splits between brokers.

Wood-Destroying Organisms Inspection Ordered. As soon as possible after loan approval, the wood-destroying organisms (WDO) inspection should be ordered. When it is completed, copies of the report should be delivered to the buyer, lender, and title-closing agent. If treatment or repairs are required, agents working with the buyer and the seller should communicate and agree on the details. If a structural inspection is required, a licensed contractor should be engaged to report on and estimate repair costs. Normally, the lender requires that treatment and repairs be completed satisfactorily before closing, so parties should act immediately in having the work performed.

Required Repairs Ordered. Many contracts require repairs other than those covered by termite damage. The appraisal could show the need for a new roof, or the buyer may have made the contract contingent on the seller's replacing a swimming pool vinyl liner, for example. As soon as loan approval is obtained, the work should be ordered.

In Practice

Don't order repairs in your name. If the transaction doesn't close, you might have to pay for the repairs ordered. The seller or the buyer, as appropriate, should contract for the work. You should limit your activities to getting estimates and putting the parties in touch.

Required Repairs Completed and Approved. When the work has been completed, the appropriate party should inspect the work to be sure that it has been done properly. A licensee who takes on this responsibility is responsible if deficiencies are discovered later.

Survey Ordered. The lender or the title-closing agent often orders the survey after loan approval. A licensee who orders the survey without written approval may be liable for the fee if the sale does not close. In case of survey problems such as encroachments, the sales associate must act quickly to help clear up the problems.

Buyer Purchases Hazard Insurance. The buyer should purchase the hazard insurance policy as soon as possible in the transaction, especially during Florida's hurricane season. If a hurricane or tropical storm develops anywhere within the "box," as shown in Figure 13.2, insurance companies stop writing insurance until the danger has passed. If there are several hurricanes at sea, the delay could be for a week or more and might cause significant delay of a closing.

Contact Buyer and Seller for Closing Appointment. Soon after loan approval, the title-closing agent should be able to set a closing date and time. The sales associate should coordinate with the buyer and the seller in setting a time agreeable to all. All parties should be notified of the date, time, and place of the closing as far in advance as possible.

F I G U R E 13.2 ■   Area of Tropical Storms and Hurricanes That Cause Insurance Delays

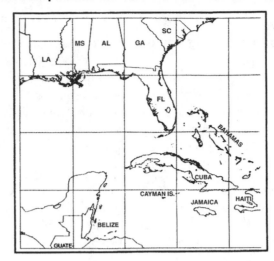

Preclosing Inspection. The buyer should make a **preclosing walk-through inspection.** The inspection is to ensure that:

- the property is ready for occupancy;
- personal property the seller is required to leave remains on the property;
- all required repairs and maintenance have been completed; and
- the property has been maintained in the condition as it existed at the time of contract, ordinary wear and tear excepted.

The sales associate should not conduct such an inspection because of the liability involved. When the inspection has been completed to the buyer's satisfaction, the sales associate should ask the buyer to sign a preclosing clearance form, such as the Preclosing Walk-Through Inspection Results in Appendix B.

**Forms
To Go**

Closing Papers Reviewed With Buyer and Seller Before Closing. Upon receiving the documents, the sales associate should arrange an appointment to visit the buyer or the seller and deliver copies of all documents that the person will sign. The sales associate should review the closing statement carefully to ensure that all items are correct and should explain each item to the buyer or the seller at the appointment. The closing will go more quickly and pleasantly for the person who has reviewed all documents the evening before.

In Practice

As soon as you get the closing documents, compare the Closing Disclosure with the sellers' net proceeds statement you prepared for the sellers, or that the lender made for the buyers. If the figures are materially different (especially if they're higher than predicted), you need to track down the difference and get ready to explain it.

Closing statements are covered later in this chapter.

Buyer Given Figure for Certified Check for Closing. This settlement check figure should be provided to the buyer as soon as possible to allow time for the buyer to wire funds to the title closing agent. Most closing agents now require that the amount due at closing be in "collected funds."

Binder Check Prepared to Take to Closing. At least one day before closing, the sales associate should get the binder check from the broker and clip it to the file folder that will be taken to the closing. Also included in the folder will be the contract and other related material, as well as copies of the inspection reports.

THE CLOSING STATEMENT

Buyers and sellers expect their sales associates to coordinate and monitor every step of the closing process. The last step is the closing itself. A sales associate must be familiar with the documents that will be presented to the parties at the closing table. One of the most important documents, the Closing Disclosure, relates to the financial side of the transaction.

A closing statement is, in effect, the purchase and sales agreement reduced to numbers. The sales associate must understand each number in the statement and be able to explain it clearly to the buyer or the seller. The material in this chapter is designed to make the process easier.

PRORATIONS AND PREPAYMENTS

In every closing, property income and expenses should be prorated between the buyer and the seller. Usually, the 365-day method is used for prorations of annual expenses. The annual cost is divided by 365 days to get a daily rate. That rate is then multiplied by the number of days involved to get the amount due.

Proration calculations should be based on the last day of seller ownership. The day of closing is charged to the buyer, although it is possible that, by negotiation or custom in an area, the day of closing would be charged to the seller.

Property tax is the most common proration on a closing statement.

Prorating Property Taxes

The buyer normally pays property taxes in arrears, so they would be a debit to the seller and credit to the buyer. If the closing occurs in November or December, it is possible that the seller has paid the tax bill already, resulting in a credit to the seller and a debit to the buyer.

Closing date—April 15
Property taxes—$2,275

	Beginning	**Closing date**	End
	1/1	**4/15**	12/31
	Seller	Buyer	
	104 days	261 days	

Number of days from January 1 through April 15:

January	31
February	28
March	31
April	14
Total	104

Daily rate—$2,275 ÷ 365 days = $6.23288 per day

Proration—$6.23288 × 104 days = $648.22

■ Debit the seller; credit the buyer.

PROPERTY TAX PRORATION EXERCISE 13.1

Do the following property tax prorations:

Closing Date	Taxes	Debit	Credit	Amount
September 12	$2,567.00			$
November 18	$4,260.00 (Paid 11/3)			$
April 24	$1,892.56			$

Prepayments for New Loan

When an institutional lender makes a new loan, and if the loan-to-value ratio is greater than 80%, the lender likely will require that an escrow fund for taxes, hazard insurance, and mortgage insurance be maintained. The borrower must deposit a sum into a lender's escrow account so that adequate funds will be available to make the payments when required. The amount of the specific charges varies with the time of the year the loan is closed. Once the escrow account is established, a monthly amount for taxes, insurance, and any required mortgage insurance is added to the monthly principal and interest payment. These funds, placed in a trust account, become the responsibility of the financial institution, which must pay such items when they are due. Some of those prepaid items are discussed here.

Prepaid Taxes

The lender normally collects taxes by adding the months of the year through closing, then adding two or three more months. For instance, if the closing is in April, the lender takes four months plus another three. In effect, the proration credit for three-plus months that the buyer receives from the seller offsets the effect of the lender's charge.

Closing date—April 15
Taxes—estimated at $2,275 for the year
Monthly taxes—$2,275 ÷ 12 = $189.58

The first payment will be on June 1. The lender will escrow seven months so that when November comes, the lender will have sufficient funds to pay the property tax bill.

monthly taxes $189.58 × 7 months = $1,327.06

■ Debit the buyer for the amount of prepaid taxes.

The buyer has received a proration credit of $648.22 from the seller, so the net from the buyer to set up the account is $678.84.

PREPAID TAX CALCULATION EXERCISE 13.2

Assuming the lender wants three extra months, calculate the amount of taxes to be escrowed.

Closing Date	Taxes for the Year	Prepaid Amount
January 18	$2,400.00	$
July 3	$4,842.30	$
September 30	$1,453.89	$

Prepaid Insurance

The buyer must pay the first year's policy in advance, plus two months. For example, if the insurance policy is $1,160, the monthly payment is $96.67 ($1,160 ÷ 12). Often the statement shows 14 months prepayment. In other cases, if the buyer has paid the premium outside closing (POC), the statement shows only two months.

■ Debit the buyer for one year plus two months' prepaid insurance.

PREPAID INSURANCE CALCULATION EXERCISE 13.3

Calculate the amount of insurance to be escrowed in the following example. The lender wants it paid in advance plus two extra months.

Closing	Insurance for the Year	Prepaid Amount
January 18	$2,400	$
July 3	$900	$
September 30	$2,200 (POC)	$

Prepaid Interest

Because the first payment covers the interest for the previous month, interest is collected at closing for the days remaining in the closing month.

Closing date—April 15

First payment on the mortgage—June 1

The first payment covers May interest. Interest must be collected on the day of closing from April 15 through April 30 (16 days).

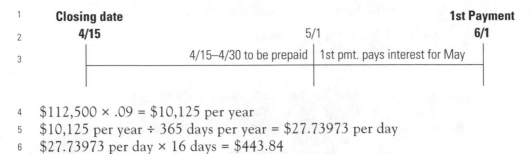

$112,500 × .09 = $10,125 per year

$10,125 per year ÷ 365 days per year = $27.73973 per day

$27.73973 per day × 16 days = $443.84

   ■ Debit the buyer $443.84 for prepaid interest.

PREPAID INTEREST CALCULATION EXERCISE 13.4

Calculate the interest prepayment for the new loans as follows:

Closing Date	Mortgage Loan Amount	Interest Rate	Prepaid Amount
September 12	$245,000	8.875%	$
January 17	$92,500	8.75%	$
December 29	$127,000	9.0%	$

Prepaid Mortgage Insurance

If mortgage insurance is required as part of an FHA or conventional mortgage loan, the borrower is charged for the coverage required.

The FHA requires homebuyers to pay two types of **mortgage insurance premiums (MIPs)**:

   1. Up-front MIP (UFMIP), which is a percentage of the mortgage amount

   2. Annual premium, which is calculated on the unpaid principal balance

The VA does not charge for guaranteeing a loan; however, it imposes a **funding fee** based on the mortgage amount. This funding fee may be included as part of the amount borrowed or paid in one lump sum at closing. A lender also may require an amount in cash adequate to open an escrow account, plus 1% of the loan amount as a maximum placement fee. Under VA loan rules, the closing costs and placement fees cannot be included in the loan amount.

Conventional lenders require **private mortgage insurance (PMI)** when a loan-to-value (LTV) ratio is more than 80%. Premiums fall into two general categories. In the first case, a single premium covers a lender's risk for a 10-year period. In the second case, a lender imposes a lower initial fee on the borrower and charges an insurance premium each year after that until the unpaid principal is reduced to a designated amount, normally 80% of appraised value. The first plan's one-time, single-premium charge or the second plan's lower initial cost is payable by the borrower at the time the loan closes. It should be noted that a PMI rate card must be used because of the different types of loans available and the different coverages required.

It is probably best not to make a large up-front payment but instead to make a higher monthly payment. In case of an early loan payoff, the premium is not refunded.

DOCUMENTARY STAMP TAXES AND INTANGIBLE TAXES

Documentary stamp taxes are collected on the deed and the note. The seller normally pays for stamps on the deed, and the buyer pays for note stamps. The deed stamps are based on the sales price and are $.70 per $100 or fraction thereof. For example, if a property sells for $140,000, the documentary stamp taxes would be calculated as follows:

$$\$140,000 \div \$100 = 1,400 \text{ increments}$$
$$1,400 \times \$0.70 = \$980$$

DEED STAMPS TAX CALCULATION EXERCISE 13.5

Calculate the documentary stamp taxes on the deed for the following sales prices:

Sales Price	Document Stamp Amount
$325,000	$
$127,415	$
$93,000	$

Documentary stamp taxes on the new note are based on the amount of the new or the assumed mortgage and are $.35 per $100 or fraction thereof. No stamps are charged on notes taken subject to the mortgage because the buyer has not assumed any of the debt obligations. For example, if the note amount on a new mortgage were $112,500, the documentary stamp tax would be calculated on the note amount as follows:

$$\$112,500 \div \$100 = 1,125 \text{ increments}$$
$$1,125 \times \$.35 = \$393.75$$

Intangible tax on the new mortgage is calculated by multiplying the mortgage amount by .002. No tax is charged on existing recorded mortgages. The buyer normally pays this charge. For example, the intangible taxes on a new mortgage of $112,500 would be calculated as follows:

$$\$112,500 \times .002 = \$225. \text{ There is no rounding.}$$

NOTE STAMPS AND INTANGIBLE TAX CALCULATION EXERCISE 13.6

Calculate the documentary stamp taxes on the following note amounts:

Note Amount	Documentary Stamp Amount	Intangible Tax Amount
$125,000	$	$
$157,415	$	$
$53,000	$	$

**Forms
To Go**

CLOSING DISCLOSURE

The Closing Disclosure is an itemized listing of the funds payable at closing (see Appendix B). Closing agents must prepare the Closing Disclosure for the parties in a federally related mortgage loan. The totals at the bottom of page 3 of the Closing Disclosure show the seller's net proceeds and the amount due from the buyer at closing.

The Closing Disclosure has five pages:

- Page 1 shows the parties, the property description, the lender, the settlement agent, and a recap of the Loan Estimate given at the time of application.

- Page 2 itemizes the settlement charges for each party, such as the broker's commission, loan closing costs, prepaid items, escrow account setup, title charges, and recording charges. Each item in the statement is assigned a separate number within a standardized numbering system. The totals for each party on page 2 are transferred to page 3.

- Page 3 summarizes the transaction and shows the amount of cash due from the buyer, as well as the seller's proceeds at closing.

- Page 4 shows additional information about the loan.

- Page 5 shows loan calculations, and provides contact information for lender, broker, and settlement agent.

Closing Disclosure Example

The following information will help the student review a completed Closing Disclosure.

Anita Wilson purchases a home from Wendy Stratton. The closing date is April 15, with the day of closing charged to the buyer. The price of the property is $125,000, and Anita is financing the purchase with a new 7.5% loan for 90% of the purchase price. She'll pay 1% of the mortgage as points and a 1% origination fee.

She gives the broker a $5,000 binder check. The seller will pay off the existing first mortgage. The payoff amount, including interest, is $74,298.60. The seller has agreed to give the buyer a $2,000 allowance for new carpeting; the lender has approved this allowance. Annual property tax, estimated at $1,750, is the only item to be prorated.

The lender requires the buyer to purchase a hazard insurance policy and pay the premium for one year ($545). The lender collects enough at closing to open the escrow account to include three months of taxes, two months of hazard insurance, and two months of private mortgage insurance. The first payment on the mortgage is due on June 1. The buyer paid outside closing (POC) for the appraisal ($300) at the time of loan application. Other typical loan closing expenses are entered on the appropriate lines.

Based on this information, Figure 13.3 shows a completed Closing Disclosure form.

F I G U R E 13.3 ■ Closing Disclosure

Closing Cost Details

Loan Costs	Borrower-Paid		Seller-Paid		Paid by Others
	At Closing	Before Closing	At Closing	Before Closing	
A. Origination Charges	**$2,250.00**				
01 1.0 % of Loan Amount (Points)	$1,125.00				
02 1.0% of Loan Amount (Origination Fee)	$1,125.00				
03					
04					
05					
06					
07					
08					
B. Services Borrower Did Not Shop For	**$302.00**		**$20.00**		**$300.00**
01 Appraisal Fee (POC) to Lafayette Appraisers					$300.00
02 Credit Report to Credit Bureau	$55.00				
03 Tax Services to Transamerica Tax Service	$59.00				
04 Underwriting Fee to First South Bank	$100.00				
05 Document Preparation Fee to First South Bank	$75.00				
06 Courier Fee to First South Bank	$13.00		$20.00		
07					
08					
09					
10					
C. Services Borrower Did Shop For	**$1,397.50**		**$225.00**		
01 Title Services to Jones & Smith (Lender)	$922.50				
02 Title Services to Jones & Smith (Owner)	$475.00				
03 Attorney Fees to Jones & Smith			$225.00		
04					
05					
06					
07					
08					
D. TOTAL LOAN COSTS (Borrower-Paid)	**$3,949.50**		**$245.00**		**$300.00**
Loan Costs Subtotals (A + B + C)	$3,949.50		$245.00		$300.00

Other Costs	Borrower-Paid		Seller-Paid		Paid by Others
	At Closing	Before Closing	At Closing	Before Closing	
E. Taxes and Other Government Fees	**$684.75**		**$881.00**		
01 Recording Fees Deed: $6.00 Mortgage: $60.00	$66.00		$6.00		
02 Transfer Taxes	$618.75		$875.00		
F. Prepaids	**$914.86**				
01 Homeowner's Insurance Premium (12 mo.) to State Farm Insurance	$545.00				
02 Mortgage Insurance Premium (mo.)					
03 Prepaid Interest ($23.12 per day from 4/15 to 5/1)	$369.86				
04 Property Taxes (mo.)					
05					
G. Initial Escrow Payment at Closing	**$1,161.65**				
01 Homeowner's Insurance $45.42 per month for 2 mo.	$90.84				
02 Mortgage Insurance $25.00 per month for 2 mo.	$50.00				
03 Property Taxes $145.83 per month for 7 mo.	$1,020.81				
04					
05					
06					
07					
08 Aggregate Adjustment					
H. Other	**$300.00**		**$8,750.00**		
01 Survey Fee to All Corners Survey	$250.00				
02 Pest Inspection to All Pest Control to All Pest Control	$50.00				
03 Commission to Tillie Evans Realty			$8,750.00		
04					
05					
06					
07					
08					
I. TOTAL OTHER COSTS (Borrower-Paid)	**$3,061.26**		**$9,631.00**		
Other Costs Subtotals (E + F + G + H)	$3,061.26		$9,631.00		
J. TOTAL CLOSING COSTS (Borrower-Paid)	**$7,010.76**		**$9,876.00**		
Closing Costs Subtotals (D + I)	$7,010.76		$9,876.00		$300.00
Lender Credits					

F I G U R E 13.3 ■ **Closing Disclosure (continued)**

Calculating Cash to Close	Loan Estimate	Final	Did this change?
Total Closing Costs (J)	$7,011	$7,011	NO
Closing Costs Paid Before Closing	-0-	-0-	NO
Closing Costs Financed (Paid from your Loan Amount)	-0-	-0-	NO
Down Payment/Funds from Borrower	$12,500	$12,500	NO
Deposit	($5,000)	($5,000)	NO
Funds for Borrower			NO
Seller Credits	($2,000)	($2,000)	NO
Adjustments and Other Credits	($499)	($499)	NO
Cash to Close	$12,012	$12,012	NO

Use this table to see what has changed from your Loan Estimate.

Summaries of Transactions Use this table to see a summary of your transaction.

BORROWER'S TRANSACTION

K. Due from Borrower at Closing		$132,010.76
01 Sale Price of Property		$125,000.00
02 Sale Price of Any Personal Property Included in Sale		
03 Closing Costs Paid at Closing (J)		$7,010.76
04		
Adjustments		
05		
06		
07		
Adjustments for Items Paid by Seller in Advance		
08 City/Town Taxes	to	
09 County Taxes	to	
10 Assessments	to	
11		
12		
13		
14		
15		

L. Paid Already by or on Behalf of Borrower at Closing		$119,998.63
01 Deposit		$5,000.00
02 Loan Amount		$112,500.00
03 Existing Loan(s) Assumed or Taken Subject to		
04		
05 Seller Credit		
Other Credits		
06 Carpet Allowance to Buyer		$2,000.00
07		
Adjustments		
08		
09		
10		
11		
Adjustments for Items Unpaid by Seller		
12 City/Town Taxes	to	
13 County Taxes 1/1/16 to 4/15/16		$498.63
14 Assessments	to	
15		
16		
17		

CALCULATION	
Total Due from Borrower at Closing (K)	$132,010.76
Total Paid Already by or on Behalf of Borrower at Closing (L)	-$119,998.63
Cash to Close ☑ From ☐ To Borrower	**$12,012.13**

SELLER'S TRANSACTION

M. Due to Seller at Closing		$125,000.00
01 Sale Price of Property		$125,000.00
02 Sale Price of Any Personal Property Included in Sale		
03		
04		
05		
06		
07		
08		
Adjustments for Items Paid by Seller in Advance		
09 City/Town Taxes	to	
10 County Taxes	to	
11 Assessments	to	
12		
13		
14		
15		
16		

N. Due from Seller at Closing		$86,673.23
01 Excess Deposit		
02 Closing Costs Paid at Closing (J)		$9,876.00
03 Existing Loan(s) Assumed or Taken Subject to		
04 Payoff of First Mortgage Loan		$74,298.60
05 Payoff of Second Mortgage Loan		
06		
07 Carpet Allowance to Buyer		$2,000.00
08 Seller Credit		
09		
10		
11		
12		
13		
Adjustments for Items Unpaid by Seller		
14 City/Town Taxes	to	
15 County Taxes 1/1/16 to 4/15/16		$498.63
16 Assessments	to	
17		
18		
19		

CALCULATION	
Total Due to Seller at Closing (M)	$125,000.00
Total Due from Seller at Closing (N)	- $86,673.23
Cash ☐ From ☑ To Seller	$38,326.77

AT THE CLOSING TABLE

The closing normally includes the buyers, the sellers, and their respective licensees, if any. Sometimes attorneys of the parties attend, and occasionally a lender's representative. The title-closing agent conducts the closing.

Separate Closings

Many licensees prefer that the buyers and the sellers close separately, rather than at the same closing table. This reduces confusion, makes it more private, and allows the title-closing agent to focus completely on each party. It is particularly appropriate if the parties have had a dispute over some issue. Sometimes separate closings occur when there is a mail-away closing package or when the buyers or sellers live out of town.

Closing Disputes

The title closer is not an advocate for any of the parties. It is the title closer's job to close the transaction based on the contract and the lender's closing instructions. If there is a problem between the buyer and the lender, the closer gets them together on the phone. If there is a dispute between the buyer and the seller, the closer will often step out of the room until the dispute is settled and the parties are ready to close.

Loan Application

Usually the lender will want a typed loan application signed at closing, verifying the information given to the lender at the time of application.

Note

The closer presents the note for the buyer's signature. The note shows the principal balance, number of payments, and the dates and the amount of the payments. The amount will be for principal and interest only. The first payment date will normally be the first day of the second month after closing. The note is not witnessed or notarized. If a signature appears on the face of the note along with the borrower's signature, that person becomes a cosigner on the note.

Mortgage

The mortgage is the security for the note. It is the document that may require the borrower to pay $\frac{1}{12}$ of the ad valorem taxes and the hazard insurance and mortgage insurance premiums, along with the principal and interest. It requires that payments be made on time, that taxes be paid, and that the property be covered by insurance and describes prepayment options. It also probably states that a transfer of the property will make the loan due immediately.

The Warranty Deed

The warranty deed is the most common deed, with the seller guaranteeing to the buyer that he has good title, without material defects or encumbrances, and will stand by the guarantee forever. Special attention should be given to the names and legal description and to any items in the "subject to" section, such as restrictive covenants and mortgages.

Other Documents

Some of the other documents the buyer may sign include an anticoercion statement that says the lender did not require that the buyer choose a certain insurance company. The lender and the title insurance company will want a compliance agreement that the parties will do anything necessary to give the lender an acceptable loan package, such as signing new documents, if required. If the loan is more than 80% of a home's value, the lender will want an affidavit that the buyer will occupy the property. The seller will be required to sign an affidavit that (1) she owns the property, (2) she has the right to convey it, and (3) it is not encumbered by any lien or right to a lien, such as a construction lien.

Disbursements at Closing

Everyone expects to be paid at closing. This is not always possible, and licensees should be prepared to explain the problem to the sellers. Perhaps an example using a broker's trust account is easier to understand. Many real estate brokers have hundreds of thousands of dollars in their escrow accounts. A broker who disburses from the escrow account before making a deposit into the account, even if the future deposit would be in certified funds, is guilty of a serious violation because the broker would be using funds that belong to others.

Title insurance companies are faced with a similar problem. Some title insurance companies agree to disburse the proceeds at closing if the certified checks will be deposited by the close of business that day. (A real estate broker may never do this.) Many title insurance companies will not disburse if the closing takes place too late to make a same-day deposit or if the lender is holding the loan proceeds check until the loan package is delivered.

Warehousing

Some companies are hesitant to insure title until the "gap" between the time of the title commitment and the time of recording is checked. Any documents filed against the property during the gap period may affect the title. A lot depends on whether the title insurance company has any reason to suspect problems.

After the closing, the title company makes all deposits, and the deeds and mortgages are copied for the lender's package before they are taken for recording. The closing package is prepared for the lender, awaiting only the recording information. The person who records the documents should ensure that the check amounts are correctly calculated, that the documents are put in the correct recording order (deed first, then mortgages), and that the "return to" address is properly entered. When the documents are recorded, the information, including the date and time and the book and page number, is entered into the final title insurance policy and the package is sent to the lender.

When the recorded instruments are returned, the closing agent will send the buyer the original deed with recording information, a copy of the mortgage (the lender gets the original), and the title insurance policy.

Signed Closing Papers Received by Sales Associate. The sales associate should be careful that the office file is fully documented. This includes any walk-through clearance papers the buyer signs for the seller and the closing statements all parties must sign. If disbursement is made at closing, the commission check also is received at this time.

Postclosing Duties

The sales associate is also responsible for the postclosing duties discussed below.

Give Commission Check to Broker. Upon returning to the office, the sales associate should give the closing file, as well as the commission check, to the broker.

Pick Up Sign and Lockbox From Property. The listing sales associate should ensure that the sign and lockbox are removed from the property and returned to the office. Often the sales associate does this just before closing. Many sales associates remove the lockbox for security reasons immediately after the contract has been signed.

Send Letter of Thanks to Buyer or Seller. The letter, which should include both the sales associate's and the broker's signatures, will be appreciated by the customer, will foster goodwill, and likely will result in future business. Many companies request that the buyer or the seller complete a questionnaire about the level of service provided in the transaction.

Visit Buyer or Seller to Follow Up. The sales associate who calls on the customer after the closing demonstrates the careful attention needed to ensure that all details of the transaction have been completed satisfactorily.

Provide Notice of Closed Sale to the MLS. Most MLS systems require that listing status changes be submitted as soon as possible. This provides brokers and sales associates in the area with the most current information about listing availability and comparable sales information.

SUMMARY

- After a sales contract is signed, the sales associate should complete a Property Sale Information Sheet to ensure all pertinent information about all the parties is in the file.

- A closing Progress Chart will help organize the closing process. Some of the most important steps are:
  - Make a deposit of the earnest money.
  - Be certain that the buyer makes loan application in the time frames of the contract.
  - Get contingencies cleared as soon as possible.
  - Order the title insurance
  - Order the WDO inspection.
  - Ensure that the buyer purchases hazard insurance.
  - Be present for the pre-closing inspection.
  - Get closing papers to the parties the day before closing.

- Understand prorations:
  - The 365-day method is the most common.
  - Prorations should be made as of the last day of the sellers' ownership.
  - Property taxes are usually paid in arrears, so the buyer pays the seller. An exception occurs when the closing is late in the year and the seller has already paid the tax bill.

- Prepaid taxes are collected from the borrower by the lender by using the months of the year that have passed and adding another three months. This amount is put into the borrower's escrow account.

- The lender requires the borrower to pay for the first-year hazard insurance premium and collects two months of insurance for the escrow account.

- Prepaid interest is collected at closing for the days remaining in the closing month.

- Documentary stamp taxes are collected on the deed (paid by seller) and the note (paid by borrower).

  - Documentary stamp taxes on the deed are $.70 per hundred dollars of the purchase price, or fraction thereof.

  - Documentary stamp taxes on the note are $.35 per hundred dollars of the purchase price, or fraction thereof.

  - Intangible taxes on the mortgage are .002 of the mortgage amount.

- The Closing Disclosure provides an itemized listing of the funds paid at closing and has five pages:

  - Page 1 shows the parties, the property description, the lender, the settlement agent, and a recap of the Loan Estimate given at the time of application.

  - Page 2 itemizes the settlement charges for each party, such as the broker's commission, loan closing costs, prepaid items, escrow account setup, title charges, and recording charges. Each item in the statement is assigned a separate number within a standardized numbering system. The totals for each party on page 2 are transferred to page 3.

  - Page 3 summarizes the transaction and shows the amount of cash due from the buyer, as well as the seller's proceeds at closing.

  - Page 4 shows additional information about the loan.

  - Page 5 shows loan calculations, and provides contact information for lender, broker, and settlement agent.

R E V I E W   Q U E S T I O N S

1. On what page of the Closing Disclosure will the prorations be found?
    a. 1
    b. 2
    c. 3
    d. 4

2. The preclosing walk-through inspection is NOT intended to ensure that
    a. personal property the seller is required to leave remains on the property.
    b. all required repairs have been completed.
    c. the property has been maintained in the condition it was at the time of the contract, ordinary wear and tear excepted.
    d. the roof is structurally sound.

3. A seller told the listing agent that the pool liner was defective. The sales associate disclosed the statement to the buyers. The contract was written reflecting that the buyers would pay for replacing the liner. The sales associate called a pool company and authorized the liner replacement at a cost of $1,750. The buyers' mortgage application was subsequently rejected and the sale did not close. The sales associate
    a. is not liable to the pool company; the buyers are.
    b. is not liable to the pool company; the sellers are.
    c. might have to pay for the pool liner.
    d. may sue the buyers because they defaulted.

4. The BEST way for a buyer to determine that the seller has moved out and the property is ready for occupancy is by
    a. requiring a home inspection company to provide a report.
    b. reading a termite report.
    c. doing a preclosing walk-through inspection.
    d. asking the sales associate.

5. To expedite a closing, catch errors made in documents, and make the buyers feel more comfortable about documents they must sign, the sales associate should
    a. obtain a hold-harmless agreement from the title insurance company.
    b. limit the time for actually doing the closing.
    c. get the papers to the parties at least 24 hours in advance of the closing.
    d. have the lender sign an estoppel letter.

6. What are the documentary stamp taxes on the deed if the sale price of a property is $214,500?
    a. $750.75
    b. $1,124.75
    c. $1,501.50
    d. $1,526.89

7. A sales associate must give the earnest money deposit to the broker no later than the end of
    a. the next business day.
    b. the second business day.
    c. the third business day.
    d. 15 days.

8. Contract contingencies should be cleared
    a. within three days of contract.
    b. within five days before closing.
    c. within five days after loan approval.
    d. as soon as possible after the contract has been signed.

9. A sales contract required that the buyer give an additional binder within 10 days of the contract date. If the buyer failed to give the additional binder, the
    a. contract is null and void.
    b. contract works like an option contract; the only remedy is the loss of the original binder.
    c. buyer has defaulted.
    d. contract should not have been accepted as written.

10. What would NOT be given to the title-closing agent when the order is given?
    a. A signed and dated listing agreement
    b. The seller's and buyer's marital status
    c. A complete legal description
    d. Property address, including ZIP code

A C T I O N   L I S T

APPLY WHAT YOU'VE LEARNED!

The following actions will reinforce the material in "Section IV—Financing and Closing Real Estate Transactions":

❏ Select a three-bedroom home that is currently for sale that you would like to own. Calculate the PITI payment, assuming you pay the listed price and make a 10% down payment. Use current interest rates.

❏ Based on the previous action, divide the PITI payment by the mortgage amount. This will give you the mortgage payment factor, including taxes, insurance, and PMI. It will probably be just under 1%.

❏ Ask a title-closing officer to show you the entire closing process (avoid doing this at the end of the month because that's a busy time). Ask to watch a title search to see what the title company looks for. Examine the closing officer's checklist for closings. See what an instruction package from the lender looks like. Watch as the closing officer enters information into the computer for the Closing Disclosure.

❏ With your broker's approval, randomly select five file folders for closed transactions. Thoroughly review each file, and list every document in the file. Do some files seem more complete to you? Are there any that you believe are *not* complete? Note what documents you want in all your closed files.

❏ Start again at the first file folder. Inspect the contract, the Loan Estimate of settlement costs and payment amounts, and the Closing Disclosure. Check to see whether the amount the sales associate estimated for the seller or the buyer matched the actual amount on the disclosure. Can you account for any material differences?

❏ Next, check every entry on the Closing Disclosure for accuracy.

❏ If you have not yet had a closing, arrange with an associate to attend one of his closings. Remember, you should listen, not talk, at the closing.

ANALYZING AND MANAGING INVESTMENT PROPERTY

CHAPTER 14 ANALYZING AND MANAGING INVESTMENT PROPERTY

Many real estate professionals focus on the sale and management of investment property. This section discusses the advantages and disadvantages of investing in income property, how the general economy affects the performance of income property, the feasibility analysis involved in purchasing income properties, and the need for professional management.

A substantial part of our country's wealth has been generated by investments in real property. Chapter 14 shows the pros and cons of different property types, and methods of evaluating the investment.

Because of the substantial amounts of capital required for real estate investments, most owners want the property managed professionally. Chapter 14 describes the relationship between owners and property managers, the employment of resident managers, and the marketing and maintenance of property.

14

ANALYZING AND MANAGING INVESTMENT PROPERTY

LEARNING OBJECTIVES

When you finish reading this chapter, you will be able to:

- itemize the four phases of an economic cycle,
- list the four major property maintenance categories,
- describe the uses and benefits of a show list, and
- itemize the four levels of maintenance operations.

KEY TERMS

before-tax cash flow (BTCF)
cash flow report
Certified Property Manager (CPM)
contraction
cycle
contract service
corrective maintenance
deferred maintenance
dynamic risk
effective gross income (EGI)

expansion
gross domestic product (GDP)
leverage
net operating income (NOI)
new construction maintenance
operating expenses (OE)
potential gross income (PGI)
preventive maintenance

profit and loss statement
random changes
recession
recovery
reserves for replacement
resident manager
routine maintenance
seasonal variations
show list
specific cycles
static risk

OVERVIEW

Real estate licensees who specialize in commercial and investment property are expected to understand the fundamentals of investment property. An investment study includes analysis of the national and local economies, specifically as they relate to real estate.

Investing in real estate has advantages and disadvantages, and each investor must evaluate the suitability of an investment. This chapter focuses primarily on investment opportunities in smaller income properties such as raw land and residential, office, and commercial properties.

Investment ratios help buyers analyze properties to help reduce risk at the time of investment. Investors may use some of these ratios to determine the appropriate amount to offer for a property.

While federal income taxes are an important consideration when weighing an investment in real estate, the property's operating economics are more important.

Professional property management is very important in maximizing the investors' returns. The professional property manager must understand the economic forces at work in the real estate market. This person must be able to evaluate the property in terms of operating income, forecast its potential for the future, and construct a management plan that reflects the owner's objectives. The property manager must be skilled in marketing rental space, understanding tenant psychology, the legal aspects of the landlord-tenant relationship, maintenance procedures, and accounting.

THE GENERAL BUSINESS ECONOMY

Timing is important in real estate investment. A good property purchased at the wrong time may result in substantial losses to the investor. Many investors also understand that a rapidly appreciating real estate market can make even marginal properties show acceptable returns, but they should carefully evaluate the market to avoid buying in a "bubble" market. Before deciding which type of real estate is right, the investor must try to understand the current economic trends.

Trends in the business economy may either originate from or result in changes in the real estate market. The condition of one directly affects the condition of the other. Changes and trends in the general economy fall into three basic categories: seasonal variations, cyclic fluctuations, and random changes.

Seasonal Variations

Changes that recur at regular intervals each year are called **seasonal variations**. Such changes arise from both nature and custom. In the northern United States, for example, construction stops during the winter months; this seasonal change affects both the general economy and the real estate economy. Customs such as the nine-month school year have a seasonal effect on residential sales. Each year, retired persons fleeing cold weather swell Florida's winter population.

Cyclic Fluctuations

Business cycles, called cyclic fluctuations, are wavelike movements of increasing and decreasing economic prosperity. A **cycle** consists of four phases: expansion, recession, contraction, and recovery (see Figure 14.1).

Production increases during **expansion** periods. High employment levels, wages, and consumer purchasing power increase demand for goods and services. Prices rise because of greater demand, and credit is easy, making more money available for purchasing.

Recession normally is defined as two successive quarterly declines in the **gross domestic product (GDP)**. GDP is the sum total of goods and services produced by the United States. The four major components of GDP are consumption, investment, government purchases, and net exports.

FIGURE 14.1 ■ **General Business Cycle**

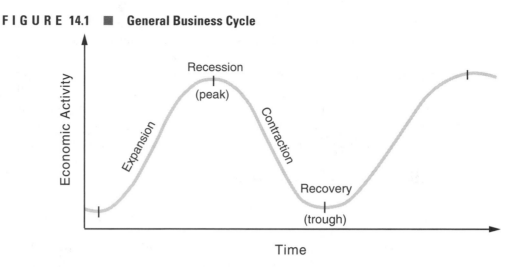

1   **Contraction** begins immediately after a recession. Confidence in the economy is
2 shaken, and consumers reduce spending in anticipation of lower earnings.

3   Slower sales cause reduced production, worker layoffs, and unemployment. Prices are
4 reduced to clear out inventories of unsold goods.

5   **Recovery**, defined as two successive quarterly increases in the GDP, begins when con-
6 sumers, lured by lower prices, venture back into the market. As business activity increases,
7 confidence begins to return. Slowly, production facilities gear up to meet the new consumer
8 demand, capital begins to flow back into business enterprises, and additional employees
9 are hired. Finally, as the gradual rise in employment generates more spendable income and
10 an increasing demand for more goods, the business cycle again enters the expansion phase.

11   Although business cycles technically consist of the four phases defined, most discus-
12 sions deal simply with expansion and contraction, measuring expansion from trough to
13 peak and contraction from peak to trough. Business cycles are recurrent, but not periodic;
14 that is, they vary in duration and timing. Economists have observed that a complete cycle
15 in the general economy may vary from 6 to 12 years.

Specific Cycles

17 **Specific cycles** are wavelike movements similar to business cycles. They occur in specific
18 sectors of the general economy, such as the real estate economy, and in individual sectors
19 of the real estate economy, such as housing starts and real estate sales. Specific cycles do
20 not always coincide with cycles of the general business economy, as the business cycle
21 actually is a weighted average of all specific cycles.

22   Regardless of the state of the national economy, certain areas boom in recessions and
23 stagnate in prosperous times because local demand runs counter to current broad eco-
24 nomic trends. Northeastern manufacturing towns were in trouble in the early 1980s, for
25 example, while an influx of new residents and industries into central Florida kept that area
26 building and growing.

Random Changes

28 **Random changes** are irregular fluctuations of the economy that may be caused by legisla-
29 tive and judicial decisions or by strikes, revolutions, wars, fires, storms, floods, and other
30 catastrophes. These changes, impossible to predict or analyze, may affect one or more

sectors of the aggregate economy. They may influence all industries in an area or one industry nationwide. Real estate activity, especially construction, is very vulnerable to labor strikes, political changes, and natural disasters. One example of a random change in regard to real estate is a zoning ordinance change allowing undeveloped land to be used for industrial purposes that would stimulate construction activity locally. Government policy changes and changes in tax laws also can cause random changes in real estate activity nationally. Investors must be aware of what is happening on both the national and local levels and have contingency plans to cope with events as they occur.

THE REAL ESTATE ECONOMY

The real estate economy is an important component of the general business economy, subject to the same four types of fluctuations. Specific cycles are the most pronounced and important trends that appear in the real estate sector. They can be observed in all phases of real estate: land development, building, sales, finance, investment, rental, and redevelopment.

Most sectors of the real estate economy are subject to both long and short cycles. Long-term cycles last from 15 to 22 years, and short-term cycles take about 3 years.

A controlling factor in the building cycle is the availability of money and credit in the mortgage and construction markets. During the years 2001 through 2006, the Federal Reserve made money very easy to get and fed the boom in real estate, all the way up to the bursting of the bubble. In general, when the economy is strong and prices are rising, the Federal Reserve tightens the money supply to control speculation. The resulting higher interest rates make real estate investment less attractive because builders must either pass the higher costs on to consumers or accept lower profits. Either situation slows the rate of construction. The Fed did not apply the brakes in time.

Additionally, the mortgage market had a huge infusion of cash from the sale of securitized loan packages called collateralized debt obligations (CDOs). The securities were so profitable to Wall Street firms that the frenzy to fund more mortgages resulted in relaxed, or even nonexistent lending standards. It was a recipe for disaster.

An extremely important indicator for forecasting the economy is the monthly report of housing starts, published by the Census Bureau between the 16th and the 20th of each month. Housing starts, along with auto sales, are the first to rise in an economic recovery and the first to drop in a recession. Not only does new housing have a direct effect on the market but housing-related purchases such as furniture and appliances also fuel a rebounding economy. In 2010, housing starts were at a 20-year low, though they have risen steadily since.

If investors believe that the general economic situation is beginning to turn around, it may be time to review the advantages and disadvantages of investment in real estate.

FLORIDA'S REAL ESTATE MARKET

Between 2003 and 2006, low interest rates fueled a real estate boom. At the same time, speculators entered into contracts to purchase real property with the intent of "flipping" the contract for a higher price even before they had to close on the purchase. Also, many unsound subprime loans were granted. Property appreciation rates were abnormally high resulting in high profits for owners and speculators who sold.

However, as the market cooled, many speculators failed to close on their purchases. This left developers and builders with large inventories of condominiums and houses. Coupled with high foreclosure rates on subprime mortgages and tightened credit standards, the seller's market turned into a buyer's market overnight in many areas of Florida. The market is only now recovering.

REAL ESTATE INVESTMENT ANALYSIS

Many of the wealthy people in this country amassed their great fortunes from real estate investments. The most significant asset of most families is the equity in their homes. Real estate may not be the right investment for everyone, however. Advantages and disadvantages exist, and should be evaluated by each individual.

Advantages of Investing in Real Estate

The advantages of investing in real estate include high leverage, good return, shelter from federal income taxes, and personal control of the asset.

Leverage. Leverage is the use of other people's money to increase the investor's return. Few other investments offer the high leverage that real estate does. Stocks and bonds typically require at least a 50% down payment; mutual funds want 100% invested. Yet real estate investments can be made with 25% down payments, and less in many cases.

Good Returns. Many careful and astute investors achieve excellent returns, often exceeding 20%.

Income Tax Shelter. Most investment opportunities such as savings accounts, bonds, stocks, and mutual funds require that investors pay taxes on all current income (dividends). Real estate investments often provide tax-deferred cash flows, primarily because of cost recovery deductions (depreciation). This allows investors to avoid paying taxes on the cash flows until they sell the property.

Exchanging and installment basis reporting are other ways to defer paying taxes. These methods will be discussed later in this section.

More Personal Control. Many investors are uncomfortable with the notion of entrusting their assets to other persons or companies with little or no control over the use of those assets. The purchase of real estate gives an investor much more control over the investment's operation and management. This is true even if the investor employs a property manager because the manager is under the investor's control.

Disadvantages of Investing in Real Estate

Disadvantages of investing in real estate include the following: management time, high capital requirements, poor liquidity, personal stress, and high risk.

Management Time. Along with the advantage of personal control comes the disadvantage of the amount of time required to manage the property. Continuing review and management of an income property's operations is essential. A prudent investor takes an active role in overseeing management. The investor must seek a higher return on the investment to compensate for the time requirements.

High Capital Requirements. Real estate requires a substantial capital investment. Not only do the investors need funds to acquire the property, they also must have reserve funds available to make major renovations when required or to cover unexpected events.

If vacancy rates are high, the investors will find it difficult to sell the property and may need to inject more money into the real estate to pay its operating costs and debt service to carry them through the hard times.

Poor Liquidity. Investment real estate is a complicated purchase, even in the best markets. Land-use requirements, environmental audits, maintenance inspections, lease reviews, and new financing all take a substantial amount of time. A seller must understand that it could be a year or more after putting the property on the market before a sale is closed. In bad markets, however, it can be close to impossible to sell property at a fair price because so many other properties are available. This is a significant disadvantage of investment real estate.

Personal Stress. Many first-time real estate investors suffer rude awakenings when they discover that property management isn't just about cash flow projections and planning, but it is also about personal interaction with tenants. Because an owner's first few properties usually are not large or profitable enough to justify hiring a manager, an owner is left with the task. When the mortgage payment is due, slow-paying tenants can become an irritation. Tenant complaints take time and interpersonal skills to resolve. Tenants sometimes leave a property in poor condition when they move, requiring a large contribution of time and money to restore the premises for the next tenant. Eviction is sometimes necessary and is usually distressing to both landlord and tenant.

High Risk. It is said that the longer an asset is held, the greater the chance of catastrophe. Many examples exist of seemingly good real estate investments gone bad. Failure could result from overbuilding in the market, causing high competition and lower rents. Environmental laws also may require expensive retrofitting. Or a major employer may relocate to another area, causing widespread unemployment. Insurance does not cover this **dynamic risk**. To overcome dynamic risk, the investor must analyze a property carefully before purchasing, and then manage it effectively.

Static risk is risk that can be insured. Examples include fire, windstorm, accident liability, floods, appliance contracts, and worker's compensation.

TYPES OF INVESTMENT PROPERTY

A wide range of property is available for investment, and the type of property suitable for an investor often depends on the investor's age, assets, and risk profile. Young investors usually are willing to take greater risks. This may be due partly to optimism that has not been dimmed by hard knocks and partly to higher energy levels. Older investors want to keep what they have because they don't have a lot of time to get it back if it is lost. They avoid high risk and are more likely to look for attractive current cash flows as opposed to speculative appreciation.

Persons with very few assets have little to lose and are often risk-takers in their efforts to strike it rich. Persons who are financially comfortable usually are more conservative in their investment decisions.

Risk-averse investors ordinarily are not comfortable with industrial property, speculative land, or new construction of income property. They are more likely to want established income property with a proven record of income.

Types of investment property discussed below are raw land, residential income properties, office buildings, commercial properties, and industrial properties.

Raw Land

Investment in raw land can be extremely profitable if good research skills, good instincts, and good luck come together in one transaction. This type of property investment also can be extremely risky for the novice investor. Cities and counties in Florida, when trying to get a handle on growth guidelines, often change land uses in an area, which may have either wonderful or disastrous consequences for the investor. Income tax laws can change the feasibility of many projects. Raw land usually does not offer a cash flow to the investor and requires continuing infusions of funds to pay property taxes and interest on mortgages. Timing is important because the longer the property is held, the lower the rate of return tends to be.

The most important determinant of value for a vacant site is location. If land is planned for commercial use, it must have access and visibility from a major arterial road. Shopping centers should have easy access to expressways. Topography is important because it can affect building costs to correct for heavily sloping land.

Residential Income Properties

A single-family home usually is the investor's initial purchase. A single-family rental home provides the investor with a breakeven cash flow or a little income if the investor combines good management with good luck. It also has some limited tax advantages from depreciation. Because the margins are so slim, however, a vacancy for even a month can wipe out all the profit for the year.

As the investor's assets and borrowing power grow, the next investment may be a multifamily property. Larger properties benefit from the efficiencies of land use and management. Where single-family homes usually are breakeven propositions for the investors, larger properties can bring substantially higher yields. Because of the much larger investment required, a buyer should make a complete and detailed investment analysis.

Office Buildings

Small investors must analyze the office building market carefully before committing their funds. What is the competition? How many new buildings are permitted? What's happening in the area economy? It is not enough to look at the overall occupancy rate. An investor should segment the market by age, location, and amenities. It is possible that vacancies are high in the older downtown buildings, while newer suburban office parks are nearly full. Prestige office buildings can be unprofitable for the investor; they're really pretty but often have low yields.

When analyzing the rent rates for competitive properties, the investor should pay careful attention to the services and tenant improvements included. Many buildings pay for utilities and janitorial service and give each tenant an initial allowance for partitioning.

Many investors prefer office buildings to residential apartments because tenants tend to occupy the properties longer, tenant complaints usually are made during business hours, and fewer collection problems occur. Smaller office buildings tend to have somewhat higher tenant turnover than buildings rented by national tenants.

Commercial Properties

Many opportunities exist for small investors as well as shopping center developers to invest in commercial properties. Small strip shopping centers, because of their rectangular shape, lend themselves well to a variety of uses. They can be converted from storefronts to offices to restaurants with relatively little expense. A typical strip center consists of a 100-by-60-foot building with four 25-foot- or five 20-foot-wide bays. The market in many areas became very soft during the last economic downturn, making new construction loans difficult to obtain for some years. The market has improved in recent years, becoming attractive again to small investors.

Larger neighborhood shopping centers usually include a grocery store or a drugstore as the anchor, along with some personal service stores such as dry cleaners, Laundromats, or restaurants.

Community shopping centers may include a Home Depot, Kmart, or Stein Mart as the anchor, along with a supermarket and other retailers, restaurants, and service companies. Management should try to arrange the mix of tenants so that each complements the others in the center and the overall effect is to generate additional traffic. Lease terms in these centers run longer than in strip centers. Professional property managers usually manage centers of this kind.

Regional shopping centers usually have three or more major department stores as anchors. They generally are located near expressways to draw more distant shoppers to the sites. The centers often have large numbers of general merchandise retailers. A professional manager is essential to enhance the value of this very large investment.

Industrial Properties

Industrial properties usually are located near expressways, airports, seaports, or railroad lines. Investment in industrial property requires substantial research and carries significant risk. Most small investors should be wary about investment in this market. Many industrial properties serve special purposes and are subject to long periods of vacancy in market downturns. However, with a successful company as a tenant, an industrial property can achieve reasonable returns.

MARKET ANALYSIS

Once the investor is satisfied that the economy is sound and begins to target the type of property for investment, a market study is the next necessary step. A regional market analysis should include demographic and economic information, such as population statistics and trends, a list of major employers in the area, and income and employment data. It should explore the economic base of the city and prospects for the future in that locale. A neighborhood market analysis should assess five major factors:

1. *Boundaries and land usage.* Rivers, lakes, railroad tracks, parks, or major highways may help define the neighborhood's boundaries.
2. *Transportation and utilities.* Transportation and utilities are crucial to the success of income property. The investor should analyze the effect of major traffic artery changes, as well as proposed or scheduled widening of streets, opening or closing of bridges, or new highway construction, all of which may enhance or hurt a location.
3. *Economy.* The investor also should review the neighborhood's economic health. Rental rates in the neighborhood are a sound indicator of the real estate market's economic strength. The investor can obtain the most reliable current rental rate information by shopping the competition.

4. *Supply and demand.* A high occupancy rate indicates a shortage of space and the possibility of rental increases. A low rate, as evidenced by many For Rent signs posted in the area, results in tenant demands for lower rents and other owner concessions.

5. *Neighborhood amenities and facilities.* The neighborhood's social, recreational, and cultural amenities can be important. Parks, theaters, restaurants, schools, and shopping centers attract potential tenants.

FINANCIAL ANALYSIS

After analyzing the market, the investor must examine the property's financial performance. This provides the basis for estimating the property's value, based on return criteria the investor establishes. Assembling the data is the most time-consuming part of the analysis process. The investor must review the property's financial history, as well as rent data, financial results, and amenities for competing properties. The first step after assembling the data is to prepare a one-year financial statement for the property.

Estimate Potential Gross Income

By multiplying the amount of space in the building by the base rental rate for that type of space, the investor can estimate rental income for each type of space found in the building. For example, the residential investor multiplies the number of studio, one-bedroom, and two-bedroom apartments by the rent for each type. The total of the estimated rent amounts from each type of space is the **potential gross income (PGI)** for the entire property.

Estimate Effective Gross Income

Effective gross income (EGI) is potential gross income minus vacancy and collection losses plus other income. Vacancy and collection losses are forecast from the experience of the subject property and of competing properties in the market, assuming typical, competent management. A good balance of supply and demand is a 95% occupancy rate. Occupancy rates change based on changing economic conditions, such as rising unemployment rates or overbuilding. Other income from sources such as vending machines and laundry areas is added to potential gross income after subtracting vacancy and collection losses.

Estimate Operating Expenses

The next step is to calculate the property's **operating expenses (OE)**. Operating expenses are divided into three categories: fixed expenses, variable expenses, and reserves for replacement (see below). Ad valorem taxes and property insurance are examples of fixed operating expenses. Their amounts normally do not vary with the level of the property's operation. Variable expenses include such items as utilities, maintenance, trash removal, supplies, janitorial services, and management. These expenses move in direct relationship with the level of occupancy. Regional norms for these expenses are available through trade journals and professional property management associations.

Establish Necessary Reserves for Replacement

If the level of expenses fluctuates widely from year to year, based on major maintenance and replacements of property components, it is difficult for the analyst to get a clear picture of typical expenses. To be meaningful, the expense figure must be stabilized. This is accomplished by establishing a **reserves for replacement** category of expenses. It is not a current cash outlay but an annual charge that should account for future expenses. The most accurate way to establish reserves is to divide the cost of each item and piece of equipment by its expected useful life in years.

Estimate Net Operating Income

The **net operating income (NOI)** is obtained by deducting operating expenses (fixed, variable, and reserves) from effective gross income.

Determine Before-Tax Cash Flow

Income properties normally are purchased with mortgage financing, so owners must make mortgage payments from the NOI. When an annual mortgage payment is subtracted from NOI, the remaining amount is called **before-tax cash flow (BTCF)**, sometimes called cash throwoff.

Constructing a Financial Statement for a Residential Investment

The following example describes the process of analyzing a residential investment.

DISCUSSION EXERCISE 14.1

Sigrid Fleming is considering an investment in an apartment property located in southeast Tallahassee. The property, which is well-maintained and about seven years old, is located near some office buildings and shopping. Many of the tenants are employed in clerical and secretarial positions. The rental rates are very competitive in the area. Sigrid's broker has given her the bookkeeper's statements for the previous two years. Based on those statements and information from competing properties, she has constructed the operating statement shown in Figure 14.2.

What is the capitalization rate for the Tallahassee Villas Apartments?

If Sigrid desires a return of 14%, what will she pay for the property?

The Capitalization Rate. Capitalizing net operating income is a basic approach to estimating value. While an appraiser uses a rate determined by verified sales in the marketplace, an investor sets the rate that provides an acceptable return using subjective criteria the investor establishes. The capitalization rate is the one-year before-tax operating return on a real property investment without considering debt service on the property. If an investor pays all cash for a $300,000 investment and the net operating income is $30,000, the rate of return is 10%. This is calculated by dividing the net operating income by the value ($30,000 ÷ $300,000).

Assume, however, that the investor would not purchase the property unless it yielded 12%. By dividing the net operating income by the rate desired ($30,000 ÷ 12%), the investor would agree to pay only $250,000.

FIGURE 14.2 ■ Operating Statement for Residential Property

Tallahassee Villas Apartments
Operating Statement
Purchase Price: $1,000,000/Mortgage $800,000

Potential Gross Income	
25 units @ $425/mo.	$127,500
12 units @ $500/mo.	72,000
	$199,500
Less vacancy and collection losses @ 5%	9,975
Effective Gross Income	$189,525
Operating Expenses:	
Property taxes	$8,700
Garbage collection	2,800
Pest control	4,500
Insurance	3,500
Maintenance	9,600
Management @ 5%	9,476
Resident manager's apartment	4,200
Reserves for replacements	$30,000
Total Operating Expenses	$72,776
Net Operating Income	$116,749
Mortgage payment ($800,000 @ 10% for 25 years)	$87,235
Before-Tax Cash Flow (cash throw-off)	$29,514

INTRODUCTION TO PROPERTY MANAGEMENT

A professional property manager may be an individual licensee, a member of a real estate firm specializing in property management, or a member of the property management department of a large full-service real estate company. She also may work within the trust department of a financial institution or within the real estate department of a large corporation or public institution. Regardless of their employment status, property managers pursue similar objectives and handle a wide variety of duties, including planning, merchandising, maintenance, and accounting. Although management duties vary according to the specific situation and particular property, a successful manager is competent in all of these areas.

The Institute of Real Estate Management (IREM) was created in 1933 by a group of property management firms as a subsidiary group of the National Association of REALTORS®. Currently, individuals wishing to join the institute must satisfy education and experience requirements, pass examinations given or approved by the institute, and adhere to a specific code of ethics. They are then awarded the prestigious designation **Certified Property Manager (CPM)** in recognition of their professional status as property managers.

CLASSIFICATION OF REAL PROPERTY

Real estate property managers manage four major classifications of real property: residential, commercial, industrial, and special-purpose. Each classification can be further subdivided and requires a different combination of property management knowledge and skills. This chapter introduces the field; it is not intended to be a complete discussion of property management. Residential property is emphasized in this introduction.

DISCUSSION EXERCISE 14.2

Relate a personal experience in renting or leasing residential property as a landlord or tenant.

Residential Property

Residential real estate is the largest source of demand for the services of professional property managers. Two principal categories of residential real estate exist: single-family homes and multifamily residences.

Single-Family Homes. Freestanding, single-family homes are the most popular form of housing in the United States. According to the Census Bureau, in July 2013, 57.5% of housing in this country were owner-occupied and did not require professional management. Although homes that are rented to other parties often are managed directly by the owners, there is a growing trend toward professional management of such properties, particularly condominiums and vacation homes. Many large corporations and their relocation companies hire property managers for homes vacated by employees who have been transferred.

Rising construction costs and a decrease in the availability of usable land have resulted in the growing popularity of town houses, condominiums, and cooperatives. Although each unit is a single-family residence, the individual owners of the units share certain responsibilities—such as maintenance of the roof, common walls, grounds, and common facilities—for the development as a whole. They usually employ professional managers to handle these jobs and maintain accounting records.

Multifamily Residences. The economy of design and land usage inherent in multifamily housing allows for a lower per-family cost of construction. Thus, multifamily residences are a rapidly growing segment of the national residential real estate market.

Multifamily residences can be held under various forms of ownership. Small properties of two to six units often are owner-occupied and owner-managed, whereas most large highrise apartment communities are professionally managed for their owners. Cooperative and condominium apartments usually are owner-occupied buildings governed by boards of directors the owners elect. These boards generally hire professional managers for their properties.

Multifamily residences can be classified as garden apartments, walkup buildings, or highrise apartments. Each type is unique in its location, design, construction, services, and amenities.

OWNER-BROKER RELATIONSHIP

Three basic relationships can exist between the individual or corporate owner of a building and the property manager: owner-broker, employer-employee, and trustor-trustee. Property managers in all categories are considered professionals, and their responsibilities are very similar. Because this section focuses on residential property management, only the principal-agent relationship is covered here.

Usually, when an owner engages a broker to be the property manager, the broker acts as a single agent for the owner. The principal-agent relationship is created by a written contract signed by both parties that empowers the property manager, as agent, to act on behalf of the owner, or principal, in certain situations. Specifically, the agent acts for the principals to bring them into legal relations with third parties. Implicit in this fiduciary relationship are the legal and ethical considerations that any agent must accord a principal. The property manager has the duties of skill, care and diligence, obedience, loyalty, accounting, disclosure, and confidentiality.

THE MANAGEMENT CONTRACT

Once the property manager and the owner have agreed on principles, objectives, and a viable management plan, it is in both parties' best interests to formalize their accord. The manager and the owner must work out the structure of their relationship, their specific responsibilities and liabilities, the scope of the manager's authority, management fees, and the duration of the management agreement. In addition, the owner must turn over management records and other information to the manager to facilitate the property's operation.

Whether the property involved is a duplex or a highrise complex, the responsibilities the manager assumes are of enough importance to warrant a written statement of intent. An agreement signed by both the manager and the owner defines the relationship between the parties, serves as a guide for the property's operation, and helps prevent misunderstandings. Management contracts have many variations, but most share the following essential elements:

- Identification of the parties and the property
- The term of the contract
- Responsibilities of the manager
- Responsibilities of the owner
- Fees and leasing/sales commissions
- Signatures of the parties

PROPERTY MAINTENANCE

Maintenance is a continual process of balancing services and costs in an attempt to please the tenants, preserve the physical condition of the property, and improve the owner's long-term margin of profit. Efficient property maintenance demands careful assessment of the status of the building's condition. Staffing and scheduling requirements vary with the type, size, and regional location of the property, so owner and manager usually agree in advance on maintenance objectives for the property. In some cases, the owner instructs the manager to reduce rental rates and expenditures for services and maintenance. Under this shortsighted policy, the manager may encounter management problems and the manager's reputation may be affected adversely. Properties can command premium rental rates if they are kept in top condition and operated with all possible tenant services.

Types of Maintenance

The successful property manager must be able to function effectively at four different levels of maintenance operations:

1. Preventive maintenance
2. Corrective maintenance
3. Routine maintenance
4. New construction maintenance

Preventive maintenance is aimed at preserving the physical integrity of the premises and eliminating corrective maintenance costs. Regular maintenance activities and routine inspections of the building and its equipment disclose structural and mechanical problems before major repairs become necessary.

Corrective maintenance involves the actual repairs that keep the building's equipment, utilities, and amenities functioning as contracted for by the tenants. Fixing a leaky faucet and replacing a broken air-conditioning unit are corrective maintenance activities.

Routine maintenance is the most frequently recurring type of maintenance activity. Common areas and grounds must be cleaned and patrolled daily. Also, cleaning and housekeeping chores should be scheduled and controlled carefully because such costs easily can become excessive.

New construction maintenance, linked closely with leasing and tenant relations, is designed to increase the property's marketability. This may be as elementary as new wallpaper, light fixtures, and carpeting. If the new construction is extensive, it might include new entryways, the addition of a swimming pool, conversion of space to a meeting room, or renovation of a previously occupied space. New construction often is performed at a tenant's request and expense. Sometimes a landlord redecorates or rehabilitates a space for a tenant as a condition of lease renewal.

Deferred maintenance is necessary maintenance that cannot or will not be performed. Deferred maintenance results in physical deterioration, unhappy tenants, and reduced rent collections.

On-Site Maintenance Staff

The manager's hiring policy for on-site maintenance personnel usually is based on the cost differential between maintaining a permanent building staff and contracting for the needed services. For example, the amount of construction activity stemming from alterations that tenants require determines the hiring policy. It makes sense to hire outside contractors for major construction jobs or for small buildings that cannot support permanent staffs.

The BOMI International sponsors instruction that leads to professional designations for maintenance personnel and supervisors. These courses are particularly instructive for on-site maintenance personnel. Property managers who wish to learn more about the technical and mechanical aspects of their properties will find these courses a good source of information.

Contract Services

Services performed by outside persons on a regular basis for specified fees are known as **contract services**. For the protection of both the manager and the owner, a service contract always should be in writing and contain a termination provision. The latter stipulation becomes important if service is not satisfactory or if the property is sold.

Before entering into any service contract, managers should solicit competitive bids on the job from several local contractors. They can then compare the cost of contracting with the expense of using on-site personnel. The management agreement terms often set a ceiling on the service contracts that managers can execute without owner approval. Window cleaning, refuse removal, pest control, and security are services that usually can be performed more efficiently and inexpensively by outside contractors. Managers should check a contracting firm's references and work history before they employ them. Managers should determine whether the firm's employees are bonded and whether it has the necessary licenses or permits.

RESIDENT MANAGER—PROPERTY MANAGER RELATIONSHIP

Most properties of 20 units or more have a manager on the premises at all times. This **resident manager** is a salaried employee who usually coordinates rent collection, tenant relations, and maintenance work on the property. Obviously, these responsibilities increase with the building's size. The resident manager reports to the property manager. With this system, a single property manager can stay current with the operations of several large apartment properties without becoming consumed by the details. In addition to reviewing the reports submitted by resident managers, the property manager should visit each building regularly to gather information on necessary maintenance and repairs. Periodic inspections show the property manager how occupancy rates may be increased, indicate where operating costs can be cut, help improve tenant relations, and provide training and feedback reviews to the on-site manager.

In the past, building superintendents not only collected rents but also served as the maintenance staff. As the property management field grows more sophisticated and building equipment becomes more complicated, managers who perform all four maintenance functions have become the exception rather than the rule. Property managers are expected to recognize when maintenance is necessary and know where to turn for help with specific maintenance problems. While a property manager need not be a jack-of-all-trades, she should understand the basic operation of mechanical and electrical systems well enough to make intelligent decisions about their care and operation. The manager also must understand the economics, staffing, and scheduling involved in the smooth performance of maintenance tasks.

The hiring and firing of employees should be under the control of the property manager, not the resident manager. When screening a potential employee or making a decision to terminate an employee, the property manager should ask for the resident manager's opinion of the person's integrity, industry, and skills.

MARKETING THE SPACE

Two basic principles of marketing are "Know your product" and "Your best source of new business is your present customer base." Thorough preparation is required to give a suitable presentation of the premises as well as to determine such items as rental rates and advertising methods necessary to attract tenants. Maximum use of referrals from satisfied tenants is the best and least expensive method of renting property and is essential to any marketing effort.

It is the property manager's responsibility to generate the maximum beautification and functional utility per dollar spent. Items such as an attractive lobby, well-landscaped grounds, and the use of pleasant colors inside and outside the building may not create greater functional utility, but they may increase marketability and profitability.

Rental space is a consumer good that can be marketed with promotional techniques like those used to sell cars or homes. Because most apartment renter prospects come to the property as a result of a neighborhood search, attractive signage and strong curb appeal are essential. Each residential property should display a tasteful sign on the premises identifying the community, the management firm, the type of apartment, the person to call for further information, and a telephone number. However, walk-ins alone will not supply all the prospects needed. Other types of advertising also are necessary to attract qualified tenants.

Advertising and Display

Even if the property is priced at the appropriate market level, the premises are clean and attractive, and the property has a good location, the building still may experience an unacceptable vacancy rate if prospective tenants are not attracted to inspect the premises. The most common advertising is newspaper classified and display ads and apartment guides. The Florida Real Estate Commission (FREC) mandates that a broker's advertising must describe the property fairly and must not mislead. It also requires that the brokerage name appear in all advertising. Other agencies also impose restrictions on ads, particularly with respect to fair housing laws.

Classified Ads. Newspaper classified advertising is the most important advertising medium for renting apartments. The property manager must keep the prospective tenant's needs in mind when composing the ad. For example, in a neighborhood where three-bedroom apartments are difficult to rent, an ad may appeal to a broader segment of the market if it offers a two-bedroom apartment with den. The classified advertisement should include the amount of rent, apartment size, property address, and manager's phone number. A brief summary of the property's major amenities also is very effective.

Display Ads. More prestigious residential projects, especially when newly built, find it advantageous to use display advertisements. These larger ads attract immediate attention, appeal to potential tenants' desire for attractive living space, and demonstrate the many amenities a building offers. The specific rental rates often are omitted, with reference to a general range.

DISCUSSION EXERCISE 14.3

Bring to class a copy of the entire classified ad section of your local newspaper. Examine the sections dealing with display ads for large residential properties and compare various ads' effectiveness. Also, examine the help wanted sections for property and resident managers.

Apartment Guides. Just as home magazines are one of the most effective ways to market residential homes for sale, apartment guides appeal to potential tenants. Color photos make the property's presentation attractive and interesting. Many management firms report that the excellent response to ads in the guides is beginning to rival the effectiveness of newspaper classified advertising.

Broker Cooperation

While all selling activities have as their ultimate objective the closing of a sale or lease with the ultimate user, the property manager will want to take advantage of all opportunities for reaching customers. This means that sales efforts should be directed not only toward prospective buyers and tenants but also toward brokers and agents who can reach rental prospects.

Broker cooperation can be especially helpful when renting or leasing a new or very large development. Managers secure that cooperation by sending to key brokers brochures or newsletters describing available properties. Compensation usually is a split commission or referral fee. A manager also can make brokers aware of a property by making a personal presentation or by sponsoring an open house.

Rental Rate Strategy

Even when the space itself is clean, attractively decorated, and in good condition, market conditions may be such that some units cannot be leased. An alert manager quickly realizes which units are renting rapidly or are not moving fast enough and either adjusts the price or changes the method of advertising and display.

The goal in establishing a rental fee schedule is to realize the maximum market price for each unit. If each apartment type is priced correctly, all types will have the same rate of demand; that is, demand for studio, one-bedroom, and two-bedroom units will be equal, and the manager will be able to achieve a balanced occupancy rate for all three types. However, this level of demand is the exception in the real market. More often than not, the manager will have to raise the base rent on the unit types that are fully occupied and decrease the rate for those units less in demand. An optimal price structure assures the manager of a 95% occupancy level for all units. For this strategy to be economically sound, the revenue from the new 95% schedule must exceed the income that was collected when some types of units were fully occupied and others had tenant levels of less than 95%. The optimum rental rates in a local market are best determined by market analysis.

Show List

To establish a reasonable rental price schedule, the manager must follow certain organizational procedures, such as compiling a **show list**. This show list should designate a few specific apartments in the building that are available currently for inspection by prospects. No more than three apartments of each type and size should be on the list at any one time; when a unit is rented, it should be replaced by another vacated apartment that is ready for rental.

The manager should use the show list both as a control guide for the marketing program and as a source of feedback on its success or failure. The features of particular units are itemized on the list so that the manager can do a better and more informed selling job. The maintenance staff will have no problem keeping a small number of vacant units on the list in top-notch condition. The limited number of show units also suggests that space is at a premium and that the prospective tenant must make her decision quickly.

The manager should review the show list and traffic count weekly to determine which units are not moving. Particular units may not rent even after several showings to prospects. The manager then should inspect these units personally to find out why they are hard to rent and then make necessary corrections. If poor curb appeal is the problem, painting or cleaning up entranceways, planting new landscaping, cutting grass, and trimming shrubs often works wonders.

It is important that managers observe fair housing laws. The limited show list must never be used as a method of illegal steering within the property.

Selling the Customer

The best advertising programs, landscaping, decorating, and maintenance may be wasted if the rental agent is unresponsive or unprofessional or does not properly show the property. Probably the most important ingredient of achieving occupancy targets is well-trained rental staff members who are personable, enthusiastic, and professional. Many large management organizations spend substantial time and money to ensure that rental agents have the technical knowledge and sales skills to best represent the property owner. The property manager should maintain records carefully, including guest books to record visitors' names. The rental agent should describe the result of each visit and record subsequent follow-up calls.

LEASES AND TENANT RELATIONS

Potential conflicts between property managers and tenants usually can be avoided when sound property management practices are employed. Sound management begins with negotiation between the property manager and the prospective tenant, the results of which should be in written form (the lease).

Essentials of a Valid Lease

The general requirements for a valid lease are similar to those for any legally enforceable contract:

- Complete and legal names of both parties (lessor and lessee)
- Legal description of the property
- Contractual capacity of the parties and legal purpose of the agreement
- Consideration or amount of rent
- Term of occupancy
- Use of the premises
- Rights and obligations of the lessor and lessee
- In writing and signed (if for more than one year)

Licensees may fill in the blanks on only the lease forms specifically approved by the Florida Supreme Court. Changing or adding to the terms of the approved forms or completing the blanks on any other lease form is considered unauthorized practice of law. Currently, there are two leases approved by the Florida Supreme Court: the Residential Lease for Single-Family Home and Duplex, and a form developed by The Florida Bar.

The manager should explain the key points in the lease agreement and be certain to cover rent collection policies. Tenants will usually pay rent promptly if the collection policy is efficient, effective, and reasonable. The manager should itemize other regulations that control the property and discuss the methods of enforcing them. The manager must be certain that the tenant understands maintenance policies and how responsibilities are divided between landlord and tenant. These policies and procedures are often outlined in a tenant brochure.

Most tenant-management problems center on maintenance service requests. When a tenant makes a maintenance request, managers must immediately tell the tenant whether it will be granted. The tenant is the customer, not an adversary, and the staff should be reminded of that fact continually. Happy tenants remain in residence, eliminate expensive turnover, protect the owner's property (which lowers maintenance costs), and promote the property's reputation (which reduces vacancy losses and promotional expenses).

A tenant request for service should be entered on a standardized request form. The top copy and a copy to be left in the unit on completion of the work are assigned to the maintenance person answering the request. The manager keeps the third copy until the job is completed. An estimated completion date should be entered on the manager's copy for follow-up. The resident manager should contact the tenant to ensure that the work was completed properly.

Landlord and Tenant Act

Chapter 83, F.S., the Florida Residential Landlord and Tenant Act, outlines the rights and duties of landlords and tenants, as well as the legal remedies available to both parties in case of noncompliance with lease terms. The law's intent was to create a reasonable balance between the two parties in their legal relationship. The law includes, among its many requirements, very specific rules for handling security deposits and advance rent. Florida licensees acting as residential managers must comply with the act. Those real estate licensees desiring to know more about this subject should obtain a current copy of this Florida law.

OPERATING REPORTS

Owners of residential rental apartments need current operating reports to measure the profitability of their investments. The annual operating budget, cash flow statement, and profit and loss statement give an owner the data necessary to evaluate his property and its management.

Operating Budget

The property manager must prepare a meaningful annual operating budget that includes all anticipated income and expense items for the property. The starting point for this year's budget most often is based on the actual data from the previous year. The annual budget is helpful as a guide for overall profitability. It must, however, be broken down into monthly budgets if it is to be useful for controlling operations. There, the manager should produce monthly statements that compare actual and budgeted amounts and should be able to explain any significant variations.

**Forms
To Go**

Cash Flow Statement

Probably the most important operating record is the manager's monthly **cash flow report** (see the Property Management Cash Flow Statement in Appendix B) on receipts and disbursements. This report includes all operating income, such as the income from parking, washing machines, dryers, and vending machines, and all operating expenses, as well as debt service. The reports show the owner how the property is doing on a cash basis. The report also can include the annual budget as well as the previous year's results, providing a budgetary control as well as a cash control.

Profit and Loss Statement

A **profit and loss statement** is a financial report of a property's actual net profit, which may differ from the cash flow. The full mortgage payment is not shown; only the interest payment is an expense. The manager usually prepares a profit and loss statement quarterly, semiannually, and yearly. Monthly income and expense reports provide the raw data for these statements. The more detail provided in the report, the better the opportunities for meaningful analysis.

Additional Reports

Managers must be completely familiar with all phases of a property's operation. Other reports, such as vacancy ratios, bad-debt ratios, showings-to-rent ratios, and changes in tenant profiles, illustrate important trends that may require corrective action. Scrutiny of the budgets and actual expenditures per account from month to month and year to year can indicate the relative performance of management personnel.

LICENSING REQUIREMENTS FOR PROPERTY MANAGERS

Chapter 475, F.S., requires that any person who rents or leases real property for another party for compensation have a current, active license. The following two exemptions exist:

1. Salaried employees of an owner, or of a registered broker working for an owner or for the properly licensed property manager of an apartment complex, who work in an on-site rental office of the apartment community in a leasing capacity
2. Salaried persons employed as managers of condominiums or cooperative apartment complexes who rent individual units, if the rentals arranged by the employees are for periods not exceeding one year

These exemptions are granted under the law to unlicensed, salaried employees. They may not be paid a commission or any form of compensation on a transactional basis.

Community Association Management

Property managers of certain community associations must obtain community association manager licenses from the Department of Business and Professional Regulation. This law does not affect apartment properties and commercial property.

SUMMARY

- Most small investors concentrate initially on small residential properties but later may investigate the opportunities in the office and commercial markets.

- An understanding of the general business economy is helpful in timing investment decisions.

- If the market is at the top of the cycle, buyers should be wary, but sellers might wish to market their properties aggressively.

- Specific cycles are the most important cycles that affect the real estate market.

- Low interest rates are a critical component of a strong real estate market.

- Real estate investing offers many advantages, such as leverage, good returns, tax shelters, and personal control.

- Some disadvantages of real estate investment include stress, management time, risk, and poor liquidity.

- When an owner hires a manager, the parties enter into one of three relationships: principal-agent, employer-employee, or trustor-trustee.

- Most management contracts share six basic characteristics and specify the duties and details of management operations that must be decided before responsibility for the property is transferred to the manager.

- To handle the property's maintenance demands, the manager must know the building's needs and the number and type of personnel required to perform the maintenance functions.

- Staff and scheduling requirements vary with a property's type, size, and regional location.

- Four types of maintenance operations exist:
  - Preventive maintenance
  - Corrective maintenance
  - Routine housekeeping
  - New construction

- Deferred maintenance is the term applied to accumulated postponed maintenance.

- The hiring policy for on-site maintenance staff depends on the cost differential between maintaining a permanent building staff and contracting for needed services.

- A show list of units available for inspection is important to a property manager's marketing program.

- Newspaper advertising is the most widely used medium for renting space.

- In addition to leasing, supervising the resident manager, and inspecting the maintenance of the premises, the property manager must provide the owner with regular financial reports.

- Property managers in Florida must meet the requirements of Chapters 83 and 475 of the Florida Statutes, unless specifically exempted.

R E V I E W   Q U E S T I O N S

1. A salaried, unlicensed manager of a resort condominium in Florida legally may rent individual condominium units if the rental periods do NOT exceed
   a. 1 month.
   b. 90 days.
   c. 6 months.
   d. 1 year.

2. A person who provides services that require licensing under the Community Association Management Act must be licensed by the
   a. Florida Real Estate Commission.
   b. Department of Administration.
   c. Department of Business and Professional Regulation.
   d. Department of Community Affairs.

3. Maintenance on a building that cannot or will not be performed when necessary is which type of maintenance?
   a. Elective
   b. Deferred
   c. Corrective
   d. Routine

4. Funds set aside to prepare for the eventual replacement of worn-out appliances, carpeting, and drapes are called
   a. contingency funds.
   b. reserves for expenses.
   c. reserves for replacements.
   d. operating expenses.

5. Changes and trends in the general business economy fall into three categories—seasonal, random, and
   a. expansion.
   b. recovery.
   c. periodic.
   d. cyclic.

6. Wavelike movements of increasing and decreasing economic prosperity in the general economy usually are called
   a. random changes.
   b. cyclic fluctuations.
   c. seasonal variations.
   d. long-term movements.

7. Apartments that are vacant and available for immediate rental are placed on the
   a. floor list.
   b. up list.
   c. show list.
   d. cleared list.

8. Most tenant-management problems are related to
    a. late or unpaid rent.
    b. maintenance service requests.
    c. conduct of tenants and their guests.
    d. handling of security deposits and advance rent.

9. Another term for *before-tax cash flow* is
    a. capitalization.
    b. effective gross income.
    c. cash throw-off.
    d. equity dividend rate.

10. Which is NOT a category of property maintenance?
    a. Elective
    b. Preventive
    c. Routine
    d. Corrective

11. The annual potential gross income for an apartment property is $291,000, other income is $480 per month, and vacancy and collection losses are 5%. What is the property's effective gross income?
    a. $276,450
    b. $276,930
    c. $281,922
    d. $282,210

12. What is NOT a requirement for a valid lease?
    a. Contractual capacity of the parties
    b. Amount of leasing commissions
    c. Term of occupancy
    d. Consideration

13. An apartment property has potential gross income of $155,000, effective gross income of $150,000, operating expenses of $58,000, including reserves for replacement of $2,400, and debt service of $40,800. What is the property's net operating income?
    a. $48,800
    b. $51,200
    c. $92,000
    d. $94,600

14. An employee of a property management firm shows prospective tenants many of the duplexes the company manages around the city and writes up leases on the court-approved forms. The employee is paid $700 per month plus $50 per signed lease. The employee
    a. must have a community association manager's license.
    b. must have a community association manager's license *and* a real estate license.
    c. must have a real estate license.
    d. need not be licensed because he is not paid a commission.

15. Total operating expenses include variable expenses, fixed expenses, and
    a. debt-service expenses.
    b. management expenses.
    c. reserves for replacement.
    d. property taxes.

16. A problem many investors have with industrial properties is that
    a. land boundaries are unstable.
    b. many properties serve special purposes and are difficult to rent once they are vacant.
    c. they rarely need proximity to airports.
    d. rates of return are always low.

17. Economic changes that recur annually are called
    a. familiar changes.
    b. long-term cyclic changes.
    c. random changes.
    d. seasonal variations.

18. The type of maintenance aimed at preserving the physical integrity of the premises is
    a. deferred.
    b. preventive.
    c. corrective.
    d. routine.

19. How many apartments should be on a show list?
    a. At least five of each type
    b. No more than one
    c. No more than three of each type
    d. All available units

20. To obtain the best and MOST reliable information about rental rates in a neighborhood, the investor should check
    a. the Bureau of Labor Statistics' survey of sample cities.
    b. competing properties.
    c. classified ads in local newspapers that cover the past 18 to 24 months.
    d. current classified ads in local newspapers for advertisements of comparable space.

APPLY WHAT YOU'VE LEARNED!

The following actions will reinforce the material in "Section V—Analyzing and Managing Investment Property":

❏ Select an apartment property in your area that has at least 30 units and learn the rental rate. Find out the typical vacancy rates in the area, then prepare a financial statement. Use an operating expense ratio of 40%.

❏ When you have completed the financial statement, capitalize the income at 10% to estimate a ride-by opinion of value.

❏ Travel on a thoroughfare and visit at least three vacant commercial buildings. Make notes about the structures and try to decide the highest and best uses. List three potential tenants for each site. Call the listing agent and get information on each property.

❏ Assume a potential buyer from out of town asks you to describe the local economy and estimate about what it will do in the next three years. Write your response as completely as possible. Get information from the local chamber of commerce and compare your description with your classmates' descriptions.

❏ If you work in residential real estate, you may often encounter potential commercial customers. Ask your broker which commercial broker he recommends for referrals. Check with a licensee in that firm to see whether the referrals could go in both directions, with you getting her residential referrals.

❏ Visit several apartment properties in your area. List the ones you would recommend to a friend looking for an apartment.

RESOURCES

The following sources are selective and not exhaustive. Numerous other available resources exist, including books, journals (e.g., FAR's *Florida REALTOR® Magazine*), periodicals, newsletters, articles, legal cases, research studies, video programs, and seminars. Consult your broker, instructor, or local board of REALTORS® librarian for further assistance.

SECTION I: LAYING THE FOUNDATION FOR A SUCCESSFUL CAREER

1. Crawford, Linda L., and Edward J. O'Donnell. *Florida Real Estate Broker's Guide*. 5th ed. Chicago: Dearborn Real Estate Education, 2013.

2. Crawford, Linda L. *Florida Real Estate Principles, Practices & Law*. 37th ed. La Crosse, WI: Dearborn Real Estate Education, 2014.

3. Lyons, Gail G., and Donald L. Harlan. *Buyer Agency Today: Keeping Your Competitive Edge in Real Estate*. 4th ed. Chicago: Dearborn Real Estate Education, 2005.

4. O'Donnell, Edward J. *30-Day Track to Success*. Tallahassee: O'Donnell Publishing, 2013.

5. O'Donnell, Edward J. *Continuing Education for Florida Real Estate Professionals*. 14th ed. La Crosse, WI: Dearborn Real Estate Education, 2013.

6. Reilly, John W. *Agency Relationships in Real Estate*. 2nd ed. Chicago: Dearborn Real Estate Education, 1994.

7. Zeller, Dirk. *Your 1st Year in Real Estate*. 2nd ed. New York: Three Rivers Press, 2010.

SECTION II: OBTAINING LISTINGS THAT SELL

1. Davis, Darryl. *How to Become a Power Agent in Real Estate*. New York: McGraw-Hill, 2002.

2. Edwards, Kenneth W. *Your Successful Real Estate Career*. 5th ed. New York: AMACOM Books, 2006.

3. Keller, Gary, Dave Jenks, and Jay Papasan. *The Millionaire Real Estate Agent*. New York: McGraw-Hill, 2004.

4. Lyons, Gail G. *Real Estate Sales Handbook*. 10th ed. Chicago: Dearborn Real Estate Education, 1994.

SECTION III: SELLING REAL PROPERTY

1. Crawford, Linda L., and Edward J. O'Donnell. *Florida Real Estate Broker's Guide*. 5th ed. Chicago: Dearborn Real Estate Education, 2013.

2. Galaty, Fillmore W., Wellington J. Allaway, and Robert C. Kyle. *Modern Real Estate Practice*. 19th ed. La Crosse, WI: Dearborn Real Estate Education, 2014.

3. Klayman, Elliot. *Real Estate Law*. 8th ed. La Crosse, WI: Dearborn Real Estate Education, 2013.

4. Reilly, John W and Marie S. Spodek. *The Language of Real Estate*. 7th ed. La Crosse, WI: Dearborn Real Estate Education, 2013.

SECTION IV: FINANCING AND CLOSING REAL ESTATE TRANSACTIONS

1. Crawford, Linda L., and Edward J. O'Donnell. *Florida Real Estate Broker's Guide*. 5th ed. Chicago: Dearborn Real Estate Education, 2013.

2. Crawford, Linda L. *Florida Real Estate Principles, Practices & Law*. 37th ed. La Crosse, WI: Dearborn Real Estate Education, 2014.

3. Koogler, Karen E. *Closing Concepts: A Title Training Manual for Settlement/Escrow Professionals*. 3rd ed. Pinellas Park, FL: Vision Quest Publications, 1996.

4. O'Donnell, Edward J. *Continuing Education for Florida Real Estate Professionals*. 14th ed. La Crosse, WI: Dearborn Real Estate Education, 2013.

5. Sirota, David and Doris Barrell. *Essentials of Real Estate Finance*. 13th ed. La Crosse, WI: Dearborn Real Estate Education, 2012.

SECTION V: ANALYZING AND MANAGING INVESTMENT PROPERTY

1. Crawford, Linda L., and Edward J. O'Donnell. *Florida Real Estate Broker's Guide*. 5th ed. Chicago: Dearborn Real Estate Education, 2013.

2. Kyle, Robert C., Marie S. Spodek and Floyd M. Baird. *Property Management*. 9th ed. La Crosse, WI: Dearborn Real Estate Education, 2013.

3. Sirota, David. *Essentials of Real Estate Investment*. 10th ed. La Crosse, WI: Dearborn Real Estate Education, 2013.

FORMS TO GO

Appendix B is intended as a resource for real estate professionals. The forms included here are presented in the order of their first appearance. While we believe the forms to be complete and accurate, we make no representations as to their legality. Before using these forms, licensees are cautioned to seek legal and other professional advice.

F I G U R E B.1 ■ **Single Agent Notice**

SINGLE AGENT NOTICE

FLORIDA LAW REQUIRES THAT REAL ESTATE LICENSEES OPERATING
AS SINGLE AGENTS DISCLOSE TO BUYERS AND SELLERS THEIR DUTIES.

As a single agent, _____ *(insert name of real estate entity)* and its Associates
owe to you the following duties:

1. Dealing honestly and fairly;
2. Loyalty;
3. Confidentiality;
4. Obedience;
5. Full disclosure;
6. Accounting for all funds;
7. Skill, care, and diligence in the transaction;
8. Presenting all offers and counteroffers in a timely manner, unless a party has previously directed the licensee otherwise in writing; and
9. Disclosing all known facts that materially affect the value of residential real property and are not readily observable.

_____

Date   Signature

_____

Date   Signature

F I G U R E B.2 ■ Consent to Transition to Transaction Broker Notice

CONSENT TO TRANSITION TO TRANSACTION BROKER

FLORIDA LAW ALLOWS REAL ESTATE LICENSEES WHO REPRESENT A BUYER OR A SELLER AS A SINGLE AGENT TO CHANGE FROM A SINGLE AGENT RELATIONSHIP TO A TRANSACTION BROKERAGE RELATIONSHIP IN ORDER FOR THE LICENSEE TO ASSIST BOTH PARTIES IN A REAL ESTATE TRANSACTION BY PROVIDING A LIMITED FORM OF REPRESENTATION TO BOTH THE BUYER AND THE SELLER. THIS CHANGE IN RELATIONSHIP CANNOT OCCUR WITHOUT YOUR PRIOR WRITTEN CONSENT.

As a transaction broker,_____ *(insert name of real estate entity)* and its Associates provide to you a limited form of representation that includes the following duties:

1. Dealing honestly and fairly;
2. Accounting for all funds;
3. Using skill, care and diligence in the transaction;
4. Disclosing all known facts that materially affect the value of residential real property and are not readily observable to the buyer;
5. Presenting all offers and counteroffers in a timely manner, unless a party has previously directed the licensee otherwise in writing;
6. Limited confidentiality, unless waived in writing by a party. This limited confidentiality will prevent disclosure that the seller will accept a price less than the asking or listed price, that the buyer will pay a price greater than the price submitted in a written offer, of the motivation of any party for selling or buying property, that a seller or buyer will agree to financing terms other than those offered, or of any other information requested by a party to remain confidential; and
7. Any additional duties that are entered into by this or by separate written agreement.

Limited representation means that a buyer or a seller is not responsible for the acts of the licensee. Additionally, parties are giving up their rights to the undivided loyalty of the licensee. This aspect of limited representation allows a licensee to facilitate a real estate transaction by assisting both the buyer and the seller, but a licensee will not work to represent one party to the detriment of the other party when acting as a transaction broker to both parties.

I agree that my agent may assume the role and duties of a transaction broker.
[Must be initialed or signed]

_____   _____

Date   Signature

_____   _____

Date   Signature

F I G U R E B.3 ■ No Brokerage Relationship Notice

NO BROKERAGE RELATIONSHIP NOTICE

FLORIDA LAW REQUIRES THAT REAL ESTATE LICENSEES WHO HAVE NO BROKERAGE RELATIONSHIP WITH A POTENTIAL SELLER OR BUYER DISCLOSE THEIR DUTIES TO SELLERS AND BUYERS.

As a real estate licensee who has no brokerage relationship with you, _____ (insert name of real estate entity) and its Associates owe to you the following duties:

1 . Dealing honestly and fairly.

2 . Disclosing all known facts that materially affect the value of residential real property which are not readily observable to the buyer.

3 . Accounting for all funds entrusted to the licensee.

_____   _____

Date   Signature

_____   _____

Date   Signature

F I G U R E B.4 ■ Designated Sales Associate Notice

DESIGNATED SALES ASSOCIATE

I have assets of one million dollars or more. I request that _____ use the

(Name of broker)

designated sales associate form or representation.

Signature:_____ (circle one) Seller / Buyer

SINGLE AGENT NOTICE

FLORIDA LAW REQUIRES THAT REAL ESTATE LICENSEES OPERATING AS
SINGLE AGENTS DISCLOSE TO BUYERS AND SELLERS THEIR DUTIES

As a single agent, _____ *(insert name of real estate entity)* and its
Associates owe to you the following duties:

1 . Dealing honestly and fairly;
2 . Loyalty;
3 . Confidentiality;
4 . Obedience;
5 . Full disclosure;
6 . Accounting for all funds;
7 . Skill, care, and diligence in the transaction;
8 . Presenting all offers and counteroffers in a timely manner, unless a party has previously directed the licensee otherwise in writing; and
9 . Disclosing all known facts that materially affect the value of residential real property and are not readily observable.

_____   _____   _____

Date   Signature   Signature

_____

Designated Sales Associate Notice

Florida law prohibits a designated sales associate from disclosing, except to the broker or persons specified by the broker, information made confidential by request or at the instruction of the customer the designated sales associate is representing. However, Florida law allows a designated sales associate to disclose information allowed to be disclosed or required to be disclosed by law and also allows a designated sales associate to disclose to his or her broker, or persons specified by the broker, confidential information of a customer for the purpose of seeking advice or assistance for the benefit of the customer in regard to a transaction. Florida law requires that the broker must hold this information confidential and may not use such information to the detriment of the other party.

_____   _____   _____

Date   Signature optional   Signature optional

F I G U R E B.5 ■ **Lead-based Paint Warning System**

Lead-based Paint Warning Statement

FLORIDA ASSOCIATION OF REALTORS®

(Use this form with contracts for the sale of residential property built in 1977 or earlier. This disclosure must be made beginning September 6, 1996, if Seller owns more than 4 dwelling units and beginning December 6, 1996, if Seller owns 1 - 4 dwelling units. Seller and licensees must keep a copy of this completed form for 3 years from the date of closing.)

Sale and Purchase Contract: This clause is incorporated into the Contract between
_____ **(Seller)** and _____ **(Buyer)**
concerning the residential Property built before 1978 and located at _____
_____.

"Every purchaser of any interest in residential real property on which a residential dwelling was built prior to 1978 is notified that such property may present exposure to lead from lead-based paint that may place young children at risk of developing lead poisoning. Lead poisoning in young children may produce permanent neurological damage, including learning disabilities, reduced intelligence quotient, behavioral problems, and impaired memory. Lead poisoning also poses a particular risk to pregnant women. The seller of any interest in residential real property is required to provide the buyer with any information on lead-based paint hazards from risk assessments or inspection in the seller's possession and notify the buyer of any known lead-based paint hazards. A risk assessment or inspection for possible lead-based paint hazards is recommended prior to purchase." For purposes of this addendum, lead-based paint will be referred to as "LBP" and lead-based paint hazards will be referred to as "LBPH."

(1) LBP/LBPH in Housing: Seller has no knowledge of LBP/LBPH in the housing and no available LBP/LBPH records or reports, except as indicated: (describe all known LBP/LBPH information and list all available documents pertaining to LBP/LBPH and provide documents to **Buyer** before accepting **Buyer's** offer) _____
_____
_____
_____
_____
_____
_____
_____
_____
_____

(2) Lead-based Paint Hazards Inspection: Buyer waives the opportunity to conduct a risk assessment or inspection for the presence of LBP/LBPH unless this box is checked (☐ **Buyer** may conduct a risk assessment or inspection for the presence of LBP/LBPH in accordance with the inspection, notice, repair and repair limits of paragraph 8(a) or H of the FAR Residential Sale and Purchase Contract or standard N of the FAR/BAR Contract for Sale and Purchase, as amended and as applicable).

(3) Certification of Accuracy: Buyer has received the pamphlet "entitled "Protect Your Family From Lead in Your Home" and all of the information specified in paragraph (A) above. Licensee has notified **Seller** of **Seller's** obligations to provide and disclose information regarding lead-based paint and lead-based paint hazards in the property as required by federal law (42 U.S.C. 4852d) and is aware of his or her obligation to ensure compliance with federal lead-based paint law. **Buyer, Seller** and each licensee has reviewed the information above and certifies, to the best of his or her knowledge, that the information he or she has provided is true and accurate.

_____   _____   _____   _____
Buyer   Date   **Seller**   Date

_____   _____   _____   _____
Buyer   Date   **Seller**   Date

_____   _____   _____   _____
Selling Licensee   Date   **Listing Licensee**   Date

Buyer (____) (____) **Seller** (____) (____) **Listing Licensee** (____) (____) **Selling Licensee** (____) (____) acknowledge receipt of a copy of this page, which is Page 1 of 2 Pages.

Ⓡ 🏠
REALTOR   EQUAL HOUSING OPPORTUNITY

FIGURE B.5 ■ Lead-based Paint Warning System (continued)

Notice from Real Estate Licensee to Seller/Landlord Regarding Responsibilities Under Federal Lead-Based Paint Law

I am notifying you of your responsibilities under the Lead-Based Paint Hazard Reduction Act of 1992 and its implementing regulations. As the owner of a residential dwelling unit built in 1977 or earlier, you have the following disclosure and other requirements (for purposes of this document, "LBP" will mean lead-based paint and "LBPH" will mean lead-based paint hazards, which are conditions that cause exposure to lead from lead-contaminated dust, soil or paint that is deteriorated or present in accessible surfaces or surfaces that rub together, like doors and windows):

1. Before You Sign a Contract/Lease.　Before a buyer or tenant becomes obligated by contract to buy or lease your housing, you must complete the activities listed in A-D below. If you receive an offer before you provide the required information, you cannot accept the offer until after the information is given. This may be accomplished by making a counter offer that allows the buyer or tenant an opportunity to review the information and amend the offer if he or she so chooses. You must:

A. Disclose　to each licensee or other agent (for purposes of this law, anyone who enters into a contract with you or your representative for the purpose of selling your home, except for buyer's agents who are paid solely by the buyer and not by you or your representative, is considered an "agent") involved in the transaction:

(1) the presence of any LBP/LBPH about which you know;

(2) any additional information available concerning the LBP/LBPH, including the basis for determining that LBP/LBPH exists, the location of the LBP/LBPH and the condition of the painted surfaces; and

(3) the existence of any available records or reports pertaining to LBP/LBPH.

B. Provide　the buyer or tenant with:

(1) an EPA-approved lead hazard information pamphlet. This means either the EPA document entitled "Protect Your Family From Lead in Your Home" or an equivalent pamphlet approved by the EPA for use in Florida; and

(2) any records or reports available to you concerning LBP/LBPH in the unit, including records and reports regarding any common areas. If the unit is in multifamily housing that you own and you had an evaluation or reduction of LBP/LBPH in the housing as a whole, you must provide available records and reports regarding other residential dwellings in that housing.

C. Disclose　to the buyer or tenant:

(1) the presence of any known LBP/LBPH in the unit; and

(2) any additional information available concerning the LBP/LBPH, such as the basis for determining that LBP/LBPH exists, the location of the LBP/LBPH and the condition of the painted surfaces.

D. Allow　the buyer time to conduct a risk assessment or inspection for the presence of LBP/LBPH. You must give the buyer a 10 day period unless you agree with the buyer, in writing, to another period of time (such as within the time allowed for property inspections) or unless the buyer indicates in writing that he or she waives the right to conduct the risk assessment or inspection. This inspection requirement does not apply to tenants.

2. Sales Contract Requirements.　You must ensure that the sales contract has an attachment having the following elements:

A. The following Lead Warning Statement: "Every purchaser of any interest in residential real property on which a residential dwelling was built prior to 1978 is notified that such property may present exposure to lead from lead-based paint that may place young children at risk of developing lead poisoning. Lead poisoning in young children may produce permanent neurological damage, including learning disabilities, reduced intelligence quotient, behavioral problems, and impaired memory. Lead poisoning also poses a particular risk to pregnant women. The seller of any interest in residential real property is required to provide the buyer with any information on lead-based paint hazards from risk assessments or inspection in the seller's possession and notify the buyer of any known lead-based paint hazards. A risk assessment or inspection for possible lead-based paint hazards is recommended prior to purchase."

B. A statement by you disclosing the presence of known LBP/LBPH in the home and any additional information available concerning the LBP/LBPH, such as the basis for determining that it exists, its location and the condition of the painted surfaces; OR indicating that you have no knowledge of the presence of LBP/LBPH in the home.

C. A list of any records or reports described in 1.B.(2) above that are available to you and that you have provided to the buyer; OR a statement that no such records or reports are available to you.

D. A statement by the buyer:

(1) affirming receipt of the information in 2.B and C above;

(2) affirming receipt of the lead hazard information pamphlet noted in 1.B.(1) above; and

(3) that he or she has either had the opportunity to conduct the risk assessment or inspection required as noted in 1.D. above or waived the opportunity.

E. A statement by each real estate licensee/agent involved in the transaction that:

(1) the licensee/agent has informed you of your legal obligations; and

(2) the licensee/agent is aware of his or her duty to ensure compliance with the law.

F. Signatures of you, the licensees/agents and the buyers certifying to the accuracy of their statements to the best of their knowledge, and the dates of the signatures.

3. Lease Requirements.　As the owner of property being rented, you must ensure that every lease for the unit contains language within the lease itself or as an attachment having the following elements:

A. The following Lead Warning Statement: "Housing built before 1978 may contain lead-based paint. Lead from paint, paint chips, and dust can pose health hazards if not managed properly. Lead exposure is especially harmful to young children and pregnant women. Before renting pre-1978 housing, lessors must disclose the presence of lead-based paint and/or lead-based paint hazards in the dwelling. Lessees must also receive a federally approved pamphlet on lead poisoning prevention."

B. A statement by you disclosing the presence of known LBP/LBPH in the unit being leased and any additional information available concerning the LBP/LBPH, including the basis for determining that it exists, its location and the condition of the painted surfaces; OR indicating that you have no knowledge of the presence of LBP/LBPH.

C. A list of any records or reports described in 1.B.(2) above available to you and that you have provided to the tenant, OR a statement that no such records or reports are available to you.

D. A statement by the tenant:

(1) affirming receipt of the information paragraph 3.B. and C. above; and

(2) affirming receipt of the lead hazard information pamphlet noted in 1.B.(1) above.

E. A statement by each real estate licensee/agent involved in the transaction that:

(1) the licensee/agent has informed you of your legal obligations; and

(2) the licensee/agent is aware of his or her duty to ensure compliance with the law.

F. Signatures of you, the licensees/agents and the tenants certifying to the accuracy of their statements to the best of their knowledge, and the dates of the signatures.

4. Record Retention Requirements.　Sellers and the licensees/agents involved in the sales transaction must keep a copy of the completed attachment described in paragraph 2 above for no less than 3 years from the date of closing. Landlords and the licensees/agents involved in the lease transaction must keep a copy of the completed attachment or lease form described in paragraph 3 above for no less than 3 years from the first day of the leasing period.

5. Impact of Law and Disclosures.　Nothing in the law or regulations requires a seller or landlord to conduct any evaluation or reduction activities. However, the parties may voluntarily insert such a requirement in the contract. Neither you nor the licensees involved in the sale or lease transaction will be responsible for the failure of a buyer's or tenant's legal representative (such as an attorney or broker who receives all compensation from the buyer or tenant) to transmit disclosure materials to the buyer or tenant, provided that all required persons have completed and signed the necessary certification and acknowledgement language described under paragraphs 2 and 3 above.

This information sheet was provided by _____

(licensee) to Seller/Landlord on the _____ day of _____, _____ .

Buyer (_____) (_____) **Seller** (_____) (_____) **Listing Licensee** (_____) (_____) **Selling Licensee** (_____) (_____) acknowledge receipt of a copy of this page, which is Page 2 of 2 Pages.

U. S. Department of Housing and Urban Development

**EQUAL HOUSING
OPPORTUNITY**

We Do Business in Accordance With the Federal Fair Housing Law

(The Fair Housing Amendments Act of 1988)

It is illegal to Discriminate Against Any Person Because of Race, Color, Religion, Sex, Handicap, Familial Status, or National Origin

---

■ In the sale or rental of housing or residential lots

■ In advertising the sale or rental of housing

■ In the financing of housing

■ In the provision of real estate brokerage services

■ In the appraisal of housing

■ Blockbusting is also illegal

Anyone who feels he or she has been discriminated against may file a complaint of housing discrimination:
    1-800-669-9777 (Toll Free)
    1-800-927-9275 (TTY)

**U.S. Department of Housing and Urban Development
Assistant Secretary for Fair Housing and Equal Opportunity
Washington, D.C. 20410**

F I G U R E B.7 ■ **Goals Worksheet**

GOALS WORKSHEET

1. During the next 12 months, I want to earn $ _____

2. That works out to be monthly earnings of $ _____
   (line 1 ÷ 12)

3. Approximately 60% of my earnings should come from listings sold: $ _____
   (line 2 × .60)

4. Approximately 40% of my earnings should come from sales made: $ _____
   (line 2 × .40)

Achieving my listing income:

5. In my market area, the average listing commission amount is $ _____
   (Get this amount from your broker.)

6. So I must have the following number of listings sold: _____
   (line 3 ÷ line 5)

7. If only 75% of my listings sell, I have to get this many listings: _____
   (line 6 ÷ .75)

8. It may take this many listing appointments to get a listing: _____
   (Get this number from your broker.)

9. So I need to go on this many listing appointments: _____
   (line 7 × line 8)

10. It may take this many calls to get an appointment: _____
    (Get this number from your broker.)

11. So I have to make this many calls per month: _____
    (line 9 × line 10)

12. Which means this many calls per week: _____
    (line 11 ÷ 4.3 weeks per month)

Achieving my sales income:

13. In my market area, the average sales commission is $ _____
    (Get this amount from your broker.)

14. So I've got to make this many sales per month: _____
    (line 4 ÷ line 13)

15. It takes about this many showings to make a sale: _____
    (Get this number from your broker.)

16. So I must show this many properties per month: _____
    (line 14 × line 15)

F I G U R E B.8 ■ Daily Activity Log

A Direct $	Hours [Goal]	Hours [Actual]	Comments
TOTAL			
B Office and Administrative			
TOTAL			
C Wasted Time			
TOTAL			
? Personal			
TOTAL			
GRAND TOTAL HOURS			

F I G U R E B.9 ■ **Exclusive Right of Sale Listing Agreement**

Exclusive Right of Sale Listing Agreement

1 This Exclusive Right of Sale Listing Agreement ("Agreement") is between

2* _____ ("Seller") and

3* _____ ("Broker")

4 **1. AUTHORITY TO SELL PROPERTY: Seller** gives **Broker** the EXCLUSIVE RIGHT TO SELL the real and personal property
5* (collectively "Property") described below, at the price and terms described below, beginning the _____ day of
6* _____, _____, and terminating at 11:59 p.m. the _____ day of _____, _____,
7 ("Termination Date"). Upon full execution of a contract for sale and purchase of the Property, all rights and obligations of this
8 Agreement will automatically extend through the date of the actual closing of the sales contract. **Seller** and **Broker**
9 acknowledge that this Agreement does not guarantee a sale. This Property will be offered to any person without regard to race,
10 color, religion, sex, handicap, familial status, national origin or any other factor protected by federal, state or local law. **Seller**
11 certifies and represents that he/she/it is legally entitled to convey the Property and all improvements.
12 **2. DESCRIPTION OF PROPERTY:**
13*   **(a)** Real Property Street Address: _____
14* _____
15*   Legal Description: _____
16* _____ ☐ See Attachment_____
17*   **(b)** Personal Property, including appliances: _____
18* _____
19* _____ ☐ See Attachment_____
20*   **(c)** Occupancy: Property ☐ is ☐ is not currently occupied by a tenant. If occupied, the lease term expires _____.
21 **3. PRICE AND TERMS:** The property is offered for sale on the following terms, or on other terms acceptable to **Seller:**
22*   **(a) Price:** _____
23*   **(b) Financing Terms:** ☐ Cash ☐ Conventional ☐ VA ☐ FHA ☐ Other _____
24*   ☐ **Seller** Financing: **Seller** will hold a purchase money mortgage in the amount of $ _____ with the
25*   following terms: _____
26*   ☐ Assumption of Existing Mortgage: Buyer may assume existing mortgage for $ _____ plus
27*   an assumption fee of $ _____. The mortgage is for a term of _____ years beginning in _____, at
28*   an interest rate of _____ % ☐ fixed ☐ variable (describe) _____
29*   Lender approval of assumption ☐ is required ☐ is not required ☐ unknown. Notice to **Seller:** You may remain liable for an
30 assumed mortgage for a number of years after the Property is sold. Check with your lender to determine the extent of your
31 liability. **Seller** will ensure that all mortgage payments and required escrow deposits are current at the time of closing and will
32 convey the escrow deposit to the buyer at closing.
33*   **(c) Seller Expenses: Seller** will pay mortgage discount or other closing costs not to exceed _____ % of the purchase
34 price; and any other expenses **Seller** agrees to pay in connection with a transaction.
35 **4. BROKER OBLIGATIONS AND AUTHORITY: Broker** agrees to make diligent and continued efforts to sell the Property until
36 a sales contract is pending on the Property. **Seller** authorizes **Broker** to:
37   **(a)** Advertise the Property as **Broker** deems advisable including advertising the Property on the Internet unless limited in
38   (4)(a)(i) or (4)(a)(ii) below.
39   **(Seller opt-out)(Check one if applicable)**
40*   ☐ (i) Display the Property on the Internet except the street address of the Property shall not be displayed on the Internet.
41*   ☐ (ii) **Seller** does not authorize **Broker** to display the Property on the Internet.
42   **Seller** understands and acknowledges that if **Seller** selects option (ii), consumers who conduct searches for listings on
43   the Internet will not see information about the listed property in response to their search.
44*   _____/_____ **Initials of Seller.**
45   **(b)** Place appropriate transaction signs on the Property, including "For Sale" signs and "Sold" signs (once **Seller** signs a sales
46   contract) and use **Seller's** name in connection with marketing or advertising the Property.
47   **(c) Obtain information relating to the present mortgage(s) on the Property.**
48   **(d)** Place the Property in a multiple listing service ("MLS"). **Seller** authorizes **Broker** to report to the MLS this listing
49   information and price, terms and financing information on any resulting sale for use by authorized Board / Association
50   members, MLS participants and subscribers; and

51* **Seller** (____) (____) and **Broker/Sales Associate** (____) (____) acknowledge receipt of a copy of this page, which is Page 1 of 4 Pages.

ERS-14tb   Rev. 11/09   © 2009   Florida Association of REALTORS ®   All Rights Reserved

Serial#:

formsimplicity

F I G U R E B.9 ■ Exclusive Right of Sale Listing Agreement (continued)

52   (e) Provide objective comparative market analysis information to potential buyers; and
53* (f) (Check if applicable) ☐ Use a lock box system to show and access the Property. A lock box does not ensure the
54   Property's security; **Seller** is advised to secure or remove valuables. **Seller** agrees that the lock box is for **Seller's** benefit and
55   releases **Broker**, persons working through **Broker** and **Broker's** local Realtor Board / Association from all liability and
56* responsibility in connection with any loss that occurs.☐ Withhold verbal offers. ☐Withhold all offers once Seller accepts a
57   sales contract for the Property.
58   (g) Act as a transaction broker of Seller.
59   (h) **Virtual Office Websites:** Some real estate brokerages offer real estate brokerage services online. These websites are
60   referred to as Virtual Office Websites ("VOW"). An automated estimate of market value or reviews and comments about a
61   property may be displayed in conjunction with a property on some VOWs. Anyone who registers on a Virtual Office Website
62   may gain access to such automated valuations or comments and reviews about any property displayed on a VOW. Unless
63   limited below, a VOW may display automated valuations or comments/reviews (blogs) about this Property.
64* ☐**Seller** does not authorize an automated estimate of the market value of the listing (or hyperlink to such estimate) to be
65   displayed in immediate conjunction with the listing of this Property.
66* ☐**Seller** does not authorize third parties to write comments or reviews about the listing of the Property (or display a hyperlink
67   to such comments or reviews) in immediate conjunction with the listing of this Property.

68   **5. SELLER OBLIGATIONS:** In consideration of **Broker's** obligations, **Seller** agrees to:
69   (a) Cooperate with **Broker** in carrying out the purpose of this Agreement, including referring immediately to **Broker** all
70   inquiries regarding the Property's transfer, whether by purchase or any other means of transfer.
71   (b) Provide **Broker** with keys to the Property and make the Property available for **Broker** to show during reasonable times.
72   (c) Inform **Broker** prior to leasing, mortgaging or otherwise encumbering the Property.
73   (d) Indemnify **Broker** and hold **Broker** harmless from losses, damages, costs and expenses of any nature, including
74   attorney's fees, and from liability to any person, that **Broker** incurs because of (1) **Seller's** negligence, representations,
75   misrepresentations, actions or inactions, (2) the use of a lock box, (3) the existence of undisclosed material facts about the
76   Property, or (4) a court or arbitration decision that a broker who was not compensated in connection with a transaction is
77   entitled to compensation from **Broker**. This clause will survive **Broker's** performance and the transfer of title.
78   (e) To perform any act reasonably necessary to comply with FIRPTA (Internal Revenue Code Section 1445).
79   (f) Make all legally required disclosures, including all facts that materially affect the Property's value and are not readily
80   observable or known by the buyer. **Seller** certifies and represents that **Seller** knows of no such material facts (local
81* government building code violations, unobservable defects, etc.) other than the following: _____
82* _____
83   **Seller** will immediately inform **Broker** of any material facts that arise after signing this Agreement.
84   (g) Consult appropriate professionals for related legal, tax, property condition, environmental, foreign reporting requirements
85   and other specialized advice.

86   **6. COMPENSATION:** Seller will compensate **Broker** as specified below for procuring a buyer who is ready, willing and able to
87   purchase the Property or any interest in the Property on the terms of this Agreement or on any other terms acceptable to
88   **Seller. Seller** will pay **Broker** as follows (plus applicable sales tax);
89* (a) _____ % of the total purchase price plus $ _____ OR $ _____, no later than
90   the date of closing specified in the sales contract. However, closing is not a prerequisite for **Broker's** fee being earned.
91* (b) _____ ($ or %) of the consideration paid for an option, at the time an option is created. If the option is exercised,
92   **Seller** will pay **Broker** the paragraph 6(a) fee, less the amount **Broker** received under this subparagraph.
93* (c) _____ ($ or %) of gross lease value as a leasing fee, on the date **Seller** enters into a lease or agreement to
94   lease, whichever is soonest. This fee is not due if the Property is or becomes the subject of a contract granting an exclusive
95   right to lease the Property.
96   (d) **Broker's** fee is due in the following circumstances: (1) If any interest in the Property is transferred, whether by sale, lease,
97   exchange, governmental action, bankruptcy or any other means of transfer, regardless of whether the buyer is secured by
98   **Broker, Seller** or any other person. (2) If **Seller** refuses or fails to sign an offer at the price and terms stated in this Agreement,
99* defaults on an executed sales contract or agrees with a buyer to cancel an executed sales contract. (3) If, within ____ days after
100 Termination Date ("Protection Period"), **Seller** transfers or contracts to transfer the Property or any interest in the Property to any
101 prospects with whom **Seller, Broker** or any real estate licensee communicated regarding the Property prior to Termination Date.
102 However, no fee will be due **Broker** if the Property is relisted after Termination Date and sold through another broker.
103* (e) Retained Deposits: As consideration for **Broker's** services, **Broker** is entitled to receive _____ % of all deposits that
104 **Seller** retains as liquidated damages for a buyer's default in a transaction, not to exceed the paragraph 6(a) fee.

105 **7. COOPERATION AND COMPENSATION WITH OTHER BROKERS: Broker's** office policy is to cooperate with all other
106* brokers except when not in **Seller's** best interest: ☐ and to offer compensation in the amount of _____ % of the
107* purchase price or $ _____ to **Buyer's** agents, who represent the interest of the buyers, and not the interest of **Seller** in

108* **Seller** (_____) (_____) and **Broker/Sales Associate** (_____) (_____) acknowledge receipt of a copy of this page, which is Page 2 of 4 Pages.

F I G U R E B.9 ■ **Exclusive Right of Sale Listing Agreement (continued)**

109* a transaction; ☐ and to offer compensation in the amount of _____% of the purchase price or $ _____ to a
110* broker who has no brokerage relationship with the **Buyer** or **Seller**; ☐ and to offer compensation in the amount of
111* _____% of the purchase price or $ _____ to Transaction brokers for the **Buyer**; ☐ None of the above (if this is
112 checked, the Property cannot be placed in the MLS.)

113 **8. BROKERAGE RELATIONSHIP:** Under this Agreement, **Broker** will be acting as a transaction broker, **Broker** will deal
114 honestly and fairly with **Seller**, will account for all funds, will use skill, care, and diligence in the transaction, will disclose all
115 known facts that materially affect the value of the residential property which are not readily observable to the buyer, will present
116 all offers and counteroffers in a timely manner unless directed otherwise in writing and will have limited confidentiality with **Seller**
117 unless waived in writing.

118 **9. CONDITIONAL TERMINATION**: At **Seller's** request, **Broker** may agree to conditionally terminate this Agreement. If **Broker**
119 agrees to conditional termination, **Seller** must sign a withdrawal agreement, reimburse **Broker** for all direct expenses incurred
120* in marketing the Property and pay a cancellation fee of $ _____ plus applicable sales tax. **Broker** may void the
121 conditional termination and **Seller** will pay the fee stated in paragraph 6(a) less the cancellation fee if **Seller** transfers or
122 contracts to transfer the Property or any interest in the Property during the time period from the date of conditional termination
123 to Termination Date and Protection Period, if applicable.

124 **10. DISPUTE RESOLUTION:** This Agreement will be construed under Florida law. All controversies, claims and other matters
125 in question between the parties arising out of or relating to this Agreement or the breach thereof will be settled by first
126 attempting mediation under the rules of the American Mediation Association or other mediator agreed upon by the parties. If
127 litigation arises out of this Agreement, the prevailing party will be entitled to recover reasonable attorney's fees and costs, unless
128 the parties agree that disputes will be settled by arbitration as follows: **Arbitration:** By initialing in the space provided, **Seller**
129* (_____) (_____), Listing Associate (_____) and Listing Broker (_____) agree that disputes not resolved by mediation will be settled
130 by neutral binding arbitration in the county in which the Property is located in accordance with the rules of the American
131 Arbitration Association or other arbitrator agreed upon by the parties. Each party to any arbitration (or litigation to enforce the
132 arbitration provision of this Agreement or an arbitration award) will pay its own fees, costs and expenses, including attorney's
133 fees, and will equally split the arbitrators' fees and administrative fees of arbitration.

134 **11. MISCELLANEOUS:** This Agreement is binding on **Broker's** and **Seller's** heirs, personal representatives, administrators,
135 successors and assigns. **Broker** may assign this Agreement to another listing office. This Agreement is the entire agreement
136 between **Broker** and **Seller**. No prior or present agreements or representations shall be binding on **Broker** or **Seller** unless
137 included in this Agreement. Signatures, initials and modifications communicated by facsimile will be considered as originals.
138 The term "buyer" as used in this Agreement includes buyers, tenants, exchangors, optionees and other categories of potential
139 or actual transferees.

140* **12. ADDITIONAL TERMS:** _____
141* _____
142* _____
143* _____
144* _____
145* _____
146* _____
147* _____
148* _____
149* _____
150* _____
151* _____
152* _____
153* _____
154* _____
155* _____
156* _____

157* **Seller** (_____) (_____) and **Broker/Sales Associate** (_____) (_____) acknowledge receipt of a copy of this page, which is Page 3 of 4 Pages.

ERS-14tb   Rev. 11/09   © 2009   Florida Association of REALTORS ®   All Rights Reserved

Serial#:

formsimplicity

F I G U R E B.9 ■ Exclusive Right of Sale Listing Agreement (continued)

158* Date: _____ **Seller's Signature:** _____ Tax ID No: _____

159* Home Telephone: _____ Work Telephone: _____ Facsimile: _____

160* Address: _____

161* Date: _____ **Seller's Signature:** _____ Tax ID No: _____

162* Home Telephone: _____ Work Telephone: _____ Facsimile: _____

163* Address: _____

164* Date: _____ **Authorized Listing Associate or Broker:** _____

165* Brokerage Firm Name: _____ Telephone: _____

166* Address: _____

167*   Copy returned to **Customer** on the _____ day of _____ by: ☐ personal delivery ☐ mail ☐ E-mail ☐ facsimile.

The Florida Association of REALTORS® makes no representation as to the legal validity or adequacy of any provision of this form in any specific transaction. This standardized form should not be used in complex transactions or with extensive riders or additions. This form is available for use by the entire real estate industry and is not intended to identify the user as REALTOR®. REALTOR®.is a registered collective membership mark which may be used only by real estate licensees who are members of the NATIONAL ASSOCIATION OF REALTORS® and who subscribe to its Code of Ethics.
The copyright laws of the United States (17 U.S. Code) forbid the unauthorized reproduction of this form by any means including facsimile or computerized forms.

168* **Seller** (_____) (_____) and **Broker/Sales Associate** (_____) (_____) acknowledge receipt of a copy of this page, which is Page 4 of 4 Pages.

ERS-14tb   Rev. 11/09   © 2009   Florida Association of REALTORS ®   All Rights Reserved

F I G U R E B.10 ■ Seller's Property Disclosure—Residential

This form must be filled out by the Seller and therefore it cannot be filled out electronically.

Seller's Property Disclosure – Residential

Notice to Licensee: The **Seller** should fill out this form.

Notice to Seller: Florida law[1] requires a seller of a home to disclose to the buyer all known facts that materially affect the value of the property being sold and that are not readily observable or known by the buyer. This disclosure form is designed to help you comply with the law. However, this disclosure form may not address every significant issue that is unique to the Property. You should think about what you would want to know if you were buying the Property today; and if you need more space for additional information, comments, or explanations, check the Paragraph 10 checkbox and attach an addendum.

Notice to Buyer: The following representations are made by **Seller** and **not** by any real estate licensee. This disclosure is not a guaranty or warranty of any kind. It is not a substitute for any inspections, warranties, or professional advice you may wish to obtain. It is not a substitute for your own personal judgment and common sense. The following information is based only upon **Seller's** actual knowledge of the Property's condition. Sellers can disclose only what they actually know. **Seller** may not know about all material or significant items. You should have an independent, professional home inspection to verify the condition of the Property and determine the cost of repairs, if any. This disclosure is not a contract and is not intended to be a part of any contract for sale and purchase.

Seller makes the following disclosure regarding the property described as: _____
_____ (the "Property")

The Property is ☐owner occupied ☐tenant occupied ☐unoccupied (If unoccupied, how long has it been since **Seller** occupied the Property? _____

		Yes	No	Don't Know
1.	**Structures; Systems; Appliances:**			
	(a) Are the structures, including roofs; ceilings; walls; doors; windows; foundation; and pool, hot tub, and spa, if any, structurally sound and free of leaks?	☐	☐	☐
	(b) Is seawall, if any, and dockage, if any, structurally sound?	☐	☐	☐
	(c) Are existing major appliances and heating, cooling, mechanical, electrical, security, and sprinkler systems, in working condition, i.e., operating in the manner in which the item was designed to operate?	☐	☐	☐
	(d) Are any of the appliances leased? If yes, which ones: _____	☐	☐	☐
	(e) If any answer to questions 1(a) – 1(c) is no, please explain: _____			
	_____			
2.	**Termites; Other Wood-Destroying Organisms; Pests:**			
	(a) Are termites; other wood-destroying organisms, including fungi; or pests present on the Property or has the Property had any structural damage by them?	☐	☐	☐
	(b) Has the Property been treated for termites; other wood-destroying organisms, including fungi; or pests?	☐	☐	☐
	(c) If any answer to questions 2(a) - 2(b) is yes, please explain: _____			
	_____			
3.	**Water Intrusion; Drainage; Flooding:**			
	(a) Has past or present water intrusion affected the Property?	☐	☐	☐
	(b) Have past or present drainage or flooding problems affected the Property?	☐	☐	☐
	(c) Is any of the Property located in a special flood hazard area?	☐	☐	☐
	(d) Is any of the Property located seaward of the coastal construction control line?	☐	☐	☐
	(e) Does your lender require flood insurance?	☐	☐	☐
	(f) Do you have an elevation certificate? If yes, please attach a copy.	☐	☐	☐
	(g) If any answer to questions 3(a) - 3(d) is yes, please explain: _____			
	_____			

---

[1] *Johnson v. Davis,* 480 So.2d 625 (Fla. 1985).

Buyer (____) (____) and **Seller** (____) (____) acknowledge receipt of a copy of this page, which is Page 1 of 4.
SPDR-1   ©2013 Florida Association of REALTORS®

F I G U R E B.10 ■ **Seller's Property Disclosure—Residential (continued)**

	Yes	No	Don't Know

4. Plumbing:
   (a) What is your drinking water source? ☐public ☐private ☐well ☐other
   (b) Have you ever had a problem with the quality, supply, or flow of potable water?   ☐ ☐ ☐
   (c) Do you have a water treatment system?   ☐ ☐ ☐
       If yes, is it ☐owned ☐leased?
   (d) Do you have a ☐sewer or ☐septic system? If septic system, describe the location of each system: _____

       _____

   (e) Are any septic tanks, drain fields, or wells that are not currently being used located on the Property?   ☐ ☐ ☐
   (f) Have there been any plumbing leaks since you have owned the Property?   ☐ ☐ ☐
   (g) Are any polybutylene pipes on the Property?   ☐ ☐ ☐
   (h) If any answer to questions 4(b), 4(c), and 4(e) - 4(g) is yes, please explain: _____
       _____

5. Pools; Hot Tubs; Spas:
   Note: Florida law requires swimming pools, hot tubs, and spas that received a certificate of completion on or after October 1, 2000, to have at least one safety feature as specified by Section 515.27, Florida Statutes.
   (a) If the Property has a swimming pool, hot tub, or spa that received a certificate of completion on or after October 1, 2000, indicate the existing safety feature(s): ☐enclosure that meets the pool barrier requirements ☐approved safety pool cover ☐required door and window exit alarms ☐required door locks ☐none
   (b) Has an in-ground pool on the Property been demolished and/or filled?   ☐ ☐ ☐

6. Sinkholes:
   Note: When an insurance claim for sinkhole damage has been made by the seller and paid by the insurer, Section 627.7073(2)(c), Florida Statutes, requires the seller to disclose to the buyer that a claim was paid and whether or not the full amount paid was used to repair the sinkhole damage.
   (a) Does past or present settling, soil movement, or sinkhole(s) affect the Property or adjacent properties?   ☐ ☐ ☐
   (b) Has any insurance claim for sinkhole damage been made?   ☐ ☐ ☐
   (c) If any insurance claim for sinkhole damage was made, was the claim paid?   ☐ ☐ ☐
   (d) If any insurance claim for sinkhole damage was paid, were all the proceeds used to repair the damage?   ☐ ☐ ☐
   (e) If any answer to questions 6(a) - 6(c) is yes or the answer to question 6(d) is no, please explain: _____

7. Deed/Homeowners' Association Restrictions; Boundaries; Access Roads:
   (a) Are there any deed or homeowners' restrictions?   ☐ ☐ ☐
   (b) Are there any proposed changes to any of the restrictions?   ☐ ☐ ☐
   (c) Are there any resale or leasing restrictions?   ☐ ☐ ☐
   (d) Is membership mandatory in a homeowners' association?   ☐ ☐ ☐
   (e) Are fees charged by the homeowners' association?   ☐ ☐ ☐
   (f) Are any driveways, walls, fences, or other features shared with adjoining landowners?   ☐ ☐ ☐
   (g) Are there any encroachments on the Property or any encroachments by the Property's improvements on other lands?   ☐ ☐ ☐
   (h) Are there boundary line disputes or easements affecting the Property?   ☐ ☐ ☐
   (i) Are access roads ☐private ☐public? If private, describe the terms and conditions of the maintenance agreement: _____

   (j) If any answer to questions 7(a) - 7(h) is yes, please explain: _____
       _____

F I G U R E   B.10 ■ Seller's Property Disclosure—Residential (continued)

	Yes	No	Don't Know

8. Environmental:

(a) Was the Property built before 1978?   ☐ ☐ ☐
If yes, please see Lead-Based Paint Disclosure.

(b) Does anything exist on the Property that may be considered an environmental hazard, including but not limited to, lead-based paint; asbestos; mold; urea formaldehyde; radon gas; methamphetamine; defective drywall; fuel, propane, or chemical storage tanks (active or abandoned); or contaminated soil or water?   ☐ ☐ ☐

(c) Has there been any damage, clean up, or repair to the Property due to any of the substances or materials listed in subsection (b) above?   ☐ ☐ ☐

(d) Are any mangroves, archeological sites, or other environmentally sensitive areas located on the Property?   ☐ ☐ ☐

(e) If any answer to questions 8(b) - 8(d) is yes, please explain: _____
_____

9. Governmental:

(a) Are there any zoning violations or nonconforming uses?   ☐ ☐ ☐

(b) Are there any zoning restrictions affecting additions, improvements, or replacement of the Property?   ☐ ☐ ☐

(c) Do any zoning, land use, or administrative regulations conflict with the existing or intended use of the Property?   ☐ ☐ ☐

(d) Do any restrictions, other than association and flood area requirements, affect improvements or replacement of the Property?   ☐ ☐ ☐

(e) Are any improvements, including additions, located below the base flood elevation?   ☐ ☐ ☐

(f) Have any improvements been constructed in violation of applicable local flood guidelines?   ☐ ☐ ☐

(g) Have any improvements or additions to the Property, whether by you or by others, been constructed in violation of building codes or without necessary permits?   ☐ ☐ ☐

(h) Are there any active permits on the Property that have not been closed by a final inspection?   ☐ ☐ ☐

(i) Is there any violation or non-compliance regarding any unrecorded liens; code enforcement violations; or governmental, building, environmental, and safety codes, restrictions, or requirements?   ☐ ☐ ☐

(j) If any answer to questions 9(a) - 9(i) is yes, please explain: _____
_____

10. ☐ **(If checked) Other Matters; Additional Comments:** The attached addendum contains additional information, explanation, or comments.

Seller represents that the information provided on this form and any attachments is accurate and complete to the best of **Seller's** knowledge on the date signed by **Seller**. **Seller** authorizes listing broker to provide this disclosure statement to real estate licensees and prospective buyers of the Property. **Seller** understands and agrees that **Seller** will promptly notify **Buyer** in writing if any information set forth in this disclosure statement becomes inaccurate or incorrect.

Seller: _____/_____   Date: _____
(signature)   (print)

Seller: _____/_____   Date: _____
(signature)   (print)

Buyer acknowledges that **Buyer** has read, understands, and has received a copy of this disclosure statement.

Buyer: _____/_____   Date: _____
(signature)   (print)

Buyer: _____/_____   Date: _____
(signature)   (print)

Buyer (_____) (_____) and **Seller** (_____) (_____) acknowledge receipt of a copy of this page, which is Page 3 of 4.
SPDR-1   ©2013 Florida Association of REALTORS®

F I G U R E B.10 ▨ **Seller's Property Disclosure—Residential (continued)**

Seller's Update

Instructions to Seller: If the information set forth in this disclosure statement becomes inaccurate or incorrect, you must promptly notify **Buyer**. Please review the questions and your answers. Use the space below to make corrections and provide additional information, if necessary. Then acknowledge that the information is accurate as of date signed below.

_____
_____
_____
_____
_____
_____
_____
_____
_____
_____
_____
_____
_____
_____
_____
_____
_____
_____
_____
_____
_____
_____
_____
_____
_____
_____

Seller represents that the information provided on this form and any attachments is accurate and complete to the best of **Seller's** knowledge on the date signed by **Seller**.

Seller: _____ / _____   Date: _____
                   (signature)   (print)

Seller: _____ / _____   Date: _____
                   (signature)   (print)

Buyer acknowledges that **Buyer** has read, understands, and has received a copy of this revised disclosure statement.

Buyer: _____ / _____   Date: _____
                   (signature)   (print)

Buyer: _____ / _____   Date: _____
                   (signature)   (print)

Buyer (_____) (_____) and **Seller** (_____) (_____) acknowledge receipt of a copy of this page, which is Page 4 of 4.
SPDR-1   ©2013 Florida Association of REALTORS®

F I G U R E B.11 ■ **Exclusive Buyer Brokerage Agreement**

Exclusive Buyer Brokerage Agreement

FloridaRealtors®
The Voice for Real Estate® in Florida

1. **PARTIES:** _____ (" **Buyer** ") grants

_____ (" **Broker** ")

Real Estate Broker   /   Office

the exclusive right to work with and assist **Buyer** in locating and negotiating the acquisition of suitable real property as described below. The term "acquire" or "acquisition" includes any purchase, option, exchange, lease or other acquisition of an ownership or equity interest in real property.

2. **TERM:** This Agreement will begin on the _____ day of _____, _____ and will terminate at 11:59 p.m. on the _____ day of _____, _____ ("Termination Date"). However, if **Buyer** enters into an agreement to acquire property that is pending on the Termination Date, this Agreement will continue in effect until that transaction has closed or otherwise terminated.

3. **PROPERTY:** **Buyer** is interested in acquiring real property as follows or as otherwise acceptable to **Buyer** ("Property"):

(a) **Type of property:** _____

(b) **Location:** _____

(c) **Price range:** $_____ to $_____.

☐**Buyer** has been ☐ pre-qualified ☐ pre-approved by _____

for (amount and terms, if any) _____

(d) **Preferred terms and conditions:** _____

_____

_____

_____

4. **BROKER'S OBLIGATIONS:**

(a) **Broker Assistance. Broker** will

* use **Broker's** professional knowledge and skills;
* assist **Buyer** in determining **Buyer's** financial capability and financing options;
* discuss property requirements and assist **Buyer** in locating and viewing suitable properties;
* assist **Buyer** to contract for property, monitor deadlines and close any resulting transaction;
* cooperate with real estate licensees working with the seller, if any, to effect a transaction. **Buyer** understands that even if **Broker** is compensated by a seller or a real estate licensee who is working with a seller, such compensation does not compromise **Broker's** duties to **Buyer** .

(b) **Other Buyers. Buyer** understands that **Broker** may work with other prospective buyers who want to acquire the same property as **Buyer** . If **Broker** submits offers by competing buyers, **Broker** will notify **Buyer** that a competing offer has been made, but will not disclose any of the offer's material terms or conditions. **Buyer** agrees that **Broker** may make competing buyers aware of the existence of any offer **Buyer** makes, so long as **Broker** does not reveal any material terms or conditions of the offer without **Buyer's** prior written consent.

(c) **Fair Housing. Broker** adheres to the principles expressed in the Fair Housing Act and will not participate in any act that unlawfully discriminates on the basis of race, color, religion, sex, handicap, familial status, country of national origin or any other category protected under federal, state or local law.

(d) **Service Providers. Broker** does not warrant or guarantee products or services provided by any third party whom **Broker** , at **Buyer's** request, refers or recommends to **Buyer** in connection with property acquisition.

Buyer (_____) (_____) and **Broker/Sales Associate** (_____) (_____) acknowledge receipt of a copy of this page, which is Page 1 of 3 Pages.

F I G U R E B.11 ■ Exclusive Buyer Brokerage Agreement (continued)

5. **BUYER'S OBLIGATIONS: Buyer** agrees to cooperate with **Broker** in accomplishing the objectives of this Agreement, including:
(a) Conducting all negotiations and efforts to locate suitable property only through **Broker** and referring to **Broker** all inquiries of any kind from real estate licensees, property owners or any other source. If **Buyer** contacts or is contacted by a seller or a real estate licensee who is working with a seller or views a property unaccompanied by **Broker, Buyer** , will, at first opportunity, advise the seller or real estate licensee that **Buyer** is working with and represented exclusively by **Broker** .
(b) Providing **Broker** with accurate personal and financial information requested by **Broker** in connection with ensuring **Buyer's** ability to acquire property. **Buyer** authorizes **Broker** to run a credit check to verify **Buyer's** credit information.
(c) Being available to meet with **Broker** at reasonable times for consultations and to view properties.
(d) Indemnifying and holding **Broker** harmless from and against all losses, damages, costs and expenses of any kind, including attorney's fees, and from liability to any person, that **Broker** incurs because of acting on **Buyer's** behalf.
(e) Not asking or expecting to restrict the acquisition of a property according to race, color, religion, sex, handicap, familial status, country of national origin or any other category protected under federal, state or local law.
(f) Consulting an appropriate professional for legal, tax, environmental, engineering, foreign reporting requirements and other specialized advice.

6. **RETAINER:** Upon final execution of this Agreement, **Buyer** will pay to **Broker** a non-refundable retainer fee of $_____ for **Broker's** services ("Retainer"). This fee is not refundable and ☐will ☐ will not be credited to **Buyer** if compensation is earned by **Broker** as specified in this Agreement.

7. **COMPENSATION: Broker's** compensation is earned when, during the term of this Agreement or any renewal or extension, **Buyer** or any person acting for or on behalf of **Buyer** contracts to acquire real property as specified in this Agreement. **Buyer** will be responsible for paying **Broker** the amount specified below plus any applicable taxes but will be credited with any amount which **Broker** receives from a seller or a real estate licensee who is working with a seller.
(a) Purchase or exchange: $_____ or _____% (select only one); or $_____ or _____% plus $_____ (select only one) of the total pur chase price or other consideration for the acquired property, to be paid at closing.
(b) Lease: $_____ or _____% (select only one) of the gross lease value, to be paid when **Buyer** enters into the lease. If **Buyer** enters into a lease-purchase agreement, the amount of the leasing fee which **Broker** receives will be credited toward the amount due **Broker** for the purchase.
(c) Option: Broker will be paid $_____ or _____% of the option amount (select only one), to be paid when **Buyer** enters into the option agreement. If **Buyer** enters into a lease with option to purchase, **Broker** will be compensated for both the lease and the option. If **Buyer** subsequently exercises the option, the amounts received by **Broker** for the lease and option will be credited toward the amount due **Broker** for the purchase.
(d) Other: Broker will be compensated for all other types of acquisitions as if such acquisition were a purchase or exchange.
(e) Buyer Default: Buyer will pay **Broker's** compensation immediately upon **Buyer's** default on any contract to acquire property.

8. **PROTECTION PERIOD: Buyer** will pay **Broker's** compensation if, within _____ days after Termination Date, **Buyer** contracts to acquire any property which was called to **Buyer's** attention by **Broker** or any other person or found by **Buyer** during the term of this Agreement. **Buyer's** obligation to pay **Broker's** fee ceases upon **Buyer** entering into a good faith exclusive buyer brokerage agreement with another broker after Termination Date.

9. **EARLY TERMINATION: Buyer** may terminate this Agreement at any time by written notice to **Broker** but will remain responsible for paying **Broker's** compensation if, from the early termination date to Termination Date plus Protection Period, if applicable, **Buyer** contracts to acquire any property which, prior to the early termination date, was found by **Buyer** or called to **Buyer's** attention by **Broker** or any other person. **Broker** may terminate this Agreement at any time by written notice to **Buyer** , in which event **Buyer** will be released from all further obligations under this Agreement.

10. **DISPUTE RESOLUTION:** Any unresolveable dispute between **Buyer** and **Broker** will be mediated. If a settlement is not reached in mediation, the matter will be submitted to binding arbitration in accordance with the rules of the American Arbitration Association or other mutually agreeable arbitrator.

11. **ASSIGNMENT; PERSONS BOUND: Broker** may assign this Agreement to another broker. This Agreement will bind and inure to **Broker's** and **Buyer's** heirs, personal representatives, successors and assigns.

12. **BROKERAGE RELATIONSHIP: Buyer** authorizes **Broker** to operate as (check which is applicable):
☐ single agent of **Buyer.**
☐ transaction broker.
☐ single agent of **Buyer** with consent to transition into a transaction broker.
☐ nonrepresentative of **Buyer.**

Buyer (_____) (_____) and **Broker/Sales Associate** (_____) (_____) acknowledge receipt of a copy of this page, which is Page 2 of 3 Pages.

F I G U R E B.11 ■ **Exclusive Buyer Brokerage Agreement (continued)**

13. SPECIAL CLAUSES: _____

_____

_____

_____

_____

_____

14. ACKNOWLEDGMENT; MODIFICATIONS: Buyer has read this Agreement and understands its contents. This Agreement cannot be changed except by written agreement signed by both parties.

Date: _____   **Buyer :** _____   Tax ID No: __ __ __ - __ __ - __ __ __ __

                        Address: _____

                        Zip: _____ Telephone: _____ Facsimile: _____

Date: _____   **Buyer :** _____   Tax ID No: __ __ __ - __ __ - __ __ __ __

                        Address: _____

                        Zip: _____ Telephone: _____ Facsimile: _____

Date: _____   **Real Estate Associate:** _____

Date: _____   **Real Estate Broker:** _____

Buyer (_____) (_____) and **Broker/Sales Associate** (_____) (_____) acknowledge receipt of a copy of this page, which is Page 3 of 3 Pages.

EBBA-5   Rev. 11/09   © 2009   Florida Association of REALTORS®   All Rights Reserved

Serial#:

formsimplicity

FIGURE B.12 ■ Residential Contract for Sale and Purchase

Residential Contract For Sale And Purchase
THIS FORM HAS BEEN APPROVED BY THE FLORIDA REALTORS AND THE FLORIDA BAR

FloridaRealtors®

1*   **PARTIES:**_____ ("Seller"),
2*   and _____ ("Buyer"),
3   agree that Seller shall sell and Buyer shall buy the following described Real Property and Personal Property
4   (collectively "Property") pursuant to the terms and conditions of this Residential Contract For Sale And Purchase and
5   any riders and addenda ("Contract"):
6   **1. PROPERTY DESCRIPTION:**
7*   (a) Street address, city, zip:_____
8*   (b) Property is located in: _____County, Florida. Real Property Tax ID No.:_____
9*   (c) Real Property: The legal description is_____
10   _____
11   _____
12   together with all existing improvements and fixtures, including built-in appliances, built-in furnishings and attached
13   wall-to-wall carpeting and flooring ("Real Property") unless specifically excluded in Paragraph 1(e) or by other terms
14   of this Contract.
15   (d) Personal Property: Unless excluded in Paragraph 1(e) or by other terms of this Contract, the following items which
16   are owned by Seller and existing on the Property as of the date of the initial offer are included in the purchase:
17   range(s)/oven(s), refrigerator(s), dishwasher(s), disposal, ceiling fan(s), intercom, light fixture(s), drapery rods and
18   draperies, blinds, window treatments, smoke detector(s), garage door opener(s), security gate and other access
19   devices, and storm shutters/panels ("Personal Property").
20*   Other Personal Property items included in this purchase are:_____
21   _____
22   Personal Property is included in the Purchase Price, has no contributory value, and shall be left for the Buyer.
23*   (e) The following items are excluded from the purchase:_____
24   _____

25   **PURCHASE PRICE AND CLOSING**

26*   **2. PURCHASE PRICE** (U.S. currency):...$_____
27*   (a) Initial deposit to be held in escrow in the amount of **(checks subject to COLLECTION)**...........$_____
28   The initial deposit made payable and delivered to "Escrow Agent" named below
29*   **(CHECK ONE):** (i) ☐ accompanies offer or (ii) ☐ is to be made within _____ (if left blank,
30   then 3) days after Effective Date. IF NEITHER BOX IS CHECKED, THEN OPTION (ii)
31   SHALL BE DEEMED SELECTED.
32*   Escrow Agent Information: Name: _____
33*   Address:_____
34*   Phone: _____E-mail:_____Fax: _____
35*   (b) Additional deposit to be delivered to Escrow Agent within _____ (if left blank, then 10)
36*   days after Effective Date ....$_____
37   (All deposits paid or agreed to be paid, are collectively referred to as the "Deposit")
38*   (c) Financing: Express as a dollar amount or percentage ("Loan Amount") see Paragraph 8 ...._____
39*   (d) Other:_____ ....$_____
40   (e) Balance to close (not including Buyer's closing costs, prepaids and prorations) by wire
41*   transfer or other **COLLECTED** funds ....$_____
42   **NOTE: For the definition of "COLLECTION" or "COLLECTED" see STANDARD S.**
43   **3. TIME FOR ACCEPTANCE OF OFFER AND COUNTER-OFFERS; EFFECTIVE DATE:**
44*   (a) If not signed by Buyer and Seller, and an executed copy delivered to all parties on or before _____
45*   _____, this offer shall be deemed withdrawn and the Deposit, if any, shall be returned to
46   Buyer. Unless otherwise stated, time for acceptance of any counter-offers shall be within 2 days after the day the
47   counter-offer is delivered.
48   (b) The effective date of this Contract shall be the date when the last one of the Buyer and Seller has signed or initialed
49   and delivered this offer or final counter-offer ("Effective Date").
50   **4. CLOSING DATE:** Unless modified by other provisions of this Contract, the closing of this transaction shall occur and
51   the closing documents required to be furnished by each party pursuant to this Contract shall be delivered ("Closing") on
52*   _____ ("Closing Date"), at the time established by the Closing Agent.
53   **5. EXTENSION OF CLOSING DATE:**
54   (a) If Closing funds from Buyer's lender(s) are not available at time of Closing due to Truth In Lending Act (TILA) notice
55   requirements, Closing shall be extended for such period necessary to satisfy TILA notice requirements, not to
56   exceed 7 days.

Buyer's Initials _____ _____   Page **1** of **12**   Seller's Initials _____ _____

F I G U R E B.12 ◼ **Residential Contract for Sale and Purchase (continued)**

57	(b) If extreme weather or other condition or event constituting "Force Majeure" (see STANDARD G) causes: (i)
58	disruption of utilities or other services essential for Closing or (ii) Hazard, Wind, Flood or Homeowners' insurance,
59	to become unavailable prior to Closing, Closing shall be extended a reasonable time up to 3 days after restoration
60	of utilities and other services essential to Closing and availability of applicable Hazard, Wind, Flood or
61	Homeowners' insurance. If restoration of such utilities or services and availability of insurance has not occurred
62 ✱	within _____ (if left blank, then 14) days after Closing Date, then either party may terminate this Contract by
63	delivering written notice to the other party, and Buyer shall be refunded the Deposit, thereby releasing Buyer and
64	Seller from all further obligations under this Contract.

6. OCCUPANCY AND POSSESSION:

66   (a) Unless the box in Paragraph 6(b) is checked, Seller shall, at Closing, deliver occupancy and possession of the
67   Property to Buyer free of tenants, occupants and future tenancies. Also, at Closing, Seller shall have removed all
68   personal items and trash from the Property and shall deliver all keys, garage door openers, access devices and
69   codes, as applicable, to Buyer. If occupancy is to be delivered before Closing, Buyer assumes all risks of loss to the
70   Property from date of occupancy, shall be responsible and liable for maintenance from that date, and shall be
71   deemed to have accepted the Property in its existing condition as of time of taking occupancy, except with respect
72   to any items identified by Buyer pursuant to Paragraph 12, prior to taking occupancy, which require repair,
73   replacement, treatment or remedy.

74 ✱   (b) ☐ **CHECK IF PROPERTY IS SUBJECT TO LEASE(S) OR OCCUPANCY AFTER CLOSING**. If Property is
75   subject to a lease(s) after Closing or is intended to be rented or occupied by third parties beyond Closing, the facts
76   and terms thereof shall be disclosed in writing by Seller to Buyer and copies of the written lease(s) shall be
77   delivered to Buyer, all within 5 days after Effective Date. If Buyer determines, in Buyer's sole discretion, that the
78   lease(s) or terms of occupancy are not acceptable to Buyer, Buyer may terminate this Contract by delivery of
79   written notice of such election to Seller within 5 days after receipt of the above items from Seller, and Buyer shall be
80   refunded the Deposit thereby releasing Buyer and Seller from all further obligations under this Contract. Estoppel
81   Letter(s) and Seller's affidavit shall be provided pursuant to STANDARD D. If Property is intended to be occupied
82   by Seller after Closing, see Rider U. POST-CLOSING OCCUPANCY BY SELLER.

83 ✱ **7. ASSIGNABILITY: (CHECK ONE):** Buyer ☐ may assign and thereby be released from any further liability under this
84 ✱ Contract; ☐ may assign but not be released from liability under this Contract; or ☐ may not assign this Contract.

85   **FINANCING**

8. FINANCING:

87 ✱   ☐ (a) Buyer will pay cash or may obtain a loan for the purchase of the Property. There is no financing contingency to
88   Buyer's obligation to close.

89 ✱   ☐ (b) This Contract is contingent upon Buyer obtaining a written loan commitment for a ☐ conventional ☐ FHA ☐ VA
90 ✱   or ☐ other _____ (describe) loan on the following terms within _____ (if left blank, then 30) days after
91 ✱   Effective Date ("Loan Commitment Date") for **(CHECK ONE):** ☐ fixed, ☐ adjustable, ☐ fixed or adjustable rate loan in
92 ✱   the Loan Amount (See Paragraph 2(c)), at an initial interest rate not to exceed _____ % (if left blank, then prevailing
93 ✱   rate based upon Buyer's creditworthiness), and for a term of _____(if left blank, then 30) years ("Financing").

94 ✱ Buyer shall make mortgage loan application for the Financing within _____ (if left blank, then 5) days after Effective
95 Date and use good faith and diligent effort to obtain a written loan commitment for the Financing ("Loan Commitment")
96 and thereafter to close this Contract. Buyer shall keep Seller and Broker fully informed about the status of mortgage
97 loan application and Loan Commitment and authorizes Buyer's mortgage broker and Buyer's lender to disclose such
98 status and progress to Seller and Broker.

99 Upon Buyer's receipt of Loan Commitment, Buyer shall provide written notice of same to Seller. If Buyer does not
100 receive Loan Commitment by Loan Commitment Date, then thereafter either party may cancel this Contract **up to the**
101 **earlier of:**
102   (i.)   Buyer's delivery of written notice to Seller that Buyer has either received Loan Commitment or elected
103   to waive the financing contingency of this Contract; or
104   (ii.)   7 days prior to Closing Date.

105 If either party timely cancels this Contract pursuant to this Paragraph 8 and Buyer is not in default under the terms of
106 this Contract, Buyer shall be refunded the Deposit thereby releasing Buyer and Seller from all further obligations under
107 this Contract. If neither party has timely canceled this Contract pursuant to this Paragraph 8, then this financing
108 contingency shall be deemed waived by Buyer.

109 If Buyer delivers written notice of receipt of Loan Commitment to Seller and this Contract does not thereafter close, the
110 Deposit shall be paid to Seller unless failure to close is due to: (1) Seller's default; (2) Property related conditions of the
111 Loan Commitment have not been met (except when such conditions are waived by other provisions of this Contract); (3)
112 appraisal of the Property obtained by Buyer's lender is insufficient to meet terms of the Loan Commitment; or (4) the

Buyer's Initials _____ _____   Page **2** of 12   Seller's Initials _____ _____

FIGURE B.12 ■ Residential Contract for Sale and Purchase (continued)

113 loan is not funded due to financial failure of Buyer's lender, in which event(s) the Deposit shall be returned to Buyer,
114 thereby releasing Buyer and Seller from all further obligations under this Contract.
115* ☐ (c) Assumption of existing mortgage (see rider for terms).
116* ☐ (d) Purchase money note and mortgage to Seller (see riders; addenda; or special clauses for terms).

CLOSING COSTS, FEES AND CHARGES

117

118 **9. CLOSING COSTS; TITLE INSURANCE; SURVEY; HOME WARRANTY; SPECIAL ASSESSMENTS:**
119   (a) **COSTS TO BE PAID BY SELLER:**
120   • Documentary stamp taxes and surtax on deed, if any   • HOA/Condominium Association estoppel fees
121   • Owner's Policy and Charges (if Paragraph 9(c)(i) is checked) • Recording and other fees needed to cure title
122   • Title search charges (if Paragraph 9(c)(iii) is checked)   • Seller's attorneys' fees
123* • Other:_____
124   Seller shall pay the following amounts/percentages of the Purchase Price for the following costs and expenses:
125*   (i) up to $ _____ or _____ % (1.5% if left blank) for General Repair Items ("General Repair Limit");
126   and
127*   (ii) up to $ _____ or _____ % (1.5% if left blank) for WDO treatment and repairs ("WDO Repair
128   Limit"); and
129*   (iii) up to $ _____ or _____ % (1.5% if left blank) for costs associated with closing out open or
130   expired building permits and obtaining required building permits for any existing improvement for which a permit
131   was not obtained ("Permit Limit").
132   If, prior to Closing, Seller is unable to meet the Maintenance Requirement as required by Paragraph 11 or the
133   repairs, replacements, treatments or permitting as required by Paragraph 12, then, sums equal to 125% of
134   estimated costs to complete the applicable item(s) (but, not in excess of applicable General Repair, WDO Repair,
135   and Permit Limits set forth above, if any) shall be escrowed at Closing. If actual costs of required repairs,
136   replacements, treatment or permitting exceed applicable escrowed amounts, Seller shall pay such actual costs (but,
137   not in excess of applicable General Repair, WDO Repair, and Permit Limits set forth above). Any unused portion of
138   escrowed amount(s) shall be returned to Seller.
139   (b) **COSTS TO BE PAID BY BUYER:**
140   • Taxes and recording fees on notes and mortgages   • Loan expenses
141   • Recording fees for deed and financing statements   • Appraisal fees
142   • Owner's Policy and Charges (if Paragraph 9(c)(ii) is checked) • Buyer's Inspections
143   • Survey (and elevation certification, if required)   • Buyer's attorneys' fees
144   • Lender's title policy and endorsements   • All property related insurance
145   • HOA/Condominium Association application/transfer fees   • Owner's Policy Premium (if Paragraph
146   9 (c) (iii) is checked.)
147* • Other:_____
148*   (c) **TITLE EVIDENCE AND INSURANCE:** At least _____ (if left blank, then 5) days prior to Closing Date, a title
149   insurance commitment issued by a Florida licensed title insurer, with legible copies of instruments listed as
150   exceptions attached thereto ("Title Commitment") and, after Closing, an owner's policy of title insurance (see
151   STANDARD A for terms) shall be obtained and delivered to Buyer. If Seller has an owner's policy of title insurance
152   covering the Real Property, a copy shall be furnished to Buyer and Closing Agent within 5 days after Effective Date.
153   The owner's title policy premium, title search, municipal lien search and closing services (collectively, "Owner's
154   Policy and Charges") shall be paid, as set forth below
155   **(CHECK ONE):**
156* ☐ (i) Seller shall designate Closing Agent and pay for Owner's Policy and Charges (but not including charges for
157   closing services related to Buyer's lender's policy and endorsements and loan closing, which amounts shall be paid
158   by Buyer to Closing Agent or such other provider(s) as Buyer may select); or
159* ☐ (ii) Buyer shall designate Closing Agent and pay for Owner's Policy and Charges and charges for closing
160   services related to Buyer's lender's policy, endorsements, and loan closing; or
161* ☐ (iii) **[MIAMI-DADE/BROWARD REGIONAL PROVISION]:** Seller shall furnish a copy of a prior owner's policy of
162   title insurance or other evidence of title and pay fees for: (A) a continuation or update of such title evidence, which
163   is acceptable to Buyer's title insurance underwriter for reissue of coverage; (B) tax search; and (C) municipal lien
164   search. Buyer shall obtain and pay for post-Closing continuation and premium for Buyer's owner's policy, and if
165* applicable, Buyer's lender's policy. Seller shall not be obligated to pay more than $ _____ (if left blank,
166   then $200.00) for abstract continuation or title search ordered or performed by Closing Agent.
167   (d) **SURVEY:** At least 5 days prior to Closing, Buyer may, at Buyer's expense, have the Real Property surveyed and
168   certified by a registered Florida surveyor ("Survey"). If Seller has a survey covering the Real Property, a copy shall
169   be furnished to Buyer and Closing Agent within 5 days after Effective Date.
170*   (e) **HOME WARRANTY:** At Closing, ☐ Buyer ☐ Seller ☐ N/A shall pay for a home warranty plan issued by
171* _____ at a cost not to exceed $_____. A home

F I G U R E B.12 ◼ Residential Contract for Sale and Purchase (continued)

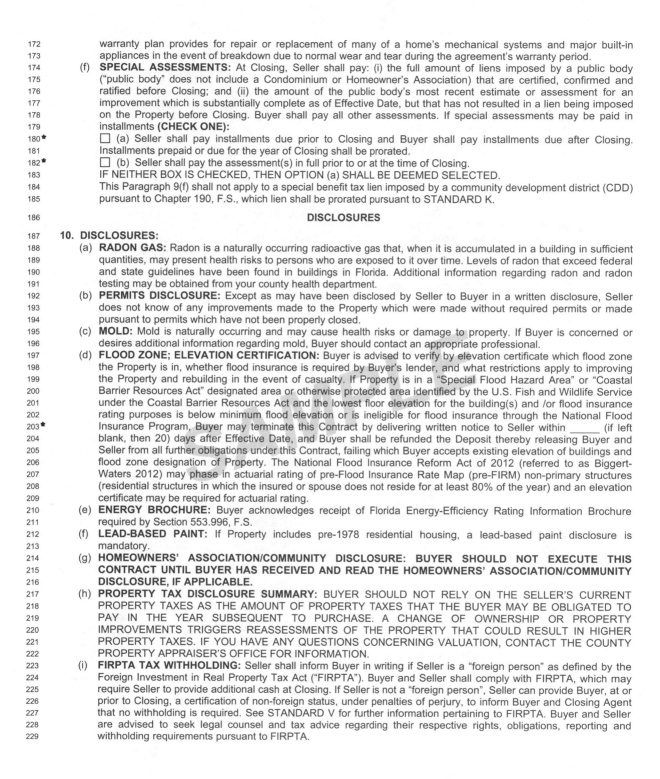

172 warranty plan provides for repair or replacement of many of a home's mechanical systems and major built-in
173 appliances in the event of breakdown due to normal wear and tear during the agreement's warranty period.
174 (f) **SPECIAL ASSESSMENTS:** At Closing, Seller shall pay: (i) the full amount of liens imposed by a public body
175 ("public body" does not include a Condominium or Homeowner's Association) that are certified, confirmed and
176 ratified before Closing; and (ii) the amount of the public body's most recent estimate or assessment for an
177 improvement which is substantially complete as of Effective Date, but that has not resulted in a lien being imposed
178 on the Property before Closing. Buyer shall pay all other assessments. If special assessments may be paid in
179 installments **(CHECK ONE):**
180★ ☐ (a) Seller shall pay installments due prior to Closing and Buyer shall pay installments due after Closing.
181 Installments prepaid or due for the year of Closing shall be prorated.
182★ ☐ (b) Seller shall pay the assessment(s) in full prior to or at the time of Closing.
183 IF NEITHER BOX IS CHECKED, THEN OPTION (a) SHALL BE DEEMED SELECTED.
184 This Paragraph 9(f) shall not apply to a special benefit tax lien imposed by a community development district (CDD)
185 pursuant to Chapter 190, F.S., which lien shall be prorated pursuant to STANDARD K.

186 **DISCLOSURES**

187 **10. DISCLOSURES:**
188 (a) **RADON GAS:** Radon is a naturally occurring radioactive gas that, when it is accumulated in a building in sufficient
189 quantities, may present health risks to persons who are exposed to it over time. Levels of radon that exceed federal
190 and state guidelines have been found in buildings in Florida. Additional information regarding radon and radon
191 testing may be obtained from your county health department.
192 (b) **PERMITS DISCLOSURE:** Except as may have been disclosed by Seller to Buyer in a written disclosure, Seller
193 does not know of any improvements made to the Property which were made without required permits or made
194 pursuant to permits which have not been properly closed.
195 (c) **MOLD:** Mold is naturally occurring and may cause health risks or damage to property. If Buyer is concerned or
196 desires additional information regarding mold, Buyer should contact an appropriate professional.
197 (d) **FLOOD ZONE; ELEVATION CERTIFICATION:** Buyer is advised to verify by elevation certificate which flood zone
198 the Property is in, whether flood insurance is required by Buyer's lender, and what restrictions apply to improving
199 the Property and rebuilding in the event of casualty. If Property is in a "Special Flood Hazard Area" or "Coastal
200 Barrier Resources Act" designated area or otherwise protected area identified by the U.S. Fish and Wildlife Service
201 under the Coastal Barrier Resources Act and the lowest floor elevation for the building(s) and /or flood insurance
202 rating purposes is below minimum flood elevation or is ineligible for flood insurance through the National Flood
203★ Insurance Program, Buyer may terminate this Contract by delivering written notice to Seller within _____ (if left
204 blank, then 20) days after Effective Date, and Buyer shall be refunded the Deposit thereby releasing Buyer and
205 Seller from all further obligations under this Contract, failing which Buyer accepts existing elevation of buildings and
206 flood zone designation of Property. The National Flood Insurance Reform Act of 2012 (referred to as Biggert-
207 Waters 2012) may phase in actuarial rating of pre-Flood Insurance Rate Map (pre-FIRM) non-primary structures
208 (residential structures in which the insured or spouse does not reside for at least 80% of the year) and an elevation
209 certificate may be required for actuarial rating.
210 (e) **ENERGY BROCHURE:** Buyer acknowledges receipt of Florida Energy-Efficiency Rating Information Brochure
211 required by Section 553.996, F.S.
212 (f) **LEAD-BASED PAINT:** If Property includes pre-1978 residential housing, a lead-based paint disclosure is
213 mandatory.
214 (g) **HOMEOWNERS' ASSOCIATION/COMMUNITY DISCLOSURE: BUYER SHOULD NOT EXECUTE THIS**
215 **CONTRACT UNTIL BUYER HAS RECEIVED AND READ THE HOMEOWNERS' ASSOCIATION/COMMUNITY**
216 **DISCLOSURE, IF APPLICABLE.**
217 (h) **PROPERTY TAX DISCLOSURE SUMMARY:** BUYER SHOULD NOT RELY ON THE SELLER'S CURRENT
218 PROPERTY TAXES AS THE AMOUNT OF PROPERTY TAXES THAT THE BUYER MAY BE OBLIGATED TO
219 PAY IN THE YEAR SUBSEQUENT TO PURCHASE. A CHANGE OF OWNERSHIP OR PROPERTY
220 IMPROVEMENTS TRIGGERS REASSESSMENTS OF THE PROPERTY THAT COULD RESULT IN HIGHER
221 PROPERTY TAXES. IF YOU HAVE ANY QUESTIONS CONCERNING VALUATION, CONTACT THE COUNTY
222 PROPERTY APPRAISER'S OFFICE FOR INFORMATION.
223 (i) **FIRPTA TAX WITHHOLDING:** Seller shall inform Buyer in writing if Seller is a "foreign person" as defined by the
224 Foreign Investment in Real Property Tax Act ("FIRPTA"). Buyer and Seller shall comply with FIRPTA, which may
225 require Seller to provide additional cash at Closing. If Seller is not a "foreign person", Seller can provide Buyer, at or
226 prior to Closing, a certification of non-foreign status, under penalties of perjury, to inform Buyer and Closing Agent
227 that no withholding is required. See STANDARD V for further information pertaining to FIRPTA. Buyer and Seller
228 are advised to seek legal counsel and tax advice regarding their respective rights, obligations, reporting and
229 withholding requirements pursuant to FIRPTA.

Buyer's Initials _____ _____   Page **4** of **12**   Seller's Initials _____ _____
FloridaRealtors/FloridaBar-2   Rev.8/13 © 2013 Florida Realtors® and The Florida Bar. All rights reserved.

F I G U R E B.12 ▓ **Residential Contract for Sale and Purchase (continued)**

230 (j) **SELLER DISCLOSURE:** Seller knows of no facts materially affecting the value of the Real Property which are not
231   readily observable and which have not been disclosed to Buyer.

232   **PROPERTY MAINTENANCE, CONDITION, INSPECTIONS AND EXAMINATIONS**

233 **11. PROPERTY MAINTENANCE:** Except for ordinary wear and tear and Casualty Loss, and those repairs, replacements
234   or treatments required to be made by this Contract, Seller shall maintain the Property, including, but not limited to, lawn,
235   shrubbery, and pool, in the condition existing as of Effective Date ("Maintenance Requirement").

236 **12. PROPERTY INSPECTION AND REPAIR:**
237 (a) **INSPECTION PERIOD:** By the earlier of 15 days after Effective Date or 5 days prior to Closing Date ("Inspection
238   Period"), Buyer may, at Buyer's expense, conduct "General", "WDO", and "Permit" Inspections described below. If
239   Buyer fails to timely deliver to Seller a written notice or report required by (b), (c), or (d) below, then, except for
240   Seller's continuing Maintenance Requirement, Buyer shall have waived Seller's obligation(s) to repair, replace, treat
241   or remedy the matters not inspected and timely reported. If this Contract does not close, Buyer shall repair all
242   damage to Property resulting from Buyer's inspections, return Property to its pre-inspection condition and provide
243   Seller with paid receipts for all work done on Property upon its completion.
244 (b) **GENERAL PROPERTY INSPECTION AND REPAIR:**
245   (i) **General Inspection:** Those items specified in Paragraph 12(b) (ii) below, which Seller is obligated to repair or
246   replace ("General Repair Items") may be inspected ("General Inspection") by a person who specializes in and holds
247   an occupational license (if required by law) to conduct home inspections or who holds a Florida license to repair
248   and maintain the items inspected ("Professional Inspector"). Buyer shall, within the Inspection Period, inform Seller
249   of any General Repair Items that are not in the condition required by (b)(ii) below by delivering to Seller a written
250   notice and upon written request by Seller a copy of the portion of Professional Inspector's written report dealing with
251   such items.
252   (ii) **Property Condition:** The following items shall be free of leaks, water damage or structural damage: ceiling, roof
253   (including fascia and soffits), exterior and interior walls, doors, windows, and foundation. The above items together
254   with pool, pool equipment, non-leased major appliances, heating, cooling, mechanical, electrical, security, sprinkler,
255   septic and plumbing systems and machinery, seawalls, and dockage, are, and shall be maintained until Closing, in
256   "Working Condition" (defined below). Torn screens (including pool and patio screens), fogged windows, and
257   missing roof tiles or shingles shall be repaired or replaced by Seller prior to Closing. Seller is not required to repair
258   or replace "Cosmetic Conditions" (defined below), unless the Cosmetic Conditions resulted from a defect in an item
259   Seller is obligated to repair or replace. "Working Condition" means operating in the manner in which the item was
260   designed to operate. "Cosmetic Conditions" means aesthetic imperfections that do not affect Working Condition of
261   the item, including, but not limited to: pitted marcite; tears, worn spots and discoloration of floor coverings,
262   wallpapers, or window treatments; nail holes, scrapes, scratches, dents, chips or caulking in ceilings, walls, flooring,
263   tile, fixtures, or mirrors; and minor cracks in walls, floor tiles, windows, driveways, sidewalks, pool decks, and
264   garage and patio floors. Cracked roof tiles, curling or worn shingles, or limited roof life shall not be considered
265   defects Seller must repair or replace, so long as there is no evidence of actual leaks, leakage or structural damage.
266   (iii) **General Property Repairs:** Seller is only obligated to make such general repairs as are necessary to bring
267   items into the condition specified in Paragraph 12(b) (ii) above. Seller shall within 10 days after receipt of Buyer's
268   written notice or General Inspection report, either have the reported repairs to General Repair Items estimated by
269   an appropriately licensed person and a copy delivered to Buyer, or have a second inspection made by a
270   Professional Inspector and provide a copy of such report and estimates of repairs to Buyer. If Buyer's and Seller's
271   inspection reports differ and the parties cannot resolve the differences, Buyer and Seller together shall choose, and
272   equally split the cost of, a third Professional Inspector, whose written report shall be binding on the parties.
273   If cost to repair General Repair Items equals or is less than the General Repair Limit, Seller shall have repairs
274   made in accordance with Paragraph 12(f). If cost to repair General Repair Items exceeds the General Repair Limit,
275   then within 5 days after a party's receipt of the last estimate: (A) Seller may elect to pay the excess by delivering
276   written notice to Buyer, or (B) Buyer may deliver written notice to Seller designating which repairs of General Repair
277   Items Seller shall make (at a total cost to Seller not exceeding the General Repair Limit) and agreeing to accept the
278   balance of General Repair Items in their "as is" condition, subject to Seller's continuing Maintenance Requirement.
279   If neither party delivers such written notice to the other, then either party may terminate this Contract and Buyer
280   shall be refunded the Deposit, thereby releasing Buyer and Seller from all further obligations under this Contract.
281 (c) **WOOD DESTROYING ORGANISM ("WDO") INSPECTION AND REPAIR:**
282   (i) **WDO Inspection:** The Property may be inspected by a Florida-licensed pest control business ("WDO Inspector")
283   to determine the existence of past or present WDO infestation and damage caused by infestation ("WDO
284   Inspection"). Buyer shall, within the Inspection Period, deliver a copy of the WDO Inspector's written report to Seller
285   if any evidence of WDO infestation or damage is found. "Wood Destroying Organism" ("WDO") means arthropod or
286   plant life, including termites, powder-post beetles, oldhouse borers and wood-decaying fungi, that damages or
287   infests seasoned wood in a structure, excluding fences.

F I G U R E B.12   ■   **Residential Contract for Sale and Purchase (continued)**

288   (ii) **WDO Repairs:** If Seller previously treated the Property for the type of WDO found by Buyer's WDO Inspection,
289   Seller does not have to retreat the Property if there is no visible live infestation, and Seller, at Seller's cost, transfers
290   to Buyer at Closing a current full treatment warranty for the type of WDO found. Seller shall within 10 days after
291   receipt of Buyer's WDO Inspector's report, have reported WDO damage estimated by an appropriately licensed
292   person, necessary corrective treatment, if any, estimated by a WDO Inspector, and a copy delivered to Buyer.
293   Seller shall have treatments and repairs made in accordance with Paragraph 12(f) below up to the WDO Repair
294   Limit. If cost to treat and repair the WDO infestations and damage to Property exceeds the WDO Repair Limit, then
295   within 5 days after receipt of Seller's estimate, Buyer may deliver written notice to Seller agreeing to pay the
296   excess, or designating which WDO repairs Seller shall make (at a total cost to Seller not exceeding the WDO
297   Repair Limit), and accepting the balance of the Property in its "as is" condition with regard to WDO infestation and
298   damage, subject to Seller's continuing Maintenance Requirement. If Buyer does not deliver such written notice to
299   Seller, then either party may terminate this Contract by written notice to the other, and Buyer shall be refunded the
300   Deposit, thereby releasing Buyer and Seller from all further obligations under this Contract.

301   (d) **INSPECTION AND CLOSE-OUT OF BUILDING PERMITS:**
302   (i) **Permit Inspection:** Buyer may have an inspection and examination of records and documents made to
303   determine whether there exist any open or expired building permits or unpermitted improvements to the Property
304   ("Permit Inspection"). Buyer shall, within the Inspection Period, deliver written notice to Seller of the existence of
305   any open or expired building permits or unpermitted improvements to the Property.
306   (ii) **Close-Out of Building Permits:** Seller shall, within 10 days after receipt of Buyer's Permit Inspection notice,
307   have an estimate of costs to remedy Permit Inspection items prepared by an appropriately licensed person and a
308   copy delivered to Buyer. No later than 5 days prior to Closing Date, Seller shall, up to the Permit Limit, have open
309   and expired building permits identified by Buyer or known to Seller closed by the applicable governmental entity,
310   and obtain and close any required building permits for improvements to the Property. Prior to Closing Date, Seller
311   will provide Buyer with any written documentation that all open and expired building permits identified by Buyer or
312   known to Seller have been closed out and that Seller has obtained required building permits for improvements to
313   the Property. If final permit inspections cannot be performed due to delays by the governmental entity, Closing
314   Date shall be extended for up to 10 days to complete such final inspections, failing which, either party may
315   terminate this Contract, and Buyer shall be refunded the Deposit, thereby releasing Buyer and Seller from all
316   further obligations under this Contract.
317   If cost to close open or expired building permits or to remedy any permit violation of any governmental entity
318   exceeds Permit Limit, then within 5 days after a party's receipt of estimates of cost to remedy: (A) Seller may elect
319   to pay the excess by delivering written notice to Buyer; or (B) Buyer may deliver written notice to Seller accepting
320   the Property in its "as is" condition with regard to building permit status and agreeing to receive credit from Seller
321   at Closing in the amount of Permit Limit. If neither party delivers such written notice to the other, then either party
322   may terminate this Contract and Buyer shall be refunded the Deposit, thereby releasing Buyer and Seller from all
323   further obligations under this Contract.

324   (e) **WALK-THROUGH INSPECTION/RE-INSPECTION:** On the day prior to Closing Date, or on Closing Date prior to
325   time of Closing, as specified by Buyer, Buyer or Buyer's representative may perform a walk-through (and follow-up
326   walk-through, if necessary) inspection of the Property solely to confirm that all items of Personal Property are on the
327   Property and to verify that Seller has maintained the Property as required by the Maintenance Requirement, has
328   made repairs and replacements required by this Contract, and has met all other contractual obligations.

329   (f) **REPAIR STANDARDS; ASSIGNMENT OF REPAIR AND TREATMENT CONTRACTS AND WARRANTIES:**
330   All repairs and replacements shall be completed in a good and workmanlike manner by an appropriately licensed
331   person, in accordance with all requirements of law, and shall consist of materials or items of quality, value, capacity
332   and performance comparable to, or better than, that existing as of the Effective Date. Except as provided in
333   Paragraph 12(c)(ii), at Buyer's option and cost, Seller will, at Closing, assign all assignable repair, treatment and
334   maintenance contracts and warranties to Buyer.

335   **ESCROW AGENT AND BROKER**

336   **13. ESCROW AGENT:** Any Closing Agent or Escrow Agent (collectively "Agent") receiving the Deposit, other funds and
337   other items is authorized, and agrees by acceptance of them, to deposit them promptly, hold same in escrow within the
338   State of Florida and, subject to **COLLECTION**, disburse them in accordance with terms and conditions of this Contract.
339   Failure of funds to become **COLLECTED** shall not excuse Buyer's performance. When conflicting demands for the
340   Deposit are received, or Agent has a good faith doubt as to entitlement to the Deposit, Agent may take such actions
341   permitted by this Paragraph 13, as Agent deems advisable. If in doubt as to Agent's duties or liabilities under this
342   Contract, Agent may, at Agent's option, continue to hold the subject matter of the escrow until the parties agree to its
343   disbursement or until a final judgment of a court of competent jurisdiction shall determine the rights of the parties, or
344   Agent may deposit same with the clerk of the circuit court having jurisdiction of the dispute. An attorney who represents
345   a party and also acts as Agent may represent such party in such action. Upon notifying all parties concerned of such
346   action, all liability on the part of Agent shall fully terminate, except to the extent of accounting for any items previously

F I G U R E B.12 ■ Residential Contract for Sale and Purchase (continued)

347 delivered out of escrow. If a licensed real estate broker, Agent will comply with provisions of Chapter 475, F.S., as
348 amended and FREC rules to timely resolve escrow disputes through mediation, arbitration, interpleader or an escrow
349 disbursement order.
350 Any proceeding between Buyer and Seller wherein Agent is made a party because of acting as Agent hereunder, or in
351 any proceeding where Agent interpleads the subject matter of the escrow, Agent shall recover reasonable attorney's
352 fees and costs incurred, to be paid pursuant to court order out of the escrowed funds or equivalent. Agent shall not be
353 liable to any party or person for mis-delivery of any escrowed items, unless such mis-delivery is due to Agent's willful
354 breach of this Contract or Agent's gross negligence. This Paragraph 13 shall survive Closing or termination of this
355 Contract.
356 **14. PROFESSIONAL ADVICE; BROKER LIABILITY:** Broker advises Buyer and Seller to verify Property condition, square
357 footage, and all other facts and representations made pursuant to this Contract and to consult appropriate professionals
358 for legal, tax, environmental, and other specialized advice concerning matters affecting the Property and the transaction
359 contemplated by this Contract. Broker represents to Buyer that Broker does not reside on the Property and that all
360 representations (oral, written or otherwise) by Broker are based on Seller representations or public records. **BUYER**
361 **AGREES TO RELY SOLELY ON SELLER, PROFESSIONAL INSPECTORS AND GOVERNMENTAL AGENCIES**
362 **FOR VERIFICATION OF PROPERTY CONDITION, SQUARE FOOTAGE AND FACTS THAT MATERIALLY AFFECT**
363 **PROPERTY VALUE AND NOT ON THE REPRESENTATIONS (ORAL, WRITTEN OR OTHERWISE) OF BROKER.**
364 Buyer and Seller (individually, the "Indemnifying Party") each individually indemnifies, holds harmless, and releases
365 Broker and Broker's officers, directors, agents and employees from all liability for loss or damage, including all costs
366 and expenses, and reasonable attorney's fees at all levels, suffered or incurred by Broker and Broker's officers,
367 directors, agents and employees in connection with or arising from claims, demands or causes of action instituted by
368 Buyer or Seller based on: (i) inaccuracy of information provided by the Indemnifying Party or from public records; (ii)
369 Indemnifying Party's misstatement(s) or failure to perform contractual obligations; (iii) Broker's performance, at
370 Indemnifying Party's request, of any task beyond the scope of services regulated by Chapter 475, F.S., as amended,
371 including Broker's referral, recommendation or retention of any vendor for, or on behalf of Indemnifying Party; (iv)
372 products or services provided by any such vendor for, or on behalf of, Indemnifying Party; and (v) expenses incurred by
373 any such vendor. Buyer and Seller each assumes full responsibility for selecting and compensating their respective
374 vendors and paying their other costs under this Contract whether or not this transaction closes. This Paragraph 14 will
375 not relieve Broker of statutory obligations under Chapter 475, F.S., as amended. For purposes of this Paragraph 14,
376 Broker will be treated as a party to this Contract. This Paragraph 14 shall survive Closing or termination of this Contract.
377 **DEFAULT AND DISPUTE RESOLUTION**
378 **15. DEFAULT:**
379 (a) **BUYER DEFAULT:** If Buyer fails, neglects or refuses to perform Buyer's obligations under this Contract, including
380 payment of the Deposit, within the time(s) specified, Seller may elect to recover and retain the Deposit for the
381 account of Seller as agreed upon liquidated damages, consideration for execution of this Contract, and in full
382 settlement of any claims, whereupon Buyer and Seller shall be relieved from all further obligations under this
383 Contract, or Seller, at Seller's option, may, pursuant to Paragraph 16, proceed in equity to enforce Seller's rights
384 under this Contract. The portion of the Deposit, if any, paid to Listing Broker upon default by Buyer, shall be split
385 equally between Listing Broker and Cooperating Broker; provided however, Cooperating Broker's share shall not be
386 greater than the commission amount Listing Broker had agreed to pay to Cooperating Broker.
387 (b) **SELLER DEFAULT:** If for any reason other than failure of Seller to make Seller's title marketable after reasonable
388 diligent effort, Seller fails, neglects or refuses to perform Seller's obligations under this Contract, Buyer may elect to
389 receive return of Buyer's Deposit without thereby waiving any action for damages resulting from Seller's breach,
390 and, pursuant to Paragraph 16, may seek to recover such damages or seek specific performance.
391 This Paragraph 15 shall survive Closing or termination of this Contract.
392 **16. DISPUTE RESOLUTION:** Unresolved controversies, claims and other matters in question between Buyer and Seller
393 arising out of, or relating to, this Contract or its breach, enforcement or interpretation ("Dispute") will be settled as
394 follows:
395 (a) Buyer and Seller will have 10 days after the date conflicting demands for the Deposit are made to attempt to
396 resolve such Dispute, failing which, Buyer and Seller shall submit such Dispute to mediation under Paragraph
397 16(b).
398 (b) Buyer and Seller shall attempt to settle Disputes in an amicable manner through mediation pursuant to Florida
399 Rules for Certified and Court-Appointed Mediators and Chapter 44, F.S., as amended (the "Mediation Rules"). The
400 mediator must be certified or must have experience in the real estate industry. Injunctive relief may be sought
401 without first complying with this Paragraph 16(b). Disputes not settled pursuant to this Paragraph 16 may be
402 resolved by instituting action in the appropriate court having jurisdiction of the matter. This Paragraph 16 shall
403 survive Closing or termination of this Contract.
404 **17. ATTORNEY'S FEES; COSTS:** The parties will split equally any mediation fee incurred in any mediation permitted by
405 this Contract, and each party will pay their own costs, expenses and fees, including attorney's fees, incurred in
406 conducting the mediation. In any litigation permitted by this Contract, the prevailing party shall be entitled to recover

FIGURE B.12 ■ Residential Contract for Sale and Purchase (continued)

407 from the non-prevailing party costs and fees, including reasonable attorney's fees, incurred in conducting the litigation.
408 This Paragraph 17 shall survive Closing or termination of this Contract.

409 <center>STANDARDS FOR REAL ESTATE TRANSACTIONS ("STANDARDS")</center>

410 **18. STANDARDS:**
411 **A. TITLE:**
412 (i) **TITLE EVIDENCE; RESTRICTIONS; EASEMENTS; LIMITATIONS:** Within the time period provided in Paragraph
413 9(c), the Title Commitment, with legible copies of instruments listed as exceptions attached thereto, shall be issued and
414 delivered to Buyer. The Title Commitment shall set forth those matters to be discharged by Seller at or before Closing
415 and shall provide that, upon recording of the deed to Buyer, an owner's policy of title insurance in the amount of the
416 Purchase Price, shall be issued to Buyer insuring Buyer's marketable title to the Real Property, subject only to the
417 following matters: (a) comprehensive land use plans, zoning, and other land use restrictions, prohibitions and
418 requirements imposed by governmental authority; (b) restrictions and matters appearing on the Plat or otherwise
419 common to the subdivision; (c) outstanding oil, gas and mineral rights of record without right of entry; (d) unplatted
420 public utility easements of record (located contiguous to real property lines and not more than 10 feet in width as to rear
421 or front lines and 7 1/2 feet in width as to side lines); (e) taxes for year of Closing and subsequent years; and (f)
422 assumed mortgages and purchase money mortgages, if any (if additional items, attach addendum); provided, that,
423 unless waived by Paragraph 12 (a), there exists at Closing no violation of the foregoing and none prevent use of the
424 Property for **RESIDENTIAL PURPOSES**. If there exists at Closing any violation of items identified in (b) − (f) above,
425 then the same shall be deemed a title defect. Marketable title shall be determined according to applicable Title
426 Standards adopted by authority of The Florida Bar and in accordance with law.
427 (ii) **TITLE EXAMINATION:** Buyer shall have 5 days after receipt of Title Commitment to examine it and notify Seller in
428 writing specifying defect(s), if any, that render title unmarketable. If Seller provides Title Commitment and it is delivered
429 to Buyer less than 5 days prior to Closing Date, Buyer may extend Closing for up to 5 days after date of receipt to
430 examine same in accordance with this STANDARD A. Seller shall have 30 days ("Cure Period") after receipt of Buyer's
431 notice to take reasonable diligent efforts to remove defects. If Buyer fails to so notify Seller, Buyer shall be deemed to
432 have accepted title as it then is. If Seller cures defects within Cure Period, Seller will deliver written notice to Buyer (with
433 proof of cure acceptable to Buyer and Buyer's attorney) and the parties will close this Contract on Closing Date (or if
434 Closing Date has passed, within 10 days after Buyer's receipt of Seller's notice). If Seller is unable to cure defects
435 within Cure Period, then Buyer may, within 5 days after expiration of Cure Period, deliver written notice to Seller: (a)
436 extending Cure Period for a specified period not to exceed 120 days within which Seller shall continue to use
437 reasonable diligent effort to remove or cure the defects ("Extended Cure Period"); or (b) electing to accept title with
438 existing defects and close this Contract on Closing Date (or if Closing Date has passed, within the earlier of 10 days
439 after end of Extended Cure Period or Buyer's receipt of Seller's notice), or (c) electing to terminate this Contract and
440 receive a refund of the Deposit, thereby releasing Buyer and Seller from all further obligations under this Contract. If
441 after reasonable diligent effort, Seller is unable to timely cure defects, and Buyer does not waive the defects, this
442 Contract shall terminate, and Buyer shall receive a refund of the Deposit, thereby releasing Buyer and Seller from all
443 further obligations under this Contract.
444 **B. SURVEY:** If Survey discloses encroachments on the Real Property or that improvements located thereon encroach
445 on setback lines, easements, or lands of others, or violate any restrictions, covenants, or applicable governmental
446 regulations described in STANDARD A (i)(a), (b) or (d) above, Buyer shall deliver written notice of such matters,
447 together with a copy of Survey, to Seller within 5 days after Buyer's receipt of Survey, but no later than Closing. If Buyer
448 timely delivers such notice and Survey to Seller, such matters identified in the notice and Survey shall constitute a title
449 defect, subject to cure obligations of STANDARD A above. If Seller has delivered a prior survey, Seller shall, at Buyer's
450 request, execute an affidavit of "no change" to the Real Property since the preparation of such prior survey, to the
451 extent the affirmations therein are true and correct.
452 **C. INGRESS AND EGRESS:** Seller represents that there is ingress and egress to the Real Property and title to the
453 Real Property is insurable in accordance with STANDARD A without exception for lack of legal right of access.
454 **D. LEASE INFORMATION:** Seller shall, at least 10 days prior to Closing, furnish to Buyer estoppel letters from
455 tenant(s)/occupant(s) specifying nature and duration of occupancy, rental rates, advanced rent and security deposits
456 paid by tenant(s) or occupant(s)("Estoppel Letter(s)"). If Seller is unable to obtain such Estoppel Letter(s), the same
457 information shall be furnished by Seller to Buyer within that time period in the form of a Seller's affidavit, and Buyer may
458 thereafter contact tenant(s) or occupant(s) to confirm such information. If Estoppel Letter(s) or Seller's affidavit, if any,
459 differ materially from Seller's representations and lease(s) provided pursuant to Paragraph 6, or if tenant(s)/occupant(s)
460 fail or refuse to confirm Seller's affidavit, Buyer may deliver written notice to Seller within 5 days after receipt of such
461 information, but no later than 5 days prior to Closing Date, terminating this Contract and receive a refund of the Deposit,
462 thereby releasing Buyer and Seller from all further obligations under this Contract. Seller shall, at Closing, deliver and
463 assign all leases to Buyer who shall assume Seller's obligations thereunder.
464 **E. LIENS:** Seller shall furnish to Buyer at Closing an affidavit attesting (i) to the absence of any financing statement,
465 claims of lien or potential lienors known to Seller and (ii) that there have been no improvements or repairs to the Real

F I G U R E B.12 ■ Residential Contract for Sale and Purchase (continued)

STANDARDS FOR REAL ESTATE TRANSACTIONS ("STANDARDS") CONTINUED

466 Property for 90 days immediately preceding Closing Date. If the Real Property has been improved or repaired within
467 that time, Seller shall deliver releases or waivers of construction liens executed by all general contractors,
468 subcontractors, suppliers and materialmen in addition to Seller's lien affidavit setting forth names of all such general
469 contractors, subcontractors, suppliers and materialmen, further affirming that all charges for improvements or repairs
470 which could serve as a basis for a construction lien or a claim for damages have been paid or will be paid at Closing.
471 **F. TIME:** Calendar days shall be used in computing time periods. **Time is of the essence in this Contract.**
472 Other than time for acceptance and Effective Date as set forth in Paragraph 3, any time periods provided for or dates
473 specified in this Contract, whether preprinted, handwritten, typewritten or inserted herein, which shall end or occur on a
474 Saturday, Sunday, or a national legal holiday (see 5 U.S.C. 6103) shall extend to 5:00 p.m. (where the Property is
475 located) of the next business day.
476 **G. FORCE MAJEURE:** Buyer or Seller shall not be required to perform any obligation under this Contract or be liable
477 to each other for damages so long as performance or non-performance of the obligation is delayed, caused or
478 prevented by Force Majeure. "Force Majeure" means: hurricanes, earthquakes, floods, fire, acts of God, unusual
479 transportation delays, wars, insurrections, acts of terrorism, and any other cause not reasonably within control of Buyer
480 or Seller, and which, by exercise of reasonable diligent effort, the non-performing party is unable in whole or in part to
481 prevent or overcome. All time periods, including Closing Date, will be extended for the period that the Force Majeure
482 prevents performance under this Contract, provided, however, if such Force Majeure continues to prevent performance
483 under this Contract more than 14 days beyond Closing Date, then either party may terminate this Contract by delivering
484 written notice to the other and the Deposit shall be refunded to Buyer, thereby releasing Buyer and Seller from all
485 further obligations under this Contract.
486 **H. CONVEYANCE:** Seller shall convey marketable title to the Real Property by statutory warranty, trustee's, personal
487 representative's, or guardian's deed, as appropriate to the status of Seller, subject only to matters described in
488 STANDARD A and those accepted by Buyer. Personal Property shall, at request of Buyer, be transferred by absolute
489 bill of sale with warranty of title, subject only to such matters as may be provided for in this Contract.
490 **I. CLOSING LOCATION; DOCUMENTS; AND PROCEDURE:**
491 (i) **LOCATION:** Closing will take place in the county where the Real Property is located at the office of the attorney or
492 other closing agent ("Closing Agent") designated by the party paying for the owner's policy of title insurance, or, if no
493 title insurance, designated by Seller. Closing may be conducted by mail or electronic means.
494 (ii) **CLOSING DOCUMENTS:** Seller shall, at or prior to Closing, execute and deliver, as applicable, deed, bill of sale,
495 certificate(s) of title or other documents necessary to transfer title to the Property, construction lien affidavit(s), owner's
496 possession and no lien affidavit(s), and assignment(s) of leases. Seller shall provide Buyer with paid receipts for all
497 work done on the Property pursuant to this Contract. Buyer shall furnish and pay for, as applicable the survey, flood
498 elevation certification, and documents required by Buyer's lender.
499 (iii) **PROCEDURE:** The deed shall be recorded upon **COLLECTION** of all closing funds. If the Title Commitment
500 provides insurance against adverse matters pursuant to Section 627.7841, F.S., as amended, the escrow closing
501 procedure required by STANDARD J shall be waived, and Closing Agent shall, **subject to COLLECTION of all closing
502 funds**, disburse at Closing the brokerage fees to Broker and the net sale proceeds to Seller.
503 **J. ESCROW CLOSING PROCEDURE:** If Title Commitment issued pursuant to Paragraph 9(c) does not provide for
504 insurance against adverse matters as permitted under Section 627.7841, F.S., as amended, the following escrow and
505 closing procedures shall apply: (1) all Closing proceeds shall be held in escrow by the Closing Agent for a period of not
506 more than 10 days after Closing; (2) if Seller's title is rendered unmarketable, through no fault of Buyer, Buyer shall,
507 within the 10 day period, notify Seller in writing of the defect and Seller shall have 30 days from date of receipt of such
508 notification to cure the defect; (3) if Seller fails to timely cure the defect, the Deposit and all Closing funds paid by Buyer
509 shall, within 5 days after written demand by Buyer, be refunded to Buyer and, simultaneously with such repayment,
510 Buyer shall return the Personal Property, vacate the Real Property and re-convey the Property to Seller by special
511 warranty deed and bill of sale; and (4) if Buyer fails to make timely demand for refund of the Deposit, Buyer shall take
512 title as is, waiving all rights against Seller as to any intervening defect except as may be available to Buyer by virtue of
513 warranties contained in the deed or bill of sale.
514 **K. PRORATIONS; CREDITS:** The following recurring items will be made current (if applicable) and prorated as of the
515 day prior to Closing Date, or date of occupancy if occupancy occurs before Closing Date: real estate taxes (including
516 special benefit tax assessments imposed by a CDD), interest, bonds, association fees, insurance, rents and other
517 expenses of Property. Buyer shall have option of taking over existing policies of insurance, if assumable, in which event
518 premiums shall be prorated. Cash at Closing shall be increased or decreased as may be required by prorations to be
519 made through day prior to Closing. Advance rent and security deposits, if any, will be credited to Buyer. Escrow
520 deposits held by Seller's mortgagee will be paid to Seller. Taxes shall be prorated based on current year's tax with due
521 allowance made for maximum allowable discount, homestead and other exemptions. If Closing occurs on a date when
522 current year's millage is not fixed but current year's assessment is available, taxes will be prorated based upon such
523 assessment and prior year's millage. If current year's assessment is not available, then taxes will be prorated on prior
524 year's tax. If there are completed improvements on the Real Property by January 1st of year of Closing, which
525 improvements were not in existence on January 1st of prior year, then taxes shall be prorated based upon prior year's

FIGURE B.12 ■ Residential Contract for Sale and Purchase (continued)

STANDARDS FOR REAL ESTATE TRANSACTIONS ("STANDARDS") CONTINUED

526 millage and at an equitable assessment to be agreed upon between the parties, failing which, request shall be made to
527 the County Property Appraiser for an informal assessment taking into account available exemptions. A tax proration
528 based on an estimate shall, at either party's request, be readjusted upon receipt of current year's tax bill. This
529 STANDARD K shall survive Closing.

530 **L. ACCESS TO PROPERTY TO CONDUCT APPRAISALS, INSPECTIONS, AND WALK-THROUGH:** Seller shall,
531 upon reasonable notice, provide utilities service and access to Property for appraisals and inspections, including a walk-
532 through (or follow-up walk-through if necessary) prior to Closing.

533 **M. RISK OF LOSS:** If, after Effective Date, but before Closing, Property is damaged by fire or other casualty
534 ("Casualty Loss") and cost of restoration (which shall include cost of pruning or removing damaged trees) does not
535 exceed 1.5% of Purchase Price, cost of restoration shall be an obligation of Seller and Closing shall proceed pursuant
536 to terms of this Contract. If restoration is not completed as of Closing, a sum equal to 125% of estimated cost to
537 complete restoration (not to exceed 1.5% of Purchase Price), will be escrowed at Closing. If actual cost of restoration
538 exceeds escrowed amount, Seller shall pay such actual costs (but, not in excess of 1.5% of Purchase Price). Any
539 unused portion of escrowed amount shall be returned to Seller. If cost of restoration exceeds 1.5% of Purchase Price,
540 Buyer shall elect to either take Property "as is" together with the 1.5%, or receive a refund of the Deposit, thereby
541 releasing Buyer and Seller from all further obligations under this Contract. Seller's sole obligation with respect to tree
542 damage by casualty or other natural occurrence shall be cost of pruning or removal.

543 **N. 1031 EXCHANGE:** If either Seller or Buyer wish to enter into a like-kind exchange (either simultaneously with
544 Closing or deferred) under Section 1031 of the Internal Revenue Code ("Exchange"), the other party shall cooperate in
545 all reasonable respects to effectuate the Exchange, including execution of documents; provided, however, cooperating
546 party shall incur no liability or expense related to the Exchange, and Closing shall not be contingent upon, nor extended
547 or delayed by, such Exchange.

548 **O. CONTRACT NOT RECORDABLE; PERSONS BOUND; NOTICE; DELIVERY; COPIES; CONTRACT**
549 **EXECUTION:** Neither this Contract nor any notice of it shall be recorded in any public records. This Contract shall be
550 binding on, and inure to the benefit of, the parties and their respective heirs or successors in interest. Whenever the
551 context permits, singular shall include plural and one gender shall include all. Notice and delivery given by or to the
552 attorney or broker (including such broker's real estate licensee) representing any party shall be as effective as if given
553 by or to that party. All notices must be in writing and may be made by mail, personal delivery or electronic (including
554 "pdf") media. A facsimile or electronic (including "pdf") copy of this Contract and any signatures hereon shall be
555 considered for all purposes as an original. This Contract may be executed by use of electronic signatures, as
556 determined by Florida's Electronic Signature Act and other applicable laws.

557 **P. INTEGRATION; MODIFICATION:** This Contract contains the full and complete understanding and agreement of
558 Buyer and Seller with respect to the transaction contemplated by this Contract and no prior agreements or
559 representations shall be binding upon Buyer or Seller unless included in this Contract. No modification to or change in
560 this Contract shall be valid or binding upon Buyer or Seller unless in writing and executed by the parties intended to be
561 bound by it.

562 **Q. WAIVER:** Failure of Buyer or Seller to insist on compliance with, or strict performance of, any provision of this
563 Contract, or to take advantage of any right under this Contract, shall not constitute a waiver of other provisions or rights.

564 **R. RIDERS; ADDENDA; TYPEWRITTEN OR HANDWRITTEN PROVISIONS:** Riders, addenda, and typewritten or
565 handwritten provisions shall control all printed provisions of this Contract in conflict with them.

566 **S. COLLECTION or COLLECTED: "COLLECTION" or "COLLECTED" means any checks tendered or received,**
567 **including Deposits, have become actually and finally collected and deposited in the account of Escrow Agent**
568 **or Closing Agent. Closing and disbursement of funds and delivery of closing documents may be delayed by**
569 **Closing Agent until such amounts have been COLLECTED in Closing Agent's accounts.**

570 **T. LOAN COMMITMENT:** "Loan Commitment" means a statement by the lender setting forth the terms and conditions
571 upon which the lender is willing to make a particular mortgage loan to a particular borrower. Neither a pre-approval
572 letter nor a prequalification letter shall be deemed a Loan Commitment for purposes of this Contract.

573 **U. APPLICABLE LAW AND VENUE:** This Contract shall be construed in accordance with the laws of the State of
574 Florida and venue for resolution of all disputes, whether by mediation, arbitration or litigation, shall lie in the county
575 where the Real Property is located.

576 **V. FOREIGN INVESTMENT IN REAL PROPERTY TAX ACT ("FIRPTA"):** If a seller of U.S. real property is a "foreign
577 person" as defined by FIRPTA, Section 1445 of the Internal Revenue Code requires the buyer of the real property to
578 withhold 10% of the amount realized by the seller on the transfer and remit the withheld amount to the Internal Revenue
579 Service (IRS) unless an exemption to the required withholding applies or the seller has obtained a Withholding
580 Certificate from the IRS authorizing a reduced amount of withholding. Due to the complexity and potential risks of
581 FIRPTA, Buyer and Seller should seek legal and tax advice regarding compliance, particularly if an "exemption" is
582 claimed on the sale of residential property for $300,000 or less.

583 (i) No withholding is required under Section 1445 if the Seller is not a "foreign person," provided Buyer accepts proof of
584 same from Seller, which may include Buyer's receipt of certification of non-foreign status from Seller, signed under
585 penalties of perjury, stating that Seller is not a foreign person and containing Seller's name, U.S. taxpayer identification

FIGURE B.12 ■ **Residential Contract for Sale and Purchase (continued)**

STANDARDS FOR REAL ESTATE TRANSACTIONS ("STANDARDS") CONTINUED

586 number and home address (or office address, in the case of an entity), as provided for in 26 CFR 1.1445-2(b).
587 Otherwise, Buyer shall withhold 10% of the amount realized by Seller on the transfer and timely remit said funds to the
588 IRS.
589 (ii) If Seller has received a Withholding Certificate from the IRS which provides for reduced or eliminated withholding in
590 this transaction and provides same to Buyer by Closing, then Buyer shall withhold the reduced sum, if any required, and
591 timely remit said funds to the IRS.
592 (iii) If prior to Closing Seller has submitted a completed application to the IRS for a Withholding Certificate and has
593 provided to Buyer the notice required by 26 CFR 1.1445-1(c) (2)(i)(B) but no Withholding Certificate has been received
594 as of Closing, Buyer shall, at Closing, withhold 10% of the amount realized by Seller on the transfer and, at Buyer's
595 option, either (a) timely remit the withheld funds to the IRS or (b) place the funds in escrow, at Seller's expense, with an
596 escrow agent selected by Buyer and pursuant to terms negotiated by the parties, to be subsequently disbursed in
597 accordance with the Withholding Certificate issued by the IRS or remitted directly to the IRS if the Seller's application is
598 rejected or upon terms set forth in the escrow agreement.
599 (iv) In the event the net proceeds due Seller are not sufficient to meet the withholding requirement(s) in this transaction,
600 Seller shall deliver to Buyer, at Closing, the additional COLLECTED funds necessary to satisfy the applicable
601 requirement and thereafter Buyer shall timely remit said funds to the IRS or escrow the funds for disbursement in
602 accordance with the final determination of the IRS, as applicable.
603 (v) Upon remitting funds to the IRS pursuant to this STANDARD, Buyer shall provide Seller copies of IRS Forms 8288
604 and 8288-A, as filed.

ADDENDA AND ADDITIONAL TERMS

606 **19. ADDENDA:** The following additional terms are included in the attached addenda or riders and incorporated into this
607 * Contract (**Check if applicable**):

☐ A. Condominium Rider	☐ M. Defective Drywall	☐ X. Kick-out Clause
☐ B. Homeowners' Assn.	☐ N. Coastal Construction Control Line	☐ Y. Seller's Attorney Approval
☐ C. Seller Financing	☐ O. Insulation Disclosure	☐ Z. Buyer's Attorney Approval
☐ D. Mortgage Assumption	☐ P. Lead Based Paint Disclosure	☐ AA. Licensee-Personal Interest in
☐ E. FHA/VA Financing	(Pre-1978 Housing)	Property
☐ F. Appraisal Contingency	☐ Q. Housing for Older Persons	☐ BB. Binding Arbitration
☐ G. Short Sale	☐ R. Rezoning	☐ Other_____
☐ H. Homeowners'/Flood Ins	☐ S. Lease Purchase/ Lease Option	_____
☐ I. RESERVED	☐ T. Pre-Closing Occupancy by Buyer	_____
☐ J. Interest-Bearing Acct.	☐ U. Post-Closing Occupancy by Seller	_____
☐ K. "As Is"	☐ V. Sale of Buyer's Property	
☐ L. Right to Inspect/ Cancel	☐ W. Back-up Contract	

608 * **20. ADDITIONAL TERMS:** _____
609 _____
610 _____
611 _____
612 _____
613 _____
614 _____
615 _____
616 _____
617 _____
618 _____
619 _____
620 _____
621 _____
622 _____
623 _____
624 _____

COUNTER-OFFER/REJECTION

626 * ☐ Seller counters Buyer's offer (to accept the counter-offer, Buyer must sign or initial the counter-offered terms and deliver
627 a copy of the acceptance to Seller).
628 * ☐ Seller rejects Buyer's offer.

FIGURE B.12 ■ **Residential Contract for Sale and Purchase (continued)**

629 **THIS IS INTENDED TO BE A LEGALLY BINDING CONTRACT. IF NOT FULLY UNDERSTOOD, SEEK THE ADVICE OF**
630 **AN ATTORNEY PRIOR TO SIGNING.**

631 **THIS FORM HAS BEEN APPROVED BY THE FLORIDA REALTORS AND THE FLORIDA BAR.**

632 *Approval of this form by the Florida Realtors and The Florida Bar does not constitute an opinion that any of the terms and*
633 *conditions in this Contract should be accepted by the parties in a particular transaction. Terms and conditions should be*
634 *negotiated based upon the respective interests, objectives and bargaining positions of all interested persons.*

635 AN ASTERISK (*) FOLLOWING A LINE NUMBER IN THE MARGIN INDICATES THE LINE CONTAINS A BLANK TO BE
636 COMPLETED.
637
638

639* Buyer: _____   Date: _____
640
641
642
643

644* Buyer: _____   Date: _____
645
646
647
648

649* Seller: _____   Date: _____
650
651
652
653

654* Seller: _____   Date: _____
655
656 Buyer's address for purposes of notice   Seller's address for purposes of notice
657* _____   _____
658* _____   _____
659* _____   _____
660

661 **BROKER:** Listing and Cooperating Brokers, if any, named below (collectively, "Broker"), are the only Brokers entitled to
662 compensation in connection with this Contract. Instruction to Closing Agent: Seller and Buyer direct Closing Agent to
663 disburse at Closing the full amount of the brokerage fees as specified in separate brokerage agreements with the parties
664 and cooperative agreements between the Brokers, except to the extent Broker has retained such fees from the escrowed
665 funds. This Contract shall not modify any MLS or other offer of compensation made by Seller or Listing Broker to
666 Cooperating Brokers.
667
668* _____   _____
669 **Cooperating Sales Associate, if any**   **Listing Sales Associate**
670
671* _____   _____
672 **Cooperating Broker, if any**   **Listing Broker**

F I G U R E B.13 ■ Loan Estimate

Save this Loan Estimate to compare with your Closing Disclosure.

Loan Estimate

DATE ISSUED
APPLICANTS

PROPERTY
SALE PRICE

LOAN TERM
PURPOSE
PRODUCT
LOAN TYPE □ Conventional □ FHA □ VA □ _____
LOAN ID #
RATE LOCK □ NO □ YES, until
Before closing, your interest rate, points, and lender credits can change unless you lock the interest rate. All other estimated closing costs expire on

Loan Terms

	Can this amount increase after closing?
Loan Amount	
Interest Rate	
Monthly Principal & Interest *See Projected Payments below for your Estimated Total Monthly Payment*	
	Does the loan have these features?
Prepayment Penalty	
Balloon Payment	

Projected Payments

Payment Calculation	
Principal & Interest	
Mortgage Insurance	
Estimated Escrow *Amount can increase over time*	
Estimated Total Monthly Payment	
Estimated Taxes, Insurance & Assessments *Amount can increase over time*	**This estimate includes** **In escrow?** □ Property Taxes □ Homeowner's Insurance □ Other: *See Section G on page 2 for escrowed property costs. You must pay for other property costs separately.*

Costs at Closing

Estimated Closing Costs	Includes in Loan Costs + in Other Costs – in Lender Credits. *See page 2 for details.*
Estimated Cash to Close	Includes Closing Costs. *See Calculating Cash to Close on page 2 for details.*

Visit **www.consumerfinance.gov/mortgage-estimate** for general information and tools.

F I G U R E B.13 ■ **Loan Estimate (continued)**

Closing Cost Details

Loan Costs		Other Costs

A. Origination Charges

% of Loan Amount (Points)

E. Taxes and Other Government Fees

Recording Fees and Other Taxes
Transfer Taxes

F. Prepaids

Homeowner's Insurance Premium (months)
Mortgage Insurance Premium (months)
Prepaid Interest (per day for   days @   )
Property Taxes (months)

G. Initial Escrow Payment at Closing

Homeowner's Insurance	per month for	mo.
Mortgage Insurance	per month for	mo.
Property Taxes	per month for	mo.

B. Services You Cannot Shop For

H. Other

I. TOTAL OTHER COSTS (E + F + G + H)

C. Services You Can Shop For

J. TOTAL CLOSING COSTS

D + I
Lender Credits

Calculating Cash to Close

Total Closing Costs (J)

Closing Costs Financed (Paid from your Loan Amount)

Down Payment/Funds from Borrower

Deposit

Funds for Borrower

Seller Credits

Adjustments and Other Credits

Estimated Cash to Close

D. TOTAL LOAN COSTS (A + B + C)

Adjustable Payment (AP) Table	
Interest Only Payments?	
Optional Payments?	
Step Payments?	
Seasonal Payments?	
Monthly Principal and Interest Payments	
First Change/Amount	
Subsequent Changes	
Maximum Payment	

Adjustable Interest Rate (AIR) Table
Index + Margin
Initial Interest Rate
Minimum/Maximum Interest Rate
Change Frequency
First Change
Subsequent Changes
Limits on Interest Rate Changes
First Change
Subsequent Changes

F I G U R E B.13 ■ Loan Estimate (continued)

Additional Information About This Loan

LENDER
NMLS/___ LICENSE ID
LOAN OFFICER
NMLS/___ LICENSE ID
EMAIL
PHONE

MORTGAGE BROKER
NMLS/___ LICENSE ID
LOAN OFFICER
NMLS/___ LICENSE ID
EMAIL
PHONE

Comparisons	Use these measures to compare this loan with other loans.
In 5 Years	Total you will have paid in principal, interest, mortgage insurance, and loan costs. Principal you will have paid off.
Annual Percentage Rate (APR)	Your costs over the loan term expressed as a rate. This is not your interest rate.
Total Interest Percentage (TIP)	The total amount of interest that you will pay over the loan term as a percentage of your loan amount.

Other Considerations

Appraisal We may order an appraisal to determine the property's value and charge you for this appraisal. We will promptly give you a copy of any appraisal, even if your loan does not close. You can pay for an additional appraisal for your own use at your own cost.

Assumption If you sell or transfer this property to another person, we
☐ will allow, under certain conditions, this person to assume this loan on the original terms.
☐ will not allow assumption of this loan on the original terms.

Homeowner's Insurance This loan requires homeowner's insurance on the property, which you may obtain from a company of your choice that we find acceptable.

Late Payment If your payment is more than ___ days late, we will charge a late fee of _____

Refinance Refinancing this loan will depend on your future financial situation, the property value, and market conditions. You may not be able to refinance this loan.

Servicing We intend
☐ to service your loan. If so, you will make your payments to us.
☐ to transfer servicing of your loan.

Confirm Receipt

By signing, you are only confirming that you have received this form. You do not have to accept this loan because you have signed or received this form.

_____   _____
Applicant Signature   Date   Co-Applicant Signature   Date

F I G U R E B.14 ■ Counter Offer

Counter Offer

1. **REJECTION OF OFFER:** ☐ Seller ☐ Buyer rejects the offer to purchase/sell dated the _____ day of _____, _____ (" Offer ") for the property described as follows (legal description):

2. TERMS: This counter offer consists of all terms of the Offer with modifications to particular clauses as follows:

Clause   Counter Offer Term

_____   _____

_____   _____

_____   _____

_____   _____

_____   _____

_____   _____

_____   _____

_____   _____

_____   _____

_____   _____

_____   _____

_____   _____

_____   _____

_____   _____

_____   _____

_____   _____

_____   _____

3. **ACCEPTANCE AND EXPIRATION OF COUNTER OFFER:** This counter offer must be signed **and** delivered back to ☐ **Seller** or **Seller's** licensee ☐ **Buyer** or **Buyer's** licensee within _____ hours from (time) _____ ☐ a.m. ☐ p.m. the _____ day of _____, _____ or it will expire.

4. **RIGHT TO WITHDRAW COUNTER OFFER:** The party making this counter offer reserves the right to withdraw the counter offer at any time prior to acceptance by the other party.

FIGURE B.14 ■ **Counter Offer (continued)**

Signatures of Parties Making Counter Offer:

_____   _____
                                                     Date

_____   _____
                                                     Date

Signatures of Parties Accepting Counter Offer:

_____   _____
                                                     Date

_____   _____
                                                     Date

| Acceptance Received by (initial): _____ Date: _____ Time: ☐ _____ ☐ a.m.   p.m. |

CO-2 Revised 10/97   ©1997 Florida Association of REALTORS ®   All Rights Reserved

Serial#:   formsimplicity

F I G U R E B.15 ■ Mortgage Loan Application Checklist

Place personal and company
information/logo here

Mortgage Lender: _____

Address:_____

Loan Officer: _____ Phone: _____

Date of Application: _____ Time: _____

Thanks for using our real estate firm to find your home. To assist you in making your mortgage loan application, we have prepared the list of items that may be needed by the lender. Additional information may be requested.

The Transaction:

☐ Copy of the signed purchase contract.

☐ If you have sold your present home, a copy of the closing disclosure. If the sale is not complete, a copy of the signed purchase contract.

Your Income:

☐ Original pay stubs for the latest 30-day period.

☐ Original W-2 forms for the previous two years.

☐ If you are self-employed or have commission income: a year-to-date profit and loss statement and balance sheet; copies of your last two years' personal and business signed federal tax returns.

☐ If you are using child support payments to qualify for mortgage: proof of receipt.

Your Assets:

☐ Original bank statements for all checking and savings accounts for the past three months. You should be able to explain all deposits not from payroll.

☐ Original statements from investment or brokerage firms for the last three months (if applicable).

☐ Original IRA or 401(k) statements (if applicable).

☐ List of real estate owned: address, market value, mortgage balance, name and address of mortgage company.

☐ List of life insurance policies with company name, face value, beneficiaries, and cash surrender value.

☐ List of automobiles, with make, model, value, amount owed, lender name, address and account number.

☐ Estimate of replacement value of household furniture and appliances.

☐ Value of other assets (collections, art, etc.).

☐ If you have sold a home in the past two years, a copy of the closing statement and a copy of the deed given.

Your Liabilities:

☐ Credit cards: name, address, account number, monthly payment; and present balance.

☐ Other liabilities: name, address, account number, monthly payment and present balance.

Payments for Housing:

☐ List of addresses for previous two years, along with names, addresses and phone numbers of landlords and/or mortgage companies where housing payments were made.

☐ Last 12 month's canceled checks for housing payments (landlord or mortgage company).

If you are divorced:

☐ Copies of all divorce decrees, including any modifications or stipulations.

☐ Child support or alimony payments: amount, duration, and proof of payment for 12 months.

If you are applying for an FHA loan:

☐ Photocopy of driver's license or other acceptable photo ID.

☐ Photocopy of Social Security Card.

If you are applying for a VA loan:

☐ VA Certificate of Eligibility.

☐ Form DD-214.

For in-service veterans or those discharged within the past two years.

☐ Statement of Service.

☐ Most recent Leave and Earnings Statement.

Other items:

☐ If you have graduated from high school or college within the previous two years, a copy of your diploma or transcripts.

☐ If you have a gap in employment for 30 days or more, include a letter explaining the reason.

☐ If part of your down payment is a gift, the lender will give you a gift letter for signature when you apply.

☐ If you have filed bankruptcy in the last seven years, give a letter explaining the reasons, a copy of the Petition Decree, a Schedule of Creditors, and the Discharge document.

☐ If you have rental property, a copy of the current lease and two year's signed income tax returns.

Your Check:

☐ Your check for the appraisal and application fee.

F I G U R E B.16 ■ **Property Sale Information Sheet**

Property Address: _____

Seller: _____   Buyer: _____

Contract Date: _____   Closing Date (Est.): _____

Seller

Listing Broker: _____

Phone: _____ Fax: _____

Listing sales associate: _____

Home Ph.: _____ Office Ph.: _____

Mobile Ph.: _____

Seller: _____

Old address: _____

New address: _____

City, State, Zip _____

Current Home Ph.: _____ Ofc.: _____

Existing mortgage for Payoff (P)

Assumption (A)

1st Mortgage holder: _____

2nd Mortgage holder: _____

Seller's Attorney: _____

Ph.: _____

Lender: _____

Title Company: _____

Appraiser: _____

Date Scheduled to Close: _____

Service Providers:

Pest inspection: _____

Home inspection: _____

Roof inspection: _____

Contractor: _____

Surveyor: _____

Buyer

Selling Broker: _____

Phone: _____ Fax: _____

Selling sales associate: _____

Home Ph.: _____ Office Ph.: _____

Mobile Ph.: _____

Buyer: _____

Present address: _____

City, State, Zip _____

Current Home Ph.: _____ Ofc.: _____

Will buyer occupy new home? _____

New Mortgage Lender: _____

Type (Fixed; ARM: FHA, VA, Conv.): _____

LTV Ratio: _____ % Interest Rate: _____% Yrs: _____

Buyer's Attorney: _____

Ph.: _____

Loan Officer: _____

Closing Agent: _____

Ph.: _____

Ph.: _____

Ph.: _____

Ph.: _____

Ph.: _____

Buyer's Insurance Company: _____

Agent: _____   Phone: _____

Property status: ☐ Occupied by seller   ☐ Occupied by tenant   ☐ Vacant

Key to property for inspection: ☐ At listing office   ☐ In lockbox at property   ☐ Call seller for appointment

FIGURE B.17 ■ **Closing Progress Chart**

Listing Sales Associate				**Closing Progress Chart**			**Selling Sales Associate**		
#	Sched. Date	Actual Date	X	Closing Duties	Done	X	Sched. Date	Actual Date	
1				"Sale pending" sign on listing					
2				Notice of under contract to MLS					
3				Binder deposited in bank $ _____					
4				Additional binder received, if required. $ _____					
5				Loan application made by buyer					
6				Contingencies cleared in writing:					
7				Home inspection by: _____					
8				Soil test from: _____					
9				Roof inspection by: _____					
10				Other (describe): _____					
11				Appraisal by: _____					
12				Loan approval from: _____					
13				Title insurance ordered from: _____					
14				Pest inspection ordered (after loan approval) from:					
15				Report received and delivered to buyer					
16				Report received and delivered to lender					
17				Treatment ordered, if required					
18				Structure inspection ordered, if necessary					
19				Work completed and approved					
20				Required repairs ordered					
21				Required repairs completed					
22				Survey ordered (After loan approval)					
23				Survey completed. Results. . .					
24				Encroachments, survey problems cleared					
25				Buyer to get hazard insurance					
26				Insurance policy to title closing agent					
27				Buyer/seller contacted for closing appointment					
28				Pre-closing inspection					
29				Closing papers reviewed with buyer/seller 1 day prior					
30				Buyer given figure for certified check for closing					
31				Binder check prepared to take to closing					
32				Closing date					
33				Signed closing papers received by sales associate					
34				Post-closing duties:					
35				Commission check to broker					
36				Sign/lockbox picked up from property					
37				Buyer/seller letter of thanks					
38				Follow-up visit to buyer/seller					
39				Notice of closed sale to MLS					

F I G U R E   B.18   ■   Preclosing Walk-Through Inspection Results

Property Address: _____   Date of Inspection: _____

Seller: _____   Buyer: _____

I have made a walk-through inspection of the property. I acknowledge that the sales associate has accompanied me to the property to make it available, and not to conduct the inspection. I take complete responsibility for the inspection and agree to hold harmless the sales associate and the brokerage firm from any liability in connection with the inspection.

My inspection shows that:

personal property items required by the contract to
be left are present in the property   ☐ Yes   ☐ No

required repairs, if any, have been completed   ☐ Yes   ☐ No

the property has been maintained in the condition as it
existed at the time of the contract, reasonable wear and
tear excepted.   ☐ Yes   ☐ No

Comments _____

I accept the property as inspected and release the sellers, sales associates, and brokers in this transaction of any further responsibility for warranting the property. I have been notified of the benefits of having the property covered by a homeowner's warranty. If the seller has not provided such a warranty, I ☐ accept   ☐ decline to purchase coverage at a cost of $ _____.

Buyer: _____   Date: _____

Buyer: _____   Date: _____

FIGURE B.19 ■ **Closing Disclosure**

Closing Disclosure

This form is a statement of final loan terms and closing costs. Compare this document with your Loan Estimate.

Closing Information

Date Issued
Closing Date
Disbursement Date
Settlement Agent
File #
Property

Sale Price

Transaction Information

Borrower

Seller

Lender

Loan Information

Loan Term
Purpose
Product

Loan Type   ☐ Conventional ☐ FHA
              ☐ VA ☐ _____

Loan ID #
MIC #

Loan Terms

		Can this amount increase after closing?
Loan Amount		
Interest Rate		
Monthly Principal & Interest *See Projected Payments below for your Estimated Total Monthly Payment*		
		Does the loan have these features?
Prepayment Penalty		
Balloon Payment		

Projected Payments

Payment Calculation	
Principal & Interest	
Mortgage Insurance	
Estimated Escrow *Amount can increase over time*	
Estimated Total Monthly Payment	

Estimated Taxes, Insurance & Assessments *Amount can increase over time* *See page 4 for details*	**This estimate includes** **In escrow?** ☐ Property Taxes ☐ Homeowner's Insurance ☐ Other: *See Escrow Account on page 4 for details. You must pay for other property costs separately.*

Costs at Closing

Closing Costs	Includes _____ in Loan Costs + _____ in Other Costs – _____ in Lender Credits. *See page 2 for details.*
Cash to Close	Includes Closing Costs. *See Calculating Cash to Close on page 3 for details.*

FIGURE B.19 ■ **Closing Disclosure (continued)**

Closing Cost Details

Loan Costs	Borrower-Paid		Seller-Paid		Paid by Others
	At Closing	Before Closing	At Closing	Before Closing	
A. Origination Charges					
01 % of Loan Amount (Points)					
02					
03					
04					
05					
06					
07					
08					
B. Services Borrower Did Not Shop For					
01					
02					
03					
04					
05					
06					
07					
08					
09					
10					
C. Services Borrower Did Shop For					
01					
02					
03					
04					
05					
06					
07					
08					
D. TOTAL LOAN COSTS (Borrower-Paid)					
Loan Costs Subtotals (A + B + C)					

Other Costs					
E. Taxes and Other Government Fees					
01 Recording Fees Deed: Mortgage:					
02					
F. Prepaids					
01 Homeowner's Insurance Premium (mo.)					
02 Mortgage Insurance Premium (mo.)					
03 Prepaid Interest (per day from to)					
04 Property Taxes (mo.)					
05					
G. Initial Escrow Payment at Closing					
01 Homeowner's Insurance per month for mo.					
02 Mortgage Insurance per month for mo.					
03 Property Taxes per month for mo.					
04					
05					
06					
07					
08 Aggregate Adjustment					
H. Other					
01					
02					
03					
04					
05					
06					
07					
08					
I. TOTAL OTHER COSTS (Borrower-Paid)					
Other Costs Subtotals (E + F + G + H)					

J. TOTAL CLOSING COSTS (Borrower-Paid)					
Closing Costs Subtotals (D + I)					
Lender Credits					

F I G U R E B.19 ■ Closing Disclosure (continued)

Calculating Cash to Close

Use this table to see what has changed from your Loan Estimate.

	Loan Estimate	Final	Did this change?
Total Closing Costs (J)			
Closing Costs Paid Before Closing			
Closing Costs Financed (Paid from your Loan Amount)			
Down Payment/Funds from Borrower			
Deposit			
Funds for Borrower			
Seller Credits			
Adjustments and Other Credits			
Cash to Close			

Summaries of Transactions

Use this table to see a summary of your transaction.

BORROWER'S TRANSACTION

K. Due from Borrower at Closing

01 Sale Price of Property
02 Sale Price of Any Personal Property Included in Sale
03 Closing Costs Paid at Closing (J)
04

Adjustments

05
06
07

Adjustments for Items Paid by Seller in Advance

08 City/Town Taxes   to
09 County Taxes   to
10 Assessments   to
11
12
13
14
15

L. Paid Already by or on Behalf of Borrower at Closing

01 Deposit
02 Loan Amount
03 Existing Loan(s) Assumed or Taken Subject to
04
05 Seller Credit

Other Credits

06
07

Adjustments

08
09
10
11

Adjustments for Items Unpaid by Seller

12 City/Town Taxes   to
13 County Taxes   to
14 Assessments   to
15
16
17

CALCULATION

Total Due from Borrower at Closing (K)
Total Paid Already by or on Behalf of Borrower at Closing (L)
Cash to Close ☐ From ☐ To Borrower

SELLER'S TRANSACTION

M. Due to Seller at Closing

01 Sale Price of Property
02 Sale Price of Any Personal Property Included in Sale
03
04
05
06
07
08

Adjustments for Items Paid by Seller in Advance

09 City/Town Taxes   to
10 County Taxes   to
11 Assessments   to
12
13
14
15
16

N. Due from Seller at Closing

01 Excess Deposit
02 Closing Costs Paid at Closing (J)
03 Existing Loan(s) Assumed or Taken Subject to
04 Payoff of First Mortgage Loan
05 Payoff of Second Mortgage Loan
06
07
08 Seller Credit
09
10
11
12
13

Adjustments for Items Unpaid by Seller

14 City/Town Taxes   to
15 County Taxes   to
16 Assessments   to
17
18
19

CALCULATION

Total Due to Seller at Closing (M)
Total Due from Seller at Closing (N)
Cash ☐ From ☐ To Seller

F I G U R E B.19 ■ Closing Disclosure (continued)

Additional Information About This Loan

Loan Disclosures

Assumption

If you sell or transfer this property to another person, your lender

☐ will allow, under certain conditions, this person to assume this loan on the original terms.

☐ will not allow assumption of this loan on the original terms.

Demand Feature

Your loan

☐ has a demand feature, which permits your lender to require early repayment of the loan. You should review your note for details.

☐ does not have a demand feature.

Late Payment

If your payment is more than ___ days late, your lender will charge a late fee of _____

Negative Amortization (Increase in Loan Amount)

Under your loan terms, you

☐ are scheduled to make monthly payments that do not pay all of the interest due that month. As a result, your loan amount will increase (negatively amortize), and your loan amount will likely become larger than your original loan amount. Increases in your loan amount lower the equity you have in this property.

☐ may have monthly payments that do not pay all of the interest due that month. If you do, your loan amount will increase (negatively amortize), and, as a result, your loan amount may become larger than your original loan amount. Increases in your loan amount lower the equity you have in this property.

☐ do not have a negative amortization feature.

Partial Payments

Your lender

☐ may accept payments that are less than the full amount due (partial payments) and apply them to your loan.

☐ may hold them in a separate account until you pay the rest of the payment, and then apply the full payment to your loan.

☐ does not accept any partial payments.

If this loan is sold, your new lender may have a different policy.

Security Interest

You are granting a security interest in _____

_____

_____

You may lose this property if you do not make your payments or satisfy other obligations for this loan.

Escrow Account

For now, your loan

☐ will have an escrow account (also called an "impound" or "trust" account) to pay the property costs listed below. Without an escrow account, you would pay them directly, possibly in one or two large payments a year. Your lender may be liable for penalties and interest for failing to make a payment.

Escrow		
Escrowed Property Costs over Year 1		Estimated total amount over year 1 for your escrowed property costs:
Non-Escrowed Property Costs over Year 1		Estimated total amount over year 1 for your non-escrowed property costs: You may have other property costs.
Initial Escrow Payment		A cushion for the escrow account you pay at closing. See Section G on page 2.
Monthly Escrow Payment		The amount included in your total monthly payment.

☐ will not have an escrow account because ☐ you declined it ☐ your lender does not offer one. You must directly pay your property costs, such as taxes and homeowner's insurance. Contact your lender to ask if your loan can have an escrow account.

No Escrow		
Estimated Property Costs over Year 1		Estimated total amount over year 1. You must pay these costs directly, possibly in one or two large payments a year.
Escrow Waiver Fee		

In the future,

Your property costs may change and, as a result, your escrow payment may change. You may be able to cancel your escrow account, but if you do, you must pay your property costs directly. If you fail to pay your property taxes, your state or local government may (1) impose fines and penalties or (2) place a tax lien on this property. If you fail to pay any of your property costs, your lender may (1) add the amounts to your loan balance, (2) add an escrow account to your loan, or (3) require you to pay for property insurance that the lender buys on your behalf, which likely would cost more and provide fewer benefits than what you could buy on your own.

Adjustable Payment (AP) Table

Interest Only Payments?	
Optional Payments?	
Step Payments?	
Seasonal Payments?	
Monthly Principal and Interest Payments	
First Change/Amount	
Subsequent Changes	
Maximum Payment	

Adjustable Interest Rate (AIR) Table

Index + Margin	
Initial Interest Rate	
Minimum/Maximum Interest Rate	
Change Frequency	
First Change	
Subsequent Changes	
Limits on Interest Rate Changes	
First Change	
Subsequent Changes	

FIGURE B.19 ■ **Closing Disclosure (continued)**

Loan Calculations

Total of Payments. Total you will have paid after you make all payments of principal, interest, mortgage insurance, and loan costs, as scheduled.	
Finance Charge. The dollar amount the loan will cost you.	
Amount Financed. The loan amount available after paying your upfront finance charge.	
Annual Percentage Rate (APR). Your costs over the loan term expressed as a rate. This is not your interest rate.	
Total Interest Percentage (TIP). The total amount of interest that you will pay over the loan term as a percentage of your loan amount.	

? **Questions?** If you have questions about the loan terms or costs on this form, use the contact information below. To get more information or make a complaint, contact the Consumer Financial Protection Bureau at **www.consumerfinance.gov/mortgage-closing**

Other Disclosures

Appraisal
If the property was appraised for your loan, your lender is required to give you a copy at no additional cost at least 3 days before closing. If you have not yet received it, please contact your lender at the information listed below.

Contract Details
See your note and security instrument for information about
• what happens if you fail to make your payments,
• what is a default on the loan,
• situations in which your lender can require early repayment of the loan, and
• the rules for making payments before they are due.

Liability after Foreclosure
If your lender forecloses on this property and the foreclosure does not cover the amount of unpaid balance on this loan,
☐ state law may protect you from liability for the unpaid balance. If you refinance or take on any additional debt on this property, you may lose this protection and have to pay any debt remaining even after foreclosure. You may want to consult a lawyer for more information.
☐ state law does not protect you from liability for the unpaid balance.

Refinance
Refinancing this loan will depend on your future financial situation, the property value, and market conditions. You may not be able to refinance this loan.

Tax Deductions
If you borrow more than this property is worth, the interest on the loan amount above this property's fair market value is not deductible from your federal income taxes. You should consult a tax advisor for more information.

Contact Information

	Lender	Mortgage Broker	Real Estate Broker (B)	Real Estate Broker (S)	Settlement Agent
Name					
Address					
NMLS ID					
___ License ID					
Contact					
Contact NMLS ID					
Contact ___ License ID					
Email					
Phone					

Confirm Receipt

By signing, you are only confirming that you have received this form. You do not have to accept this loan because you have signed or received this form.

_____   _____   _____   _____
Applicant Signature   Date   Co-Applicant Signature   Date

F I G U R E B.20 ■ Property Management Cash Flow Statement

Your firm logo here

PROPERTY CASH FLOW STATEMENT

Owner: _____   Report period: _____

Property location: _____   Prepared by: _____

Item	%	Actual	Budget	Comments
Cash Receipts				
Gross rents collected				
Other:				
Other:				
Total cash collected		$	$	
Cash Disbursements				
Accounting & Legal				
Advertising				
Insurance				
Management fee				
Payroll				
Property taxes				
Repairs and maintenance				
Services: janitorial lawn pest control trash				
Supplies				
Utilities: electric gas & oil water & sewer				
Other:				
Other:				
Other:				
Other:				
Monthly mortgage payment				
Total cash disbursements		$	$	
Cash flow (deficit)		$	$	

PRACTICE FINAL EXAM

Before you take the end-of-course examination, test your readiness by completing this 100-question, multiple-choice practice exam that is similar to the course exam. The questions are drawn from the 14 chapters in this book; they are of the same type and in the same form, with a similar degree of difficulty, to the end-of-course exam questions. If you score 75 or higher without using any reference material (in other words, if you simulate exam conditions), you are in a strong position to pass the course exam. Your instructor can discuss the correct answers to each question. Be certain to review those subject areas you miss.

1.   A sales associate who has been licensed for eight years did not renew his license this year. What is his status?
a.   Void
b.   Suspended
c.   Voluntary inactive
d.   Involuntary inactive

2.   When selling his property, a sales associate failed to disclose the fact that a person died in the home last year. The sales associate
a.   and his broker are legally liable to the buyer for damages.
b.   and his broker are subject to disciplinary action by the FREC.
c.   and his broker can have the court dismiss the suit.
d.   is liable; the broker is not.

3.   Which duty is owed by the broker to a principal in a single-agency relationship that is NOT owed to a customer in a transaction broker relationship?
a.   Skill, care, and diligence
b.   Dealing honestly and fairly
c.   Loyalty
d.   Accounting for all funds

4.   A broker who works with a seller is legally presumed to be
a.   a disclosed dual agent.
b.   a transaction broker.
c.   a single agent.
d.   an attorney-in-fact.

5.   A broker was a transaction broker in the sale and purchase of an office build-
     ing. The broker felt an obligation to tell the buyer about the seller's need to sell
     quickly. As a balance, the broker helped the seller get a better price from the buyer
     because of some comments the buyer made during the property inspection. What is
     correct?
     a.   Because the disclosures were balanced and both buyer and seller were treated
          fairly, no violation has occurred.
     b.   Disclosure of such information violates Chapter 475.
     c.   While an ethical violation has occurred, no statutory violation has taken
          place.
     d.   While allowed to disclose motivation information, the broker may not discuss
          specifically what price a seller might accept or the buyer might pay.

6.   A person who authorizes another person (the agent) to represent her in a real
     estate transaction is the
     a.   customer.
     b.   prospect.
     c.   principal.
     d.   third party.

7.   If a single-agent residential seller's broker wishes to provide limited representation
     to a buyer, what must the broker do?
     a.   Have the seller sign the Consent to Transition to Transaction Broker Notice
          and give the buyer a Transaction Broker Notice.
     b.   Have the buyer sign the Consent to Transition to Transaction Broker Notice
          and give both parties a Transaction Broker Notice.
     c.   Give both the seller and the buyer a Transaction Broker Notice.
     d.   Become a single agent for the buyer also.

8.   A commercial broker allows one sales associate to act as a single agent for the
     buyer and another sales associate to act as a single agent for the seller. Both the
     buyer and the seller have assets of more than $1 million, and each agrees to this
     form of representation. The situation describes a
     a.   transaction broker relationship.
     b.   single agency.
     c.   dual agency.
     d.   designated sales associate.

9.   A person wishing to avoid liability under the Comprehensive Environmental
     Response, Compensation, and Liability Act of 1980, claiming innocent purchaser
     status, must
     a.   pay for an insurance bond issued by the Department of Environmental
          Regulation.
     b.   require that the seller obtain an insurance bond issued by the Department of
          Environmental Regulation.
     c.   exercise due diligence by investigating the property, usually in the form of an
          environmental audit.
     d.   obtain certifications from the local planning commission that the property
          never has been used as a gas station or dry-cleaning establishment.

10.   A married couple who file jointly and who have owned and occupied their personal residence for three years sells a property. Which statement is TRUE about their tax liability?
       a.   They must pay taxes at a 20% rate on the amount that the property's adjusted sales price exceeds the property's new price.
       b.   They may exclude up to $600,000 of any gain before becoming liable for taxes.
       c.   They may exclude up to $500,000 of any gain before becoming liable for taxes.
       d.   Their maximum capital gains rate is reduced to 10% because it was a personal residence.

11.   An investor sells an office property he has owned for three years and has a capital gain of $125,000. His ordinary income tax rate is 28%. His long-term capital gains are taxed at a maximum of 15%. Using just this information, how much will his taxes be for this transaction?
       a.   He may exclude up to $500,000 of the gain before calculating taxes.
       b.   He will pay $12,500 in taxes.
       c.   His taxes will be $18,750.
       d.   His tax payment will be $35,000.

12.   A broker who sends a fax must have
       a.   had a transaction with the recipient within the previous 18 months.
       b.   requested permission from the recipient before the message was faxed.
       c.   purchased a no-fax list from the Federal Trade Commission.
       d.   an established business relationship with the recipient.

13.   A licensed sales associate employs a salaried, unlicensed personal assistant. The assistant hands out brochures at an open house but does not do any selling, nor does she write contracts. Which is correct?
       a.   The sales associate and her assistant have both violated Chapter 475.
       b.   This activity is allowed.
       c.   This is illegal only if the sales associate makes a sale.
       d.   The broker, the sales associate, and her assistant have all violate Chapter 475.

14.   A sales associate hires a licensed personal assistant. The personal assistant is paid a salary of $1,000 per month and 15% of the sales associate's share of commissions. Which is correct?
       a.   The broker must pay both the salary and the commission to the personal assistant.
       b.   The sales associate may pay both the salary and the commission to the personal assistant.
       c.   The salary may be paid by either the sales associate or the broker. The broker must pay the commission.
       d.   Sharing commissions with a licensed personal assistant is a violation of Florida license law.

15.   A lead-based paint hazard disclosure must be made if the house being sold was built before
       a.   1963.
       b.   1975.
       c.   1978.
       d.   1998.

16.   The BEST way to acquire product knowledge is to
       a.   be in the marketplace.
       b.   read the many books available through NAR.
       c.   give on-the-job training classes.
       d.   attend a class at the community college.

17.   Joining Toastmasters is an effective way to improve which skill?
       a.   Written communication
       b.   Oral communication
       c.   Nonverbal communication
       d.   Product knowledge

18.   Unlicensed personal assistants
       a.   may not be present at an open house or hand out brochures to visitors.
       b.   who are directed by the sales associate in how to do their jobs cannot be classi-
            fied as independent contractors, and must pay withholding taxes.
       c.   may be classified as independent contractors if they are able to determine
            working hours, even if the employer directs how they are to do their job.
       d.   are usually not a worthwhile expense for sales associates, according to major
            real estate associations.

19.   The MOST probable price a property should bring in an arm's-length transaction
       in a competitive and open market is called the
       a.   market price.
       b.   market value.
       c.   exchange value.
       d.   sales price.

20.   A sales associate should normally avoid spending time on a FSBO prospect who
       a.   does not need to sell.
       b.   is moving to another city.
       c.   is realistic about pricing.
       d.   tells the agent he does not want to list right now.

21.   Shady Acres neighborhood has had 103 homes sold last year out of 560 homes in
       the area. Sunny Hills neighborhood has had 87 homes sold with 400 total homes.
       Windy Woods neighborhood has had 150 homes sold with 800 total homes. Still
       Waters neighborhood has had 145 homes sold with 625 total homes. All are in the
       same general price range in well-kept areas of the city. Which neighborhood would
       be the BEST farm area based on likely reward-to-effort ratios?
       a.   Shady Acres
       b.   Sunny Hills
       c.   Windy Woods
       d.   Still Waters

22.   MOST listings expire because they are
       a.   not easy to show because of uncooperative owners or tenants.
       b.   poorly maintained by the owners and don't show well.
       c.   overpriced for the market.
       d.   listed by sales associates who fail to properly market the property.

23. Writing ads for a new listing would be considered what type of activity in the daily activity log?
    a. Direct $
    b. Office and administrative
    c. Wasted time
    d. Personal

24. A sales associate works an average of 9 hours each day. Last year, he worked for 260 days and made gross income of $102,000. What was his hourly rate?
    a. $18.40
    b. $22.94
    c. $43.59
    d. $392.31

25. Which FSBO activity is more likely to generate a listing?
    a. Mailing a letter
    b. Telephoning
    c. Visiting
    d. Advertising

26. A potential seller has a home worth $240,000 with a mortgage balance of approximately $199,000. The sales associate assures him that a 6% commission should be acceptable. The commission as a percentage of the seller's equity is
    a. 6.
    b. 14.
    c. 24.
    d. 35.

27. Sensitivity to the thoughts and feelings of others is
    a. feelings.
    b. courtesy.
    c. empathy.
    d. sympathy.

28. Under federal do-not-call rules, licensees may
    a. call FSBOs and past customers, even if they're on the list.
    b. not call either FSBOs or past customers, even if they are on the list.
    c. call FSBOs but not past customers.
    d. not call FSBOs, but they may call past customers for up to 18 months, even if they are on the list.

29. High interest rates usually result in
    a. more properties in listing inventory and a buyers' market.
    b. fewer properties in listing inventory and a sellers' market.
    c. higher home prices.
    d. lower total mortgage payments.

30. Which is the LEAST likely to help a sales associate obtain a listing?
    a. Persuasiveness
    b. Sympathy
    c. Persistence
    d. Empathy

31.   Targeted strangers in your database should be contacted at LEAST
       a. six times monthly.
       b. every other month.
       c. twice a month.
       d. twice each year.

32.   To ensure maximum future value of the properties, subdivision restrictions rely on
       the principle of
       a. contribution.
       b. substitution.
       c. conformity.
       d. competition.

33.   A comparative market analysis (CMA) with adjustments assumes that
       a. the subject property sold recently in the same neighborhood.
       b. adjustments for differences have been made to the subject property.
       c. adjustments for differences have been made to the comparable property.
       d. the sales associate knows construction costs for this type property.

34.   A person who sends a fax
       a. must allow the recipient to opt out of getting more faxes.
       b. may have received the recipient's number from a fax-spamming company.
       c. may send the fax only between 9 am and 5 pm.
       d. must have paid for the consumer data do-not-fax list.

35.   The principle of value that says improvement to a property is worth only what
       it adds to the property's market value, regardless of actual cost, is called the
       principle of
       a. substitution.
       b. conformity.
       c. contribution.
       d. competition.

36.   A basic principle of value stating that a property's maximum value tends to be set
       by the cost of acquiring an equally desirable property is known as the principle of
       a. anticipation.
       b. conformity.
       c. increasing returns.
       d. substitution.

This information is to be used for questions 37–39:

A comparable property sold two months ago for $138,000. It has four bedrooms (the subject property has three) and is 160 square feet larger as a result. An analysis shows that the additional room/space makes an $8,000 difference. The subject is newer and in slightly better condition, so you estimate a difference of $5,000.

37.   Due to the difference in square footage and bedrooms, you make a
       a. plus $8,000 adjustment to the comparable.
       b. plus $8,000 adjustment to the subject.
       c. minus $8,000 adjustment to the subject.
       d. minus $8,000 adjustment to the comparable.

38. The resulting net adjustment for size and physical condition is
     a. plus $3,000.
     b. minus $3,000.
     c. plus $5,000.
     d. minus $5,000.

39. The adjusted sales price of the comparable property is
     a. $130,000.
     b. $135,000.
     c. $138,000.
     d. $143,000.

40. Trees, landscaping, driveways, fences, pools, and other improvements of a home
     should be valued by the listing sales associate at
     a. their original cost.
     b. their original cost, less their physical depreciation.
     c. their contribution to value.
     d. the seller's best representation of their value.

41. Properties that should be rejected as comparables for determining a subject prop-
     erty's value include all properties EXCEPT
     a. those sold within the previous six months.
     b. those that differ in quality of construction.
     c. those that are much different in size.
     d. those in which the buyers and the sellers were relatives.

42. When making adjustments to sold properties in a CMA, the licensee's goal is to
     find the
     a. monetary difference in features between the subject property and the compa-
         rable property.
     b. subject property's characteristics.
     c. price the subject property should sell for.
     d. current market influences.

43. After completing a review of the CMA, a sales associate and seller agree on a
     list price of $240,000. Sellers' expenses, including brokerage fee, are estimated
     at $17,600, and prorations for taxes and interest paid in arrears are estimated
     at $6,700. The mortgage payoff is expected to be $196,500. What is the seller's
     equity?
     a. $19,200
     b. $25,900
     c. $32,600
     d. $43,500

44. Using the information from the previous question, what is the estimated net pro-
     ceeds to the seller?
     a. $19,200
     b. $25,900
     c. $32,600
     d. $43,500

45. The BEST location for making a listing presentation to prospective sellers is the
    a. sofa in the prospects' living room.
    b. kitchen or dining table.
    c. hood of your car.
    d. lunch counter at a busy restaurant.

46. What is the MOST persuasive argument to help get a FSBO to list her house?
    a. The buyer needs to get financing.
    b. Writing a contract may be difficult.
    c. She is unlikely to "save" the commission.
    d. Handling the closing details are too time-consuming.

47. The first step when meeting the sellers for a listing appointment is to
    a. break the ice.
    b. shown them the sellers' net statement.
    c. go over the listing agreement.
    d. recommend the right price to sell the property.

48. A property is likely to sell faster if it is priced at the
    a. "expired" section of the CMA.
    b. "sold" section of the CMA.
    c. "currently listed" section of the CMA.
    d. median value from all sections of the CMA.

49. Which is FALSE about listing agreements in Florida?
    a. Listing contracts for less than one year are covered by the statute of frauds.
    b. All written listings must have definite expiration dates.
    c. Oral listing contracts are enforceable.
    d. Listings are personal service contracts.

50. An agreement between a seller of real property and a real estate broker that authorizes the broker to sell the property on specified terms in return for a sales commission if the broker is successful is
    a. a single agency contract.
    b. a sales contract.
    c. an option contract.
    d. a listing contract.

51. A real estate contract given to one broker as sole agent for the sale of an owner's property, with a commission going to that broker regardless of who actually sells the property during the contract period, is
    a. a unilateral agreement.
    b. an exclusive-representation agreement.
    c. an exclusive-agency listing.
    d. an exclusive-right-to-sell listing.

52. At the time a listing agreement is negotiated, the listing broker should NOT discuss with the seller the
    a. pros and cons of subagency.
    b. seller's religious preference.
    c. use of the local MLS.
    d. seller's attitude toward the broker sharing the sales commission with a cooperating broker.

53. Sales associates should spend MOST of their time working with buyers who have
    a. to move into the area in 60 days from out of town.
    b. a lease expiring in six months.
    c. not been on the job for at least two years.
    d. their house listed with a good friend.

54. If a buyer raises an objection to a property, the associate should first
    a. ridicule the objection to ensure the buyer is serious.
    b. refute the objection.
    c. confirm and isolate the objection.
    d. ask the customer whether he wants to continue their business relationship.

55. When presenting an offer, a sales associate is in a better position to get an acceptance when the buyer has
    a. just started a new job.
    b. been prequalified by a lender.
    c. been preapproved by a lender.
    d. given a good-faith deposit of $1,000.

56. Callers who are asking about property they saw from a sign usually ask for the
    a. address.
    b. price.
    c. square footage.
    d. owners' names.

57. Where the agreement of the parties is contrary to any of the provisions or standards in a preprinted sales contract, it is BEST to
    a. line out the particular provision or standard affected.
    b. insert one or more special clauses in an addendum to the contract.
    c. renegotiate the contrary item(s) with the parties to the contract.
    d. prepare a nonstandard contract.

58. Yesterday, a broker obtained a 90-day listing contract that has a self-renewing provision extending the agreement an additional 60 days after expiration unless either party cancels in writing. The listing contract is
    a. void.
    b. unconscionable.
    c. valid.
    d. implied.

59. Which is NOT allowed under the CAN-SPAM Act?
    a. Emailing sellers about marketing efforts on their homes
    b. Failing to include an opt-out method in commercial advertisements
    c. Emailing a newsletter without advertising
    d. Text-messaging information

60. The state requires that sales tax be collected on personal property sold as part of a real estate transaction when the property is
    a. depreciated for income tax purposes.
    b. itemized and valued in the sales contract.
    c. mentioned in the contract.
    d. used to determine the broker's compensation.

61. The law requiring that certain types of contracts be written to be enforceable is
    a. Chapter 455, F.S.
    b. the statute of frauds.
    c. the statute of limitations.
    d. the "Little FTC Act."

62. What is MOST important in a sales contract?
    a. Seller's marital status
    b. Serial number on each major appliance
    c. Buyer's maiden name
    d. Subject property's legal description

63. What is a contract that may be terminated at the option of one of the parties?
    a. Voidable
    b. Implied
    c. Option
    d. Dual representation

64. Which is FALSE about fair housing?
    a. A real estate agent may not limit a home search to certain neighborhoods based on the customer's race.
    b. An apartment building owner may assign families with children to one particular building if older people live in the other buildings.
    c. A loan officer may turn down a Hispanic applicant because of the applicant's lack of steady income.
    d. An apartment building owner may turn down an applicant because of the applicant's poor housekeeping habits.

65. A bilateral agreement spelling out the complete terms between a buyer and a seller for the transfer of a parcel of real property is
    a. a representation agreement.
    b. a sales contract.
    c. an option contract.
    d. a wraparound mortgage.

66. An agreement to hold open for a set time period an offer to sell or lease real property is
    a. a contract for deed.
    b. an option contract.
    c. an installment contract.
    d. an agreement for deed.

67. Under which contract does the seller warrant appliances to be in working order?
    a. Quasi
    b. Executory
    c. Florida REALTORS®
    d. Implied

68. The Florida REALTORS® contract requires that the seller warrant appliances, heating and cooling systems, and plumbing systems to be in working order
    a. at closing.
    b. on the date of contract.
    c. as of 10 days before closing.
    d. as of three days before closing.

69. A very important social media site for uploading and viewing videos is
    a. YouTube.
    b. WordPress.
    c. LinkedIn.
    d. IDX.

70. In the Florida REALTORS® contract, if a survey shows an encroachment, the
    a. encroachment will be treated as a title defect.
    b. encroachment will be a breach of contract on the seller's part.
    c. seller must pay damages to the buyer for any delays due to the problem.
    d. buyer is responsible for any expenses associated with curing the problem.

71. The component in an adjustable-rate mortgage that does NOT change from year to year is the
    a. margin.
    b. index.
    c. calculated rate.
    d. rate charged.

72. Most conventional residential mortgage lenders have adopted the Fannie Mae suggested housing expense ratio and the total long-term obligations ratio calculated from gross income amounts for underwriting loans. The Fannie Mae ratios for housing expense (HER) and total obligations (TOR) currently range from
    a. 3 to 1 (HER) and 4 to 1 (TOR).
    b. 28% (HER) and 36% (TOR).
    c. 30% (HER) and 30% (TOR).
    d. 40% (HER) and 40% (TOR).

73. The ratio of monthly housing expenses to monthly income is the
    a. housing expense.
    b. income and expense.
    c. total obligations.
    d. total consumer credit.

74. A buyer expects to live in his new home for about five years. He is shopping for a new $100,000 mortgage. With no points, he can get a 30-year 8% fixed rate mortgage with principal and interest payments of $733.76. Another lender has a 7.75% mortgage (payments of $716.41) with one point. How many months will it take the buyer to break even on the points if he takes the lower interest loan, using simple arithmetic?
    a. 48.5
    b. 57.6
    c. 68.6
    d. 69.2

75.   The process of evaluating the risks involved in issuing a new real estate mortgage is commonly called
   a.   buyer/borrower qualification.
   b.   loan risk evaluation.
   c.   buyer/borrower prequalification.
   d.   loan underwriting.

76.   A mortgage note normally shows the amount required to pay monthly
   a.   principal and interest only.
   b.   principal, interest, and one-twelfth of annual property taxes.
   c.   principal, interest, and one-twelfth of annual hazard insurance.
   d.   principal, interest, and one-twelfth of annual taxes and insurance.

77.   The three components of a full property title report are a physical inspection of the property, a search of the public records, and
   a.   a survey.
   b.   a legal description.
   c.   a valid conveyance from all previous owners.
   d.   an abstract or opinion of title.

78.   What is NOT a good reason to make a preclosing walk-through inspection?
   a.   To determine that no encroachments exist
   b.   To determine that the property has been maintained in the same condition it existed in when the contract was written, reasonable wear and tear excepted
   c.   To ensure that all required repairs have been made
   d.   To determine that all items of personal property are on the real property

79.   A licensee should work hard to clear contract contingencies
   a.   within five days before closing.
   b.   within five days after loan approval.
   c.   within three days of contract.
   d.   as soon as possible after the contract has been signed.

80.   How does the appraisal cost usually appear in the Closing Disclosure when a new institutional mortgage has been used for the purchase?
   a.   Debit to the seller
   b.   Credit to the buyer
   c.   Debit to the buyer
   d.   POC

81.   The Fair Housing Act applies to
   a.   a religious organization that limit rentals of its properties to members of its religion.
   b.   private clubs that limit rentals to its own members in noncommercial lodgings.
   c.   a For Sale by Owner selling his personal house (his only real property).
   d.   an owner who lists his personal house (his only real property) with a broker.

Use the following information to answer questions 82 through 88.

Susan lists her home with Broker William for $90,000 on March 16. On August 1, Henry makes an offer of $85,000, accompanied by a binder deposit of $5,000, and asks the seller to pay points on a new loan of $80,000. Susan counters at a price of $87,500 and agrees to pay four points on a loan of $82,500. Henry accepts.

Henry qualifies for the loan at an interest rate of 9% and agrees to pay a 1% origination fee. The monthly payment for principal and interest is $663.81. Henry also will be charged for prepaid interest for the balance of the month of closing. The closing date is September 15, and Henry is charged for the day of closing.

Henry will purchase an insurance policy for $720. City and county taxes are $760. Susan agreed to pay her own attorney's fees of $125. Henry must pay $130 for attorney's fees, $56 to record the mortgage, $6 to record the deed, and $640 for title insurance.

The payoff on Susan's existing mortgage will be $64,455.16 on the day of closing. Broker William's fee is 6%. Doc stamps and intangible taxes are paid according to custom. Use the 365-day method for prorations.

82. How are the points to be handled on the closing statement?
a. Credit Henry $3,500.
b. Debit Susan $3,500.
c. Debit Susan $3,300; credit Henry $3,300.
d. Debit Susan $3,300.

83. If the lender wants a three-month tax escrow plus the number of months through the day of closing, what is the amount of prepaid taxes the lender collects at closing?
a. $190.00
b. $696.67
c. $760.00
d. $773.33

84. What is the proration of taxes between the seller and the buyer?
a. Debit Henry; credit Susan $535.12.
b. Debit Henry; credit Susan $224.88.
c. Debit Susan; credit Henry $535.12.
d. Debit Susan; credit Henry $224.88.

85. What is the amount of documentary stamp taxes on the note?
a. $288.75
b. $306.25
c. $577.50
d. $612.50

86. Using the 365-day method and the exact number of days in the month, how will prepaid interest be handled on the closing statement?
a. Henry must pay $325.48 in prepaid interest at closing.
b. Susan must pay $325.48 in prepaid interest at closing.
c. Henry must pay $330.00 in prepaid interest at closing.
d. Henry must pay $535.12 in prepaid interest at closing.

87.   How are the documentary stamp taxes on the deed handled on the closing statement?
       a. Debit Henry $306.25.
       b. Debit Susan $306.25.
       c. Credit Henry $612.50.
       d. Debit Susan $612.50.

88.   Assuming the mortgage insurance premium is $50.18 per month, what is the total monthly payment (PITI) on the mortgage?
       a. $663.81
       b. $725.89
       c. $787.14
       d. $837.32

89.   The point where the business cycle, at its highest point, levels off and begins to fall is called
       a. expansion.
       b. recession.
       c. contraction.
       d. recovery.

90.   When calculating a property's net operating income, such items as depreciation, income taxes, and property financing costs are
       a. included in variable operating costs.
       b. included in fixed operating costs.
       c. considered as funds reserved for operations or replacements.
       d. excluded from consideration.

91.   When annual debt service is subtracted from net operating income, the resulting amount is the
       a. after-tax cash flow.
       b. before-tax cash flow.
       c. cash flow.
       d. net spendable income.

92.   The relationship between a property's net operating income and its present value is the
       a. cash throwoff.
       b. debt service.
       c. capitalization rate.
       d. return on investment.

93.   Which is NOT a type of operating expense?
       a. Fixed expenses
       b. Reserves for replacements
       c. Depreciation
       d. Variable expenses

94. Which illegal statement would MOST likely be termed *steering*?
    a. "I can list your house and get it sold before any more minorities move into this neighborhood."
    b. "I'm sorry, we won't be able to make the loan in that Hispanic neighborhood."
    c. "Are you certain you'll be comfortable in this predominantly white neighborhood?"
    d. "I'm sorry, we don't rent to non-Christians here."

95. The optimum rental price for standard space in a local area is determined by
    a. market analysis.
    b. property analysis.
    c. neighborhood analysis.
    d. surveys of past, current, and projected tenant population figures.

96. The monthly report of housing starts is
    a. an extremely important economic indicator.
    b. a lagging economic indicator.
    c. not able to be forecast by the previous month's building permit data.
    d. prepared by the Department of Veterans Affairs.

97. What is the difference between effective gross income and net operating income?
    a. Before-tax cash flow
    b. Vacancy
    c. Operating expenses
    d. Cash throwoff

98. The relationship between supply and demand for a particular type of multifamily property at its current rental level is reflected by the
    a. rental market's equilibrium.
    b. turnover of tenants whose leases expire.
    c. area's location quotient.
    d. occupancy rate for that type of property.

99. The BEST and least expensive method of renting or leasing residential properties is the use of
    a. referrals from satisfied tenants.
    b. newspaper classified ads.
    c. radio ads of 30 seconds or less.
    d. short, relatively inexpensive television commercials.

100. A woman is searching for a new apartment. When she drives up to a particular apartment complex, she gets a wonderful impression and decides to rent if the price is right. The woman's first impression is called
    a. market value.
    b. eye invitation.
    c. curb appeal.
    d. comparative market analysis.

GLOSSARY

A

accessible Easy to approach, enter, operate, participate in, and/or use safely and with dignity by a person with a disability.

accommodation A change to a dwelling that the housing provider must provide. An example would be a tenant's request for a handicap-accessible parking space near the tenant's apartment.

adjustable-rate mortgage (ARM) A loan that allows the borrower's interest rate to fluctuate based on some external index beyond the control of the lender.

adjustments The method used by brokers and appraisers to account for differences in comparable properties. If a subject property is superior, the appraiser makes a dollar adjustment increasing the sale price of the comparable. If the subject property is inferior to the comparable property, a negative adjustment is made.

after-tax cash flow The amount remaining to an owner of income property after all expenses, debt service, and income taxes have been paid.

agency The relationship of agents and their principals.

agent A person who represents another person in a fiduciary relationship.

Americans with Disabilities Act (ADA) A federal law that guarantees equal opportunity for individuals with disabilities in public accommodations, employment, transportation, state and local government services, and telecommunications.

annual percentage rate (APR) An expression of credit costs over the life of a loan, taking into account the contract interest rate plus lender fees for originating, processing, and closing a mortgage loan.

antitrust. Federal law that prohibits monopolistic practices such as price fixing.

appraisal An unbiased estimate of a property's market value.

appraising The process of estimating the market value of property.

arm's-length transaction A business transaction in which the parties are dealing in their own self-interest, not being under the control of the other party. One of the requirements before a comparable sale should be used in an appraisal.

assets Things of value owned by a person or organization.

automated underwriting The evaluation of a mortgage loan application using predetermined formulas and credit scores. Fannie Mae's Desktop Underwriter performs automated underwriting.

automated valuation The use of computers and linear regression formulas to calculate the market value of property based on large numbers of comparable sales.

B

before-tax cash flow (BTCF) The amount of spendable income from an income property after paying operating expenses and debt service, but before the effect of income taxes. Sometimes called cash throw-off.

bilateral contract A contract that requires both parties to perform, such as a sales contract.

biweekly mortgage A mortgage that requires that the borrower make payments every two weeks (26 payments per year). The payment is calculated by dividing the monthly mortgage payment by two. The effective result is that the borrower makes 13 monthly payments per year.

blockbusting The illegal act of a licensee who frightens homeowners into selling by raising fears that minority homeowners are moving into a neighborhood.

body language Nonverbal communication expressed by the position of the body, hands, arms, legs, or facial expressions.

buyer agency The fiduciary relationship between a buyer and the buyer's single-agent broker.

buyer brokerage agreement An agreement between a buyer and a broker for the broker to provide services to a buyer for compensation. The broker may be acting as a single agent, a transaction broker, or a nonrepresentative.

C

calculated interest rate The interest rate in an adjustable-rate mortgage that is calculated by adding the margin to the index.

canvassing Prospecting for buyers or sellers by telephoning or walking door to door.

cap The maximum amount that an interest rate can increase per year, or during the life of a loan.

capitalization rate The net operating income divided by the property value. A percentage representing the return on the investment, assuming the property was purchased for cash.

cash flow report A property manager's monthly report to the owner, showing cash receipts and cash disbursements of an income property.

Certified Property Manager (CPM) A professional designation awarded by the Institute of Real Estate Management (IREM) to a property manager who has successfully completed required education and experience.

Civil Rights Act of 1866 A federal law that prohibits discrimination based on race.

Closing Disclosure A detailed accounting of charges and credits for the buyer and the seller in a real estate transaction.

Coastal Construction Control Line (CCCL) An imaginary line established by Florida counties a specified distance from the mean high-water mark of the Atlantic Ocean or the Gulf of Mexico that prohibits construction seaward from the line.

codes A method used by persons to discriminate in employment and housing. An employer may pencil in a series of numbers on an application form (for example, the number 11 may mean "Asian" and the number 15 may mean "African American"). These tactics are illegal.

collateral Something of value given as security for a debt. In real estate, the mortgage pledges the property as collateral for the repayment of the loan.

collected funds Checks or wired funds that have become actually and finally collected and deposited into the escrow agent or closing agent's account.

commission Compensation for professional services that is usually calculated as a percentage of the property's sales price.

community association A residential homeowners association in which membership is a condition of ownership of a unit in a part of a residential development that is authorized to impose a fee that may become a lien on the parcel.

community association manager An individual licensed by the Department of Business and Professional Regulation who is paid to perform certain functions for a residential homeowners association.

comparable property A similar property in the same market area that may be used to help estimate the value of the property being appraised.

comparative market analysis (CMA) Similar to the comparable sales approach used by appraisers but usually less detailed. Used by brokers and sales associates to estimate the most likely selling price of properties they are listing or selling.

Consent to Transition to Transaction Broker Notice A disclosure form that allows a single agent to become a transaction broker. The notice must be signed by the principal before the broker can make the change.

contingency A condition in a contract that, unless satisfied, may make the contract voidable by one of the parties.

contract An agreement between two or more parties to do or not do a specific act.

contraction The phase of a business cycle that begins after a recession when economic conditions worsen.

contract service A property maintenance service that is done by an individual or company not in the employ of the property manager.

contraction A component of an economic cycle that follows a recession and that experiences reduced sales, slower production, worker layoffs, and unemployment.

cooperative sale Sale of a property by a broker who is not the listing broker. Normally, commissions are split between the two brokerage firms.

corrective maintenance The repairs to a building's structure and equipment following breakdown.

counteroffer A substitution for the original offer made by the offeree who changes the price or terms offered, sending it back to the offeror. The original offer is terminated. The original offeree becomes the offeror.

credit scoring A method of credit reporting using a numeric score. A higher score reflects a person with better credit history.

cross-defaulting clause A mortgage clause that results in a default of a junior mortgage in case a senior mortgage becomes delinquent.

curb appeal The impression, good or bad, that is made when a person first looks at a house from the street.

customer A person who works with a sales associate or a broker. While the person could be a principal, the usual definition is that the broker is either a transaction broker or has no brokerage relationship with the person.

cycle Periodic fluctuations in the overall economy, or any part of the economy, between good times and bad. The four parts of a general cycle are expansion, recession, contraction, and recovery.

D

deferred maintenance Maintenance that needs to be done but that has not been done for some reason, usually economic.

designated sales associate A sales associate who is appointed by a broker as a single agent for a buyer or a seller in a nonresidential transaction when another sales associate in the firm has been appointed as the single agent for the other party in the transaction. Both buyer and seller must have assets of at least $1 million and agree to the arrangement.

disability An individual with a disability is a person who (1) has a physical or mental impairment that substantially limits one or more major life activities, (2) has a record of such an impairment, or (3) is regarded as having such an impairment.

documentary stamp taxes A tax on a real estate transaction that may be levied on the sales price of a property or on the amount of a mortgage note.

dual agency An illegal arrangement whereby the broker tries to represent both the buyer and the seller in the same transaction.

dynamic risk The uninsurable risk in owning real property. For example, changes in environmental or tax laws, of loss of a major employer in the area. This risk can sometimes be avoided by careful analysis before the property is acquired.

E

effective gross income (EGI) The amount of rent and other income actually collected by the owner. When preparing an income statement, vacancy and collection losses are deducted from potential gross income, and other income such as vending machine collections is added.

equity The amount of the owner's portion of the property value after deducting mortgages and other liens.

ethical The right thing to do. Usually a higher standard than legality.

exclusive-agency listing A listing that requires that the owner pay the listing broker if the property is sold by any broker but allows the owner to personally sell the property without being liable for a commission.

exclusive-right-of-sale listing A listing that requires that the owner pay the listing broker no matter who sells the property. The broker is automatically the procuring cause of the sale.

executed contract A contract in which nothing else remains to be done. All requirements have been performed by the parties.

executory contract A contract in which part of the agreement remains to be done. It has not yet "closed."

exercised Used in connection with an option contract. An option contract is a unilateral contract until the optionee agrees to purchase and is then said to have "exercised" the option.

expansion The phase of a business cycle that begins after a recovery when economic conditions improve.

express contract An oral or written agreement where the words specifically describe the intent of the parties.

F

fact of execution The acceptance of an offer. The offeree or his licensee must communicate the fact of execution to the offeror in order to make a valid contract.

Fair Housing Act Title VIII of the Civil Rights Act of 1968 is commonly called the Fair Housing Act. This federal law, as amended, provides for equal housing opportunities regardless of race, creed, or national origin, sex, persons with disabilities and families with children.

Fair Housing Amendments Act of 1988 This federal law expanded the Fair Housing Act to include protections for families with children and persons with disabilities.

fallback list A list of properties similar to the property being advertised that can be used by the licensee if the advertised property does not appeal to the person responding to the ad.

false or misleading statement In real estate, a statement made by a licensee or party in a real estate transaction that is not factual.

farm A geographic area selected for special prospecting attention by a real estate licensee.

federally related transaction A real estate-related financial transaction which falls under a federal financial institutions regulatory agency and which requires the services of an appraiser.

fee Compensation, either as a fixed dollar amount or as a percentage of the sale price.

FICO score A proprietary numeric credit score used to evaluate a prospective borrower, developed by Fair, Isaacs, & Co.

fiduciary relationship A relationship of trust and confidence between an agent and principal.

fixed-rate mortgage A loan secured by real estate that has the same rate of interest for the life of the loan.

Florida Americans with Disabilities Act A state law that implements and mirrors portions of the Americans with Disabilities Act.

Florida Fair Housing Act A state law, modeled after the federal Fair Housing Act, that prohibits discrimination based on race, color, religion, sex, national origin, familial status, or handicap.

For Rent by Owner (FRBO) An owner who attempts to rent his own property without using a broker.

For Sale by Owner (FSBO) An owner who attempts to sell her own property without using a broker.

funding fee A charge levied by the Department of Veterans Affairs to veterans who use VA loans.

G

gross domestic product (GDP) The sum total of goods and services produced by the United States. The four major components of GDP are consumption, investment, government purchases, and net exports.

H

handicap A physical or mental impairment that substantially limits one or more major life activities.

Housing for Older Persons Act An act that describes housing intended and operated for occupancy by older persons where at least 80% of the occupied units are occupied by at least one person who is 55 years of age or older. Properties that fall within these guidelines are exempted from the familial status requirements of the Fair Housing Act.

I

implied contract An agreement not spelled out in words, where the agreement of the parties is demonstrated by their acts and conduct.

index An indicator beyond the control of a lender to which the interest rate on an adjustable-rate mortgage is tied.

innocent purchaser status An amendment to the Comprehensive Environmental Response, Compensation, and Liability Act (CERCLA) that exempts from liability landowners who made reasonable inquiries about hazardous substances before purchasing the property.

intangible tax A tax of 2 mills (.002) levied on the amount of new mortgage indebtedness.

J

jargon A word or expression related to a specific vocation or profession that a layperson may not understand.

K

key safe A lockbox holding the key to the home, usually attached to a door handle, allowing licensees who are members of the MLS easy access to the property.

L

latent defects addenda A disclosure by the seller that informs the seller of a duty to disclose known property defects and to hold the licensee harmless for the seller's failure to disclose.

leverage The use of borrowed money with the intent to increase the investor's return on the cash invested. If the return on the investment is greater than the interest rate paid by the borrower, the owner has positive leverage.

liabilities Amounts owed by a person.

listing agreement An agreement between a seller and a broker whereby the seller agrees to pay the broker a commission if the broker is successful in selling the property.

Loan Estimate A required disclosure that shows the amount of cash needed at closing as well as the annual percentage rate of interest charged on the loan.

loan processing procedure Steps taken by a lender to ensure that underwriting and documentation of a mortgage loan are done in a manner that reduces the lender's exposure to loss.

loan underwriting The evaluation of risk when a lender makes a mortgage loan to reduce the lender's exposure to loss.

lockbox A secure box holding the key to the home, usually attached to a door handle, allowing licensees who are members of the MLS easy access to the property by using a special access key to the box.

M

margin The additional percentage added to the index on an adjustable-rate mortgage, resulting in the calculated interest rate.

marketing knowledge A licensee's knowledge of the sales process, including the psychology of selling, advertising, personal marketing, and prospecting.

material fact An important fact that may affect a buyer's decision to buy or a seller's decision to sell. Licensees must disclose facts that materially affect the value of residential property.

misrepresentation A false or misleading statement made intentionally or unintentionally, or the failure to disclose a material fact.

modification In the case of a person with disabilities, a modification is a change that the housing provider must allow the tenant to provide at the tenant's expense.

mortgage insurance premium (MIP) The amount paid by a borrower for insurance that protects the lender against loss in case of the borrower's default. FHA mortgage insurance is called MIP.

mutual recognition An agreement between states to recognize a licensee's education obtained in another state. Florida has mutual recognition agreements with several states that exempt licensees in those states from taking a Florida pre license course if the licensee can pass a 40-question test on Florida real estate law.

N

negative amortization A situation occurring, usually under a graduated payment mortgage, where the payment on the loan is less than the amount required to pay the accrued interest. The unpaid interest is added to the principal balance of the loan, and the loan balance gradually increases.

net operating income (NOI) The income from an investment property remaining after operating expenses have been paid from the effective gross income.

net proceeds The amount available to a seller after paying the expenses of the sale and satisfying liens on the property.

net worth The amount remaining when liabilities are subtracted from assets.

new construction maintenance Work done on an income property designed to enhance the property's appeal to tenants. Includes adding new wallpaper, carpeting, and light fixtures.

No Brokerage Relationship Notice A disclosure that must be given by a licensee who does not represent a buyer or a seller before entering into an agreement or showing a property.

nonverbal communication Unspoken communication expressed by the position of the body, hands, arms, legs, or facial expressions, commonly called body language.

O

open listing A nonexclusive agreement in which a seller agrees to pay a broker if the broker sells the property. The broker is not paid if the seller or another broker sells the property.

operating expenses (OE) Costs of operating an income property. Includes property taxes, maintenance, insurance, payrolls, and reserves for replacements.

opinion of value A broker's price opinion, usually based on a comparative market analysis.

option contract An agreement that allows one party to buy, sell, or lease real property for specified terms within a specified time limit.

oral communication skills The ability to speak effectively one on one or in a group presentation.

P

paperless mortgage A mortgage that is "signed" electronically, using digital signatures.

passive prospecting A method of prospecting that does not include direct face-to-face or telephone conversations. Advertising and direct mail are examples of passive prospecting.

performance The completion of a contract's requirements.

PITI payment The payment required of a borrower that includes principal, interest, taxes, and insurance.

point A lender's charge to the borrower that increases the lender's yield. One point is equal to 1% of the loan amount.

potential gross income (PGI) The total annual income a property would produce if it were 100% occupied, with no vacancy or collection loss.

power prospecting A type of prospecting that seeks to make contact with many more buyers and sellers and that results in much higher income levels.

preclosing walk-through inspection An inspection of the house by the buyer, done sometime before the sale closes, to determine that the property is in the same condition as it was when the contract was signed and to ensure that all required repairs have been completed.

prequalification The preliminary process during which a prospective lender evaluates the buyer's ability to obtain a mortgage loan. Most licensees want a buyer to be prequalified or preapproved before showing properties.

preventive maintenance A work program designed to preserve the physical integrity of the premises and eliminate the more costly corrective maintenance.

previewing properties The activity a licensee uses to stay abreast of the market and to find specific properties to show to a prospective buyer.

principal (1) The person who enters into a fiduciary relationship with a single-agent licensee. (2) The amount of money remaining due on a mortgage loan.

prioritize To set up a list of activities in an order based on their importance.

private mortgage insurance (PMI) The amount paid by a borrower for insurance that protects the lender against loss in case of the borrower's default. Conventional lenders use the term private mortgage insurance; FHA mortgage insurance is called MIP.

product knowledge A licensee's familiarity with the real estate market and specific properties available for sale.

professional ethics A body of accepted codes of behavior for a specific industry.

profit and loss statement A detailed report of the income and expenses of an investment property over a stated period.

property characteristic The features of a property that are used as a basis of comparison in an appraisal or comparative market analysis.

property condition disclosure A form designed for disclosure to a buyer of any property defects. The form is normally signed by the seller, and the buyer signs a receipt that the buyer has received the disclosure.

Q

qualifying The process used by a licensee to determine whether to spend time working with a buyer or a seller. For example, a buyer would first be qualified financially, and then based on motivation to buy.

quality of income A lender's analysis of factors that reveal the likelihood of the borrower's income continuing over a long period.

quantity of income The total amount of a borrower's income from all sources.

quasi-contract A contract that is imposed by law to prevent unjust enrichment. For example, if a person's bank made an error in the person's favor, the quasi-contract invented by the courts would require that the person repay the bank.

R

radon gas A colorless, odorless gas occurring from the natural breakdown of uranium in the soil. Many experts believe radon gas to be the second leading cause of lung cancer.

random changes Irregular fluctuations of the economy that may be caused by legislative and judicial decisions, wars, weather, et cetera.

Real Estate Settlement Procedures Act (RESPA) A federal law requiring disclosure of loan closing costs in certain real estate financial transactions.

recession Two successive quarterly declines in the gross domestic product (GDP). This is the point at which economic activity has peaked and will be followed by a contraction.

reconciliation The final step in the appraisal process before the report is prepared. The correlation of property values derived from each of the three appraisal approaches into a single estimate of value.

recovery Two successive quarterly increases in the gross domestic product (GDP). This is the point at which economic activity has bottomed and will be followed by expansion.

redlining A lender's refusal to loan money in an area based on illegal discrimination.

refinance Placing a new mortgage on a property to replace another mortgage.

Regulation Z The part of the Truth in Lending Act that requires that lenders calculate and disclose the effective annual percentage rate to the consumer.

reserves for replacement A portion of an investment property's income that is set aside to pay the cost of replacing major building components when necessary.

resident manager A salaried individual employed for specific management functions for a single investment property.

rider An attachment to a contract.

routine maintenance The most common maintenance performed on an investment property, such as grounds care and housekeeping.

S

sales contract A bilateral agreement in which a buyer agrees to purchase a seller's property at a specified price and terms.

seasonal variations Changes in the economy (for example, winter tourism in Florida) that recur at regular intervals at least once a year.

seller agency The relationship of a single agent and his principal, the seller.

seller's net proceeds form A form used to show the seller's equity, expenses, and prorations, as well as the net amount the seller is estimated to receive as proceeds from the sale of the property.

servicing the listing The actions of a licensee who stays in touch with a seller regularly, getting feedback from licensees who have shown the property, sending the seller copies of advertisements, and generally keeping the seller informed of the marketing efforts.

show list A selected inventory of apartments that are available for inspection by prospective tenants.

single agent A broker who represents either the seller or the buyer in a real estate transaction, but not both.

Single Agent Notice A disclosure form informing the principal of the duties of his single agent.

specific cycles Wavelike movements similar to business cycles that occur in specific sectors of the general economy, such as the real estate market.

static risk Risk that is quantifiable and insurable. For example, the risk of fire is a static risk. Fire insurance will transfer the risk from the owner to the insurance company.

statute of frauds A body of law that requires certain contracts, such as those for the sale of real property, to be written.

steering The illegal, discriminatory act of a sales associate who brings buyers into an area based on the racial or ethnic makeup of the neighborhood.

subject property The property being appraised.

T

targeted strangers Persons not known to a licensee who are qualified as prospects by income, occupation, or residence address.

technical knowledge The knowledge needed by licensees to properly conduct their business that relates to filling out contracts, preparing seller's proceeds estimates, doing comparative market analyses, et cetera.

time is of the essence A contract clause that requires strict compliance with all dates and times specified in the contract. If a party fails to perform some act by the time specified, the person may be in default.

time management The organization of a person's day to maximize efficiency. It includes planning, scheduling, and prioritizing.

title insurance A guarantee to reimburse a loss arising from defects in title or liens against real property.

to-do list A daily list, usually designed in priority order, of tasks to be completed that day.

transaction broker A licensee who has limited representation to the buyer and/or the seller in a transaction. Instead of being an advocate for the buyer or the seller, the licensee is working for the contract.

transactional characteristic The factors related to a real estate transaction itself, such as time of sale, and financing terms.

Truth in Lending Act A federal law that requires that lenders inform consumers of exact credit costs before they make their purchases.

U

Uniform Standards of Professional Appraisal Practice (USPAP) Strict requirements for appraisers interpreted and amended by the Appraisal Standards Board. Florida appraisers and brokers who prepare appraisals must follow the guidelines.

unilateral contract A contract in which only one of the parties is required to perform, such as an option contract. The optionor must sell if the optionee exercises the option, but the optionee is not required to buy.

V

voidable contract A contract that allows the buyer and/or the seller to void a contract based on some predetermined action or event.

W

warranty of owner clause A hold harmless clause in a listing agreement whereby the seller warrants that all information given to the broker is correct.

written communication skills The ability to communicate effectively in letters, emails, and other documents.

INDEX

Notes